CREEVEY
LIFE AND TIMES

A FURTHER SELECTION FROM
THE CORRESPONDENCE OF
THOMAS CREEVEY

BORN 1768—DIED 1838

EDITED BY
JOHN GORE

NEW YORK
E. P. DUTTON AND COMPANY, INC.

FIRST EDITION . . . 1934

PRINTED IN GREAT BRITAIN.

THOMAS CREEVEY.
From a portrait in the possession of Miss E. L. Blackett-Ord,
Brownside, Alston.

[Frontispiece.

INTRODUCTION

WHEN, thirty years ago, Sir Herbert Maxwell first examined the Creevey Manuscripts with a view to publishing some portion of them, he reported that they contained sufficient fresh and interesting material for six volumes on the lines of Greville's *Memoirs.*

He was invited to skim so much of the cream as would fill two volumes, and his *Creevey Papers* became famous, a source of endless entertainment to the reading public, of considerable value to the social historian, and of much interest to the student of politics.

With the publication of Sir Herbert Maxwell's book,* Thomas Creevey came back to a generation that knew less than nothing of his years of notoriety in the society of his day. Beyond a brief reference by way of obituary in Greville's *Memoirs* and a few words by Brougham, Hobhouse, Abbot and one or two more contemporary writers, nothing remained in print to recall his name or memory.

Now, a century after his death, " every schoolboy " could write the requisite " three lines " upon him in a general knowledge paper, but the best informed might find a difficulty in filling a full page of foolscap with facts concerning his career. Sir Herbert Maxwell had not space at his disposal for such details. He allowed Creevey to tell his own tale, but in the exigences of his imposed task he subordinated the man to the matter and used him very much as a peg on which to hang his sparkling raiment. What he published represents little more than one-fortieth of the available material and only a small part of the " cream."

* If the publication had taken place half-a-dozen years earlier, *The Creevey Papers* must inevitably have been a chief authority in scores of contemporary notices in the *Dictionary of National Biography,* and space would surely have been found there for Creevey himself.

In March 1933 I was invited to re-examine the papers with a view to further publication, and as I worked my gay way through the endless succession of bundles, it became clear to me, first, that the industry of this vivacious letter-writer must triumph over all attempts to cram him into two, or even more, volumes, and that there was cream and to spare for more books ; and secondly, that the career of an opportunist so amusing, frank and shrewd would afford an entertaining theme even apart from the colour and sparkle of his commentaries on men and things.

With the political aspect Sir Herbert Maxwell has dealt faithfully, and it seemed best to me to serve in the present volume the interests of the social historian before those of the student of politics, and, while documenting Creevey's career, to paint as full and vivid a picture as possible of the social life of that privileged and select circle of Whig aristocracy in which he lived. It appears to me that the twentieth century, which has had a restricted opportunity to revalue Thomas Creevey, has allowed his reputation to go by default. His published writings have been accepted for all they claim to be ; the man has been left out in the cold, left like a pedlar to kick his heels in the porch while the ladies examine his wares in the drawing-room. While no writer has yet troubled to investigate the career of the man since *The Creevey Papers* were published, one popular Victorian biographer, Lytton Strachey, either deliberately or in lighthearted carelessness, tied a very one-sided label round his neck.

One thing is clear after reading through the whole extent of Creevey's MSS. They reveal the man who wrote and collected them to an extent which compels comparison with *Pepys' Diary*. His robust humour, shrewd judgment and untiring industry were employed to delineate his contemporaries and to paint a very complete picture of Whig society, and the painter himself stands out, lifelike and complete, the central figure in the landscape. Every line and shade in his character stand out ; those lighter social qualities which the world admits, his frailties and limitations which his admirers concede, and, underlying them, it seems to me, a hint of more substantial virtues. It is to be regretted that the organised collection of letters and papers dates only from his marriage and that he himself did not contribute anything like the lion's share until after his wife's death in 1818. There is, however (as I ventured to prophesy before I examined the unpublished papers), quite enough material to enable us to set forth and document almost continuously his progress from boyhood to youth and from youth to apprenticeship and from apprenticeship to office ; after 1822 one can almost hear him breathe in his letters.

When *The Creevey Papers* first enchanted the public thirty years ago, they brought back to life a social and political era which even then seemed remote and strange, though Sir Herbert Maxwell was born only a few years after Creevey's death. But since 1903 what changes have we seen ! There seems nothing left to-day to connect us with the social life of the first years of the reign of Edward VII, let alone of the Reform Bill era. The Edwardians had their roots in that age of privilege in which Creevey lived and died, and did indeed view with an indulgent smile the narrow prejudices and the serene belief in the divine right of a privileged aristocracy which distinguished those remote pioneers of democracy. Such indulgence comes less easily to us.

Yet first steps are the hardest, and we ought not to forget it. While admitting that too many politicians of Creevey's age rode with a slack rein and set no curb upon their tongues, and that some of his intimates in Parliament were but spoiled darlings of fortune, I am yet convinced that those ancestors of ours were not so primitive as a new school of biographers would have us believe. In the opinion of that school, to be dead is to be ridiculous. Yet experience of the last decades leads some of us to wonder whether the laugh is not on the farther bank of Styx. The world is slow to change for the better, and it is our duty to bear in mind the prevailing conditions of political and social life and thought when we read the annals of Whig society.

I, too, must acknowledge my debt to the pioneers in Creeveiana. My task was much simplified by Sir Herbert Maxwell's labours with the first skimming. His concise précis and lucid notes smoothed the way for my own efforts to link up the letters and explain their allusions ; and the excellent transcription and arrangement of the papers by their owner * still further reduced the toil and added to the pleasure of the task.

In this attempt to recreate Creevey and his times, common sense guides me to follow Sir Herbert's principles. Creevey and his correspondents tell his story, from the point at which the letters by their number and length become self-explanatory and afford a continuous record, and they tell it with the bare minimum of interpolation by the editor. I have tried to keep the footnotes short and to limit them strictly to explanation of allusions relevant to the main (biographical) purpose of the book or falling outside the ready recollection of the educated reader of average intelligence, and I have strenuously avoided pointing facile comparisons between the institutions and fashions of Creevey's day and of our own. So far as the plan of my book admits, the division of years adopted by Sir Herbert is retained, not only for my own convenience but for that of the reader who may desire to follow the narrative with Sir Herbert's book at his elbow. In respect to orthography I have continued his rules : to retain the characteristic archaisms of the period, to correct for the sake of identification *serious or confusing* misspellings of proper names (which are many), and for orderliness the *obvious* slips in spelling, punctuation and grammar, inevitable in letter-writing. An amended table of Creevey's nicknames for his contemporaries, to cover the new material, is also inserted for guidance. Every precaution has been taken to print no

* Mr. John Blackett-Ord, of Whitfield.

excerpt used by Sir Herbert Maxwell. If any reader should recognise in some sentence a familiar ring, let him remember that Creevey in his heyday as a letter-writer sometimes wrote twice a day to Miss Ord and thought nothing of dashing off half a dozen eight-page letters between breakfast and dinner, and in consequence he occasionally repeated the sense of his commentaries on the events of the hour.

Finally, I must urge in mitigation of criticism that I, too, am restricted by considerations of space. The Creevey Papers, if published entire, would fill a three-foot bookshelf ; and only the most determined students of history would search through the chaff for golden grains ; my present instructions limit me to a single volume. To achieve my double aim, to write Creevey's biography and to paint a picture of his times, an elaborate and drastic selection is called for, and it has been impossible to avoid breaking up the text with those irritating dots, indicating omissions, which are a bug-bear of research.

As for those readers whose interest in Creevey is confined solely to his social gossip, they must, I am afraid, restrain their impatience or skip to Chapter VII. Until he was turned fifty-five he was far more interested in party and world politics than in society, and his reputation as a sparkling letter-writer rests on the huge output of his last fifteen years.

JOHN GORE.

PITFOLD,
    HASLEMERE,
        1933.

ACKNOWLEDGMENTS

CONSENT to publication was sought from all ascertainable representatives of the authors of letters appearing in the following pages, except in cases where fragments of one or two letters only were involved. I offer my thanks to those who took the trouble to reply. My grateful thanks are also due to Mr. Roger Fulford and my father, Sir Francis Gore, for many valuable suggestions and corrections in the proof stage, and to my wife for her constant help.

NICKNAMES USED BY CREEVEY

Barney . .	12th Duke of Norfolk; also *Twitch, Scroop*.
Beau, The . .	Duke of Wellington.
Billy, Our . .	William IV.
Bruffam . .	Henry Brougham; also *Wickedshifts, Beelzebub*, and finally *Guy Vaux*.
Ciss . . .	Lady Cecilia Underwood, daughter of 2nd Earl of Arran. 2nd wife of H.R.H. Duke of Sussex, created Duchess of Inverness in 1840.
Cocky . .	Hon. H. G. Bennet.
Cole, Old or Mrs.	G. Tierney.
Cole, Young .	James Abercromby, Speaker 1835–9.
Comical Bob .	Lord Robert Spencer, son of 3rd Duke of Marlborough.
Dear Eddard .	Hon. R. Edward Petre.
Doctor, The .	Henry Addington (Lord Sidmouth).
Fergy . .	General Sir R. Ferguson of Raith.
Frog, The . .	King William I of Holland.
Frog, Young .	The Prince of Orange.
Jack the Painter .	Thomas Spring Rice.
Jaffa . .	General Sir Robert Wilson.
Jenky . .	Lord Liverpool.
Jockey . .	11th Duke of Norfolk.
King Jog . .	J. G. Lambton (afterwards Lord Durham); also *The Monarch*. "*One can jog along on £40,000 a year*."
King Tom . .	Coke of Norfolk (afterwards Lord Leicester).
Madagascar .	Lady Holland.
Mull . . .	Lord Molyneux, son of Lord Sefton.
Niffy Naffy .	Lord Darlington (afterwards Duke of Cleveland).
Og . . .	Lord Kensington.

P., Mrs.	. .	Princess of Wales (Queen Caroline).
Prinney	. .	The Regent. (This nickname originated with the Misses Ord, who saw much of the Prince in childhood.)
P, Young	. .	Princess Charlotte.
Pet, The	. .	Lord Sefton.
Pie and Thimble	.	Lord John Russell, also *Widow's Mite*.
Pop, The	. .	Lady Darlington; also *Poplolly, Haradan*.
Punch	. .	Charles Greville.
Roscius	. .	Lord Henry Petty (Lord Lansdowne).
Sally	. .	Sarah, Lady Jersey.
Sally, Old or Dow :		Emily Mary, Lady Salisbury.
Scroop	. .	12th Duke of Norfolk.
Slice	. .	H.R.H. Duke of Gloucester.
Snip	. .	Lord Goderich.
Squire, The *Stiff-rump.* }		C. Western ; also *The Turkey*.
Suss	. .	H.R.H. Duke of Sussex.
Taffy	. .	W. J. Hughes, Lord Dinorben.
Twitch	. .	12th Duke of Norfolk.
Vesuvius	.	Hon. Douglas Kinnaird.
Vic or Viccy	.	Queen Victoria.
Wickedshifts	.	H. Brougham.
Widow's Mite	.	Lord John Russell.

CONTENTS

                                                                    PAGES

INTRODUCTION . . . . v-ix

ACKNOWLEDGMENTS xi

NICKNAMES USED BY CREEVEY . . . . . xiii-xiv

PART I

CHAPTER I

1768-1805

Birth and parentage—Newcome's school—Cambridge—Called to
the Bar—Doctor Currie—Progress in the law—Elected for
Thetford—Marries Mrs. Ord—Progress in Parliament—Pitt's
return—Addington resigns—Melville's disgrace—Trafalgar
and Pitt's death blow 3-25

CHAPTER II

1806-1808

" All the Talents "—Creevey secretary of Board of Control—
Advice to Petty—Fox's death—Sheridan's frenzy—Mac-
mahon—Sir Sidney Smith—Duke of Portland's ministry
—Creevey and Sir Arthur Wellesley—The Fleet at Rio—
Convention of Cintra 26-40

CHAPTER III

1809-1813

Sir John Moore's death—James Moore's defence—Walcheren—
Sir Francis Burdett—Mrs. Clarke and Lord Folkestone—
William Cobbett in Newgate—The Regency—Creevey's
speech on India—Henry Brougham—Perceval remains—
Offer to Grey and Grenville—Creevey and Brougham for
Liverpool—Creevey's address—The Liverpool Election—
Brougham and Creevey defeated—Southill—Creevey as
Parliamentary reporter—Prosecuted for libel—Convicted—
Cobbett on libel 41-71

CHAPTER IV

1814–1815

PAGES

The Creeveys leave England—And the Princess of Wales—
Bonaparte abdicates—Brussels in 1815—Rumours and
alarms—Lady Holland's commissions—Creevey's account
of Waterloo—The Battlefield—Cumberland's marriage—
Whitbread's suicide—Miss Ord's account of Waterloo—
Praise of the Duke—Hamilton's daily bulletin—Bonaparte
surrenders   72–96

CHAPTER V

1816–1819

Creevey urged to return—Anne Hamilton's marriage—Mrs.
Creevey's illness—Rumours of dissolution—A new evening
paper—Mrs. Creevey's death—Creevey's devotion—His
finances—Sefton defeated at Liverpool—Creevey loses his
seat—Protest to Duke of Norfolk—The growth of Brighton—
Tierney as party leader—Creevey returns to England   97–117

PART II

CHAPTER VI

1819–1821

Correspondence with Miss Ord—George III's death—Lady Jersey
—Creevey's Pamphlet—Samuel Romilly's Journal—
Brougham and the Queen—The green bag—Bill of Depriva-
tion shelved—Public rejoicings—The King's speech—Burdett
sentenced—Creevey called out—The Queen at the Abbey—
Queen Caroline's death—George IV in Ireland—Lady
Glengall's account—Brougham's daughter. .   . 121–147

CHAPTER VII

1822

Creevey, the man-of-fashion—Sir B. Bloomfield—Lambton and
Mde de Flahault—A very bad joke—O'Meara on Bonaparte—
Creevey's Waterloo memoir—Durham clergy case—Castle-
reagh's suicide—George IV at Edinburgh—The enigma of
Canning—His dilemma—Duke of York's opinion—The St.
Leger—Lambton snubbed—Harewood House—Lady Ann
Clifford—Bolton Abbey—A visit to Croxteth .   . 148–174

CHAPTER VIII

1823

PAGES

Newspaper circulations—Duc de Reichstadt—Brougham's great speech—Irish affairs—News from France—A question of precedence—Stoke and Windsor—The Spanish Fête—A day of blunders—Lady Oxford—A seat at Appleby ?—Windsor tradesmen entertained—Lord Grey challenged . . 175–190

CHAPTER IX

1824

The Mansion House—Lord Mayor's banquet—The Derby— Ascot—A royal dinner-party—Lady Londonderry's pearls— Doncaster races—A duel averted—Lambton's luck—Lord Derby at Knowsley—Dean Shipley 191–206

CHAPTER X

1825–1826

Miss Creevey—Lord Thanet's death—A hunt from Raby—Duchess of Richmond and Mr. Tighe—Ascot again—Lord Darlington's dinner—Mrs. Brougham—Two famous Dowagers— Mrs. Coutts—Creevey's reprieve—Hopes of another seat— Lady Bland—Murat and Jaffa Wilson—Another pamphlet— Lambton in darkness—The depression of 1826—*The Times* —Sefton's loss—Lady Salisbury—The King and Lady Conyngham—The King Fisher—Croxteth—The Foley crash
207–231

CHAPTER XI

1827

Liverpool resigns—Canning Premier—Duke of York's funeral— The King and Canning—Brougham and London University— Wellington declines office—Canning's difficulties—The anti-Catholic condition—A Government formed—Canning's death —Lord Grey on the situation—Lowther Castle—Princess Lieven at Wentworth—Raby—Wickedshifts—Tories at Howick—Count Montrond—Brougham's methods—Navarino—Miss Creevey's drum—Goderich resigns . . 232–256

CHAPTER XII

1828

PAGES

George IV's last Government—Sydney Smith—Sefton on Wellington—Gin drinking—Wellington overworked—Lord Dudley as Foreign Minister—The King at Ascot—A rowdy dinner—Lady Salisbury at Eton—Duchess of St. Alban's party—Greville's reversion falls in—Goodwood meeting—Goodwood House—Arundel—Woolbeding—Cowdray Park—Petworth's early hours—The servants—Catalogue of pictures—A famous fountain—Mr. Poyntz—Lord Egremont's heir—Windsor again—The wits compared . . . 257–281

CHAPTER XIII

1828 (continued)

Dublin—Lord Melbourne's civility—At the Chief Secretary's—The charm of Bessborough—The Duncannon family—Kilkenny Players—Kilfane and the Powers—A conversational butler—Glendalough and Tom Moore—Lady Erroll—Croxteth—Knowsley and Lady Derby—Back in Whitehall 282–296

CHAPTER XIV

1829

The Catholic question—Wellington surrenders—Lady Foley's extravagance—The Duke of Norfolk—Harrington House theatricals—Lady Grey—Wellington's duel with Winchelsea—A racing record—Grey's position—Zingalee—A trip to Calais—Cumberland's outrage on Lady Lyndhurst—Greville's evidence—Wellington and Cumberland—An adventure at Walmer—Fanny Kemble—Lord Derby—Montrond on Josephine—George IV and Salamanca . . . 297–313

PART III

CHAPTER XV

1830

Death of George IV—Two beauties at Lady Salisbury's—Creevey baulked of a seat—The new King—An informal procession—Lady Glengall and Mde de Berri—The turn of the Whigs—Grey's Government—Creevey rewarded—Treasurer of Ordnance—Brougham's help—In Port at last—An office in Dublin 317–331

CHAPTER XVI

1831

PAGES

Progress of the Reform Bill—The lions at the Tower—The King and Creevey—The House of Orange—Alava—*John Bull* on Creevey—Taylor's reward—Lord Chancellor Brougham —The Borough-mongers—Talleyrand and the King— William IV opens Parliament—M.P. for Downton—House of Commons revisited—A quarrel over Hyde Park—Leopold elected King—Lord Grey's happiness—The Lords throw out the Bill—Dublin again—The Irish survey .   .   .   332–352

CHAPTER XVII

1832–1833

Reform Bill year—Sir Hudson Lowe—Defeat in the Lords—Grey resigns—And returns in triumph—The Bill passed—Road speed—Western a peer—Crockford's—The Duke of Sussex's marriage—Creevey to lose his job—Orléans and Wellington— Duchess of Sutherland—Windsor and Eton—The Dino and the Lieven—Duchess of Kent's demands—Lord Wellesley— Lord Durham's secret aims—Viceroy and Lady Wellesley 353–375

CHAPTER XVIII

1834

Brougham's intrigues—Creevey hears of Greenwich—And introduces the Prime Minister—Cupping—Miss Martineau— Lord Lansdowne—Lady Holland's flattery—Creevey's house at Greenwich—Ude of Crockford's—Miss Creevey—Woollen stockings—Lord Grey in retirement—Peel summoned from Rome—Grey and Sefton—Lady Grey discusses politics 376–400

CHAPTER XIX

1835–1836

Creevey's last phase—The omnibus—Abercromby chosen Speaker —Tyranny of Lady Holland—The Sheridan sisters—Miss Creevey's death—Lady Grey asks a favour—Lady Salisbury burnt to death—Lord Melbourne—The fire at Hatfield— Melbourne and Mrs. Norton—Lady Jersey abroad—Lady Holland's daughter—The de Ros case .   .   .   401–422

CHAPTER XX AND LAST

1837–1838

PAGES

The Victorian Age—D'Orsay—Brougham's papers—The young
Queen—The new Court—Hayter's impressions—The Queen
and Melbourne—Guildhall banquet—Holkham—American
manners—Creevey lays down his pen—A mysterious bequest
—Greville's note—Creevey's will—Mrs. Murray—An
estimate of Creevey   423–450

LIST OF ILLUSTRATIONS

THOMAS CREEVEY . . . . . *Frontispiece*
From a Portrait in the possession of Miss E. L. Blackett-Ord, Brownside, Alston

TO FACE PAGE

CHARLES WILLIAM, 1ST EARL OF SEFTON . . . 4
From a Picture in the possession of the Earl of Sefton

MRS. CREEVEY 66
From a Miniature in the possession of John Blackett-Ord, Esq., at Whitfield

LT.-COLONEL ANDREW HAMILTON 100
From a Miniature in the possession of John Blackett-Ord, Esq., at Whitfield

ST. JAMES'S STREET, ABOUT THE TIME OF CREEVEY . 178
From an old Print. By courtesy of Messrs. Francis Edwards, Ltd.

CROXTETH, LIVERPOOL (QUEEN ANNE FRONT) . . 230
By courtesy of Helena, Countess of Sefton

MARIA, VISCOUNTESS DUNCANNON 286
From a Painting by SIR THOMAS LAWRENCE, P.R.A., in the possession of the Earl of Bessborough at Stansted

FACSIMILE OF CREEVEY'S HANDWRITING . . *page* 314

MARY ELIZABETH, COUNTESS GREY 334
From a Miniature in the possession of Mrs. Lascelles at Woolbeding

GREENWICH HOSPITAL AND PARK, SHOWING LONDON IN THE DISTANCE 386
From a Drawing by W. WESTALL, R.A.

H.R.H. DUKE OF SUSSEX 436
From a Lithograph by E. Desmaisons, 1841

PART I
PARTY-MAN

CHAPTER I

1768–1805

THE life-story of Thomas Creevey begins and ends with a note of interrogation. The facts of his birth and details of his last hours will probably never be elucidated beyond question, and although his active life is as copiously documented as any, there are a few blanks which can never be filled in the story of his childhood, his youth, and professional apprenticeship. Some light is thrown on the dark places by autobiographical observations culled from the later Creevey Papers and reasonable inferences may be drawn still further to narrow the gaps in the narrative. The details of his death will come to be considered in their proper place. The mystery of his birth may be referred to here once and for all.

It is not in question that in March * 1768 a son was born to the wife of William Creevey, merchant of Liverpool, and that that child was Thomas, the subject of this biography. Sir Herbert Maxwell, when he published *The Creevey Papers*, had no reason to suppose that William Creevey was not the father of Thomas, but shortly afterwards he was informed by a member of the Molyneux family that Creevey was in fact the illegitimate son of Charles William, 1st Earl of Sefton, and that before the child's birth a Liverpool tradesman or merchant was induced to marry the mother. Sir Herbert made no attempt to secure further proofs of this assertion ; neither accepting it as proved nor rejecting it, he recorded his opinion that, if true, it helped to explain Creevey's warm acceptance by the Whigs.

---

* A letter written by Creevey and clearly dated March 6th, mentions that he " was sixty yesterday." Sir Herbert prints a letter which suggests a later date in March. I have relied on the first named letter which fixes 5th March as the date of birth.

My own opinion is that Creevey's career was in no way influenced by this question of his birth and that his acceptance by the advanced Whigs can be distinctly traced to other causes. For that reason I have been at no pains to probe deeper into what is of all problems the least open to absolute proof.

While it is true that no one, reading through the Creevey MSS. in ignorance of the Sefton tradition, would discover suggestive pointers, I am bound to admit that to a reader seeking evidence to bastardise Creevey, there are a number of passages capable of being interpreted that way, and not a few deletions by Creevey or Miss Ord not less suggestive. Some of these passages appear in the correspondence which follows, and the inquisitive reader can put his own interpretations upon them. On the other hand, it may be said that at the time of the suggested liaison, Lord Sefton was still short of nineteen years of age ; that Creevey's intimacy with the family of his reputed father did not begin until he was well over forty, and had held ministerial rank ; and that there is no evidence that any assistance was forthcoming from the Molyneux family in furthering his education or advancement.

After this somewhat lengthy and early digression I return to a statement of facts.

Thomas Creevey was born in Liverpool on March 5, 1768. William Creevey, merchant and sometime sea-captain, was a native of Northern Ireland, his own father, an officer in the Army, having migrated thither from Galloway, the cradle of the family. Whether the Creeveys were an ancient stock in Galloway, as Creevey was given to believe on one occasion when he was enquiring into his pedigree, is a question rather for genealogists than biographers.

One other child was born to the William Creeveys, a daughter, Jane, who passed the whole of her life in Liverpool and died unmarried. It seems that there were no other relations bearing the name of Creevey, but the papers reveal the existence of a tribe of

CHARLES WILLIAM, FIRST EARL OF SEFTON.
From a picture in the possession of the Earl of Sefton.

[To face p. 4.

cousins, mostly in humble circumstances, who put in occasional appearances at family functions, or recalled their existence in times of need. Their company Creevey neither sought nor shunned. Sometimes he went out of his way to hunt one out, and there is no instance of any attempt on his part to conceal the humbleness of his mother's origin.

William Creevey died while Thomas was still a child, and the boy's upbringing devolved, if the evidence of the Creevey Papers is to be believed, upon a Committee of Management which comprised his mother, an uncle and aunt, Mr. and Mrs. John Eaton, a life-long friend and adviser, Dr. James Currie, and last but not least, Thomas Creevey himself.

At the age of twelve or thirteen he persuaded his mother to send him to school in London in order that he might see the world on a larger scale, and he was accordingly sent to Newcome's * school in Hackney. In later life, it became a habit with him, whenever any signal mark of respect was paid him, to make reference to " Old School Lane " as indicating the extent of his progress from this seat of learning. Certain it is that he carried away from " Old School Lane " an imperfect knowledge of spelling, an execrable handwriting, and a very fragmentary grounding in history and general knowledge.

On the other hand, he early acquired, or else inherited, a real love of good literature and an absorbing interest in family and local history and traditions. Of any language but his own he never learned more than a smattering.

In his eighteenth year he was entered at Queen's College, Cambridge, and his academic career was by no means despicable. He graduated B.A. as Seventh Wrangler in 1789, and in November of that year was admitted student of the Inner Temple, transferring on November 7th, 1791, to Gray's Inn.

* According to Stratford Canning, who left in 1795, Richard Newcome was a priggish potentate ; the school buildings antiquated ; and the younger boys mere slaves, pilferers of turnips. . . .

In 1792 he took his M.A. degree in Cambridge and was called to the Bar by Gray's Inn on June 27th, 1794. There is evidence in a letter of this time,* preserved in the Creevey Papers, that he deliberated long on his choice of a career and at one time favoured the idea of taking Holy Orders.

The records of Cambridge University show that between 1786 and 1792 few of the great Whig families had sons at that seat of learning. Charles Grey had been admitted a fellow commoner of Trinity in 1781, but during Creevey's undergraduate days small opportunity presented itself, if he sought it, to recommend himself to the Whig aristocracy by friendship with its cadets.

There are references in his papers to acquaintances made at Cambridge who occasionally enlisted his interest on their behalf, but with one important exception he seems to have made no friendship which survived beyond his school and university days.

He elected to practise at the Chancery Bar, which he considered offered a better scope for his abilities and in his circumstances, and soon after his call, he set up in chambers at 7 Holborn Court, Gray's Inn, and divided his time between London and Liverpool,

---

* J. Bewshar to Creevey. ". . . I cannot forbear mentioning to you my sentiments with regard to your determination. . . . Your present scheme is a just mean between the easy life of a Clergyman, and the trouble and confusion which necessarily attends the business of pleading. You have been educated with the prospect of being one day called to the Bar ; your views, I believe, have been chiefly directed to that end ; and no doubt your Friends have endeavour'd to procure you such connections as may be of service to you in this line. When these circumstances are considered, altho' I believe there is something in your Temper which would highly relish the tranquility of a *Parsoner* life, still a habit of fickleness, I doubt not, would be likely to ensue from a total alteration of your plan at this age. It is true you have deviated a little, but only into a different branch of the profession. The same friends who could assist you at the Bar, will no doubt be able, by their advice or interest, to help you forward as a conveyancer. Your project upon the whole seems to ensure you success and much comfort. . . . There is, moreover, should you reside at Liverpool, the most extensive range for an ambitious mind. . . ."

working at his profession and enjoying the society in both cities of a number of able barristers who went the Liverpool circuit.

A few letters have survived under dates between 1792 and 1802, from which quotation will now be made. They suggest that the social and literary circle built up by Dr. Currie was an important influence in Creevey's career.

James Currie, M.D., was a not unremarkable man. He was a busy specialist whose theories on the treatment of fever were advanced and widely noticed, and a much travelled, intelligent, and liberally minded man. He attracted to himself such men as Romilly, Scarlett, and Michael Angelo Taylor * ; included among his acquaintances Sir John Moore and his sailor brother, Graham Moore ; and was held in high esteem by many families of influence in the neighbourhood of Liverpool.

As the years went on Creevey's circle rapidly widened and his letters to Dr. Currie are filled with the names of new friends. Among these was a charming widow, Eleanor, daughter of Charles Brandling of Gosforth, M.P. for Newcastle-on-Tyne, and widow of Charles Ord, sometime M.P., of Fenham, Newminster Abbey and Whitfield. Mrs. Ord, who was married to Ord in 1779, had been left with five children, two sons and three daughters, and a life interest in a comfortable fortune. She was several years older than Creevey and her elder son and eldest daughter were already nearly grown up in 1800.

The first few letters in the collection in point of time prove that in 1792 a very close and affectionate friendship had long existed between Mrs. Ord and the family of Charles Grey, the Prime Minister of the Reform Bill. It is a point not without value in an examination of the causes contributing to Creevey's start in political life.

* Son of a well-known architect ; he married Miss Vane, an heiress and a beauty. Their house in Whitehall and their country house, Cantley, became important centres for the Whig Party.

One quotation from these earliest records will suffice :

Hon. Chas. Grey,* M.P., to Mrs. Ord

" Fallodon, Novr. 8th, 1792.

" . . . I shall be extremely happy if I can be of the smallest use in assisting you to place your son advantageously at Eton. I am convinced that Eton is the best public school (none of them are so good as they ought to be) and that the situation you have chosen is the best at Eton. I have written to Dr. Heath the Headmaster, to whom a recommendation will be of great service, and who I know will pay attention to a recommendation from me. He is one of the best and most amiable men that ever lived ; you must not be disappointed if you find in him an awkwardness of manner, which the life of a school must almost inevitably occasion. But it is amply compensated by real learning, and honest discharge of the duty imposed on him, and a mild and benevolent disposition. To him I owe all that I have of good. . . .

" All here join in affectionate regards to you. . . .

" God bless you and Believe me, my dear Mrs. Ord,

" Your sincere and affectionate friend

" C. GREY."

The first of Dr. Currie's letters to Creevey is addressed to Felix Hall, Kelvedon, where the latter was staying at the end of the year 1795, with his friend Charles Western. This Western was the " exception " to which I referred above when discussing Creevey's school friendships. A few months older than Creevey, he was the elder son of Charles Western of Rivenhall in Essex, names which will occur constantly in these Papers.

He, too, was educated at Newcome's School,

* Afterwards 2nd Earl Grey and Prime Minister.

Hackney, where Creevey first made his acquaintance, and later on at Cambridge.   He represented Maldon in Parliament from 1790 until 1812.[*]

Dr. Currie to Creevey

"Liverpool, 30th Dec. 1795.

" . . . Your pleasant letter from Felix Hall . . . has arrived. . . .

" You make a sort of apology for writing me nonsense, that is, giving me the thoughts of the moment and the occurrences of the day.   The apology is out of place, for I desire nothing else and I like nothing so well.   If an apothegm comes across you, put it down, tho' it have an air of wisdom and of research, but for men like you and me, to study what we say to each other and to write dissertations, instead of chit-chat, would be a stupid sort of a business. Besides, I live out of the great world, I want incident and life ; and the scenes you move in have to me both interest and amusement. . . . I would have given five pounds to have heard your election song at Maldon.   Do send it to me. . . . Did I mention to you that I kept Pemberten Milnes of Wakefield alive 36 days without his swallowing meat or drink, and without his complaining of hunger or thirst. . . ."

It is possible to glean from the few available papers covering the next five years that Creevey continued to follow his profession of the law, that he was already taking an assured place in a circle of rising barrister-politicians and was gaining some political experience on the hustings in support of friends who were standing for Parliament.

Political events in France occupied a great deal of

[*] A Whig of independent spirit and a champion of the agricultural interests, he ended his career as Lord Western of Rivenhall (1833). Died unmarried 1844.

his thoughts ; he was deep in Voltaire and discussing French politics and philosophy with Erskine, Parr and Mackintosh at the close of the century. For the rest he was looking round for a seat in Parliament and paying his addresses to Mrs. Ord, and he found a very firm ally and backer, in both projects, in Charles Western, who seems often to have brought the couple together under his roof. They became engaged in February 1802 and their marriage took place in the summer.

The year 1802 was indeed a milestone in Creevey's career, for it saw also his entry into Parliament ; and here again Western's good offices must be acknowledged. Creevey obtained a nomination for the pocket Borough of Thetford in the joint gift of the Duke of Norfolk * and of Lord Petre, and it is clear that the influence of Lord Petre worked the oracle. Lord Petre was a neighbour of the Westerns in Essex. He was also the 12th Duke's brother-in-law. Western brought Creevey and Petre together and at a propitious moment. For Creevey was now by no means without recommendations as a candidate for Parliament. He was getting some work as a conveyancer, and already Western and soon Petre employed his services ; he was gaining a name for shrewdness and address on the hustings, he was well regarded by several rising men in the ranks of the party, and his impending marriage would bring him into relationship with the Brandlings who, at that time, possessed considerable political patronage. Thetford's handful of electors duly returned the Duke's nominee.

Such is the solution of the " mystery "—for so it has always been regarded—of how an unknown " attorney or barrister " † secured a ducal nomination to a seat in Parliament.

---

* Charles, 11th Duke of Norfolk ("The Jockey"), was a Whig and died a Protestant in 1815. Bernard, 12th Duke (" Scroop," " Twitch," etc.), was his third cousin and a Roman Catholic.

† *Greville Memoirs*, I, 235. Lytton Strachey takes the same line in *Books and Characters*.

Dr. Currie to Creevey, at Gray's Inn

" Liverpool, 19th October, 1799.

" . . . In spite of the French, the Devil and the Dutch, there is yet another summer I hope in store for us. I am quite sure that if it is not your fault, I shall have seen Mrs. Ord before the summer is over. . . . We are confoundedly gloomy here. The news from Hamburgh are worse and worse. Corn rises, the harvests have failed everywhere on the continent and in America. This winter lowers dreadfully as it approaches.

" Adieu my dear friend ! "

Charles Western to Creevey

" Felix Hall, May 28, 1801.

" Thank you much for my voluminous testa-ment, the comparison with the original is rather droll. As a professional *friend*, I have thoughts of naming you as one *Trustee*, have you any objection ? I shall be extremely glad to see you at any time you have no *good* job in hand, but if you have any fun going, put off your journey till you have less to do. . . ."

Dr. Currie to Creevey

" Liverpool, 11th Feb. 1802.

" . . . I have at length received your long expected letter, and can truly say that I never received one from you that gave me so much pleasure. I could very easily suppose that you would find it difficult to write, and while uncertainty hung over you, readily excused your not writing at all. It never occurred to me that you had any suspicion of my reserve. I very seriously and solemnly assure you I conducted myself with perfect prudence. . . . I

3

could not indeed help hearing the report in question. It was very general before you last came to us from the north, for people here take a great interest in you, and knowing our friendship talk much of you to me. . . . I have been lately attending your Mother or rather calling on her as I passed, in consequence of the state of the eye, which you saw, and which continues. *She* mentioned the subject to me, and afterwards what you said to her about it ; which I desired her not to repeat to any other ; which she assured me she would not. . . . Every part of your letter gave me true pleasure. This young squire * rises upon me much. Upon my soul he has done the thing most handsomely. But let everything be signed and sealed. Generosity is a vigorous plant, but shortlived. Self interest is a little shrub, that gradually increases, and that becomes at length the monarch of the forest. . . .

" And your success at Morpeth too ! upon my soul it is quite the thing. On this one may look a step further. Orde may, will very likely, bring in two members. Be this as it may, your way is clear. Creevey will come in before long, etc., etc. I am truly happy you are taking root. I know you well and love you very much, and have thought of you at times not without some anxiety.

" In your progress upwards, the first steps are the most difficult to a man like you—to a man of pride and sensibility. Give you a firm footing, enable you to stand secure, and your rise, your consideration, will be speedily secured. The connection you are about to form is in every way desirable. I am a fool if it is not preferable to your marrying a Liverpool or a London Miss with £30,000. . . . I never had an oppor-

---

* William Ord, Mrs. Ord's elder son.

tunity of thanking you for your skill in showing off
Mackintosh * in such a stile.   He is a wonderful Lion :
not what you would call a Scotchman—but an indolent, thoughtless, innocent sort of man that will be
continually in scrapes, and that will not get forward
with all his extraordinary talents, unless somebody
take him up and push him on. . . .

" Say a word or two of politics when you write—
kind regards to our friend Scarlett † to whom I shall
write soon.   Adieu my Creevey.   Thou art a damned
knowing one after all. . . ."

Soon after their marriage the Creeveys settled in
London in Great Cumberland Place.   A few short
extracts from the remaining letters of the period
under review reveal sufficiently clearly the first steps
which Creevey took to recommend himself to leaders
of the advanced Whigs.

Creevey to Dr. Currie

" Great Cumberland Place,
" November the 8th, 1802.

" I have broken my word with you I know, but I
know likewise you will forgive me when I tell you that
during my very short stay at Thetford and at Lord
Petre's I was too much occupied to give you any
satisfactory account of myself.   My journey to both
these places I consider as having been very prosperous ; I had long interviews on different days with the
leaders of my constituents and tho' they have been
abandoned on a late occasion by my Patron as I was
nearly by him at the election, and of course are much
disgusted, they have nevertheless formed a treaty of
alliance with me offensive and defensive, against

* Sir James Mackintosh (1765–1832), barrister and philosopher.
† Lord Chief Baron of the Exchequer (1834) ; created Lord Abinger
(1835).

future occasions, I guaranteeing his support to them in Corporation struggles, and they theirs to me in electioneering ones. He however knows nothing of this, but in our conversations he yielded as much as I could expect to my discipline of him ; then they both took mightily to my wife, and Lady Petre too is I am sure my steady friend. I have by today's post a proof of their reliance on me by the absolute discretion which he vests in me over affairs of his of very considerable moment, so, as I said before, our visit of three days to them has answered perfectly. . . .

" P.S. from Mrs. Creevey

" I hope my picture goes on well—indeed indeed I must have it—in return you shall hear how good Mr. Creevey is about going to Westminster Hall, tho' at present it is too soon to boast of his getting up at 8 o'clock every morning. . . .

                                        " E. CREEVEY."

Creevey to Sir Francis Burdett *

                                        " Nov. 20, 1802.

" I have thought a great deal upon the subject of our conversation the other day, and have made up my mind to decline the offer you made me of being your Nominee . . . My total want of experience in the practice of Election Committees and the duties of Nominees . . . and . . . the necessity there is for the person being your Nominee to possess weight with the Committee . . . make me perhaps of all men the least qualified to render you any service. For these reasons I beg you to consider of some more efficient person to assist you."

* 1770–1844. Radical politician and champion of public speech ; imprisoned in 1810 for breach of privilege.

Creevey to Dr. Currie

"Nov. 25th, 1802.

"Do be so good as to state to me whether Gascoigne's * account of last night is correct—' that so far as relates to Liverpool there is a diminution 'of trade since the peace.' I should like to have this fact ascertained or disproved and to be in possession of the documents for deciding the question. Fox was still more admirable last night than ever. Everything goes well. God continue Fox's prudence and Pitt's gout.

"Yours for ever
"T. C."

S. Whitbread † to Creevey

"I hope you will send me your paragraph by the bearer as I want to have the whole copied before I go out. After what I have said to various persons about my amendment, I should be very sorry not to move it, and yet I am determined not to speak before Canning; now this might issue in no debate at all, which would be a very awkward circumstance to me. I call upon your friendship therefore in such a case, to take your own line, and to fire into them about finance, so as to provoke a debate at least. I beg of you not to refuse me this."

Creevey to Dr. Currie

"Dec. 8th, 1802.

". . . The damned disturbers of the public peace have been so exposed by the superior lights of old Fox, that you may have perceived, in the House of

---

* Bamber Gascoigne, M.P. for Liverpool, 1780–1796.

† Of Southill, Beds. (1758–1815). The well-known leader of the advanced Whigs in opposition. Married Elizabeth, daughter of 1st Earl Grey. At this stage he supported Addington.

Commons and in the public prints, the Thieves have taken to the most malignant misrepresentation of his opinions.   In consequence of this and of what I heard Lord Hawkesbury say on Thursday night in the House of Commons when neither Fox nor any of his immediate friends were in their places, I was induced to write the letter, a copy of which I enclose to you, to Fox last Saturday, signed only with my initials, and I think you will perceive by the report of his speech at the Whig club yesterday in the ' Chronicle ' of to-day, it has had its effect.   If anything more comes of it in to-night's debate, you shall hear of it.   I supplied Vansittart and Addington * with your little official scrap respecting the duties, tonnage etc. of your ports for which they were very grateful and requested to keep the possession of it.   I have two excellent channels of pouring into their ears and councils, all kinds of arguments you may furnish me with respecting your trade. . . ."

[The enclosure, addressed to Fox and initialled " T. C.," urged on him in sonorous periods the importance of denying publicly the statement attributed to him by Lord Hawkesbury in the House that " the aggrandisement of France constituted the security of England."]

At the beginning of the year 1803 the Creeveys moved to 8 Park Place, St. James's.

Creevey entered the House of Commons at a moment of grave anxiety.   War clouds hung over Europe.   The Treaty of Amiens, signed in March 1802, held no guarantee of even temporary respite ; the shadow of Bonaparte reached across the Channel, and the nation was preparing for invasion.

Pitt had been for more than a year in retirement,

* Chancellor of the Exchequer and Premier respectively.

and Addington, who had taken his place, had already
proved his incompetence to cope with a situation so
fraught with dangers. Coached by Canning and
other Tory leaders, he made a tardy effort to induce
Pitt to return by offering him a share in the responsibilities of government. But Pitt, though fretting for
action, declined. Early in 1803 our delay in evacuat-
ing Malta under the terms of the Treaty once more
precipitated the country into war with France, and
Pitt came back to the House, from which he had long
held aloof, to support the war and to find himself in
uneasy alliance with Fox in a common purpose, to
overthrow Addington. Such opposition was irresistible ; Addington resigned in May 1804 and Pitt
succeeded him. But the King refused to accept Fox
in the new Government.

Creevey entered political life with few illusions
about politicians and with his opinions formed. He
had thrown in his lot with Fox and his lieutenant,
Grey, and that signified with the old gang of the
Pavilion, including its royal master, of whose patronage
the advanced Whigs still had hopes.

There is little in the papers preserved during the
first phase of Creevey's career which reveals the
sparkling letter-writer of later years. The amusement
they afford is rather as a record of an ambitious
politician's carefully laid plans and his progress towards
recognition by his leaders. He had resolved to take
his native Liverpool under his wing and to fight its
battles on every possible occasion, with the hope of
one day representing it in Parliament ; and in general
to make a name for himself by calling attention in the
House to abuses of all kinds and by harassing the
Government whenever occasion offered.

In March 1804 he made his first important speech,
when he moved to enquire into the war in Ceylon.
This speech is carefully preserved among his papers ;
it is of some length, and, if the truth be told, savours
rather of midnight oil than Attic wit.

Creevey to Dr. Currie

" Ap. 18, 1803.

" Well this fellow Pitt you see has not carried his point at last.   The following account of his defeat I learnt from Falkner (the Secretary to the Privy Council) at his sister Mrs. Bouverie's * yesterday. The King was never informed till Thursday of any-thing that had been passing for the preceding fortnight between the Dr.,† Pitt, the Grenvilles, etc. and he was asked by Addington if his Majesty would permit his servants in the present crisis to call in any assistance, to which he replied ' they might do so and that he had no exceptions to make ' ; he was then asked whether Mr. Pitt might be named to him, and he observed he had said before he had no exception to any man.   It was then proposed that Mr. Pitt should be spoken to and the result of the Conference reported to the King on Friday ; on the last mentioned day the King was told Mr. Pitt would be happy to serve him *if he (Mr. P.) named his administration,* to which the Monarch replied, ' *Then he must wait till my death ; I desire to hear no more of this business.*'   So that you see the aspiring Billy is distinctly *rump'd,* but what the Devil Addington is to do God only knows. . . .

" If you see Scarlett during the Sessions this week, I hope he will give favourable accounts of me.   I am getting some money in my trade and have several clients ; I think and indeed am sure that I shall do in time.   The whole of the Petre family behave admir-ably to me, we are become domesticated, their family and mine, and they *must* become a source of profit to me.   My Lord has presented me to the King at his

* Henrietta, daughter of Sir E. Fawkener ; married, first, Hon. E. Bouverie ; secondly, Lord Robert Spencer.
† The Doctor, Addington.

Levée, where I go again next Wednesday, and on Thursday I am to be presented to the Queen ; rare mummery all this, is it not ? . . ."

Lord Henry Petty * to Creevey
" Bowood Park, August 4th.

" . . . Is it true that Addington said he would not speak a word more unless the King bid him ? He always seems to walk in leading strings, but now appears to have had them more conspicuous than ever.

" I am going thro' the slavery of a military education and am only in the first rudiments as yet.   I have raised three hundred men in Calne and the neighbourhood. . . ."

Creevey to Dr. Currie
" Aug. 22nd.

" . . . The King is convinced Pitt and Fox will attempt to storm him by a Coalition and is quite prepared and determined in that event to dissolve Parliament, but no such step can by possibility take place, tho' from the thirst of revenge in Pitt's friends any one thing might happen as far as concerns them. Canning and his friends latterly have taken it into their heads to be hugely civil to me as a kind of brother wit at the Doctor's expense, and their professions of admiration of Fox as Minister instead of Addington, and their pacific language, are (considering the quarter from whence they come) really too ridiculous.   I had an excellent letter from the excellent Graham Moore † on Saturday, you can have no conception how highly we all of us estimate our good fortune and our obligation to you for having given us

---

* Succeeded as 3rd Marquis of Lansdowne.   He held a number of important offices in Whig Governments.

† Captain (afterwards Admiral Sir Graham) Moore, Sir John's brother.

this most valuable acquaintance and friend ; as for the women I believe they are all in love with him, Mrs. Creevey and all. . . . Do you know, after what passed at Dr. Brandreth's last summer, when the lofty peeress of Derby * showed no inclination to become acquainted with Mrs. Creevey tho' she saw her lord talking to me, she came without rhyme or reason to call upon her when she came to town in the winter ; and so we have all been there three or four times, and we always found the little man very good and the Countess, Mrs. Creevey says, can really behave very well and be very agreeable, but it seems she has a Hell of a temper. . . ."

" Jan. 31, 1804.

" . . . Sheridan dined here and alone with me at his own request last Friday and I suppose we had good four hours sober talk ; he gave it as his opinion that Addington was further removed from Fox than ever and that finally Pitt and the Doctor would unite again. . . . Sheridan and Erskine with some of these Parliamentary youngsters, Petty, Ossulston, King etc., are coming to dine here on Saturday, so I think we must have some sport. Poor Burdett was here yesterday and evidently much hurt at not being able to prevail upon anyone to be his nominee, it is really hard upon him, very hard, for with all his political intemperance he is an amiable, innocent, excellent creature, but the Archfiend Tooke † has put him in this unpleasant dilemma by his infamous counsels to him ; I am sure you will approve of my persisting to refuse being his nominee. . . ."

* Eliza Farren, the actress, second wife of the 12th Earl.

† Rev. John Horne Tooke possessed at one time considerable influence as a political thinker of a radical type and as a philologist. But he was by nature timid and happiest among his books, and does not merit the label " Archfiend."

" May 1st.

" I was present in the House of Lords last night at the interesting discussion that developed the downfall of the Dr.* . . . The state of parties and their respective views I think are these—Pitt has involved himself too deeply in hostility with the present administration to listen to any participation with them in their power ; he knows too the King's hatred of him and he knows the King's precarious life ; to take the Government upon himself alone would have a most powerful Opposition, would preclude the possibility of reconciliation with the Prince of Wales and could not in its nature be of long duration. This he will never do, and always take for granted, what you may rely upon is true, that the Grenvilles and Wyndhams † will not join him, they are I believe really determined to go with Fox. The next question is, can Fox (was he offered such a thing), together with the Grenvilles, make an Administration ? They think during the King's life they could not with such an Administration fight the Pitts and Addingtons. What then is to be done ? Pitt will be sent for and indisputably he will offer to Fox and the Grenvilles seats in the Cabinet. What is Fox to do ? Had I to advise him, I would say ' don't accept it ' ; never, was I Fox, would I sit in the same Cabinet with Pitt. . . . If Pitt was compelled by Fox's refusal to take the Government himself, there is nothing he is not capable of doing to reconcile the Prince ; he would give him a military command, maybe would betray the King and give the Prince a Regency ; what could we do against such powerful engines ? You would be surprised at the suspicion the Grenvilles openly express

 * Addington.
 † William Windham, 1750–1810. A follower of Burke, he joined Pitt's Government in 1794 and resigned with him in 1801.

of Pitt, they all profess to hate him and I believe they do so as much as we do. . . ."

                   " June 2nd.

    " . . . I really believe I have played my cards excellently. . . . I can never be sufficiently obliged to Tarleton for his foolish conduct about the Liverpool Dock Bill, he openly espouses the side of the Corporation, and because I fight for the petitioners, he has seen fit to announce me as his future opponent for Liverpool. . . . If the Corporation and town could agree together upon plans of improvement for either port or town founded upon fair and impartial grounds, I would then most willingly fight their common battles against either or both of the Potentates at the North and South of Liverpool, Lord Derby or Lord Sefton. . . .

    " I know you will be pleased to learn that I can find my tongue in a Court of Law as well as in other places ; Scarlett and I were heard before the Privy Council last Monday and Tuesday in behalf of Richard Lake of Jamaica against John Dawson of Liverpool, an appeal from a decree made in Jamaica against Lake ; we were opposed by Dallas and Romilly ; I spoke almost an hour and the partial Scarlett was highly complimentary ; I however was sufficiently gratified in doing without much hesitation all I had determined to do ; we shall certainly have the decree reversed and save Lake above forty thousand pounds.

    " . . . You will perceive from this letter an alarming alteration from my quondam profession of modesty. . . ."

                   " June 21st.

    " . . . I have thought it prudent at different times lately, when I have acquired a little publicity, such as

by my speech respecting Ceylon and my victory over
the Liverpool Dock Bill, to communicate my success
to my worthy *relations Mr. and Mrs. Eaton* and it
seems by their answers to my letters that I have
produced the happiest effect upon them. . . . And
increased of course my chance of ultimate substantial benefit from my very good friends and
relations. . . .''

The political events of 1805 gave Pitt his death-
blow.

In the spring the disgrace of his old friend, Melville,
following the Parliamentary proceedings which led
to impeachment, hit him hard.

Then and throughout the summer, preoccupied as
he was with foreign policy and diplomatic negotiations
to secure a coalition against Bonaparte, he was a
constant target for opposition critics organised to
press for Reform and to lay bare abuses. The news
of the capitulation of the Austrians at Ulm on October
20 destroyed his hopes of a coalition with Austria and
Russia, which but a month before had seemed to be
nearing fruition.

Trafalgar followed and brought him a personal
sorrow not less deep than his relief. Then on December 2 came the news of Austerlitz, and with that he
lost his will to live.

In these grave matters, Creevey played his small,
important part, a very active gadfly on the Government's flanks. In September Mrs. Creevey and the
Misses Ord moved to a house in Brighton for the
autumn and immediately entered the royal circle at
the Pavilion, resuming a friendship with the Prince
which had begun when the children were in the
nursery. Creevey remained for the most part in
their London house, attending to his parliamentary
duties and more rarely appearing in causes at Westminster Hall. He gave bachelor dinners to members
of his party, Henry Petty and Sheridan being frequent
guests. He wrote very few letters at this period and

those chiefly concerned with politics. His wife and stepdaughters supplied him with the gossip of Brighton, such as it was; but it happens to be a dull interlude in a sufficiently outworn theme and the material available is too slight to merit publication.

A brief résumé of the family's activities will serve. During the spring Creevey was co-operating with Whitbread in the " active pursuit of Melville " and in further harassing the Government by bitter opposition to the Athol * Bill. For his activity in this matter he received the formal thanks of the House of Keys. Thetford's thirty-one electors showed a similar appreciation of a live-wire member, and during one of his visits to the Pavilion, Creevey was chosen by the Prince as ambassador to enlist for the " Prince's party " the high-minded Romilly.

At the beginning of September 1805, Dr. Currie died at Sidmouth and the papers reveal the depth of Creevey's sorrow for the loss of his earliest friend and benefactor.

Mrs. Creevey stayed on in Brighton, her friendship with Mrs. Fitzherbert quickly ripening to intimacy. From her on November 7th she received the news of Nelson's death and victory which Harry Grey † brought down to the Pavilion and by her was impressed with the genuineness of the Prince's sorrow.

The Ord girls made the most of a company of aged and infirm beaux. They walked out on the Steyne with old Lord Thurlow, accepted and retailed the good-natured chaff of the Prince, or nervously filled a gap at the dinner table of their next-door neighbour,

* The brief details of the Athol case are as follows : The 3rd Duke married his cousin, daughter of the 2nd Duke. She brought with her the Barony of Strange and the sovereignty of the Isle of Man, derived from a Stanley of the fifteenth century. The 3rd Duke sold the sovereignty to Government for £70,000, reserving a landed interest. The 4th Duke in 1805 jobbed through Parliament a Bill settling on himself and the heirs-general of the 7th Earl of Derby a valuable part of the Island's customs.

† Afterwards 3rd Earl.

the exacting Lady Holland with her more easy Lord
and her tame Dr. Allen.   And they danced cotillions
at the Pavilion and constantly deplored in their
" dear, dear Beau Père " a condition of mind which
could prefer Briefs to Belles and the air of London to
that of Brighton.

CHAPTER II

1806–8

THE year 1806 carried off two giants from the political scene. Pitt survived until January 23rd and the King was forced at last to admit the Foxites to a share of the responsibilities of government. Grenville was invited to form a coalition, which is known to history as " the Ministry of All the Talents." Fox went to the Foreign Office, Grey to the Admiralty, Henry Petty became Chancellor of the Exchequer. Addington, now Lord Sidmouth, was Privy Seal.

Creevey's zeal did not go unrewarded. There was no doubt from the first that a minor post would be found for him, although his political experience was of little more than two years. He was appointed Secretary to the Board of Control. The post, which yielded a salary of £1,200 a year, did not entail re-election, and carried with it the duties of Government Whip.

Thus with surprising quickness he won his way to a position of some power and consequence and to an easy affluence.

But it was to be " light come, light go " ; the sweets of office were destined to be for Creevey considerably shorter than his novitiate. Before summer Fox was a dying man ; on September 13th he died, universally mourned. His frailties were many and in his day venial, and he never sought to hide them. His virtues were of the kind that cannot be hidden and everywhere claim admiration and love ; stoutness of heart, charm of manner, simplicity of character. His death knocked the stuffing out of the Coalition, which survived the year indeed but went to pieces on the rocks of Roman Catholic relief in March 1807.

Somewhat quixotically (as several of his colleagues felt) Grenville refused to the King to pledge his

Government to consider no measure of relief for the Catholics. So the Tories returned under the Duke of Portland, and returned to stay. Whitbread succeeded to the leadership of the advanced Whigs in opposition, while the affairs of Spain and the Peninsular War claimed the chief attention of Parliament.

Creevey in office and Creevey in opposition were two very different persons. From the moment when his own position in the new ministry was announced until the death of Fox, there is almost a blank in his correspondence. He spared a few days at the end of January to canvass for Lord Henry Petty, who was being opposed for Cambridge University by Althorp and Palmerston, but, once established in his office at the Board of Control in February 1806, he had no leisure or inclination to accumulate material for his history of his own times, and there is not much to draw on throughout the whole of 1806 and the following year. What little there is seems to show that in the first flush of office, Creevey was rather too zealous with advice to his colleagues, notably to the Chancellor of the Exchequer. A temporary estrangement between Grey and Creevey—the only one ever recorded—occurred also and was happily ended during this period. The cause of it was Grey's unwillingness to wage Party warfare in times so critical for the country.

Creevey to Lord H. Petty

" 1806.

" I have thought with great uneasiness since we parted of the information you gave me of your intention of raising the Property Tax * to 10 per cent., and I am certain you know my regard for yourself and your fame so well as to let me tell you precisely how I feel about it.

" Rely upon this, that of all existing Taxes the Property Tax is the most odious. It is new (or was so

* Now familiar as Income Tax.

4

when first imposed) in its nature to the people of England, and the one I am certain that, in its principle and in its collection, is the most offensive to the general feelings of the country.   It is Pitt's child, and it was worthy of him.   He has been stigmatised as its author by all our friends in and out of Parliament, and now alas ! we are to adopt it in a more frightful and aggravated form, with an enormous addition to its weight, and with a removal of the only part of it that had any pretension to humanity, the abatement in favor of persons under £200 per annum.   Upon my soul ! Petty, I dread such a beginning of your reign.   The measure has all the air of the oppressive, unfeeling policy of the Grenvilles, and was I in your situation I would have nothing to do with it.   Rely upon it, it will make the Devil of an outcry in the country. . . .

" . . . Whatever sound policy there may be in raising a considerable portion of the supplies within the year, it is not worth the sacrifice you are about to make for it.   For the first year at least, I would go on by loans, and loans only. . . .

" I do believe if the people see the new administration have nothing better to give them on financial measures than bad editions of Pitt's worst taxes they will turn away with disgust and despair, and have done with you and their hopes for ever.

" Labelled by Creevey :—
" This letter was written by me to Ld. Lansdowne in 1806, he being then Chanc: of the Exchequer in the Cabinet.   I, Secretary of the Board of Controul. He had dined with me that day, and mentioned his intention of raising the Property Tax.   We were then as intimate as two persons could be, but he never

answered my letter, and what is still more to his discredit, I am quite sure he never forgave me for it.

" T. C. 1822."

Mrs. Creevey to Miss E. Ord

" Monday, Sept. 15.

" My last letter would quite prepare you for the sad event which took place on Saturday afternoon, a quarter before six o'clock. I have ever since felt less afflicted than when I knew there was no hope and conceived he might be suffering and his family and friends in the most dreadful of all states round him, but these afflictions to himself and them were all softened by his death being easy and happy to a degree perhaps more honourable to him than all the great acts of his life. He happily suffered no pain and pre- served his senses and his speech to the last. He had many private conversations with Lord Holland after he knew there was no chance of recovery and he sent for every friend in the house (even to two boys, the sons of Lord Holland and Genl. Fox) and as they approached his bed in their turn he shook hands with them in token of taking leave ; probably he spoke to some of them but I know not that he did. I believe his last words (looking on Mrs. Fox and Lord Holland) were ' I die quite happy but I pity you.' It was hardly known when he died, he so quietly ceased to breathe and it was with such a calm smile on his countenance as was actually fixed there after he was dead in a way that Lord Henry said perfectly astonished him when he saw his body yesterday. All this is very affecting but surely it is very consoling to think that he died as he had lived, with most singular happiness. I believe he never suffered from a great and heartbreaking affliction (such as many of his friends must now submit to) and as for the lesser evils of life no man perhaps ever could so soon and so completely set them aside. One lingers over the remembrance of him and it is fully his due, but it is right also to think of his friends and the great public consequences of his death ; so let us try to do so. Poor Mrs. Fox has requested his relations to remain in the house ; they are doing so (that is Lord and Lady Holland, and Genl. Fitzpatrick, Miss Fox etc.). She is greatly praised for her conduct and has the comfort of thinking that his friends were not of a sort to desert her in her distress. . . . I fancy Lord Holland is greatly overcome and it is true (what you will see in the papers) that Lord FitzWilliam fainted and remained senseless for some time and was taken home very ill and, like Wyndham, he has the feelings of having once deserted this great man, giving him perhaps the greatest pain he ever suffered. I pity them the more. Lord Robert * returned yesterday to Woolbeding, Lord John paid Mr. Creevey the great compliment of coming here yesterday to talk of his late friend. I did not see him but amongst other things he told of his being opened (no doubt by his own desire) and of its being proved beyond a possibility of doubt that since this last illness no human power could have saved him. Clive says ' he hardly ever before saw a liver in so diseased a state ' . . . that it must have been years since it was sound. . . . I hear the King said ' I am very sorry, it is a great loss to me and the Country and *it will give me a great deal of trouble*,' probably alluding to the intrigues for a new ministry, but it also looks as if he was not dis-

---

* Lord Robert Spencer, of Woolbeding, son of the 3rd Duke of Marlborough.

posed to enter into such troubles. The Prince is not
returned. . . . We had a very good quiet day at
Sir Robert Barclay's on Saturday, no one but the
MacMahons,* and we were all prepared for the sad
news that reached us before we came away. It came
by a letter from Sheridan to MacMahon, evidently
written under the most violent and frightful agitation,
beginning by lamentation over his old friend but soon
going to his own ambitious projects and (as he said)
to his ' Revenge.' Wanting to see the Prince the
first moment of his arrival and entreating Mac to come
to him instantly. . . . None of the present party wish
. . . to quarrel with him, yet perhaps they may all
think (as Lord John very sensibly expressed to Mr.
Creevey yesterday) that with his present ambitious
hostility he might make the being member for
Westminster a most troublesome engine for mischief, with his friend Cobbett etc. to help him. Most
heartily do I wish he may be tamed for his own
sake as well as that of others. I think he ought
to recollect that those persons who have given him
and Tom £8 or £9000 a year † for no one service
to be performed in return, could have no illwill to
him. . . ."

Creevey to Miss E. Ord

" Sept. 15th, 1806.

" MY DEAREST BESSY,

     " I am willing to confess as indeed I did in
my last letter to Anne that I have used you like a dog
and that I am quite unworthy any longer of being a
pet of yours or indeed of mine. You know however
how disturbing the late vicissitudes in poor Fox's

* Sir John MacMahon, the Prince's private secretary.
† Sheridan was Treasurer of the Navy.

health have been . . . Now this great and wonderful
creature is gone, we must make the best of it. It
really is a most delightful thing to think of that
although he has been unfortunate beyond all conception in proportion to his claims, he has been perhaps
one of the happiest men that ever lived. His great
mind put him beyond the power of fortune and he
enjoyed life to the extreme in the midst of all its
perverseness. . . . Would you believe it, the wretched
Sheridan was yesterday in the midst of two physicians,
and an apothecary, Dennis O'Brien, Cobbett, Graham
. . . and a deputation from Westminster all in Somerset Place, consulting first of all whether he could live
and secondly if he could be Member for Westminster
in the place of his departed friend—in the mean time
all the Cabinet and all our friends have sent to Lord
Percy and he is to be our Candidate, so that Sheridan
after committing himself to stand to supply Fox's
place, will not be supported by a single friend of Fox
—I am convinced he is mad from what I have lately
seen, from liquor, vanity and passion, and he has
worked himself up to such a frenzy that he really
believes (now Fox is gone) or at least professes to
believe that he can turn out all the Government and
rule the country himself.

" Our leading men, Ld. Howick, Fitzpatrick &c.,
are so mad with him that they are for cutting at once
and turning him out of his office.* This however
would be very rash and I shall do all I can to make
them think so ; I have just been working upon
Morpeth upon that tack whom I find furious against
him. He (Morpeth) has shown more feeling and
apparently more sincere distress over this terrible loss

* Treasurership of the Navy. Sheridan succeeded Fox at Westminster, but lost the seat in 1807.

to us than I thought him capable of. . . . Petty too
is every thing one could wish him to be, and probably
your mother will tell you that Mc.Mahon read me a
letter from the Prince or at least part of it which was
really in every respect most excellent. As far as I
recollect, one sentence is ' Was there ever so irreparable
a calamity to me, to England, to Europe and the
World ? Where am I to look for such another
friend, what age, what country is to give to the world
his equal ? '

" I found however by Mac's silence when he came
to some parts of the letter, and by conversation with
him afterwards, that our Prinney thinks he might
have been consulted by the Ministers about the
successor to Fox . . . He may be unreasonable but
certainly they are very deficient in ordinary civility
to him considering how much it is his due, how grateful
he is for it and above all considering the cheapness of
the commodity—I have already impressed Petty with
this and he promised me they should mend. It is a
most fortunate circumstance for them if they chuse
to use it that I have got the confidence of Mac and
can know by such means the real sentiments of
Prinney, for, strange to say, this poor Mac goes about
the streets unheeded by a single soul . . . whilst he
is the only human being to whom the Prince unbosoms
his whole soul. . . . I went over Carlton House with
him yesterday which you know is all new done up and
it certainly is amazingly handsome. Your Mother's
name was put down in a book as having liberty to come
there when she likes, so when you return we will all
go look at it. . . . I asked Petty yesterday if it was
settled who succeeds poor Fox in the Foreign Office
and he said it had not been discussed yet, but that he
hoped it would be Lord Holland. I shall be furious if

it is not him or Grey,* but I won't permit myself to think it can be otherwise. Did you hear of all our blunders about my dinner on Friday ? The Chairman of the East India Company, Mr. Elphinstone, for whom my dinner was made, never came nor has he sent an apology. . . . Ld. Howick and Jn. Ponsonby went into the country ; the ' dirty devil,' jockey of Norfolk,† came on Saturday instead of Friday, when we were dining at Sir Robert Barclay's, and Tierney came whom I did not expect and Piggott stayed away by mistake. . . ."

Mrs. Creevey to Miss E. Ord

" Park Place, Sep. 20th.

" . . . I waked your Beau Père out of a sound sleep this morning to tell him it was Bessy's Birthday and tho' he is not in general pleased with such a *liberty*, he took it rather as a *compliment* and said directly—' Oh *my* sweet child, is it her Birthday ? Well, I wish her many happy returns of it and I am very sorry she is not here '— . . . He said he would *get drunk*—but I assured him he should not but come up stairs prettily to the Dowager Lady Petre who invited herself to dine with me today . . . When your Beau Père went out he *said* he would write to you in return for the cover to him but he went with Mr. Western which *might* produce idleness, so pray excuse him if he does not do what I am certain he intended and wished. They are both very intent upon seeing people to whom they may suggest what *they* think the most proper and touching honors to their Great Leader at his funeral

---

* On his father's elevation to an earldom at the beginning of the year, Grey took the title of Viscount Howick. He played little part in politics, however, until he entered the House of Lords as Earl Grey on his father's death in November 1807.

† Charles, 11th Duke (1746–1815).

. . . Sheridan came here again yesterday to get Mr. Creevey to dine with him, so I flatter myself he begins to be ashamed of having committed himself so indecently.   We are not his enemies, so rejoice that it is so—and attribute as *much as we can* to drunkenness and the nervousness occasioned by it. . . ."

From Capt. Graham Moore, R.N., to Creevey

" *Marlborough*, off the Tagus.*
" Nov. 28th, 1807.

" I have no idea of this affording you very great satisfaction but I suppose you would rather hear from me than not, which is so powerful an inducement for me to write that I cannot resist.   We have been off here eight or ten days, I am not sure to what end, but here we are with eight Line of Battle Ships, a Frigate and a Corvette, under the Christian Knight † who is busy negociating in the old way.   He began by smuggling Lord Strangford off and has since that sent the Confiance twice in with proposals, and the last time, I believe, Lord Strangford ‡ is gone to Lisbon in her.   I know no more than you do what we are to do, indeed I do not see what we can do that is worth the risk.   We hear the French have entered Portugal and as we cannot drive them out with our ships they will dictate what terms they please, for until I see it, I will never believe them equal to the Brazil speculation. In the mean time we have detained a few Portuguese

---

* Moore was appointed to the *Marlborough*, 74 guns, in August 1807. He sailed on November 29th for the Brazils with a convoy and carrying the Royal Family of Portugal, the Brazils being then a Portuguese colony.

† Sir Sidney Smith, Admiral, defender of Acre.   Senior naval officer to the Tagus in 1807 and at Rio.   In constant dispute with Strangford, he was recalled in 1809.

‡ British minister at Lisbon, who advised the removal of the Court to Brazil.

Ships, I have a Lieutenant and 22 men on board a Brazil Ship of about 600 tons, which I am very sorry for, as we can very ill spare the men and we shall get nothing for it. Sir Sidney keeps these Ships with the Squadron, which will not do long. Meanwhile he is negociating. He is a very singular man, and Altho' I by no means go along with him in his vagaries, yet there is a certain merit in the fellow's bravery to excess, in his good nature and his never ceasing good humour. . . . I have a very flattering and, certainly, to me acceptable letter from Scarlett, whom I never saw but at your house, recommending a Gentleman to my good offices. I have answered him to tell him how much Currie dealt in Poetry when he spoke of one he loved.

" I have scarce room left to desire my love to Mrs. Creevey, to Anne, Bessy, and Eleanor. When you see Western, my kind regards to him. . . ."

In the year 1808 this country was once more committed to prolonged military operations on the Continent. The last remaining territory bordering on France, where a fresh stand against Bonaparte might succeed, was Spanish, and Spain at the beginning of the year was still in nominal alliance with France.

The Duke of Portland, whose Government had succeeded the " Talents," with the idea of weakening or detaching Spain, had perfected plans to stir up the Spanish Colonies in South America to revolt, and at the beginning of May a force of 9,000 men lay at Cork awaiting orders to sail for South America. Suddenly news came that the Spanish nation had risen in revolt against the French, and the Government decided to divert the expeditionary force to the Peninsula. Sir Arthur Wellesley, who since the Copenhagen campaign of 1807 had been acting as Secretary for Ireland and had already been consulted concerning the equipment of the force, was appointed to command it, with general instructions to restore the Spanish king's authority, to encourage a general rising against the French and to give what aid he could to Portugal. Three months later, despite constant interference, Wellesley with his small force was in a position to dictate terms to the French. The Convention of Cintra, under the terms of which Junot's army evacuated Portugal, was, however, bitterly resented in England, and Wellesley was unjustly credited with full responsibility for it.

It is well perhaps that the Creevey Papers throw little light on 1808, for the condition of the Whig Opposition was unhealthy and its policy inglorious. The party was disintegrating into factions and was weakened by personal squabbles. Whitbread, leading the advanced Whigs, with Creevey as his lieutenant, opposed the Government's war policy and missed no opportunity for obstruction. Grey, considering the times too critical for party tactics, retired to the seclusion of Northumberland.

It may be well to set down here in Creevey's own words, taken from a fragment of reminiscences which he wrote in 1822, his relations with Sir Arthur Wellesley during the years 1806–9. He says : " I had seen a good deal of the Duke of Wellington in 1806, and in a very amicable way. He was just returned from India and brought into the House of Commons to defend his brother, Lord Wellesley's, Indian government. I was Secretary of the Board of Controul at the time, so that all Indian papers moved for on either side came through me. . . . Afterwards in 1807–8 and –9 I took a very decided part in Parliament against Lord Wellesley which produced such angry words between Sir Arthur and myself that I was quite prepared for there being no further intercourse between us."

Graham Moore to Creevey

" *Marlborough*, at sea, June 25th, 1808.

" . . . I sailed from Rio Janeiro a week since on a cruise ; I have only got *Marlborough* and *Foudroyant* with me, the rest of the squadron with the brilliant Sir Sidney are in Port. Sir Sidney has established himself on shore and is playing off his old game upon the Portugueze. I was very glad to be allowed to take his ship and my own to sea and to leave him to play off his tricks which no longer amuse me . . . tho' at the same time I believe there is a very fine game to be played here, if the Government knew the real state of affairs and could employ a sensible, clear-headed and rightheaded fellow to conduct it ; Sir Sidney, certainly, in my opinion, is not the man. . . . He will disgust the Portugueze, by his pretensions and his intermeddling with what he ought to have nothing to do, and I am afraid he will neglect what [is], I think, the right line we ought to follow. I believe there is in Spanish America a very considerable body who are anxious to shake off the connexion with the mother Country and I think, as the game seems to be completely up in Europe for the present, it would be a great point for us to enable them to effect that object ; not for the purpose of subjecting them to England, which is impossible, or to the weak and arbitrary government of the Brazils, but to leave them to settle that for themselves, as all that we can want, at least all that can be beneficial to us, is the liberty to trade with them. Now I believe Sir S. is spiriting up the Government here to attack the Spanish Settlements, which I think is the way to unite them against us. To be sure, if we must chuse between the Spanish Settlements continuing subject to Spain or France, or the Court of Portugal, there could be no doubt what line we should adopt ; but, in my opinion, it would be infinitely better and more liberal and more likely to succeed to attempt to render them their own masters. No good is to be

expected from any expedition by the Portugueze ;
their government is weak and indolent and inefficient ;
it has strength enough to oppress its own subjects, but
is certainly deplorably weak either for attack or
defence.   We can defend it with the aid of its natural
advantages from any attack likely to be made on
the Brazils ; but they are not the stuff of which con-
querors are made.   I think it would be of great consequence for the English to have possession of Monte
Video with a view to exciting and feeding a revolution
in Spanish America. . . .

" Lord Henry Petty has done very right, he has
married a very pretty and very sweet girl.*   I knew
her a little some years ago and thought her very
amiable.   I dare say he will not make a bit the worse
Chancellor of the Exchequer when you all come in
again.   When is that to be, pray ?   A Dio."

Lord H. Petty to Creevey

" Tunbridge, Septr. 25th.

" . . . I am really anxious to hear some better
account both of you and Mrs. Creevey, since your
journey to the North.   I hope you will both manage to
recruit during this long recess, as I think it promises
to be, notwithstanding the weight of public expendi-
ture, which these multitudinous expeditions must
have considerably increased.   I do not take Ld.
Derby's cook to be a Minister of Health, but if you
have escaped from Knowsley without a relapse, I shall
have good hopes of you.

" I conclude the same sentiment prevails all over
the country respecting the Portuguese convention.
Cobbett's dissertation upon it is excellent, tho' it by
no means explains, nor can any thing explain the

* Lady Louisa Fox-Strangways, daughter of the 2nd Earl of Ilchester.

mystery. I grieve for the opportunity that has been lost of acquiring National glory, but am not sorry to see the Wellesley pride a little . . ."

(Corner torn off the MS.)

H. Brougham to Creevey

"Temple, Decr. 1808.

" . . . No news here. Lords Grey and Lauderdale *won't* come to town at all, they say, and they give as a reason Tierney's * account of the state of the party. —Dissensions &c. &c.—No good to be done.—Game up and so forth. If Tierney really wrote this, he is a very bad counsellor—I could say more—but the people who can listen to it, are not very wise—I conceive that this d——d faulty half-secession will not only finish the ruin of the Party—but deservedly exclude them from all public confidence. Pray do what you can to counteract the resolution of not coming. I presume they will after all come to town. But if they tell everybody they don't intend it, what sort of effect must it have on the body of your voters ? I learn that the King growls at his Ministers for having done so little agt. the enemy in Spain. . . ."

* George Tierney (1761–1830) was an able Whig Statesman even among his contemporary giants, but his career was a failure. He was leader of the Opposition, 1817–21.

CHAPTER III

1809–13

ONE of the chief references in the correspondence for the year 1809 is to the death on January 16th of Sir John Moore at Corunna, a loss deeply felt by Creevey and his circle. In April Wellesley returned to the Peninsula in supreme command. In August Castlereagh's ill-conceived and ill-fated expedition was despatched to Walcheren. In September the quarrel between Castlereagh and Canning on the question of the Government's war policy ended in a duel and the resignation of both ministers.

Lord Wellesley was brought back from Spain * to succeed Canning at the Foreign Office and Perceval replaced Portland at the head of the Government. He immediately approached Grenville and Grey with offers to join the Government and each returned an uncompromising refusal. In defence of his conduct in the face of rumour and criticism, Grey sent his brother-in-law, Whitbread, copies of the correspondence between himself and Perceval, together with a summary of the grounds of his refusal. This correspondence and Whitbread's approving reply are preserved among Creevey's papers, having been passed on to him by his leader and copied. The Creeveys were now established in a house in Great George Street, and Creevey continued to give his wholehearted service to his section of the party under Whitbread's leadership.

Earl of Derby to Creevey

"Thursday, Jan. 24, 1809.

" I am very much obliged to you for your Letter which gave us all the greatest pleasure, but alas the

* In 1809 Lord Wellesley was British Ambassador at Seville while his brother, Sir Arthur, was in command of the Army in the Peninsula.

vision of yesterday is limited, and we feel it the more from having conceived the Danger happily over. I personally was very little acquainted with General Moore, but his whole Military Character and particularly the last traits of it, are sufficient to make me feel his Loss is a great National Calamity, and I sincerely condole with you and Mrs. Creevey upon it, as being his private friends. If you have any further particulars relative to him or his army you will much oblige me by a Line and I shall be particularly grateful to you if you could obtain for us any Information of the Fate of Captain Burgoyne.*   His sister is naturally very much alarmed for his safety, especially as she has had no Letter since He marched for Portugal. . . ."

S. Whitbread to Creevey

" Ward told me last night that Burdett had it in contemplation to move the thanks of the House of Commons to Wardle.†   After what I have said on that subject,ʻI need not now add that I hope he will not do it ; and that you will be able to dissuade him from it. It is in principle highly objectionable to thank a Member of Parlt. for the simple performance of his Duty. . . . In the case of Managers they are the deputed Servants of the House, to whom a trust is confided ; if they do their duty to the satisfaction of the House they have no claim to thanks. . . . On

---

* (Sir) John Fox Burgoyne, illegitimate son of Rt. Hon. J. Burgoyne. He was brought up by his cousin, the 12th Earl of Derby. In the retreat to Corunna, he was Moore's chief engineer.

† On January 27th, 1809, Colonel Wardle, the disreputable M.P. for Salisbury, moved in the House for a Committee to investigate the conduct of the Duke of York, Commander-in-Chief, in respect to appointments, promotions, etc. The private life of the Duke and the notorious Mrs. Clarke afforded a fine scandal for the public and a useful handle for the Whigs. The Duke was acquitted but resigned.

the Resolution of April 1805 * I had a *Majority* of
the House and the whole Country with me, but nobody
thought of thanking me.   Pray stop it."

Creevey to Graham Moore

"Gosforth, July 26.

" I am infinitely obliged to you for your invaluable
present of your brother's Book.†   I never read any
thing in my life with more interest or so much real
anguish as the concluding part of it.   It is a perfect
and unanswerable case for your poor Brother the
General and the most damning one that can be
imagined for the Government that plan'd the Expedition. . . . What are we to say to those who told the
General he was to have 40,000 British Troops and
assist a Nation enthusiastically devoted to the Defence
of their country and left him with his limited army of
26,000 without the assistance of a single Spaniard, to
fight the united armies of France with Bonaparte at
their head? Indeed, my dear Moore, never was there
a case of such cruelty as that of General Moore. . . .
It is to me quite marvellous how he saved as much of
his Army as he did. He was a great and noble
Creature. Everything he wrote under his difficulties
is quite affecting. It will always be a great delight to
me to think I knew him, slightly even as I did. . . ."

Graham Moore to Creevey

"Brook Farm, Cobham,
"July 31st.

" . . . Some time ago, about a month, James had
a letter from the Duke of Portland, informing him
that it was the intention of His Majesty to settle

* Attacking Melville and Navy administration.
† James Moore's defence of his brother, Sir John.

5

£1000 a year on him from the Civil List, my Mother
having declined anything for herself or her Daughter.
James was advised not to give this a refusal, tho' he,
as well as all the family, thought it was not an
honorable way of testifying to the sense entertained
of the General's services.   He thanked the Duke for
the *communication* and requested he would convey
to the King the gratitude of our family for the protection he had always afforded the General while
living, and for the *grief* he had shewn on his *death*.
He said not a word about the £1000 and I was in
hopes they would have let the matter drop ; however,
three days ago, he had the Pension notified to him in
the usual form.   I do not blame James . . . but I
certainly wish them and their £1000 damned, for
such paltry and miserable conduct. . . ."

G. Tierney to S. Whitbread

"Wimbledon, Sept. 25.

"I had the satisfaction to hear from Lord Holland
that you were in high health and spirits about ten days
ago.   I did not know you were in Town or I should
not have omitted to pay my respects to you as a
mark of proper attention to the Leader of the Opposition.   I wish I could comply with your request and
tell you what is going on ; all I hear and see only
puzzles and perplexes my weak understanding. . . .
Mr. Whitbread, it is said, declined an opportunity of
making a Speech at Sheffield.   Mr. Wardle has
indicted Mrs. Clark for a Conspiracy, and they shoot
one another in the Cabinet.   The D. of Portland and
Messrs. Canning, Huskisson, Stenger, Bowen and Rose
are I believe all actually out or have at least tender'd
their Resignations.   Who is to succeed them I know
not—that indeed is most extraordinary, as I do not

even know, what a number of my friends are sure of, that I am Chancellor of the Exchequer and have been so this last week.   Grey is I fancy equally ignorant that he has been appointed First Lord of the Treasury —a fact very currently reported. . . .   Parliament I believe will meet in November and I should presume you would have a stirring time of it. . . ."

All through 1810 Perceval's Government, weaker still by the loss of Canning and Castlereagh, survived in spite of itself ; the country at least enthusiastically supported its policy of carrying on the war, and the Opposition, divided by dissensions, remained totally ineffective.

The enquiry by a Committee of the whole House into the Walcheren débâcle* occupied most of the attention of politicians at the beginning of the year. Wellington, with scanty encouragement from the Government, was in the Peninsula, secretly fortifying the lines of Torres Vedras.

In May, Sir Francis Burdett's arrest made him for a time a popular idol as a courageous friend of liberty, and William Cobbett also served this year a sentence in prison for his outspoken criticism.

Creevey, as assiduous as ever to the interests of his party and of his personal friends, was much in London, while Mrs. Creevey spent a large part of the year at Brighton for the sake of her health.

Graham Moore to Creevey

"*Marlborough* in the Downs.   Jany. 9th, 1910.

" . . . I have been here this fortnight in hopes of collecting my men from the Gun Boats where they have been for their sins these six months.   It has been

___

* The combined military and naval expedition to Walcheren, commanded respectively by Lord Chatham and Sir Richard Strachan, ended in disastrous failure and heavy loss of life from fever and other-wise.   The quarrels and self-justification of the commanders at the enquiry produced the famous doggerel.

bitter hard service for them, poor fellows, who after having displayed the greatest spirit and gallantry while offensive operations were going on, have been obliged to play the part of advanced Picquets until the end of Decr., very much exposed to the weather, not a little to the enemy's shot, and cooped up in a vessel not much bigger than a sentry box. It has ruined my Ship's Crew. . . . Nothing could have been weaker or more absurd than delaying the evacuation of the Island after the great object of the Expedition was given up. . . . I cannot help thinking that Lord C. never had any intention of attempting any more than was done, and my reason is that from the beginning it must have been felt that if they succeeded against Antwerp and the Fleet it could only be by great rapidity of execution before the enemy could have a force collected and means of defence prepared ; and he remained quiet at Flushing or Middleburgh, I do not know how many days after the former had surrendered. I believe he was in the right to return, but he would have been still more in the right if he had not stirred from England. . . . But what excuse can Ministers have for giving such a command to Lord Chatham ? . . . As to Enquiry it is a farce. What could possibly have been expected from an expedition so commanded ? As to the Navy it did all and more than ought to have been looked for from it. . . ."

R. B. Sheridan to Mrs. Creevey

" House of Commons, Mar. 7.

" I can't resist the Pleasure I have in telling you that William* has just sat down after making as neat

* Her son, William Ord.

and as spirited a short speech as ever I heard . . . and
with very great effect and general applause.

"Yours ever,

"R. B. S.

"Tell my nieces * all."

Graham Moore to Creevey

"April 27th.

"You politicians . . . seldom hear much of public
opinion, except in Parliament ; you mix only with
your own set, and you all crow in the same note.   I
hear many different opinions, and the result is that,
whether Burdett is right or wrong in the question of
the Speaker's Warrant, his resistance went too far and
gives room for attributing mischievous designs to him.
And that the popular applause has elated him so as to
turn his head. . . .   There can be no doubt that he
has for some time done all in his power to bring the
House of Commons into contempt. . . .   I always
inclined to think him an honest, well meaning, wrong-
headed man, of considerable talents and much firmness and intrepidity.   I now have more than doubts
of his good intentions. . . .   You cannot see the
folly of the House in a stronger light than I do. . . ."

Viscount Folkestone † to Creevey

"June 12th.

"Thank you extremely for your information :
but I want a little now.   Is the letter a *damned*
foolish one ? does it make me appear ridiculous ? is
it worse or better than you expected from my account
of it to you ? I told you my best recollection of it—
is it the one wherein I say ' it will do no good to the
family ' ? Do other people think much of it ? and

* Mrs. Sheridan was related to Mrs. Creevey.   † See note next page.

do you ? Pardon these inquiries, but after the excessive nervousness you witnessed in December you will not wonder at them. Does the bitch hint at my sleeping with her ? or say anything else about me ? *

" I shall not write to Wardle on the subject unless you write to me expressing a wish that I should do so . . .

" . . . Don't mind giving me your real opinion, however unfavorable it may be to me—I repeat my thanks for all your kindnesses. If you see Burdett and have any talk with him on the matter, you may explain it to him, as, the truth is, I have never done so.

" I have just heard from Cobbett that his trial comes on on Friday."

" July 1.

" . . . On Friday I perceived in the paper an advertisement of the second edition of ' the Rival Princes ' ' with 8 interesting letters from Ld. Folkestone,' and though I feel perfectly assured that there is nothing in them that can affect my character—Here the post arrives and I find the Paper is full of these said letters. Do let me hear what people say and think of them—I shall be anxious to hear and direct to me at Coleshill House. Do not disguise the truth.

" There is enough in several of these letters to raise the laugh—but the only things in them of any serious tendency are the letter about Sir Richard Phillips's letter, and this long one about the publication of the book. You know the story of the first case—and of the latter I can only say, that I never

---

* William, 3rd Earl of Radnor (1774–1869), was a fearless Radical. As Viscount Folkestone he sat for Salisbury 1802–1828. He had been closely associated with Wardle in pressing the investigation into the conduct of the Duke of York, whose mistress, the notorious Mrs. Clarke, had long trafficked in army commissions. Unfortunately

advised her to change her price or to higgle for more,
tho' I advised her to sell the book if they made it
worth her while to do so . . . I could appeal to the
letters, which I drew up for her to write to Lord
Chichester (demanding a particular price and for that
offering to do certain things), whether the proposals
then made are not perfectly fair and candid. . . .

"Pray let me hear what the world say of all this."

"Coleshill House, July 5th.

"I know not whether or no I have been ridicu-
lously nervous and fidgetty—but I have been, I
confess, in a great quandary in consequence of not
having seen you since the publication of my 8 letters
by Mrs. Clarke. . . . I have at times fancied that
as you are silent, these last 8 damned letters have
been thought damning to me, but I confess I do not
see that they prove anything more against me, than
what Lord Holland expected : and I have had the
pleasure of finding that all the sentiments, which
have come to my knowledge on the subject, are the
same—I trust that is your opinion too and the
Squire's.

"I wonder whether the Bitch will come out with
any more of the 210 which she says she has. I do not
dread it so much for the contents, because I have no
doubt, seeing the motive which has directed this last
selection, that if they had contained anything more
ridiculous than those published, she would at once
have published them . . . but because it is abomin-

---

for Lord Folkestone, it came out that he himself had had a liaison with
her. Her book, *The Rival Princes*, was her counter-attack to the
Wardle Enquiry. In it, she discussed the relations of the Dukes of
York and Kent, and attacked the characters of both Wardle and
Folkestone.

able to be thus posted in all the cursed Newspapers
and to be made the subject of universal talk. . . ."

Wm. Cobbett to Creevey

"Newgate, Sepr. 24th.

" I am much obliged to you for your franks and
more so for your note. I have thought a great deal
about the Affairs of India, and, as you must have
perceived, I look upon that ' Empire ' (as the impudent and the foolish call it) as one of the great, one of
the Cardinal, Curses of the Country. I should very
much like to see the *cheat* exposed to the public. I
should suppose that it cannot be very long disguised ;
but the sooner the exposure takes place the
better. . . ."

R. B. Sheridan to Mrs. Creevey

"Decr. 28th.

" I am infinitely obliged to you for the kind
interest you take in Charles * and for your letter
respecting B. You may rely on his not having a hint
from me of any such communication. I will say
nothing on the subject now as I shall have the Pleasure
of seeing you in a few days, meaning to pay my Duty
to the Prince to wish him all manner of good from the
approaching new year. I hope Creevey keeps good
hours and is abstemious in the article of wine ; any
other course of Life ' will not do, it will not do,
' it really will not do ! '

"Your sincere and obliged

"R. B. SHERIDAN.

" Remembrance to my young friends."

* Charles Sheridan was R. B. Sheridan's son by his second wife,
Esther or Hester, daughter of Dean Ogle. The boy was at Brighton
with a tutor and Mrs. Creevey was keeping an eye on him. The B.
referred to was Baker, the tutor.

George III became permanently insane at the end of 1810, and the first business of Parliament in 1811 was the Regency Bill. The Prince was at last to have a say in affairs of State, and the Whigs began to count their chickens and dispose of offices.

But their hopes in their royal party-leader were soon dashed. The Regent was in no hurry to upset the existing government, and as the prospect of their sojourn in the wilderness lengthened, their irritation with the Prince, with the Government, and with each other increased.

Creevey appears to have concealed his disappointment even from his wife and in the course of the session made a notable speech on Indian affairs. For the rest, he continued to act as handyman for his party.

Robt. Waithman * *to Creevey*

" Bridge St., Jan. 2d, 1811.

" . . . We have presented a requisition for a Common Council . . . I think it may be useful to express an opinion on recent measures and our confidence in the Prince. I should be glad of any suggestions from you on the subject, but what I particularly wish you to turn your attention to is, whether it would be desirable and practicable for the Livery to address the Prince upon His appointment ? . . . If the Prince would receive them it would greatly tend to endear Him to them and the Country. You are most likely acquainted with Those who are most in His confidence, and could ascertain his feelings on the subject so as to give me timely information. Lord Grey, I have been told, is gone off in dudgeon—Ld. Grenville is disliked by the Prince, Ld. Holland, Moira and Erskine are most in His confidence and He will probably form an administration independent of Grey and Grenville. . . ."

* 1764–1833. Political reformer, and linen-draper. Some time Member for the City of London and Lord Mayor.

Creevey to Mrs. Creevey

" Great George Street,
" Saturday, Feby. 23rd.

" I am afraid of tiring you by giving you any further account of the effect of my speech after all I wrote yesterday and yet it is so unexpected to myself that I must. The truth is, so little attention did I fancy I should excite upon anything connected with this odious India * that, contrary to my established custom, I went to Bed on Wednesday without even an arrangement in my own mind of such facts as I thought would be most impressive and it was from waking from uneasiness at this recollection at three o'clock and walking about my bed room for two hours that I made up my mind to say precisely what I did, but this again I did without the slightest expectation of any impression from it. . . . Of my admirers for my mode of doing the job I find none more vehement than Burdett ; he seems thunderstruck at my power, as he says, of selecting and condensing and making facts perspicuous. He told me this morning he was quite convinced my two speeches of this session were by far the best thing that had been done and, as he said, the best specimens of good old parliamentary statements —this becomes I find a fashionable doctrine, that I am the real fellow for a statement ; Brougham told me he heard it with the greatest pleasure. . . . Sheridan said it was like myself . . . *because it contained nothing but good sense and good taste*—what think you of that ? Whitbread was the only person who has raised a Cavil at it—the Ponsonbys and Abercrombys are *mute*. . . . God bless you . . . my dearest Nelly."

* Lord Minto's viceroyalty was notable for military annexations, which drew the attention of Whig politicians to the expense of the Indian administration and to the urgent need for reform of its fiscal system. Minto was superseded in 1813 by Lord Moira, the Regent's favourite.

Henry Brougham, who bulks large in the Creevey Papers, first emerges as a power in politics in 1812. He was now thirty-four years of age and had been for some seven years settled in London and accepted in Whig Society as a brilliant conversationalist, a rising star in the legal, political and literary world, and as the chosen adviser of the Princess of Wales.

The Creevey Papers contain a large miscellaneous correspondence between Brougham and Creevey, and many other contemporary politicians, which reveals to an extent not hitherto realised how very much he relied on Creevey's judgment and also (from the cynical opportunism of his expressed opinions) how thoroughly justified were the nicknames coined for him by Creevey and his friends.

After only two years in Parliament he lost his seat at Camelford at the dissolution of September 1812, and, standing at once for Liverpool against Canning and General Gascoigne, was forced to retire from the polls and to his chagrin remained for three years out of the House.

Creevey was now forty-four years old. Though he held a safe seat at Thetford he was easily persuaded to fly higher to representation of his native Liverpool, whose interests he had never ceased to sponsor. As entitled to do under the existing electoral law, he stood and was re-elected for Thetford, before joining Brougham in the unsuccessful attempt on Liverpool. He thereupon fell back on Thetford. The Liverpool election brought the two defeated candidates closely together, although each in private cited the other as the cause of his own defeat.

The Regent still clung to Perceval, and the only gesture of goodwill by the Royal Patron of the Whigs was an offer to Grey and Grenville to join Perceval's administration " on the usual terms " of no measures towards Catholic Emancipation.

This condition had brought about Wellesley's resignation from the Government in January, and in February Grenville and Grey refused on the same grounds to join the Ministry. The Regent was now very unpopular with the nation, and the assassination

of Perceval on May 11 revived the political crisis.
The Prince, after negotiations with Perceval's cabinet,
sent again for Wellesley and instructed him to offer
four cabinet seats to Grenville and Grey. The offer
was refused, and on June 9th Lord Liverpool succeeded
to Perceval's place. George Ponsonby * continued
to lead the official opposition and Whitbread the
advanced Whigs.

Mrs. Creevey to Creevey
" May 10th, 1812.

" I have some pleasure in Lord Grey's not being so
much to blame as I thought, but still he is very weak
and wrong to give way to people who if he had been
steady must have given way to him. Brougham ought
to tell him so, and I hope he does do all he can to
injure Canning and Wellesley—really Lord Grey is
worth saving if it could be done, and I hope you urge
Brougham to try to do him good—if Canning has been ·
intriguing with Liverpool it might be a fine opportunity for Grey to be off—Oh ! if he could but quarrel
with the Grenvilles ! As for the Prince, I expect to
hear of his becoming quite mad and I think Hertford
House has it all to answer for. His Love for that
Woman has been madness from the beginning, and I
have no doubt she and her son are now exerting a
secret influence that will overpower Moira and every
one else if they cannot bring about entire separation. . . .
· " Houston has made every one here believe today
that all was settled the night before last in a 3 hours
consultation with Grenville and Grey at Carlton
House, and his authority was the Duke of Norfolk,
but I sadly stagger'd him forth just now by telling

* 1755–1817. Formerly Lord Chancellor of Ireland. Brother of
1st Lord Ponsonby and uncle of Lady Grey and of George Ponsonby
who married Lady Robert Spencer's daughter.

him of the yesterday's visit of . . . Sidmouth and
Westmorland. . . ."

Creevey to Mrs. Creevey

" June 3rd.

" . . . ' The high and honorable conduct of
Wellesley and Canning throughout the whole of this
business.' This was the language of our friends. . . .
This is capital, two fellows without an acre of land
between them, the one an actual beggar, both bank-
rupts in character, one entirely without Parliamentary
followers, the other with scarce a dozen.   These two
bucks I say in the abundance of their high honor and
character condescend to offer to Earl Grey of spotless
character, followed by the Russells and the Caven-
dishes, by all the ancient nobility, and all the great
property of the Realm and by an unshaken phalanx
of 150 of the best men in Parliament, these honorable
worthies offer Earl Grey so circumstanced four seats
in the Cabinet to him and his friends.   Oh dear, oh
dear, this is too much, to have voted as our poor
friends did, to reserve to themselves such a degrada-
tion must surely produce much suicide amongst
them ! . . .

   " I would not have acted the foolish dirty part they
have done for the world.   What an escape for the
honest sturdy old Premier—how much better he is
off . . . than with these shattered politicians in
London.—What this *new* Government is to do I
know not ; Wm.* learnt from Petty that Moira† and
Sheridan were to join them.   I can have no resentment at any thing the latter does under all the
circumstances of his unhappy case and great trans-

   * William Ord.
   † Earl of Moira and 1st Marquis of Hastings, K.G.   Supporter of
the Regent.   Appointed Commander-in-Chief, India, 1812.

cendant talents nor can I feel very much interested in
Moira's preferring the outside pitch of consistency to
his own interest, if after all his sacrifices he should
resolve either to gratify his ambition or repair his
fortunes.   As every thing is interesting that relates
to these passing events, I enclose you two notes I
received this morning. . . ."

Hon. H. G. Bennett * to Creevey

" Hurrah ! the whole thing is abroad and afloat.
Ld. Wellesley was commissioned to offer Lds. Grey
and Grenville 4 seats, and the Chancellorship not to
be one of them, and a limitation of the Catholic
Question,and God knows not the insults—so come up
to Town as soon as you can. . . ."

S. Whitbread to Creevey

" June 3rd.

" Many thanks for your letter. The same Postman
put into my hand a letter from Grey written from the
Hs. of Lords telling me that a final refusal would be
given to Lord Wellesley's proposal to himself and Lord
Grenville last night. . . . Of course you will have
heard long before this reaches you what that proposal
was. It does appear pretty impudent for Wellesley
to take the Treasury, that *he*, Canning, Moira, and
Erskine should be the Prince's nominees, Grey and
Grenville to add *two* to themselves and the balance to
be extracted by the Marquis. You need not quote
me.

" I am glad of anything that extricates Grey from
a situation which could not fail of being most irksome
to him, and which could not have conduced to his

* Second son of 4th Earl of Tankerville ; M.P. Of Creevey's party
and circle.

reputation : and I am perfectly well satisfied with the decision I made.

" I thank you for your kind enquiries after my health.   It is very good and I feel quite disposed to occupy the Watch Tower and be as much upon the alert as ever.

" I believe it is the post in which I shall die. . . ."

W. Roscoe * to Creevey

"Liverpool, 23rd July.

" . . . Since I wrote to you (I think) I had a letter from Lord Sefton, in the most friendly terms towards yourself and Brougham with a view to Liverpool, to which in my reply I gave all possible encouragem't. . . . That it would be as easy or easier to carry two as one I am convinced, for reasons which you have clearly stated.   One point must however be strictly guarded ag't.   You are at present secure and this security must not be given up on a speculation. . . .

" This confounded ill timed Declar'n † of war by America has thrown us all back into gloom. . . ."

"22nd August.

" We have determined to give Brougham a public dinner in Liverpool for his services about the Orders in Council, on the 4th Sept. next, and as this will certainly afford an opportunity of saying something about the representation of Liverpool, it would have given us all great pleasure if you could have made it convenient to have been present on the occasion.

" I have written by desire of the Stewards to Lords Derby, Sefton, Stanley, &c., and you must also consider this invitation as *official*. . . ."

* Banker, of Liverpool.
† June 18th.

Brougham to Creevey

" Aug. 25th.

" . . . Let me ask you what you think of this celebration on the 4th of Septr. ? I have many doubts, chiefly from the American news . . . I have begged it might be postponed in case bad news continues to arrive . . . but before finally resolving, should like to know your sentiments. If the reports are true of this day, all doubt is at an end—but tho' I have never been *at all* apprehensive of the war lasting long, yet the appearance of the last 3 weeks makes me dread lest it should last until our bungling ministry and their idiotical envoys settle it by negotiation. Therefore I am at present rather prepared for a new battle, to last half the next Session— than for any rejoicings on our last successes. . . .

" I take it for granted that all your doubts are now removed and that you now believe I was rather too desponding in my report. Indeed I think so myself. . . .

" Your journey must be as quick as possible. Settle with Thetford and come—I go to L'pool immediately on hearing of the Dissolution.

" Yrs. ever

" H. B.

" The formal invitation to us JOINTLY arrived here yesterday signed by *Sefton and them all.* I conclude you have got a duplicate. An ample fund is ready.

" Don't speak too confidently to people—but learn if you can what J. Calcraft * is doing—without giving to any one the slightest hint respecting me. . . ."

* Rt. Hon. John. Sometime M.P. for Wareham and Rochester. A staunch Whig, who once turned Tory. Committed suicide, 1831. Brougham was anxious to secure a " second string " in Wareham.

Creevey to Mrs. Creevey

" Fornham [Duke of Norfolk's], Oct. 2nd.

" Well, my pretty, I finished the Thetford campaign for the present, and nothing can be better than every thing is there. I am now in a fidget till my address goes off to Liverpool, which must be this evening by *express* from this place ; as they have subscribed so handsomely they can afford to pay for this express as the devil is in it.

" I see by one of the papers that Canning is stated to have declined standing for Liverpool and this I pray likely. Tomorrow I will send you my address, at present I am affraid of being too late for the post.

" God bless you, and excuse more from Diddy [i.e. himself] at present. . . ."

Lady Petre * to Creevey

" Brentwood, October 4th.

" I did not write yesterday as I wrote to my Brother and was in a great hurry. I am quite pleased with the disposition of Thetford, and sincerely wish you success at Liverpool, tho' I certainly shall regret your loss to us. . . .

" We all join in best and kind wishes to you ; my Brother will have told you what I have done with regard to Dudley North, in the event of your being elected for Liverpool. . . ."

Creevey to Mrs. Creevey

" . . . I send you my *Address* . . . any display of my particular political opinion would have been inconsistent with that *modesty* which *Diddy* flatters

* Wife of 10th Baron and sister of 12th Duke of Norfolk. Another Lady Petre, mentioned by Creevey, is Julia Lady Petre (" Dow. Julia "), the second wife of the 9th Baron. These ladies were sisters.

6

himself he has put off with reference to school days and Diddy the elder having been Captain of the good ship *Black Prince*, a *guineaman!* . . .

" . . . Considering what trash and unmeaning things these addresses generally are, I think it *fair* and likely to soften the Liverpool Tories, to touch ' *The Jackets* ' and to melt the old Bitches who read it over their tea. . . .

" So good bye to you, my pretty. *Diddy* has been up since seven o'clock this morning and has derived the greatest benefit to his health by jauntering about upon a poney that in shape and make is the very image of him. . . ."

" Knutsford, Oct. 7th.

" Well, my pretty, here I am within thirty miles of Liverpool all safe and sound, and Canning is expected here any instant. Horses have been ordered for him and waiting some hours—it would be funny enough if he was to come in to this room just now ; I think it is rather better for us confederates that he should come than not, it divided the interest more. . . .

" Liverpool,
" First day's poll, Oct. 8.

Canning	.	.	.	. 139
Brougham	.	.	.	. 137
Creevey .	.	.	.	. 135
Gascoigne	.	.	.	. 117
Tarleton .	.	.	.	. 5

" I got to Prescot at ½ past eleven last night—sent over with the Lark to know from Roscoe when the poll began, and received for answer at eight that it begun at half past eight—I was there at nine, White-head* and I brought on in our chaise and four with

* His servant.

a procession, band of musicians and enthusiastic
applause ; when I got to the Hustings I had been
nominated by *Tom* Earle and seconded by Ashton's
son-in-law—I instantly made a speech—the poll
began and ended at five when I made a speech from
Roscoe's Bank to thousands of people and was
received with great applause—I did this very well . . .
Canning instantly put his hand out to shake with me,
and we have been cracking jokes all day particularly
upon an old cobler who voted for him and me—we
were all good humoured as ever we could be ; my
addresses have done much good, not one of the
enemy who did not come up and shake hands with
me—the people on our side, even Tom Earle says we
are certain to win. . . . I now must gobble down
a mouthful and be off to the *Clubs* which operation
they say lasts till 12 or 1.

    " God bless you . . . Diddy never was better."

                    " Clayton Square, Sunday, Octr. 11th.

    " . . . I have no canvassing today but I have
people to call upon, such as the Earles and the
Derbys and then I am to dine and stay all night at
Sefton's. I can't sufficiently regret that Charles or
any of the girls is not here to see the perfect beauty of
the scene of our election—Canning and his friends,
Granville Leveson* and Charles Ellis†, who are with
him, say they never saw any thing like it. We are
all as amiable as ever we can be, there is not a particle
of bad blood and I never beheld so flattering a picture
of mankind as this presented by the Voters of all sides
who come to Poll—at 5 o'clock when the Poll closes
each party moves off, the one after the other with his
friends, his band of musick, his profusion of beautiful

* Lord Granville Leveson-Gower, afterwards Earl Granville.
† M.P. Created Lord Seaford, 1826.

flags and his followers—oh if you could but have seen us yesterday, the ocean of people who came home with us and the good temper of them in leaving room enough for Brougham and me in the middle of them to walk unmolested, then we spoke to them from the windows of this house, as is the custom, every day, and they took to my jokes hugely and every body within the room I spoke from, Sefton, Tom Earle, Shepherd, Roscoe &c., &c., were much pleased with me . . . As soon as we swallow our dinner we go to the Clubs and speak there . . . These establishments are without a single exception almost entirely with us and indeed we fight against a hired enemy ; the Corporation and the Boltons, Gladstones &c., &c. *form* the people who vote against us. . . .

" Since writing the enclosed I have been at Church in my Sister's Church, Brougham and Canning were at the Corporation one—then I came out here,* Lord Sefton's, and we have all just returned from a visit to Knowsley where we found Lord Derby looking old but very well, and My Lady tho' she was wrapped up with the Mumps, was most gracious to me as well as in her enquiries after you—she condescended to tell me stories of Lady Mary being so anxious for me that she rode about Prescot and the neighbourhood in pink ribbons canvassing for me, with a crowd following her and shouting, and as I afterwards met the little girl on horseback, I stopt her and found her Mother's account quite true. . . ."

" Oct. 16th.

" Well, now we have struck our colours and every thing is at an end at one o'clock this day, speechifying and all—and I never was more heartily glad to get

---

* Croxteth.   His host was William, 2nd Earl of Sefton.

out of a business in my days, tho' *for such an affair* it
has been conducted in a manner infinitely flattering
to myself—but by God I would not have to go thro'
the same again for a little.   My conscience ! to have
to speak to thousands of people every day after
Brougham, and to speak to hundreds at night, and
twelve times over after him likewise—this has been the
severity of the Campaign.   I am only surprised how I
got on so well as I have done in a trade so new . . ."

                                   " Croxteth, Oct. 17th.

    ". . . As to the result of the campaign . . . it is
impossible not to consider the whole as favourable to
me. . . . It is a connection . . . built upon the most
solid foundation, the 1050 supporters whom I have
found there, are devoted admirers of my publick
conduct, . . . they recognise my claims to be one of
its members, and they all say had I come alone my
return had been certain . . . Brougham has heard
nothing from Calcraft about Wareham, and as two
gentlemen appear returned for that place, he considers
himself as jilted by our friend Jack ; you see Romilly's
fate at Bristol, it is you know what I always expected ;
we shall now see whether Petty will let Abercromby *
remain in Calne to the exclusion of Romilly . . .

    " Let me say a word or two of my host † here. He
certainly keeps the best and most *sensible* house I have
ever been in, . . . his two elder Daughters are perfect
patterns for all young women in their unaffected and
pretty manners, and the whole thing in short is
comfort and good sense itself, with every thing that
is quite first rate in the eating and drinking part of it
. . . Tuesday at my Sister's ; Wednesday and Thursday I shall be at Knowsley, Friday and Saturday at

    * James ; afterwards Speaker.   † Lord Sefton.

Roscoe's, and then for London on my way to Brighton, and now Good bye to you, my pretty. I hope you don't mind my having been so beat at Liverpool, it is quite sufficient matter of congratulation to myself to think that I have not had a single mortification during this trying process nor have I done or omitted to do one single thing of which I repent. . . ."

" Southill.*

" Why should not I write a *line* to my Dearest Dear *Divine*, whilst Lock is getting ready; so you know I can carry it with me and put it in the post when I reach the Capital. I have breakfasted, read the papers, sat and had a good prose with Whitbread in his room, and yet the Clock is only striking eight at the moment; to be sure never human being was so improved in early rising as Diddy and yet he was making Cocky Bennet and Whishaw split their sides with laughing at his jokes so late as nearly one this morning. . . .

" Upon my soul this is a charming place, and improves in beauty every time one sees it; it is now at its very best, and so is Sam, but there is some . . . unfortunate defect in his Constitution, his tendency to manufacture blood and fat is beyond anything I ever heard of, and the disposition evidently increases. He is never in bed above six hours and lives or rather starves by rule and yet increases in weight; with his small limbs and tho' so very little fatter than some, he weighs fifteen stone 2 pounds whilst I am barely 14 stone, and I was struck beyond measure just now at the prodigious Gills and Collops in his Neck. . ."

"St. Albans—London.

" Welcome Diddy, welcome Home. Welcome Diddy, welcome home &c. &c.! To be sure there is

* Mr. Whitbread's.

nothing in life like taking time by the *fetlock* ; since I began this I called at Wrotham and had a pretty long and very comfortable prose with Mrs. Byng, who abused me like a pickpocket for not staying to dine a Wee, all night, but no, no, no such thing.   Diddy knew better than all that and now he has been talking and walking with Graham Moore, Sir John Aubry, Senr., Julia Lady Petre, . . . Sir Wm. Montgomery, Jasper Fonblanque &c. &c., and meantime been up to Folkestone to make an epigramation with him for tonight ; he must just look in at new Drury and in the morning he expects to be off for Brighton in the eight o'clock coach, as he sent Whitehead to take a place for him.   Lock of course stays to do his little business with the kitchen maid."

Brougham to Creevey

" Nov. 4.

" Pray did it strike you that Sam * is *well pleased* at all of us being out ?   Among other marks, I was with him about a week and he never said a syllable by way of condolence or regret at my being out, or Romilly &c.

" The Holland House folks, I plainly perceive from some things, don't relish attacks on Pitt . . ."

The tale of the Regent's married life has been told *ad nauseam*. The quarrels between the tarnished Prince and his dingy Caroline were public property for a decade, and in 1813, as once again in 1820, held the excited interest of politicians for months on end.

The Creevey Papers contain a large number of still unpublished letters on the subject, some of them in the Princess's handwriting addressed to Brougham. It is difficult now to bring any interest to the reading

* Whitbread.

of them ; indeed, perhaps the most remarkable fact they bring out is the reliance Brougham placed on Creevey's opinion on this matter—to the professional eye so highly confidential between lawyer and royal client.

Yet, it must be admitted, it was not professional zeal but political opportunism which induced Brougham to champion the Princess of Wales. He saw in the drab tragedy a trump card to lead in the party game, and we are left to speculate, in no great uncertainty, what would have been the attitude of the advanced Whigs towards her, if in the year 1811, when the Regency was confirmed, the Royal hope of the party had dismissed his father's Ministers and filled their places with Foxites. Then the position would have been reversed. The Regent would have been in the eyes of Whitbread, Brougham and Creevey the first gentleman of Europe, and Caroline no better than she should be. Such was the game of party politics as too many of the politicians of that day viewed it.

In 1813 another and more personal cause drew Brougham and Creevey closer together. During his Liverpool candidature, Creevey had repeated in public a trenchant attack which he had earlier made in the House and under its privilege, on a Mr. Kirkpatrick, of Liverpool. A prosecution for libel resulted, Brougham was retained for the defence, and Creevey and his friends, judging the proceedings to be a political move by the hated administration, awaited the verdict with the gloomiest forebodings.

Mrs. Creevey was still settled in Brighton and in a bad state of health. The letters written by her to her husband in this anxious time charmingly bring out her great devotion, her good sense, and her courage. Creevey himself docketed them with a note that they should be carefully preserved. But considerations of space forbid their publication, and the progress of the year must be sketched in with brief excerpts from half a dozen letters. The Brighton period is fully documented in *The Creevey Papers*.

MRS. CREEVEY.
From a miniature in the possession of John Blackett-Ord, Esq.,
at Whitfield.

[*To face page* 66.

Creevey to Mrs. Creevey

" March 6th.

" I am so tired with writing last night that you must not expect much from me today.   I was determined to try how far I could proceed in reports of Debates when the professional Reporters were excluded, so I took my pen, ink, and paper into the Gallery and in the face of the whole House set to work at six o'clock, and when I had finished my notes of Johnstone, Castlereagh and Whitbread's speeches I retired to write them out fair, and I did not finish till one this morning when they went to the ' Chronicle ' and are there you see in that paper of to-day.   I was relieved by Parnell who finished the rest and I have been complimented universally and most warmly today for the ' Chronicle ' and my part of this report . . . Never was there such a night of triumph for a woman as last night was for the Princess . . .

" Whitbread made quite the best speech I ever heard from him and won the hearts of all who heard him, from his noble courage and justice about this poor persecuted devil of a Princess.

". . . Was not honest Wortley's speech quite invaluable, one sentence that he spoke is omitted in the report, viz. ' That he was glad he was saying what he did in the presence of one (looking at Lord Yarmouth) who no doubt would speedily convey it to Carlton House.' . . ."

" Brooks's, March 7th.

" Just as I had finished my letter yesterday Lord Grey came in here, and there was a full assembly, amongst others Abercromby looking as mad as fire at me, both on account of the success of the Princess and of my having taken down and published the Debate ;

however Lord Grey came smash up to me and, aloud and in every one's hearing, said, ' Well, Creevey, you had a famous night of it last night ; I hear Whitbread made an admirable speech, did not he ? ' and I said ' *that* he did, indeed the best I ever heard,' upon which he replied, ' I'm damn'd glad of it.' . . ."

Mrs. Creevey to Creevey

" March, 1813.

" There is no use in talking of what is past, dearest, and perhaps as little in my troubling myself about what is to come—but the latter cannot be prevented and there has certainly nothing taken place in this Trial to make me have any confidence in your going to the King's Bench unless you could tell me that the Injustice of your Judge and the malice of Ellenborough are without the *Power* to send you to a worse place—if they can do it (and I suppose they can) I have no doubt they will. I daresay the Lord Chief Justice wishes to be an Earl, and he knows the man who can make him so, well enough to be sure of pleasing him if he could send any friend of the Princess to spend the summer in Newgate . . . I am so persuaded of this that I very naturally think of how I may make it most tolerable to myself and the poor girls . . . and as you can do little for me when you are once confined, I hope you will *now* help me to prepare for the worst. I know the impediments there may be about money but I have no plan that I think can eventually increase our expenses—for no one doubts that for 6 months (from June) I might get £300 by letting this house and I fancy there is no doubt that for the same period I might get a small house or a good lodging for much less in London. I should like a lodging quite as well, as I would not venture upon housekeeping in London—I would not have more than 4 or at most 5 servants and they sh'd be at board wages which would not be more than 3 guineas a week ; and I am sure the girls and I could live for very little compared with what we do here— that they would think it rather fun to have the management of our little establishment and that it would be an excellent opportunity of breaking up all Whitehead's profuse habits and finally of parting with him . . .

". . . Charles * would stay and walk about with them at least till August—and our coming up directly for the evident and sole purpose of being near to you is quite a sufficient reason for any scrambling way it is done in. Of course you shall at all events directly have John and I suppose you would like him better than Whitehead, and then (at board wages) Whitehead might for a time do for us in London . . .

". . . I must just say I hope you are not too much guided by Brougham—it does not signify my trying, I *cannot* trust him honestly towards you . . . In short pray do nothing on the suggestion of Brougham alone —for law you have Sir S. Romilly—but I am quite exhausted by this long letter, dearest, and Mrs. Fitzherbert has proposed coming to take leave of me this even'g and I could not refuse—indeed felt no inclination—she has been so kind and affectionate— and she wants me to come to London. . . ."

Mr. Tindal† to Creevey

" 31st March.

" Mr. Tindal was requested by his friend Mr. Brougham whom he left at Lancaster late on Monday

---

* Her younger son.

† Afterwards Sir Nicholas and Chief Justice of the Common Pleas.

evening, to send Mr. Creevey the earliest account in his power of the unfortunate result of the trial of the King *v.* Creevey.

" The case came on, on Monday. Brougham moved to put it off, on account of the absence of Mr. Bennet, but the prosecutor agreeing to admit all that Mr. Bennet could have proved if he had been there, namely that the Libel with which Mr. Creevey was charged was [*erased*] a true account of a speech spoken by him in Parliament, and was published by him as such speech, the Trial of course proceeded.

" Mr. Justice Le Blanc directed the Jury, that it was no excuse for the publication of matter which was defamatory to the character of an Individual, that it was published by the party as a true account of a speech spoken by him in Parliament, and that in his opinion the publication in question was a Libel. The Jury thereupon found the Defend't guilty.

" Brougham tendered a Bill of Exceptions to the Judge for the direction he had so given to the Jury : Le Blanc hesitated about granting it, because he thought it did not lie in a criminal case, but he said he would consider that point, and give his opinion the next day. . . .

" Nothing could exceed the judgement shown by Brougham in arguing the point ; or his strength afterwards when he was put to the Jury. . . ."

Mrs. Creevey to Creevey

" . . . As for the £100 I w'd give twice that if I thought your appearance had given old Ellenbro' an uneasy moment—Your Friends delightfully good indeed—Thank God it's no worse, however ; but no more libels, Diddy, whatever you do."

William Cobbett * *to Creevey*

" Batley, 9th May.

" . . . You owe your present trouble to the old cause : The damnable doctrine, that ' truth is a libel.' † Where this is allowed to pass for Law, no man can be safe. If you could have proved the *truth* in justification, all would have been right, and yet you will hear no *lawyer* say that such a justification *ought* to be admitted. But, until it be, honest men will always be liable to be put into jail by rascals. . . ."

* 1762–1835. Ex-soldier, journalist, politician, and agriculturalist, he owed his influence to his commonsense and pugnacity.

† In *criminal* libel truth was no defence until Lord Campbell's Act. Truth was always a defence in civil actions.

CHAPTER IV

1814-15

In 1814 several factors contributed to lessen Creevey's political enthusiasm and industry. All present expectation of a return to power was over when the Regent dished his Whig supporters. The hope of the party had become its enemy and butt, the Tories were once more entrenched, and the Opposition more than ever divided in council. Creevey, too, was still hurt and humiliated by his prosecution and conviction, and was inclined to shun the House and sulk in his tent. His finances were strained and his wife's failing health gave him cause for great anxiety.

In the autumn, after a preliminary survey in Belgium, he transported the family to a house in Brussels ; and before the year was out, his party's trump card, the Princess of Wales, after still further dividing the Whigs and refusing the offer of an increased allowance, left England for the Continent, to the great relief of the Regent and his Government.

The allied armies had entered Paris at the end of March, and in April Napoleon abdicated and retired to Elba. In London the season was stimulated by the proclamation of peace and the presence of Louis XVIII, the Emperor of Russia and the King of Prussia.

Yet, despite this wealth of material, Creevey's correspondence is meagre and too disjointed to be worthy of record in a single volume. Creevey the inimitable letter-writer, the inexhaustible gossip, is yet to emerge. The fruits of his industry remain still to be harvested.

The year of fate—1815—found the family entrenched in Brussels at the centre of affairs. The

coming struggle overshadowed all other events, and
Creevey's interest in party tactics fell from lukewarm
to cold.   At the best he viewed with an indulgent
smile, from the Olympus where history was making,
the little scores and set-backs of his group.   The
" Mountain " was but a molehill, after all.   He settled
down to enjoy the fun while it lasted and squired his
stepdaughters to balls and parties until news came
that Napoleon had landed in France.   Then the
candles were snuffed out in gay Brussels and Creevey
used his ears and eyes to find his way in the darkness.
As already indicated, he had little expectation of being
noticed by the Duke and was agreeably surprised by
the attentions paid him and the confidence reposed in
him.   Whether it was due to his own merits or to the
deference proverbially paid by soldiers even to minor
politicians, the fact remains that no civilian on the
spot was deeper in Wellington's confidence at this
historic juncture.   He was not to be the only great
letter-writer in the family.   Bessy Ord now proved
herself a worthy partner in the great undertaking,
and her Waterloo letters, written while the events
were still fresh in her memory, are hardly inferior in
interest and value to Creevey's famous narrative,
written down many years afterwards.   The burning
minute came and went, and when the tide rolled back
to Paris, his son-in-law elect, Hamilton, fed him from
General Barnes' headquarters with daily bulletins
more authoritative than club gossip.

The letters which follow are not without touches
of unconscious humour—the omniscient Pope of
Holland House sending out commissions for cambric
on the eve of Waterloo ; Wedderburn Webster, spread-
ing panic among the ladies ; the politicians at home
absorbed in domestic trifles ; and Creevey himself
deaf to the stuttering of the party machine, as was to
be expected of one who rode in the whirlwind and (it
almost seemed) directed the storm.   It was surely
luck or a blessed sense of proportion which saved him
from enduring for the rest of his life the nickname
" Waterloo " Creevey.

Hon. H. G. Bennet to Creevey

"March 16th, 1815.

" Why, what a fellow you are not to write one word after all my fine letters and news. Now what think you of Boney, we are all here in a terrible state and the ' Moniteur ' of the 11th has done our business. As you may imagine, we are most anxious for further news, but nothing is come this day. . . . Castlereagh has taken to his bed with the news, so the political state of Europe is withheld from us ; we are however going on merrily in the tax line. . . . Sam and I go on most agreeably together, I think I am in favour, and I try to keep it. The Grenvillites seem inclined for war to keep out Boney, but you see Sam has declared for neutrality ; it is generally credited— that we have offered Lewis Baboon our Brabant Army and that it is to be put in motion if wanted. If you can get any information upon that subject, be so good as to let the faithful know it here as soon as you can, for it is of consequence. If Boney can hold his head up a fortnight, it is our opinion here that the Bourbons are done, which God forbid. Not that I like those personages, but peace with them is better than War with Napoleon. . . ."

Major Hamilton to Creevey

"March 21st, 1815.

" Bonaparte was expected to enter the gates of Paris about 1 o'c. on the 19th of March. The King was on his route towards Bordeaux. The Troops would not fight against Bonaparte. The esteem of all classes for Louis alone saved him thus long, but all France seems implicated in the act of dethroning him, and the plan has been deeply and well laid."

" March 22nd.

" A Courier is just arrived from Mons, sent by
Dorneberg to state that two emissaries of Bonaparte
have been seized there this morning on their way into
this country.   Their papers are of consequence, and
are before the Prince.*   They have caused sufficient
alarm to *induce my* man † to write circular letters to
the Officers Command'g. on the frontier, to be
extremely vigilant. . . .

" . . . The Guards have received orders to march
on the shortest notice. . . ."

Lady E. Whitbread to Mrs. Creevey

" March 22nd.

" . . . We are *all* very anxious to know how you
feel at this moment—are you afraid of Bonaparte ?
I should like also to know all the news and how your
Master is.   I hope he has not been again guilty of the
same behaviour which you told me of ; tho', no
doubt, he is rather pleased with it than otherwise or
he would not have desired the letter to be *shown
about.* . . . I should rather GUESS that you are a
little afraid, and you would be of little use in defending your Master if defence *was required.*"

Lady Sarah Lennox ‡ to Major Hamilton

" I am desired by Papa to thank you for your
kind note.§   Mama begs you will read the enclosed,
notwithstanding which we shall wait till we hear from
you or Genl. Barnes."

* The Prince of Orange.   He was Commander-in-Chief of our forces
in Brussels until Wellington superseded him in April.

† General Sir Edward Barnes, Adjt.-Gen. ; Major Hamilton, who in
1816 married Miss Anne Ord, was on his staff.

‡ Daughter of 5th Duke of Richmond.   Married, 1815, Sir Peregrine
Maitland.

§ Annotated by Major Hamilton.   My note to the Duke was, " that
all is tranquility."—A.H.

7

Enclosure. Wedderburn Webster to Mrs. Creevey

"March 24, 5 o'clock.

" Mr. Webster * is this inst. returned from Ghent —where he has had an interview with the Duke of Orleans who evacuated Lisle at 2 o'clock this morning—and he is desired by him to inform the Prince that the sooner he is off—the better, and that every body anxious for their safety will immediately quit Brussels—The Duke proceeds to Antwerp from thence to Helvootstress, I suppose to embark for England.

" Excuse this intrusion, my dear Madam, but as I imagine every body must be anxious at such a critical moment—I have taken the liberty of giving you the first information."

Lady Holland to Creevey

" Holland House, May 14th.

" I am very anxious to hear how Mrs. Creevey has sustained the horrid shock. I hope you got there before the news arrived.

" We have moved from Town, and consulted the Calendar, not the thermometer, in occupying the Summer Apartments, for I literally sit shivering in the spacious library ; how is the temperature at Bruxelles ? . . .

" What is the amount of my debt to you for Gina's under raiment ? I must tell you that your packing was not famous, as every one of the little garments has three or four small, *very small* holes in them, of no consequence as the seams can be cut out easily. I wish Lady Charlotte Greville could be requested to

* Probably James W. W.—a bore and a buffoon. It was to his wife, Lady Frances, that Byron addressed the lines " When we two parted," a fact which he disclosed in 1823 in a (recently published) letter to Lady Hardy.

bring me two pieces of fine Cambrick, which perhaps Miss Ord would choose for me and give her, if she will *really* promise to bring them securely."

Creevey to Charles Ord

" Bruxelles, Sunday, June 25th.

" The girls tell me I ought to give you a bit of a Diary* of our two days of trouble after you left us, and so without further preface, here goes.

" When you left us yesterday week at about 3 o'clock in the afternoon, you know we thought all was well, and our belief was the French Army had retreated—it was about half an hour after that Juarenais † called, and came up to your Mother and me and told us things were looking very ill, that he had seen a man just returned from Head Quarters, who reported that Blucher's Army and ours were separated, that ours was retreating to take up a position in advance of Waterloo, and that the French were advancing upon us. In the afternoon during dinner and after it, there was an evident falling back of baggage and troops; every thing came *down* the Rue de Namur, nothing went up; the Place Royale was filled with Cavalry, bivouacing in it, our street and the ground between Belle Vue and the Park the same. I went and talked with the soldiers, who all looked gloomy and told me things were looking but badly when they came away. Night arrived, and with it Hamilton, who confirmed every part of Juarenais' report and my own suspicions; he was graver than usual, left us with his opinion that a most infernal battle for Bruxelles would be fought the next

* It is interesting to compare this letter with Creevey's reminiscence of Waterloo written down at Cantley in 1822 and published in *The Creevey Papers*, Chapter X.

† Marquis Juarenais.

day, and as you may well suppose, we all thought his life was certain of being lost in it.

" On Sunday, this day week, my only consolation was to see nothing more coming *down* the Rue de Namur, and about twelve every thing begun to move *up* it. I walked some way out of the Gate, the road was covered with troops and baggage going to the army, and I heard no firing ; all this was well. At four, however, as I was dressing, Bessy ran into my room to tell me the French were in the Town, and to beg me to come to your Mother. Our blinds were closed, the door shut, and I came with all possible dispatch to your Mother to be present when the French entered the House. I had, however, a strong impression it could not be true from what I had seen on the Namur Road, and I turned out to be right. A body of foreign Cavalry from some villainous desire of plunder or from actual cowardice, proclaimed this advance of the French to Bruxelles and they came in at the Namur Gate, down the street and thro' the place at full speed, with swords drawn and upsetting every thing that came in their way. It was in this piece of villainy that Hesse's horses and baggage were lost, and that Barnes' carriage was overturned, left in the road and plundered. This delusion, however, was not of ten minutes duration in this place ; I went out and found every thing right again, the people convinced the alarm had been a false one, and every thing going *up* the Rue de Namur as formerly. At dinner I heard a noise again, but I soon found it arose from another and a pleasanter source, it was a large body of French prisoners coming under escort down the Rue de Namur with two color or Eagles ; another hour produced another larger body of prisoners, and another Color. We were now all at our best. I went out and talked with the soldiers, and they were in the highest possible spirits.   It was not till I saw Legh,* about eight in the evening, and who had been all day looking at the battle, that I began again to have my fears.   He said he left things in the most ticklish state possible, that the French were fighting like Devils, and that he did not like it.   I talked to a Life Guards man just come, and he said when he left, we were retreating.   I went to Juarenais' and found him and Madame Juarenais supporting an officer of our Guards just billeted upon them, very much wounded.   The Officer said, The French Army were pushing on when he left the field, and as he believed would be in Bruxelles that night.   Seeing Barnes's four carriage horses in a chaise going by at full speed towards the Namur Road, I ran off to his house, where I found a German Orderly had come from the field of Battle for Barnes's carriage.   He told me the General was very badly wounded, that Erskine† had lost an arm, and that Hamilton was safe ; of the fate of the Battle he could tell me nothing.   At night, however, after Hamilton had *walked* here from the field of battle leading the horse on which he had put Barnes, and after being himself wounded both in the head and foot, he came in here ; his impression was that when they left the field the battle was lost, that the Prussians had not come, and that all was over or nearly so.   I need not describe to you the night we spent, the girls never taking off their cloaths and all expecting the French every moment.   I was very much surprised on looking at my old signal post, the Rue de Namur, between four and five on Monday morning, to see nothing coming down, all was quiet

* Of Lyme.   M.P. for Newton.
† Hon. E. S. Erskine, 6oth Foot. D.A.A.G.

too, and presently things were moving up. This gave me a ray of hope. At a quarter past six I was at Juarenais where I found Madam Juarenais among all the horses and servants, and who told me all was well. I could not believe my ears, and she took me to the Marquis who was in bed, and he told me General Alten was wounded and there in his house, and that he had had an express at three o'clock stating the French were flying in the greatest confusion. I still doubted, and in going downstairs with Madam de Juarenais we met Duc D'Ursel, who came from the Secretary of State, Capellan, and who had received the same account with that of General Alten. I flew to Barnes's, saw him, poor fellow, as gay as a lark in the midst of his blood, and both he and Hamilton were convinced my news was true, as the French must have been in Brussels before that hour, had they not been beat. They had heard the report of my news, and Major Evatt* had been sent off to Head Quarters to ascertain all about it. From this time all was sunshine, and you know the rest as well as I do. In the course of that morning (Monday) Wellington came over here to write his dispatch, and as you have learnt from Bessy he beckoned to me out of his windows to come up to him, and having shook hands, he very gravely told me how very *critical* the battle had been, and with what incredible gallantry our troops had conducted themselves. He walked about uttering expressions of astonishment at our men's courage and particularly at the Guards keeping their position in a Chateau and garden in front of the left † of his position.

"On Tuesday morning, nothing would serve Barnes and Hamilton but I must ride over and see

* G. Evatt, 55th Foot A.A.G. to General Barnes.
† Hougomont was on the right of Wellington's position.

their positions, so I was mounted on your old friend the *Curate*, accompanied by Barnes's groom on a Boss Coach Horse. Two miles on this side Waterloo Wellington overtook me in his curricle with Harvey, so we went on together and he said Harvey would mount his horse at Waterloo and shew me over the field of battle, and all about it, which he did with Lord Arthur Hill, Barnard, Cathcart and others. Terrible as this sight was in prospect and in fact, it was most interesting, and I would not have missed it for the world. I talked with various French soldiers lying among the dead, but not dead or dying themselves. They were very gay, and Lord Arthur got off and gave three or four of them some gin and water out of a bottle he had, and they all called him ' Mon Général ' and said he was ' bien honnête.' Harvey told me in riding home he thought the French left on the field were 15,000, and here ends my story.

" If you see Bennet tell him I got his last letter, and that I have neither ' *lost my senses* ' nor ' *am I bit.*' His letter was rather a pert one, and you may give a little hint I think so."

Miss E. Ord to Charles Ord

" My Mother begs you will do no such thing Charley, my dear—I have little to add to this dispatch but that General Barnes is going on well, as are the wounded generally. Hesse * is still in bed but doing well. Erskine is surprisingly so, but I cannot consider him as perfectly safe till a few more days are over. . . . I suppose now the Army is so much advanced, you have more news of them in England than we have here. We suppose the Head Quarters are at St. Quentin, but no position dispatches come to

* Capt. Hesse, afterwards of Queen Caroline's Household.

any one here.   I trust in Heaven Ld. Wellington will not risk this little body of men without the other Allies doing what they ought, which I confess I doubt. Nothing can look more favourable than the report made in the French H. of Commons of the insurrections in all parts of France.   John Grey* is nearly well, he w'd. have dined with us today but we chose he should be on the over cautious side and keep himself quiet a day or two longer. . . .

"We have just heard that the Duke of Bedford has arrived.   Mr. Creevey has called on him and written to him, but we have no answer yet. . . .

"P.S.   Have heard nothing, so the Duke must be gone to see the field of Battle, and it will be late before he returns. . . ."

Hon. H. G. Bennet to Creevey

"July 5th.

"What an age we live in ; we fare victorious here, as you do at Waterloo—think of our triumph over the Duke of Cumberland † . . . Nothing ever was better done—having got rid of the old drone Ponsonby, Cole ‡ became factious and announced an opposition, every stage of which was carried into effect, and you see we have thrown out the bill by one vote. . . . I believe, however, the Queen was our best ally as she was furious and kept many away, so it was the old court against the new ; she refuses to see the Duke and Duchess, and there have been terrible scenes between her and Prinney, so much so that the

* Capt. 10th Hussars.

† The Duke's marriage to the Princess of Solms was very much disliked by the Royal family and the country.   Parliament refused by one vote to increase the Duke's allowance on marriage.   The affair afforded almost as much interest as the Battle.

‡ Tierney.

Princess says that there is no chance of a reconciliation. . . . Prinney is much discomfitted at this, and
the Tories say it is the commencement of a revolution
—We are looking out for news from Paris, there are
many rumours afloat such as the Bombardment of
Paris—it being taken by assault—the escape of
Boney to America—but there are no official accounts
come—tho' if the allies were in Paris on Sunday we
ought to have learnt the news last night.   In all events
we . . . are all against Louis le Desiré, and young
Cole * is in tears and prophesies the end of the world
on account of the restoration of the Bourbons—we
are all for Napoleon the 2nd., versus the legitimate
monarch. . . .

" . . . Sam looks and is very ill. . . . I never saw
him so low.   He leaves town next week for Southill
—this makes me wretched.

" Brougham is doing well, and Sefton who huzzaed
old Cholmondeley all up the street the evening of the
Duke's defeat—the Taylors too are stout and are
going to Little Hampton for the year.   Ferguson
desires to be remembered.   Let me hear from you,
tho' Brussels must be a dull place now.   Maitland
has returned and likes Peronne, and is the hero of the
day ; every one praises him. . . ."

" July 7th.

" I write by this day's Mail per the Horse Guards,
and send this per post.   It is to tell you that you have
lost your friend Whitbread, who died yesterday
morning. . . . I hardly know how to tell you that
the blow, great and over-whelming as it is, is much
increased by the manner of his death.   He destroyed
himself in a paroxysm of the disease in the head which

* James Abercromby.

was an aneurism under which he laboured. He had
been long in a low and declining way, and the damned
theatre* and the worries attendant on it so over-
powered him as to lead to this fatal step. Gracious
God, what is not the loss to us all, take it any way,
public or private ? Who is like him, who was ever
like him ? . . . The purity and honesty of his life and
character ; there is not a person in the kingdom but
the vile and base, who does not deplore his loss. You
can form no notion of the general feeling here. I
never saw people so agitated. Poor Lady Elizabeth
is in a dreadful state ; she has not spoken since. I
can write no more. God help you. . . ."

Lord Ossulston † to Creevey

"July 7th.

" I wish to join with the other persons who I
understand mean to write to you today, and communicate to you by far the most deplorable event
which has happened in our time, not excepting the
death of Mr. Fox, viz. the death of *poor Whitbread*
which took place yesterday morning. . . . I cannot
hope to save you the pain of knowing what wd. come
to you from so many quarters, viz. that Sam's sensibility of mind on that important subject which so
unaccountably enfused his whole thought, viz. Drury
Lane Theatre, and an idea that he had been the cause
of distress to persons who had embarked their profit
in it at his suggestion, precipitated (by his own hand)
what his broken state of health was preparing. . . .
For three or four weeks he was much altered in looks
and manner, complaining that he could not attend to

* He was on the Drury Lane Theatre Committee, and its leading
spirit.

† Succeeded in 1822 as 5th Earl of Tankerville ; brother of Henry
Bennet.

business &c. and there was a particular tenderness in
his manner to his friends. . . .

" . . . On Wednèsday night, the night before his
death, he passed the whole even'g with Wiltshire and
Burgess who with diff'y. persuaded him that to lose
one part dividend was not absolute ruin either to
those who had Drury Lane Shares. On going to bed,
however, he returned to his old arguments with Ly.
Eliz., and I understand passed the most restless night,
as he had done for a long time, and on the following
morning on getting up he went into his Dressing
Room where with what he found on his Dress Table
he˗ put an end to his life. He was found slashed on
the floor abt. ten o'clock by one of the servants whose
screams made known the event. . . .

" I find the ' Morning Post ' has the credit of being
the only paper that notices the manner of the death."

Miss E. Ord to Wm. Ord at Florence

" Brussels, July 9th.

" . . . Considering how very uncomfortable we
have been, I assure you we deserve great credit,
particularly my Mother, for our good behavior, and
when I think of all the other circumstances and events
of the last two months, in addition to her anxiety
about you, I am almost astonished to see her sitting
in her corner really not much affected in her health.
. . . I do not know where to begin my story. You
have heard how the landing of Bonaparte put a stop
to all our gaieties, how in Easter week the alarm of
his intending to make a dash at this country made
almost all the English families fly off to Ostend,
Antwerp, and England, and that after serious delibera-
tion and taking the advice of all those who were considered authorities both civil and military, Boss and

British, it was decided that under the circumstances of my Mother's health we were more likely to meet with inconvenience by running away than by staying. . . . This storm and all the clouds attending it soon blew over, Ld. Wellington arrived, almost all the fugitives came back, Brussels became as gay as ever, and if possible pleasanter when one could avoid thinking of what was to come. Ld. Wellington had delightful Balls every week, and of course military of all nations abounded at them. Troops from England were arriving every day, and I think one saw every officer almost one had ever seen or heard of. At last on the 15th. of June we were all invited to a Ball at the Duchess of Richmond's, and in the middle of that day Ld. Wellington received the account of the Prussians having been attacked and beat by Bonaparte, who was advancing towards one end of the English lines as fast as possible. To give an idea of this take-leave Ball is impossible, it was too dismal ; but I must not begin to talk of our feelings in any part of these three or four days or I should never be able to stop, or even then to do them the least justice. It was *principally* misery for our friends—the fright for ourselves was only occasional, and never I believe as great as it ought to have been, as I think it was not till it was all over that the consciousness of what we had escaped came upon us in its full force. . . . On the 16th. for several hours we had a canonade, the concussion of which on the Air we felt as if it was close at hand. It was frightful, and our only comfort was the idea that our troops were so spread that it was impossible they should have reached the ground where the fighting was said to be. About 12 o'clock at night, however, we were cruelly undeceived by the arrival of Major Hamilton (with whom we had been dancing the night before)—our Army, or rather parts of it as fast as they came up after most fatiguing marches, had had some very severe fighting, and had beat the French, but as not a man of the Cavalry had arrived on the ground, no advantage could be taken of it.   Major Hamilton, who is on the Staff, A.D.C. to Genl. Barnes, had not gone to bed after the Ball, had rode to the field of Battle, fought all day, had his horse killed under him with other hair-breadth escapes, had seen Ld. Wellington sit down to supper at Genappes 28 miles from here, and had then rode off here to tell us the news.   In two hours, he started again.   On the 17th. we were less unhappy from not hearing guns ; some of the Staff came into Brussels in good spirits at the performances of the day before, and I could tell you many interesting stories of the gallantry of both officers and men, if they could be put into a letter, that would make you doat upon them.   You never saw anything like the state of this town night and day.   The streets jammed full of horses, waggons, artillery, soldiers, and people of all sorts—bivouacs even in our little quiet street.   Our house commands a side view of the street leading to the Namur Gate thro' which everything passed to the Army and according as baggage &c. &c. went *up* or came *down* this street, we had a very accurate means of judging how matters went on. . . .

" On Sunday the 18th. of June we, amongst many others, shall never forget it, and it is impossible to describe—it was passed in a sort of stupid state of despair, now and then enlivened by reports spread to create confusion, that French Dragoons were actually in the Town, Waggons, Baggage, &c. &c. were over-turned in the fright, the road was blocked up, and the infamous villains who had raised the cry (composed of

stragglers of all nations) plundered everything at
their leisure, and above half the Officers of the Army
have lost everything they had ; those who were left
to guard taking fright and galloping off in every
direction, and assuring every one the French were at
their heels. Every hour brought the name of some
Officer either killed or wounded, that the fighting was
desperate, &c. &c. Mr. Creevey every time he went
out returned with a more dismal face, till at last we
sat looking at each other without venturing to ask
any questions. Again at night Major Hamilton
arrived having just walked from the field of Battle,
leading a horse with two balls in it, and his poor Genl.
on it severely wounded, and himself slightly so in the
head and foot. His account was that never was there
such fighting from the Duke down to the Drummer,
but he feared from the Prussians not being yet in
action when he left the field, and the immense
superiority in numbers, particularly in cavalry, of the
French, that things would not end well, and that, as in
that case Brussels could not be kept, we must make
up our minds what to do, and that if we determined to
go, he wd. press a carriage &c. &c. Our manner of
passing the night I leave you to guess—Anne and I
never took off our cloaths ; not having slept much for
the two nights before, this was spent in trying to
decide what we ought to do, there being great danger
in either determination. By five in the morning we
had Mr. Creevey in the Drawing room, and as soon as
it was possible to have a chance of seeing anybody,
he went out to hold a final consultation with a Boss
friend. There he heard what had taken place after
Genl. Barnes and Hamilton had left the field, and that
never was there so complete a Victory. In the course
of the morning he saw Ld. Wellington, who was

everything that he ought to be, grave, awed, astonished—walking up and down the room making
exclamations about the wonderful conduct of the
Army, and yet what a cold dispatch he wrote ; but
tho' he can't write he is an astonishing man.   His
personal conduct on this occasion was our great
means of gaining the battle.   The scenes after such a
battle fought within so short a distance have been
dreadful, thousands of wounded brought in hourly.
Hearing a horse at our door I looked out and saw an
officer supported by a Dragoon.   He was so pale and
covered with dirt that it was not till the second look
I knew poor Hesse ; he came to know where we wd.
recommend him to go, but of course as Chas.'s bed
was vacant he went no further.   The wound is
through his right arm just below the elbow, both his
life and his arm have been in danger, but I trust both
are now entirely safe tho' he has suffered dreadfully
and has never left his bed till today for a few hours.

" Our greatest happiness was now to be useful to
the sufferers.   We had five dying Prussians billetted
upon us, and we could not get them into an hospital
for two days, and if it had not been for Hesse's
Surgeon, they wd. never have had their wounds
dressed ; all we could do was to wash and feed them.
Then we offered the use of our dining room with a bed
in it to the Duke's surgeon (as by the most extraordinary luck all our most particular friends were
safe) and a week after the battle a little interesting
Captn. Dumaresq,* A.D.C. to Genl. Byng, was brought
from a farm house at Waterloo on a litter on men's
shoulders.   He is shot thro' the lungs, and the ball is
still in him, but tho' still confined to his bed and likely
to be for some time, he is considered to be out of danger,

* 9th Foot.

and his spirits are so good that our only difficulty is to keep his tongue quiet for two minutes. Our whole time is taken up with our Out and Indoor Patients, for to the astonishment, and rather dismay, of Mrs. Greathed, we go and sit by the beds of any who like to see us, and you cannot think how it seems to please them. John Grey whom you wd. see in the list, is now quite well and going to join in a few days—Col. Vigoureux we visit daily and he is more interesting than I ever saw him from the manly way he bears a very painful wound in his leg. The wounded, generally, are doing well, the weather has been most favorable, and there have been no fevers, notwith-standing there have been 30,000 wounded of different nations in the town at one time. The attention and devotion of the natives to the English common men as well as Officers is most touching, and is a most flattering proof of their good conduct since they have been quartered here. But, Good God what a Battle it was, and if it should not be the conclusion ; and as long as Bonaparte is in France I cannot persuade myself it can be. I trust in Heaven he will not get to America as I think he wd. be very dangerous there, but I must not write Politics. . . ."

Mrs. Creevey to W. Ord

" Lest you should think my dearest William that the Battle of Waterloo has had some extraordinary effect on your old Mother, you shall at least see her handwriting to tell you that nothing has so much cheer'd her as the letter she got from you yesterday. Indeed I was beginning to have all sorts of un-comfortable fancies and no doubt they might be the stronger from my nerves having got a considerable shake by being so *very near* to the horrors of War, and

most people may think I deserved some punishment
for braving such dangers, but the truth is that our
great Duke himself was taken by surprise, or he
would not have been at the Duchess of Richmond's
Ball on the morning of the Battle of Genappe . . .
I think I must tell you of one change that has taken
place in me—I am become a more devoted and
enthusiastic admirer of the Duke of Wellington—
most deeply impressed with his extraordinary skill and
heroic bravery in the late Battle, and full of admiration of his moderation since he got to Paris, but I will
follow your wise example and go no further on public
matters. . . . I wish I could meet you at Florence or
Rome, but alas ! lame legs are unfit for going so far,
and mine get lamer I think every day, so I must hope
that Brussels will be as pleasant next winter as it was
the last, and then I shall have no reason to complain
of my situation.   Mr. Creevey talks of a short trip to
Paris (for himself only) whilst our Army is there, for
he is sure of meeting with such a reception at Head
Quarters as wd. add greatly to the pleasure of seeing
sights. . . ."

Major Hamilton to Creevey

" Port Saint Maxance,
" July the 15th.

" I send you a paper of 14th, which arrived here
from Paris as we did about an hour ago.   We shall
get in tomorrow at 4 o'clock.

" The Prince of Orange will stop here tomorrow
night—one of his Belgic A.D.C.'s arrived at Roye this
morning as we were quitting it, and says the Prince is
as well as a wounded Prince can be.

" My General is getting on well, and has wanted
nothing to make his journey pleasant to him but you.

8

I shall soon tell you when to come to Paris, and come
you ought, for Paris will be seen to much advantage
by you when the allies are there—but how would this
answer for my friend in the corner ?

" I recollect once to have heard the General say
that ' Creevey's family must be the happiest in the
World,' and I have very often since abused him for
wishing you to quit it, even for so long a time as to
see Paris, therefore the best thing to be done is to
move thither with *every body*."

> " No. 4 Rue D'Anjou,
> " St. Honoré, Paris,
> " July the 17th.

" We are got into a very delightful billet, and will
have every thing very comfortable and snug very soon,
and all prepared for you when the spirit moves you to
come hither.

" The Duke of Wellington is continually employed
in conferences with the Kings and Emperors, and
seems to think of nothing else—what they are all
doing is not for us to know.   Every body seems intent
on the pursuit of their own amusements, and very little
business is thought of.

" Blucher has asked the 8 Millions mentioned in
the papers for his own Army only, and without the
knowledge of the Duke—at least he pretends to know
nothing about it. . . ."

Mary Lady Petre to Creevey

> " July 17th.

" I fear you will think me very inattentive in being
so long without answering your kind letter, and
congratulating you upon having *survived* the terror
you must have been in the day of the terrible Battle,
which quite makes me shudder at this distance when

I think of it. I trust, however, it will promise us Peace, but a Dear bought one it is indeed. Charles's having gone to America (which at the time I thought so hard) has properly preserved him to me, as I am sure the 14th. would have been there if they had not just returned from America. My Nephew, Henry Petre, who is in the Inniskillings, luckily escaped. . . .

"Thetford I have heard but little about lately, but I do not think *we* are very popular there. The Duke of Grafton always behaves in the most handsome manner upon the subject. . . ."

Major Hamilton to Creevey

"July 18th.

"The report has just reached us that Bonaparte was embarked on board a French friggate, and pursued into a harbour in the Isle of Rhé, where he was closely watched by our Cruisers for several days, but getting tired of waiting there, he sent to the Captain of the Belona* to ask if he would permit his passage to America, to which demand a negation was given.

"Bony immediately put to sea and gave himself up to the Belona. He has been sent to England, and dispatched a message to the Prince Regent to ask permission to proceed to America.

"The eight millions demanded by Blucher has caused a good deal of talk, but the old Gentleman holds out, and Lord Wellington will not interfere. . . ."

"July 20th.

"All the world are gone to a Review of two regiments of Austrians, and the Duke has just passed with the Emperors and Kings. After the show is over they all go to their conference as usual. I cannot

---

* Bonaparte voluntarily surrendered to Capt. Maitland of *Bellerophon* on July 15th.

pick up any news this morning. Harvey thinks we shall be here six weeks or two months, and even then it is a question whether old Louis can hold his own without us.

" The Prussians torment the natives dreadfully, but the least complaint against an Englishman is attended to and the latter is sure to come off second best. The town is as full of all sorts and conditions of men as if all Europe had been collected in one spot. . . ."

" July 22nd.

" I have just heard that the Allied Chiefs have sent to Davoust to desire he will order the French Army into cantonments, and await further instructions from his Sovereign—his answer is expected tomorrow, which of course must be in the affirmative as far as regards the first article, but whether he will take Louis' orders is a question.

" We saw about 15,000 Prussian Guards reviewed this morning, and it is quite impossible to describe the beautiful appearance they made in every respect. . . ."

" July 23rd.

" I have just heard from Fagal that a note *is said* to have been written to the Ministers assembled here, by Louis 18th, stating that as he perceives it is not the wish of the French people to have him or his family, he would willingly resign the Throne and retire into Spain. This was asked of Lord Clancarty to confirm, and his Lordship did not deny the fact, but it is not yet spoken of as fact. . . ."

" July the 25th.

" The Review lasted yesterday from 10 o'clock until 5 o'clock in the evening—about 69,000 men,

composing Duke Wellington's Army, passed the
Emperor of Austria, and made a very good appearance.   The French people seem to become more and
more averse to Louis, and all this show of troops in the
Capital seems to exasperate them.

" Davoust's answer has not been made known,
but it would seem that the Austrians are moving to
attack the French Army.   Like a cunning Frenchman he pretends to have nothing to do with the
spirit prevailing in the army, and sends in his submission to the will of the King, but this does not blind
the Allied Chiefs.   There will be a blow up yet before
all is settled.

" Lady Castlereagh has commenced giving Balls
and Suppers, and they talk of one at Hd. Qrs., but we
all seem to agree that Paris is becoming a very stupid
place. . ."

" July the 27th.

" . . . Whilst the British Field Marshal is unfortunately confined by ill-health, the Prussian Chief
thinks it right to be on the qui vive, and was poking
about—no doubt with good intent—when he stumbled
upon a place where twenty two stand of Prussian and
Austrian Colours were secreted.   The Marshal took
his measures most prudently, and, not liking to trust
his secret, as in the case of the blowing up of the
bridges of Gena and Austerlitz, he kept his own
council, and sent a regt. in the night and laid hold of
the standards without any fuss.

" The most perfect collection of models of all the
fortified places of Europe have fallen into the hands of
the Allies as being implements of War, and Colonel
Smith of the Engineers has been employed in sending
to England our share of the prizes, which is very
valuable in a military point of view.

"*July the* 28*th*. Papers have been (just) recd. from England to the 25th.   Bony's letter to the Prince (which I copy) will at least insure him the *Garter*.

" ' Exposed to the factions which divide my country and to the enmity of the great powers of Europe, I have terminated my political career, and I come like Themistocles to throw myself upon the hospitality of the British people.' . . ."

" August 1st.

" Bonaparte is to go (has gone I believe ere this time) to St. Helena. Old Hudson Lowe is named Governor, he has arrived at Marseilles with 4,000 or 5,000 men, but what force he is to have as a garrison at his new post I know not—perhaps these very men. . . ."

CHAPTER V

1816–1819

THE hopes of Creevey's friends revived in 1816 and 1817, the position appearing to grow more favourable for attacks on the Government over the Treaties and the Property Tax. One by one they joined their entreaties to Creevey to return and join in the fun, and the sooner the better. Brougham held out the bait of the representation of Liverpool or shook his head over the desertion of the faithful thirty at Thetford, but he left it to the others to whisper that the principal objective of that inscrutable mind was the leadership of the party.

But Creevey—though he made one effort to dash to London for an important division—was deaf to their entreaties and remained at his wife's bedside, a source of strength and comfort to all the sorrowing family. And Lady Holland's commissions for millinery continued relentlessly.

Lady Holland to Mrs. Creevey

"Holland House, Jany. 1st, 1816.

" I have sent you ' Emma,' * . . . be good enough to make enquiry about it, for if things are as long in getting there as in coming from there, it will be a stale forgotten work before it reaches its destination. Mr. Greville Junr. has offered to bring over any thing. Will you give him the 12 half cambrick cravats which I begged you to order. . . . I should like some Valenciennes edging about an inch broad, 12 or 20 English yards. . . .

" Lord John Russell has seen poor Ly. Elizabeth.†

* Jane Austen's fourth novel was published anonymously in 1816.
† Whitbread.

He describes the interview as painfully affecting. . . . What a deplorable hopeless condition is hers ; she is going to change her house which will be a good scheme, as the sights of the objects in Dover Street must be a perpetual source of fresh pain. . . .

" Lord Buckinghamshire is dying, sent to Bath without any hope of recovery.

" Lord Fife is going to be married.

" Dr. Baillie when he returned from Weymouth where he was sent to see Pss. Charlotte, says he perceived no illness, but an obstinate determination against going to the Fêtes at Brighton. . . .

" The papers of today announce the arrival of La Valette at Brussels ; if he should really be there, give me some acc't. of him, how he is received and whether he is likely to come here. I should be glad to see him in this country, as he would find the respect for his private character would far exceed any political animosity that might be felt for his principles, as the interest and respect he has inspired is universal. I should be glad to show him how sensibly we remember his civilities to us, both at Dresden and Paris. . . ."

Hon. H. G. Bennet to Creevey

" February 2nd.

" . . . I wish you joy of Miss Ord's marriage, every one speaks well of Col. Hamilton, and I think he is a very lucky man. Pray make my congratulations to Mrs. Creevey upon the subject. . . .

" I find all the *party* intent upon the subject of the proposed 5 per cent. Property Tax. Fitzwilliam last night was saying that every town and county, nay every village, ought to petition and that every effort sh'd be made—how can then the excuse be made out without your Horner and Tierney both protesting ag't. attack on the sinking fund, which if not done and no Property Tax left existing, how the establishments can be paid I know not. Baring however says that you can safely take off it 7 millions, so he is at issue with our two financiers and I prefer his opinion, from having some little more interest in the aforesaid funds, to the other two great theorists—we shall make a great fight however and we all hope to see you join in the battle as soon as possible. . . ."

Brougham to Creevey

" Feb. 6th.

" I marvel much at your not feeling the necessity of coming speedily. In the first place, as you are to come for some part of the Session, why not take the best, the hottest and most interesting part ? Next, you would like naturally to be here when the treaties come on, that is, Thursday senight. But chiefly, I must tell you we are in great want of you : seriously, there is much to be done. I never saw as good a spirit among the young ones and the elders of the Cole School and their adherents are evidently disposed to *let good* be done tho' not to assist it much themselves. I could give you dozens of anecdotes proving how useful, not to say indispensable, your presence is—for once *take them in trust*—I don't much like committing them to paper.

" Another reason is that if we ever mean to have you in for Liverpool, you must not be out of sight of the publick so long. . . ."

Earl of Sefton to Creevey

" March 5th.

" . . . My present object is not correspondence but to see your mischievous face in its proper sphere. There never was such a moment for you. Ministers are really at their last gasp, and your appearance would give them their coup de grace. . . .

" The Prop. Tax comes on next Monday. They don't expect to carry it by above 20, and I don't believe if common exertion is used they can carry it at all. Think of the civil list as well as the expenses at Brighton &c. and stay at Brussels if you can. Come immediately, and come to this house. You will find a room and a hearty welcome ready for you. . . .

". . . I want to see you much on private affairs. I meditate going abroad for 3 years to save money. You must tell me what one could do at Brussels upon £7,000 a year. . . ."

Mrs. Creevey to Wm. Ord

" March 26th.

" . . . I was not *merry* when your letter came, for Mr. Creevey had just set off for England ; he stayed a few days to console Bessy and me for the loss of Anne, and still expected to be in time for a vote upon the Income Tax—but it has died more suddenly than we hoped for—by a majority of 37. . . . The Ministers talked big to the last and really expected to carry it. Mr. Western writes in astonishment and ecstacies at it, but says no one expects any change of Ministry. . . ."

Mrs. Hamilton to Miss E. Ord

" Malines, 29th March.

" . . . I think you will by this time be beginning to look out for a letter from Mrs. Hamilton herself, and having *order'd* my *better half* to improve his mind for a few moments with the ' Edinburgh Review,' I mean to devote that time to informing you that having

LT.-COLONEL ANDREW HAMILTON.
From a miniature in the possession of John Blackett-Ord, Esq.,
at Whitfield.

[*To face p.* 100.

had now one *whole* week's experience of the married
state, I have not yet discover'd any just cause for
repentance, either for the loss of my liberty or in the
choice of my Lord and Master. . . . You know of
course that after the terrible business at the Ambassador's, we set off for this place . . . I know, my
dearest Nelly, that when I felt his arms round my
neck, I felt the want of yours too, and after having
been kiss'd by my dear old Duke, Mr. Creevey and my
warm hearted little Brother Alick,* I believe I stood
still expecting Fawther † and Charley and Mary and
little Willy. . . .

" We went on Tuesday to Antwerp, saw all the
Lions there except the Pictures which have been
brought from Paris, as the Museum in which they
have been exhibited was shut up, and the Pictures
are now to be restored to their old stations in the
Churches. Antwerp is much the finest and most
striking Town I have seen on the Continent, the
Cathedral is beautiful, the streets broad and handsome, and all Bonaparte's works, tho' left in an
unfinished state, quite worthy of him. . . .

" Give my tenderest love to my Fawther, and tell
him I don't know how to thank him enough for all his
beautiful, kind and affectionate messages—but assure
him that they are not lost upon me, or upon his
Brother Hamilton who has exactly the heart and
feeling to value and love him as he deserves. . . ."

Lady Holland to Mrs. Creevey

" Holland House, 4th June.

" I have sent you by Mrs. Abercrombie a shirt of
your friend Henry's, and will thank you to order 16

* Hamilton's young brother.
† Her elder brother, William Ord.

to the mode with the additions in point of size as mentioned by the paper, the frill of Cambrick. I shall trust to your finding some conveyance to bring them over, only do not let them be *rubbed* so as to make holes. Mrs. A. is going to stop a few months in the Netherlands, and will divide her time between Spa and Aix la Chapelle. . . .

" We are full of stories and reports about the P. of Wales, who is to be summoned they say upon a charge of high treason, which, if made out, is to pave the way to the Throne for Pss. Sophia of Gloster. There will be a change in the destinies of that family hitherto so crushed and humbled. . . .

" The Novel * and its writer is almost forgotten, nothing in this great town goes beyond a nine days wonder. I believe the Authoress is to have Melbourne House. . . ."

Mrs. Creevey and Miss Ord to William Ord

" Brussels, June 11th.

" I am most mercifully supported by a long preparation and fixed expectation of the worst—and by submission to the will of God, who alone knows what it is best for us all to suffer. . . . I have a great debt to pay to Eleanor, to you and to Mary who have done what it was my duty to have performed if my infirmities had permitted it. I am unable to write more today than that my blessing is upon you all. Bessy must say the rest in answer to your letter. . . ."

" You will see by the above, my dearest William, the resignation of our beloved Mother, and the exertions she makes. I have seen so much of her goodness that I was sure she would do her utmost,

* Lady Caroline Lamb's *Glenarvon*, published anonymously in 1816.

but she has surpassed even my expectations, and I
trust I shall never forget or cease to try to profit by
the example she has set me in the most violent
moments of agitation. . . . In short every thing she
does or says is affecting from the beauty of the
feeling and motive that suggests it ; it has the effect
she so much desires, giving every consolation they are
capable of receiving to those about her.   I can never
be sufficiently grateful for the unceasing support and
assistance Mr. Creevey has been to us both, he has
never from the day he came back left her, but for me,
for a moment.   His attentions, his consolations, and
his affection have been most invaluable, indeed without him I do not know what would have become of
me. . . ."

Hon H. G. Bennet to Creevey

" July 12th.

" . . . The plot thickens here every day.   Lauderdale shewed me last night the acc't. of the Revenue of
the last quarter, which, contrasted with that of last
year, stands as follows—whereas in the last quarter
accruing to this last year the deficiency was about
£400,000, this quarter it loses two millions.   Government however say that things are to improve, and
that the funds are to be at 76, but at present houses are
failing on all sides, in the country everyone is out of
work, there is no foreign trade and little home
demand for our manufactures, and in all the trading
districts thousands are without bread. . . .
" Now as to politics in general.   It seems clear
that the Government is very rash and not much
augmented in strength by Canning, who has commenced his intrigues, and the general belief is Ld.
Liverpool is to retire. . . . People talk of a dis-

solution and of a divorce—Queen C. denies stoutly that in the latter event any step has been taken, but it is generally understood that ample materials are come near to warrant one, and that there is a disposition here to further the view of Prinney; our answer is there are many who w'd. go great lengths agt. Mrs. P., and I don't feel I am so warm for her as I did. . . ."

Earl of Sefton to Creevey

"Jany. 17th, 1817.

" I am pressed by everybody to add my feeble solicitations to those of all others who are anxious for your arrival here. It will really be most grievous if you are absent at such a moment; a good pull altogether would do wonders. The whole country is with us on the subject of retrenchment, and will support us to any extent, not, God damn them, from any patriotic motive but because they are pinched. Pray come and lend a hand. I am aware of the motives which make it difficult for you to come, but I think even Mrs. Creevey, if she was quite aware of the state of the case, would be desirous you should come. Brougham is expected every day, but that wise man is such a fool that till I see his bewitching countenance I shall not believe in his coming.

" The Derbys are in the greatest affliction, as their son James is in the last stage of dropsy and consumption.

" We are just arrived in town. I never heard one word of John Eaton, Esq. of Edgehill. . . ."

Brougham to Creevey

" 16th March.

" I lament to hear from H. Brand that Mrs. C.'s eyes have been troubling her like Kinnaird's, for it must interrupt her amusing herself. I cured myself twice by applying flannel dipped in water as *hot* as I could bear every half hour or oftener. It is refreshing and agreeable also. . . .

" My Trade Debate last night has been peculiarly successful in every way, and I delight and glory in having at length spoke out my mind fully agt. the damnable system of Castlereagh & Co., towards all foreign countries. I told him in the parchest terms how he is execrated and abhorred every where. The ' Chronicle ' reports it BELOW the truth, and my reply (being the cream of it) is wholly omitted. ' The Times ' has given it.

" Tonight we expect Canning to take advantage of our exhaustion and fire off a speech he has long been bottling up, but *some of us* are ready for him. Last night neither he nor Husky took the field. . . .

" Mark that our success, as usual, was in spite of our leaders, who first threw cold water on the motion, then tried to put it off, then tried to prevent a division, and when *forced* by me into it, gave it no support. Tierney to be sure is ill. C. Wynne and Fremantle would not touch it, so we mean to bring that set to an explanation.

" Joe Phillimore comes in under Lord B. for Horner's seat. Sefton spoke admirably and replied still better t'other night. If he don't make a capital hand, never trust me. . . ."

" March 25th.

" . . . I hope you approve of what I have done this last week (or rather 4 days). We have actually down upon paper £4,500 for a new Evening Paper— for reports of debates generally—of *good principles*— and we have above £1,500 more we are *quite sure* of

—Lambton began with £500 and the D. of B. has just sent the same. It takes beyond measure, and I expect to see it out immediately after Easter, having got excellent people for publishers, editor, &c. The estimate was £3,000—but we keep the overflow for similar purposes—therefore—don't quite believe those who tell you nothing has been done. We have done (every thing considered) a great deal, and tho' I go about complaining, because I am provoked at some people's slackness and think much more might be done, yet I don't quite approve of *others*, such as Bennet &c., from mere silliness complaining in the same way. *They* have no right to say a word—for they know what has been done, and for one, I have worked like a negro—e.g. my falling on Canning at one in the morning the *night after* my exhausting motion on modern manufacturers, and which I never should have done (for I was literally knocked up) had I not been waiting a fortnight for him, and saw that he came out of port after Romilly and Ponsonby had spoke—and when Tierney was away, and he reckoned on me being unfit for service.

" Don't fear our committing poor Whitbread's error and making ourselves conductors after setting the paper once agoing ; we only start it, and then leave it to the people as a mercantile concern. . . ."

" April 1st.

". . . The Newspaper (*Guardian & Evening Reporter*) will soon be out in great style . . . Sefton and all of us are *most clear*—that your coming *is no longer a matter of choice*—There is indubitably to be a dissolution this summer—Govt. hardly deny it—Now do you ever mean to be in Parlt. again ? . . . Your own presence is *plainly* essential—in ways I can't go

thro' in a letter—Your coming after the summer and
at a dissolution is quite preposterous. . . ."

Earl of Sefton to Creevey

"Dec. 30th.

" . . . I am really very much vexed at the little prospect you hold out of coming over this year. My illness has prevented my attending to Liverpool matters,
but I have no doubt a Whig will succeed . . .
Nothing but a certainty of success without expense
would induce me to put Molyneux forward, and upon
the whole I think you would be the best candidate.
. . . You not shewing in Parliament will, as you must
be aware, be a great impediment. In the meantime
what a state we are in, in party matters ! I don't
foresee what can happen. Old Bruffam certainly
lost ground last session, and is so unpopular with the
House that they very often don't hear him. His last
motion, to be sure, was the Devil. . . ."

The letters of 1818 are self-explanatory. Mrs.
Creevey died at the end of May, after many years of
suffering endured with a courage and gaiety and
unselfishness to which her own and the family letters
testify. After her death Creevey and his stepdaughters moved to Cambrai. Miss Ord in correspondence with her brother pays tribute to Creevey's
devotion, and while she reveals the financial straits to
which her mother's death brought him, she makes it
clear that his conduct towards them all had more than
justified their respect and affection for him.
    In the election of that summer his seat at Thetford
was otherwise bestowed by the Duke of Norfolk. The
letter which Creevey wrote to the Duke in consequence,
is strong evidence that those who have regarded him
as a toady or hanger-on, are wide of the mark. It is
true that the Duke might fairly have replied to the
indignant exile that Creevey himself had not been

9

more faithful to Thetford than Thetford to him ; for this year Creevey once more (reluctantly) consented to stand for Liverpool, but his efforts were half-hearted and the new Parliament did not number him among the elect.

He returned to England at last in the autumn of 1819.

Earl of Sefton to Creevey

"Feb. 10th, 1818.

" . . . Now for Liverpool. A Candidate is absolutely wanting . . . I am as convinced as I am of my existence that if you were boldly to present yourself and to canvass the houses within 2 or 3 months from this time you would be *sure of succeeding.* I should certainly *walk over* and am equally determined not to meddle with it, but in hopes of preventing other candidates I shall not positively declare that, till you make up your mind. The Canningites would infinitely prefer you to Gascoigne. . . . There never was such an opening and you owe it to yourself not to neglect it. You would be most respectably attended in your canvass. Heywood, the Earles &c. and the whole body of the Whigs. Scarlett is nibbling at it by Roscoe's *invitation*, but that of course would signify nothing. . . ."

" What think you of Broggam and Westmoreland? I cannot conceive his succeeding tho' he is very sanguine. If he fails he throws himself out of Parliament.

" My Ladies all desire to be kindly remembered to you. I fear, as you don't mention Mrs. Creevey, you had nothing favourable to say. . . ."

Miss E. Ord to William Ord

" You must take comfort, . . . dearest William, our poor dear sufferer prayed for the release that has been granted to her. I think with thankfulness even of the event which deprives me of the object of my greatest respect and affection, the very best of Mothers.   Had you seen her as we have done, you would take consolation.   Lengthened life afforded no prospect but of the most dreadful kind—ten years of suffering such as hers have been, and borne in such a way, were surely enough to subdue all selfish feelings even in those who are the most conscious of what they have lost. . . .

". . . We none of us had any idea that the event could be so near. . . .

". . . Thank God, Anne was able to come when she did.   It will be a comfort for her to think of, all the days of her life, that the sight of her happiness and of her dear sweet infant cheered the few hours that remained.   Her good Husband, too, devoted himself to us and has established us in the house with himself and Anne.   Mr. Creevey remains at home, but we prevailed upon him to come to us yesterday evening and it was much better for us all.   He has every consolation he can enjoy from the reflection of all he has done for her.   I cannot write any more now, but I will next post.   God bless you. . . ."

Earl of Sefton to Creevey

" June 12th.

" You will always have the satisfaction of knowing that your unparalleled kindness and unwearied attention prolonged the existence and rendered less acute the sufferings of her who has at length been released from a life of torment.   I trust you will not accuse me of impertinent curiosity if I express the greatest anxiety as to your future lot, and if I beg you to tell me what your prospects are of returning to your friends.

" Alas, your address to Liverpool arrived too late ; a fortnight sooner it might have seated you, but now I have yielded to the solicitations of the Whigs there, no other cock being to be found, and they are hard at work, *as they say* with every prospect of success, but I don't believe it.   I take no part either in purse or person, but my son who is to abstain from canvassing, is to appear on the hustings to receive and thank the voters. . . ."

Miss E. Ord to William Ord

" June 23rd.

". . . In my last letter I mentioned to you our first feeling as to staying abroad as long as Anne does. . . . If she returns soon to Cambrai *we* are very well off here if Mr. Creevey will stay with us, and it appears to me that our reason for staying abroad and our all keeping together must appear right and *reputable* to everybody who takes an interest about us. . . . When you have a little spare time you will much oblige me if you will enter a little into the detail with me and let us know exactly what we each have, for as it has hitherto been a matter of great indifference to me, I am very ignorant on the subject, and as when one is young and in health is the time when one can do without many indulgences that one wants afterwards, now is the time I mean to be stingy.   The most painful part of this subject is what I feel for Mr. Creevey.   Since we came abroad I have had so much the management that I know much more than I did before.   We all know then that our debts were great— he has been since that time most anxious to pay them, but, like himself, even with that object in view, never thought himself entitled to lessen any comfort or indeed luxury we enjoyed, and tho' in the last year of suffering particularly his own probable situation must frequently have presented itself, there was nothing any one could suggest or no fancy of our beloved Mother's that was not instantly gratified if money could procure it.   In this way the sum he fixed to spend here has been exceeded and of course less remained to pay debts at home.   £4,000 I know has been paid, how much remains I do not know, nor of course shall I ask, but I am sure there must be a good deal.   He is unwilling to let me talk to him on that part of the subject *now* tho' he says ' Oh never mind that, I have hopes in time to get thro' it.' . . . He then shewed me a letter he had received from his Sister with all sorts of generous, kind offers, and also two or three others she had written lately with details of his Uncle's* will leaving his fortune, £10,000 or £12,000, between them ; this Uncle is 81. . . . He is unwilling to stay with us because he says he will not live upon us, but for the present I have made him promise.   I consider his debts ours as much as his, for the money has gone much more to gratify us than anything else, but this he won't hear me mention . . .

" I do not see *any thing* Mr. Creevey has to live upon at present.   I wish he had thought more of himself, but as that is past we must think for him, and as long as I live I consider myself bound by *duty* to do so. . . ."

Earl of Sefton to Creevey

" June 26th.

". . . The Contest at Liverpool has been most severe, but I suppose is now ended. . . . The numbers on the 6th. day at 3 o'clock were : Canning 1405,

* John Eaton.

Gascoigne 1295, Sefton 1162, . . . I am most gratified by hearing that Molyneux has acquitted himself
there with very great success, and has acquired great
personal popularity.

" I am very anxious for your answer to my last
letter as I begged you to state your prospects to me,
in which I am sure you will not suspect me of idle
curiosity. . . ."

Creevey to Duke of Norfolk

" Cambrai, August 3rd.

" MY DEAR DUKE,

" You will probably be surprised at receiving a
letter from me, and you will not be the less so when I
tell you beforehand, that my letter is to contain
articles of impeachment against you.   If there is anything like presumption in my venturing to arraign you,
let me refer for my justification to our acquaintance
of sixteen years duration, to my belief that our
opinions upon all political subjects are substantially
the same, to my wishes that upon my return to
England I may live with you upon the same friendly
terms as heretofore, and to my conviction that in
order so to do, it is better you should learn from
myself the free expression of the grievance I complain
of than from any other person. . . .

" . . . You are not the only member of the Whig
Aristocracy who has wanted in his time a loan of
money, or who may want it at this present moment,
yet in no other instance than your own can you
recognise on the part of the Whig Aristocracy a
money transaction in any of their Parliamentary
returns.   Suppose the Dukes of Bedford and Devonshire, the Lords Fitzwilliam, Landsdowne and others
had adopted your precedent, in such a case, every

opposition man that has rendered himself useful by experience, by talent, or by fidelity to publick principles must equally have given way to some money lender, and in addition to much the most valuable publick man that England can boast of, I mean Sir Samuel Romilly ; such persons as Tierney, Brougham, and Mackintosh must also have been sacrificed. . . .

" It appears to me . . . that my sixteen years of service and fidelity in Parliament gave me a stronger claim upon your Parliamentary patronage than any loan of money from Mr. Phillips can have established for himself and his family.

" But allow me, Duke, to mention another ground of claim that Romilly and myself had upon you, and which I sometimes think can never have presented itself to you. Have you forgotten that in 1807, long before Mr. Phillips was in Parliament, the Administration of that day and under which Romilly and myself both held official situations, voluntarily abandoned their offices upon a pure and insulated case and point of honor to the Catholic Body ? Now altho' I can justly say to the honor of that administration that I never heard an expression of regret at their Government being destroyed in such a cause, yet I am justified on this occasion in reminding you of the fact and in closing this part of my case by shortly stating, first, that you and Lord Petre, the only Catholic Peers with Parliamentary patronage, are the only Peers of the Whig Aristocracy who turn out their old members upon the express grounds of pecuniary arrangements with new connections, and secondly, that the Members you so sacrifice, viz. Romilly and myself, happen to be persons who themselves sacrificed in 1807 every interested consideration for no other object than that of serving yours, the Catholic Cause.

" I now come to the claims I have upon you, Duke, of a more private nature, during my sixteen years representation of Thetford. . . . It is you who know better than any man in England (because I sent expressly for you to be present on that occasion) the danger the Petre interest was in, in 1806, and I am sure you will do me the justice to admit that had it not been for what I then did, Lord Petre would have had no members to return at the present day. Let me say, too, that in addition to my successful exertions in those times, I have expended £2,000 of my own money in the borough of Thetford. . . ."

Duke of Norfolk to Creevey

" Worksop Manor, August 22nd.

" Tho' I readily acknowledge the pleasure I have heretofore enjoy'd in your acquaintance and tho' I may regret that you are not in any situation which you desire . . . yet I cannot admit the claim which you seem to think you have upon me . . . You will therefore, I hope, not deem it inconsistent with my good wishes towards you and the desire I have of renewing our acquaintance, that I should avoid any controversy or correspondence upon subjects of such a nature and treated with such extraordinary and unmerited asperity as those contained in your letter. . . ."

Mrs. Fitzherbert to Miss E. Ord

" Sept. 15th.

" . . . I often think of you, my Dr. Bessy, and am most anxious to know something about you, therefore I beg you will write to me. It was only the other day that I heard from Sefton you were all assembled at Cambray. . . .

" . . . Do you recollect, my dear friend, that I have several boxes belonging to some of you. I shall take great care of them till I know what your wishes are respecting them. Before I bid you adieu let me implore of you to give me a line, for I really am anxious to the greatest degree about you all, and I can with truth assure you that no friend you have can feel a greater regard and affection for you all, than I do.

" A thousand loves to Mr. Creevey, and your sisters. . . ."

Mrs. Fitzherbert to Creevey

" Brighton, Decr. 28th.

" . . . I am delighted to hear Dr. Mrs. Hamilton is recovered and that Bessy and Eleanor are so well. I cannot tell you how anxiously I am looking forward to your arrival here, to see you all once more inhabitants of this country. . . .

" You would scarcely know Brighton, it is so enlarged since you were here, and is at this moment so full there is not a house to be had. I cannot boast of much good society which formerly we abounded with at this season. When I tell you that fifty-two public coaches go from hence to London every day and bring people down for six shillings, you will not be surprised at the sort of company we have ; besides which the Royal Palace attracts numbers who are puzzled to know what to make of the appearance of the building which it is impossible for me, or indeed any one else, to describe.

" The Regent and all his household are here, but as he never stirs out of his parlour and no one sees him, it makes no alteration in our proceedings.

" Minny desires me to assure you and all her kind friends of her best wishes. . . ."

Creevey to Hon. H. G. Bennet

" December 30th, 1818.

" I owe you a thousand apologies for not having answered long before this time the kind letter I received from you months ago at Cambray. In summer, however, all the world is in motion, and I am more likely to catch you now in London when your new Parliament is on the eve of assembling. . . .

" . . . If you must *elect* a Leader of the Whigs, let me with all the impression I have of Tierney's* talents and great utility in Parliament mention some objections to your choice of him. Tierney began his publick life by joining in the clamour of that day in favor of the Crown and the East India Company against Mr. Fox, the Leader of the Whigs ; there was nothing he did not do against him. . . .

" In 1793 Tierney was a Reformer of the first water. He was the organ of the friends of the people and the author of that celebrated report on the state of our representation, so erroneous and anti-Whiggish as I contend it was in its principles, and so injurious as I am sure it has been in its effects. It is in that report that Tierney employs all his talents in exciting the feelings of the publick against the aristocracy and the gentry of the country possessed of or connected with Parliamentary influence, a doctrine in defiance both of Whiggism and common sense. . . .

" In opposition to all his former opinions he voted for the War of 1803, after hearing the most powerful and conclusive speech against it that Mr. Fox had ever delivered in Parliament, and what is more he was

---

* George Tierney now became leader of the Whigs. The contemporary of Pitt, Burke and Fox, his high abilities were overshadowed and he was never trusted nor rewarded. He was perhaps a victim of the exclusiveness of the politics of his day.

made Treasurer of the Navy and a Privy Councillor for having so voted.   It is true that in 1806, after the death of Mr. Fox, Tierney took office under the Whigs and has remained with them since.   I very readily give him every advantage he can desire from his two years' fidelity to his new connections, the Whigs, and as readily admit his distinguished talents, and great utility in the ranks of any party, but believe me, my dear Bennet, that with the facts before our eyes, such as I have stated them, to make him *Leader of the Whigs*, is only involving the Party and himself in derision. . . ."

Eight months later Creevey and his family returned to England.

PART II

MAN OF FASHION

CHAPTER VI

1819-21

AFTER a continuous absence of more than five years, Creevey came back to England in the early autumn of 1819, and his stepdaughters began with his help to look out for a home for themselves. After a trial of Tunbridge Wells, they settled down ultimately at Rivenhall in Essex, where their landlord was Creevey's oldest friend, Charles Western, " the Squire." Creevey was now fifty-two years old. He had left England in 1814 an ex-Minister and M.P., a man of family and substance. He returned home without a seat, without political expectations, and without a shilling to call his own or a cupboard for his clothes. The state of his finances was clearly revealed in Bessy Ord's letter to her brother after her mother's death in 1818, and the same letter mentioned his determination to make no calls on such part of their mother's income as remained to be shared among her daughters. They wished him to make his home with them, but such a proposal he very naturally rejected, although he remained for the rest of his life their constant adviser on all matters, financial, legal and general.

There now began that correspondence between Creevey and Bessy Ord which forms the bulk of the later Creevey Papers, and was from the first intended to be preserved to form the material for Creevey's *History of his Times*, an idea which got no nearer realisation than the form in which the letters and diary fragments are preserved, arranged and annotated, and a few isolated memoranda. In times of political excitement, and even on social occasions of more than usual interest, he would write her sometimes twice a day letters of enormous length, judged even by the standards of his day ; and although he wrote easily and naturally, he had one eye on posterity. So he returned to England and to London, a free-lance, to begin as he had begun when he first settled in Gray's Inn more than thirty years earlier. But if he had no material assets at his disposal, he was not lacking in less tangible resources. His wonderful health was unimpaired, his spirits and energy and enthusiasms as boundless as ever. He had besides many loyal friends, some rich, some influential, and all devoted to his interests. Whether he would or no, they had been working on his behalf during his last year in Belgium. Those whom he counted as friends, and many more who would have valued his friendship, now sought him out, not in pity for his plight, but for the varied gifts which he had to offer; that fund of high spirits and good humour, that resource and shrewd judgment on men and things in politics and social life. He had the offer of free quarters in half a dozen great houses in London and in the country.

When, on January 29, the long reign of George III came to an end, the interest of Lord Thanet had been secured and Creevey represented Appleby in the first Parliament of the new reign. For if the sweets of office seemed to the Whigs as far distant as ever, Creevey's reputation as a party fighter and strategist had not been forgotten, and even his political opponents admitted his merits as a speaker * and his adroitness in debate.

Once more the trump card of the Whigs had turned up with the prospect of Queen Caroline's return. The sordid details of her trial were to occupy the attention and interest of all classes for the whole of the year, and to overshadow every other topic, whether political or social. Creevey's letters during 1820 make a formidable bundle and 90 per cent. of the contents deal with the trial.

It is an outworn subject to-day; it was never otherwise than shabby, and now it is threadbare. On that account it is the less to be regretted that, vast as

* Lord Colchester's *Memoirs.*

is the bulk of the 1820 letters, Sir Herbert Maxwell so
dealt with them that what remains is of secondary
interest.   The excerpts which follow, in so far as
they touch on the business of Queen Caroline, are
restricted to a summary of events to date drawn up
by Creevey before the trial, and one or two letters
that describe the popular demonstrations of sympathy
with her cause during the trial.

It only remains to add that the Whigs' trump card
won them no trick, the party being quite unable to
combine to use it.   The old Whigs under Lord Grey
revolted from exploiting the dirty business in the
party game, and even " the Mountain," while admir-
ing Brougham's resourcefulness and brilliance, came
to realise that he was espousing first and last not the
cause of his injured client but his own.

At the beginning of the year Creevey, with no
home and no settled plans, availed himself of an offer
to join Brougham in a round of visits.

Creevey to Miss E. Ord

" Middleton.*
" January 21st, 1820.

". . . Brougham and I had a most agreeable drive
here. . . . I must reserve, till we meet, the account
he gave me of efforts that have been made to bring
me into Parliament, hitherto quite unknown to me.
One agreeable thing, however, I must tell you of ; he
is obliged to go to the Princess of Wales on business
either at Easter or after the session of Parliament is
over.   Whenever it takes place, I am to go with him,
if I am so disposed, which I certainly shall be.   She
is at Milan, but all this is a secret at present. . . .

" We have been the last hour in my Lady's † own
appartments, which are most beautiful, and she is

---

* Middleton Park, Bicester : Lord Jersey's.

† Sarah, daughter of the 10th Earl of Westmorland.   She inherited
her grandfather's, Robert Child's, fortune and controlled his Bank.
Both she and her mother made runaway marriages.

10

now laying down to rest herself, which I don't wonder
at having talked at least six or seven hours to her
own share since our arrival.   I know nothing of the
length of our stay here, I leave everything to *Bruffam*,
and am quite content."

"Liverpool, February.

"Would you believe it ; I have sent a '*Brochure* '
by tonight's coach of my writing to Bruffam.   Its title
is, ' A guide to the Electors of Great Britain upon the
Accession of a new King, and the immediate prospect
of a new Parliament.'   Whether it will ever see the
light, I know not.   Its facts are very good and strong,
and the reasoning upon them both just and important,
but it is ' careless and *indeed slovenly* in its address,'
and as a ' *Guide* ' I am afraid somewhat *windy*.

"I have begged Bruffam to let it appear either by
detachments in the ' Chronicle ' or as ' a work '
published by Ridgeway."

Brougham to Creevey

"Feb. 7th.

"I take this opportunity of telling you that after
much teazing and delay, you are to be out to-morrow
morning.   *It is excellent*, and I have taken care to
have it puffed—I altered a very few words, and added
one or two sentences or bits thereof here and there."

Viscount Folkestone to Creevey

"Feby. 13th.

"Bruffam says your work is excellent and calculated to do much good.   It strikes me it would do
much more if your name was to it.   Why should it
not be ? and why should you not move up to town
to receive the applauses of your friends and to be

ready in the way of a seat if any thing propitious was
to turn up ?   It seems mighty foolish to stay poking
about at Liverpool."

Earl of Sefton to Creevey

"February 15th.

" What the devil are you at ?   Is John Eaton *
lying in state ?   Are you sitting up with the body ?
I wish you could tell me you had been canvassing
Liverpool with success.   I assure you there is nothing
else could make me take any part in a Liverp'l.
Election. . . .

" It is my belief Parlt. cannot be dissolved
speedily ; besides the innumerable things that must
arise, I believe the King's health will stop their
eagerness for it.   He certainly gains no strength, and
is in a state of great exhaustion."

Brougham to Creevey

"Appleby Castle,† March 12th.

" These are to require that you come here with
the Earl—who is expected anxiously. . . . You can
be conveyed to town from hence easily—as I go at all
events alone, and Ld. T. has a whole coach empty.

" Your tract I had puffed in the Chronicle and I
wrote to enjoin Burdett to take it with him to the
Hustings as his manual—to prevent him from speaking any nonsense of his own.   He has done so
admirably.

" You are aware that in this season of bustle if
St. John had written his Apocalypse in the form of
an address to the Electors it would have been over-
looked, but all things considered your revelation has

* Creevey's uncle from whom he had expectations.
† Lord Thanet's.

done pretty fairly. The Holland House tone (where I took it and spoke of it) is of course unfavourable, at least they all delight so dearly in jobs and disregard so entirely every reform of any size or value, that this was to be expected. But Lauderdale alone is furious —the others are more decent in their dislike ; Allen is of course rather favorable."

Viscount Folkestone to Creevey

" March 14th.

" . . . I hereby certify to you . . . my great satisfaction at the perusal of ' The Guide.' That work is, I think, calculated to do a great deal of good at the present time, and ought to be universally read. . . .

" There is a report that your old friend Prinney is gone mad, that he is so haunted by the apprehension of seeing his Wife that he is under the constant delusion of supposing her by his side ; that the only thing that gives him pleasure and satisfaction is tumbling over (not Lady Hertford or Lady Conyngham) but trinkets and jewels. This report receives, I think, confirmation from the paragraph lately inserted in the papers, that the Crown Jewels had been sent down to the Pavilion. I wonder who would be responsible if they were to find their way out of the Pavilion by some back stairs, to France for instance. . . ."

J. Whishaw * to Creevey

" April 30th.

" . . . You are already aware that poor R.[omilly] † was extremely pleased with your letter of congratula-

---

* J. Whishaw, M.P. Friend of Romilly and habitué at Holland House.

† Sir Samuel Romilly, sometime Solicitor-General, committed suicide in 1818. He was the third of Creevey's friends to do so.

tion to him on the Westminster Election ; but it may be worth while to transcribe for you the passage of his Journal, in which he mentions this circumstance :—

" ' 1818—July 27. I have received numerous letters from my friends on the result of the Westminster Election. The two, which from the view they take of the subject, are most worth preserving, are from my friend Creevey at Brussels, and from Mr. Otter, my Son's tutor. . . .'

" In the course of your letter something is said of the Whig Aristocracy not having provided R. with a seat ; upon which there is this marginal note :— ' This is certainly an unjust reproach. I had no claims on what C. calls the Whig Aristocracy. The D. of Bedford, however, as I afterwards learnt, had made an arrangement to provide a seat for me, if I were not returned for some other place.'

" You may recollect what passed in 1805, (which you mentioned to me at the time), relative to the communication from the Prince, of which you were the *medium*. He preserved, and has left a particular account of this transaction." *

Memoranda by Creevey respecting the Queen, her Trial, etc. etc.

"Gosforth, Dec. 15th, 1820.

" In the month of January last, Brougham and I left London together upon a visit to Lord Essex at Cashiobury, and from thence to Lord Jersey's at Middleton. During our journey he told me he should be obliged to go the approaching Easter to see the Queen at Milan upon business of importance, and he was kind enough to press me to accept a seat in his carriage and to accompany him on that occasion ; an

* See résumé for the year 1805.

offer which I most willingly and heartily accepted. On the 28th of the same month the late King died, and I being at Liverpool when I heard of that event, wrote a letter to Brougham suggesting to him whether it would not be for the Queen's interest to bring her to this country ; to which letter I received an answer stating that he had on the very morning after the King's decease and as soon as he could procure a passport for such purpose, dispatched Sicard to the Queen, imposing upon her his most positive injunctions to return to England without loss of time. . . .

" . . . I had my suspicions at this time that Brougham never meant to bring the Queen to England, and that this movement of hers was only meant by him to gain for her the best terms as to money &c. For observe, at this time she was absolutely pennyless, owing to her late income of £35,000 per annum having been settled upon her for the *joint lives* of herself and the late King. . . . Soon after this it was discovered that Lady Anne Hamilton and Alderman Wood had left England, and it turned out they were both gone to meet and accompany the Queen to this country. Lady Anne had been formerly in Her Majesty's service, the Alderman was a perfect volunteer. I found Brougham greatly incensed at this measure of Wood's whom he abused without mercy.   On Thursday June the first . . . I learnt . . . that Brougham and Lord Hutchinson had left London *together* to meet the Queen at St. Omers. . . .

" Tuesday, June the sixth, was a day of great expectation. Lord Sefton, Lord Kinnaird, Lambton and myself went about noon to Westminster Bridge expecting the Queen would be arriving about that time, as she was known to have slept at Canterbury.

. . . At 5 in the evening Lord Castlereagh entered the House of Commons with a *green bag* * in his hand ; he announced at the bar ' A message from the King.' The message was read, the Bag was laid on the table, and Lord Castlereagh moved that the House should the day following take into its consideration His Majesty's message. All was silence for a few seconds after this question was put, the House was very full both of Members and expectation. Bennet at last rose and with much warmth and agitation made the first attack. . . . Castlereagh in answer to him repro-bated his warmth, deprecated all discussion *then* as premature. . . . I supported and justified Bennet, and made as strong a speech as I could against any proceeding whatsoever upon the message and bag that night brought to the House, and attempted to show the certain inevitable and disastrous consequences of any such course being adopted. Pending this dis-cussion Brougham entered the House, having just got out of his chaise on his return from St. Omers. I have often wondered at what disposition it was of mind with which he so entered the House. He had made a great point of arriving there in time, he had been completely baffled both by the Queen and Wood at St. Omers, and I found at night in conversation with him his indignation at the highest pitch against each of them. I must always, I own, have my suspicions and those strong ones too, that on entering the House on Tuesday, his intention was to wash his hands of the Queen, to say that Wood's counsels with Her Majesty were preferred to his, and that to such advice he must thereafter leave her, but he arrived too late, the skirmishing had begun. He heard very decided

* The " green bag " contained the evidence secured by the Govern-ment's agents who followed the tracks of the Princess across Europe.

marks of approbation given both to Bennet and myself in what we said, and he paused and took a night to consider of his course.   At night he was evidently out of temper with me, but the next day he was all sunshine, and in the evening made the first of that series of incomparable speeches by which he so essentially served or rather saved both the Queen, the Lords, and the Constitution. . . ."

Creevey to Miss E. Ord

"Brooks's, August 16th.

" As my labors as an *Historian* begin from this day, it is necessary one should begin betimes in the morning, you know.   I got to Mrs. Hurrell's * last night between eight and nine. . . .

" In coming here I called at Ridgeway's where the first thing I saw was a *fifth* edition of the *Guide*, and which still continues to sell, and I hope the success of this work will make me persist in my intention of giving to the world ' a history of the trial of Queen Caroline with all parliamentary proceedings connected with it &c. &c.,' so as I said in my last letter to you, if you value my fame and wealth, keep every thing I write to you respecting the Queen, as notes to refresh my memory. . . ."

Day after day, as the trial dragged on in the Lords, Creevey was in his place registering impressions of every phase and turn and recording his criticism of the speeches.   When each session ended, he hurried away to feed his stepdaughter and a dozen hungry friends on the rich fare of the day's proceedings.   He allowed himself scant leisure for meals, sat writing far into the night, and was at it again when the late revellers were turning into bed.

* Another of Creevey's many landladies in the St. James's area.

The bare details of the autumn proceedings are as follows :

In July Lord Liverpool announced a Bill of deprivation and dissolution of marriage against the Queen. It was read a first time in August, and the taking of evidence began on August 21. On November 6 the Lords divided on second reading, which was passed with a majority of twenty-eight. On November 8 the Divorce clause was carried.

On November 10, the day of the third reading, Liverpool announced suddenly the shelving of the Bill. The Queen's supporters hailed the decision as an acquittal and Brougham's fame as an advocate was established.

Major A. Hamilton to Creevey

"Colombo, October 10th.

" I thank you from my heart for all your kindness to my children and Anne, and for the nice account you have given me of them in your letter of the 17th. of May. . . . If you cannot give me credit for being very grateful to you for your recollection of me, and for the trouble of writing to me, you must turn to the dear and magnanimous Elizabeth to answer for me, and to convince you how grateful I am. I know the value you are of to the two dear girls, but it would be presumption in me to thank you in their names for being so constant in your attentions and considerations for them ; but you must allow me to say, that for all you are doing for me in supporting the spirits of Anne, and being a protection to her children, and to herself, I shall ever feel, I trust, as I know you deserve from me. Your letter is so delightful that I can read it over and over with pleasure, but certain points of it are peculiarly gratifying. Your own triumph and success in getting the seat in Parliament in the way you have, ought to make you very conceited, and sincerely do I

congratulate you, nor will I now hesitate to acknowledge that I was before very *low* about you in this
point, because I thought you deserved better at the
hands of your friends. They have now made the
amende honourable, and I forgive them, and am more
happy than I can here express to think you are where
you ought to be, and ' God keep you so.' . . ."

Earl of Sefton to Creevey

"Nov. 12th.

" I am really drunk with joy. What an unheard
of triumph over villainy. What is to be done now ?
I shall be most anxious for your next accounts. . . .
I certainly thought with you that the divorce vote of
our friends was of doubtful policy, but it has done the
business. . . ."

W. J. Hughes * to Creevey

"Kinmel Park, 13th November.

" Not three times three, but nine times nine, My
Dear Creevey, or as often as the mystick numbers
can be multiplied. Never was consummation of folly
and wickedness more complete. Why Liverpool ever
brought the Bill out of the Committee is to me a
marvel. . . .

" However, that the accursed Bill is lost I most
heartily rejoice. . . .

" I am now anxious to know what will be the next
step. Shall we meet on the 23rd. and will the call be
inforced or will Ministers wait until after Xmas ?
Yet some provision must be made for the Queen, and
is it possible after all that has happened, the present
Ministers can be the proposers of it, but they have
been kicked and disgraced so often they are become
quite callous ?

* Of Kinmel. Created Lord Dinorben in 1831.

" I have no great inclination for a journey to London unless some good and substantive measure is to be proposed, and I think you must have had enough of London which will become insipid after the fine incitement of the late extraordinary proceedings. . . .

" I really cannot express to you the obligation I feel for your punctual and most interesting reports. . . ."

Creevey to Miss Ord

" Felix Hall, November 17th.

" I have not much time for you today because you know it was quite impossible to leave the hounds when they were running so *sweetly* ; then Mr. Honeywood had them brought over here on purpose for me, and I was mounted on his tip-top hunter into the bargain, and I must say a more perfect animal I never rode, and a very charming gallop I have had. Ferguson was mounted by the Squire, and we all enjoyed the fun as much as if we had been 30 years younger.

"Western and I arrived here on Monday within half an hour of each other, he from Thorndon (Lord Petre's) and I per coach from London. Altho' we were quite alone (save Shirley, Western's Brother) we lost no time in calling for the attention of the Public. We amused ourselves with illumining every window of the House with candles. A waggon load of wood and faggot was conveyed to the *highest* part of the Park, and set fire to, and the Bailiff was dispatched to Kelvedon with orders to the four Public Houses to open the campaign with ale for the people at the Squire's expense. I am sure 20 minutes could not have elapsed before we heard the cursedest clatter of voices, shoutings, and bells coming towards the house, and on looking out of the window it was the entire population of Kelvedon with a huge *Green Bag*, ' All lies ' written upon it, carried at the end of a pole by a man with a bell. After a sufficient exposure the bag was committed to the flames. . . ."

C. C. Western to Creevey

"Brooks's, November 29th.

" The Queen has this instant passed on her return. I was here as she went, and afterwards fought my way on foot with Folkestone, and his Brother through Lanes and Alleys till we came out of them *in* St. Paul's Churchyard, to witness her arrival there, which we did. It is difficult to convey to you an idea of the scene—the myriads that crowded the street, filled the windows, and loaded the roofs of the houses, not only in the main line of the procession but in every street leading into the line of march. The people were all stretching their necks out of windows, and waving their *white handkerchiefs*. The white handkerchiefs out of the windows of the Strand were the most extra-ordinary sight, from the countless numbers of them that were flying in all directions, and all the ways we threaded along running parallel to the Strand &c. were also crowded to excess. In short, the whole population was out. I saw men streaming down in the morning through Hanover Square from the other side of Oxford Street ; Bond Street was crowded at nine in the morning, all going one way, with anxious earnest haste. Now, with all this, everything was *perfectly* quiet, not an angry word, nor hissing, nor any symptoms of savage feeling. The mass seemed quite to understand that solemnity and quiet conduct on this occasion were essential. . . .

". . . You are a . . . *rum* fellow . . . to go away and leave such an exhibition. . . ."

The Queen's tragedy dragged on to its climax and close in 1821. The new session opened with the customary speech from the throne, all too mild for the fighting element of the opposition whose D'Artagnan was Creevey. He was constantly on his feet, and his audacity delighted his friends ; if it did not greatly disturb the Government, it appears to have succeeded in embarrassing and annoying individuals.

The times were as bad as could be, distress and discontent were everywhere apparent, and Parliament voted an outrageous sum to stage a suitable coronation. This " million dollar " pageant was fixed for July 19, and on that day the Queen made her last gesture at the Abbey door, and returned to her house to die and to be forgotten, like her trial, " in 48 hours." There is nothing unjust or deliberate in the juxtaposition of the last three papers printed in this chapter. The Queen's funeral and the King's Irish revels were concurrent topics which kept the town agog.

It was the nadir of the British Monarchy.

Creevey to Miss Ord

" Jan. 23rd, 1821.

" *Prinney* was received with very considerable applause, but his admirers were as drops in the ocean compared with those of his Wife. His speech is all *muggery*. He thanks for the supplies of last year, and says, as the Queen's annuity has ceased, he submits to the House of Commons to make such provision for her under *present circumstances* as they shall think fit."

" January 24th.

" Well, you see the campaign was opened last night, and so far so good. Was there ever anything like the amiable mildness of the speech ? I can't resist sending you the ' Morning Post ' Newspaper of today that you may see how gentle the Government *Press* is become too all at once. . . ."

"Jan. 27th.

" Well, our fight ended this morning at 7 o'clock in what I must consider as a ruinous blow to the character of the Honorable House. The Ministers of the Crown (with all their power) dare not assert that their own measure of striking the Queen's name out of the Liturgy was an ' expedient one,' and one of their own body modestly proposes to *adjourn*, and give no opinion upon the matter, and to which 300 Members, every one of them in his own judgement and familiar discourse condemning it as most *inexpedient*, give their assent and vociferous support. The Boodle's Politicians, I understand, are all cock a hoop at this victory, which victory is none ; neither they nor their masters, Castlereagh & Co., are out of the wood yet, they may rely upon it. Wetherell's speech was the great feature of the night, a most triumphant, unanswerable, legal, argument, and supported with great ability. Scarlett was rum, and to say the truth Bruffam was no great thing either.

" I send you the ' Times ' Newspaper that you may tell me if you recognise the style of a friend of yours in a few observations upon the House going into a Committee of Supply. . . .

" Lady Jersey and Lady Sefton were there, and Bennet tells me the former has pronounced me a tip top Jeroboam."

"February 1st.

" We had a rare breeze last night, or rather a collection of breezes. The presenting of petitions on the subjects of the Liturgy, Reform of Parliament

&c. are quite capital ; it gravels the Government to the greatest degree, and every discussion on them ends in the defeat of one or other of their supporters. The Queen's message produced hotter work still. I did not know till the last that it was to come. I was not sure it was a right course for her to pursue, but I presume it *was* by the rage into which Castlereagh was evidently thrown by it. The poor Queen herself yielded to the advice of her advisers on this occasion with *great reluctance*. I should really be very sorry for this step if I did not know that this £50,000 per ann : voted to her last night must in truth, and before it is long, find it's way into her pocket. Western, I assure you, made a capital speech ; Tierney one of his very best speeches, and Brougham *at last* took his House of Lords tone, and clearly proved to me that by continuing so to do, he might rule and govern the House of Commons as successfully as he did the House of Lords. The whole ended by a Billingsgate attack by Mr. Holme Sumner upon the Queen, and a very successful exposure and refutation of him by *Wood*. . . .

" Burdett * was brought up for judgement today, and upon an argument of Scarlett's in arrest of judgement, the Judges have deferred giving it till Saturday, so that under all these circumstances of delay, and doubts, and difficulties, I still hope he may escape a prison, or at least be sent there for a very short time. . . ."

" February 3rd.

" . . . I disported myself in the Committee of Supply to the infinite horror of Brother Bragge,

* For his criticism of the authorities on the affair of Peterloo, Sir Francis Burdett was sentenced at Leicester Assizes to 3 months' imprisonment and a fine of £2000.

Mouldy,* Warrender & Co., and to the convulsion of Sefton and my other ten bottle-holders with laughing. It was considered a most successful exposure of the Honorable House, the Big Whigs of course are horrified at the Radical nature of the proceeding, but the great mass are quite enchanted, and only mortified they were not there. The Government are to the greatest degree annoyed and I believe alarmed at this prospect of our people providing for the Queen. She is entitled by her marriage settlement to £50,000 a year in the event of her surviving the King, so we have only to buy an annuity of £50,000 for the *joint lives* of herself and the King, and this it is said may be done for £250,000 or £300,000 at the outside, a sum which all agree may be raised by subscription.

" John Smith, the Banker, in presenting the Mansion House Petition last night, gave notice of a motion for Tuesday week to restore the Queen's name to the Liturgy, and coming from him this motion may be considered as made from that City Meeting, and must consequently produce a great impression. . . .

" Bennet tells me Lord Grey told him he quite approved of what I did last night which pleases me much.   Old Cole † is furious with me."

" Feb. 10th.

" I dine with the *Queen* today at 3 o'clock.   She sent me a message last night by Brougham to come out with him ; so Keppel Craven is to carry us both out in one of Her Majesty's carriages.

" You will see by the papers that I was not idle last night.   My followers should have been much more numerous, had it not been that on finding the Committee of Supply being put off I announced positively

---

* Nicholas Vansittart, Chancellor of the Exchequer.   † Tierney.

my intention to withhold my fire, in consequence of
which Sefton, Ossulston, Bennet, Lambton, and
various others went away, and were afterwards to
the last degree provoked at having been absent.   I
think, however, I may be quite content with my 48.
I and my system of attack are becoming quite the
fashion with our lads, and indeed with the old ones
too. . . ."

"Feb. 16th.

" . . . Enclosed I send you two documents to
shew you the different *pint* of view in which we
publick men are liable to have our Parliamentary
conduct considered.   The amicable one came to me
in the House the day before yesterday, with the
Writer's printed card enclosed.   The note from *Lord
Binning* was sent up to me in my place last night,
within five minutes after my arrival, and whilst I was
entangled with the Lord Advocate.   My impression
at first was, it was a *hoax*, but as Sefton and Ferguson
who were by me denied all knowledge of it, I went up
stairs immediately, and there true enough I found Ld.
Binning waiting for me, so after having found an
empty Committee Room, and shut the door, his Lordship with dramatic gravity said, after what had
passed in the House of Commons the preceding
evening, he was commissioned by his friend Sir
George Warrender to deliver me a letter, which he
produced from his pocket, and which of course I knew
from the moment I saw Binning, was a demand of an
apology ; so having read it, (and it was sufficiently
windy), I said that of course I had nothing to do with
it, and that I would send Genl. Ferguson to him as my
friend.   So up went *Fergy*, and after two hours and
a half, he returned with the first *protocol*, and from
which it was clear there would be no blood spilt, and

I I

Binning took it off to consult Warrender upon, which took up two hours more, and I have the pleasure to inform you that about eleven o'clock, this serious affair was finally settled under the hands of Binning and Ferguson annexed to as damned long winded a business as you ever saw. . . . You never saw a more ridiculous figure than Ferguson has made Warrender cut in this great state paper, so much so as to convulse Sefton and Roslyn who saw it, but still I should hate exceedingly any publishing of such nonsense. The history of the affair is this :

" Warrender was so cursed sore upon my fire into him last Friday, that he did nothing but bluster and vow vengeance upon me at his Club at White's, telling every one that the very first opportunity, he would blow me up sky high in the House of Commons. . . . I thought it would not be amiss to anticipate his shot, and so acted accordingly to the great amusement of my audience on both sides, and to the utter discomfiture of Warrender who looked like the damnest idiot you ever saw, and could not produce a single word in reply. . . ."

Enclosure 1

" The Individual whose card is enclosed, begs very respectfully to state, that himself and a few City Friends, forming a private circle of acquaintance, are subscribing a short Address of Thanks to Mr. Creevey for his recent conduct in the House of Commons. . . ."

Enclosure 2

" Lord Binning presents his compliments to Mr. Creevey and would be glad to have a moment's conversation with him. Lord B. waits for him in the Smoking Room, and perhaps Mr. Creevey will be so obliging as to follow him into one of the Committee Rooms."

Captain Hesse * to Creevey

"July 19th.

" By H.M.'s desire and my inclination I inform you that *she* went *towards* Westm'r : Abbey this morning. She was in her State carriage with Ly. Hood and Ly. A. Hamilton, and in a second carriage Ld. Hood and your humble servant.

" We tried two different doors to get admission, but were told no one could gain admittance without a ticket. When Ld. Hood said the Queen desired to be admitted, they said, ' They had not the pleasure of knowing the Queen.' After two unsuccessful attempts we entered the carriages and amidst a tremendous concourse of people who were *all* in our favour we drove back to South Audley St. On our way all the houses that had G. R. with lamps, had their windows broke. Before Carlton House tremendous groans and hisses. All this happened between ½ past five and seven o'clock.

" Her M. is gone to bed while the better and stronger half is in the act of getting crowned.

" Brougham and I are now on our way to the sight, merely as spectators and not as actors.

" I believe every thing will go off quietly enough tonight, unless John Bull is really as enraged as they swore themselves this morning he ought to be."

Creevey to Miss Ord

"Cantley,† July 22nd.

" I had no letter from Brougham yesterday. The different letters to this house were certainly unfavor-

---

* In attendance on Queen Caroline. See *ante* (Waterloo letters).
† M. A. Taylor's.

able to the Queen's reception the other day, and according to custom, when a measure is supposed not to have answered the measure itself is condemned. For one, however, I am certain, that having declared she would go, she was perfectly right to persist, and I go further, and think, that without having made any such pledge she was right in going.

"I became converted by her message to me ' that I had never been a Queen.' The argument is irresistible. If she only has nerves sufficiently strong to act upon it, if she does not mind hissing and hooting, they don't affect in the slightest degree her right as Queen, or one of the Royal Family to be present at a Coronation. The King and his Court and the higher orders of the Nation, have in the most villainous and blackguard manner attempted to destroy her, first under the appearance of Law, and having failed in that, are now trying to hunt her down like a wild beast. To talk of *conciliating* such a collection of Monsters is perfectly contemptible.

"I see ' The Times ' Newspaper mentions ' some hideous monster at a window in George Street who indulged himself in the most frightful paroxysms of rage as Her Majesty passed his window.' This no doubt was Stracey—a perfect model of a Queen's enemy. . . ."

Brougham to Creevey

"Hampton Court, Aug. 6th.

"I came here last night with Mrs. B., whom it was absolutely necessary to bring away from London. She is a little more composed, and tho' she has had an alarm or two of premature labour, I believe it will not happen. If she weathers today, indeed, there is no chance. Nothing could prevail on her to stay in town. . . .

"Give my kind remembrances to the Taylors, who are extremely to be envied in having no children. I look upon it as a prime blessing, and as I never can see the one I've lost I hope never to see another."

Dr. Holland * to Brougham

"Mount Street, August 8th.

"You will hear it from other quarters, but I write a single line also, to tell you that our painful duties are at an end. During the morning of yesterday, the Queen became suddenly and rapidly worse ; the pulse sunk ; great restlessness and oppression came on, and a consciousness of approaching death. At 4 o'clock, Baillie, Maton and I wrote a bulletin. At 6 o'clock the indications of more acute suffering were over. The remaining 4 hours of life were tranquil with respect to all outward expression, the last 20 minutes so much so, that it was difficult to say when she drew her last breath. I believe I felt her last pulse.

"Lushington † will probably tell you all that is needful about other matters. He and Wilde ‡ were there till 2 in the night. He is, I fancy, already married this morning, and is to see Lord Liverpool, as I presume, at 11.

"I left Brandenburgh House two hours ago. Every thing has been done there, since the event, as

---

* Sir Henry Holland. Physician to Queen Caroline, 1814–21. He married secondly Sydney Smith's daughter. Sydney Holland, Lord Knutsford, was his grandson.

† Stephen Lushington, 1782–1873, reformer, advocate and judge.

‡ One of the Queen's advocates. Afterwards Lord Chancellor and Lord Truro. His second wife was the Duke of Sussex's daughter, Augusta D'Este.

correctly as circumstances allowed. Lord Hood has shewn great discretion and propriety throughout the whole."

Report from the Countess of Glengall *

"Dublin, September 5th.

" A true account of His Majesty George the 4th's visit to the Curragh of Kildare, and of the previous arrangements made by the stewards appointed by the Hon'ble. and Rev'd. the Turf Club to prepare for his reception.

" On Wednesday last His Majesty was expected at the Curragh, but he gave a grand dinner the day before to the Knights and Todies of St. Patrick, at which he shewed evident signs of uneasiness in his Royal stomacher, and was thereby *obligated* to send an excuse early in the morning to his expectant worshippers, who were mounted cap-a-pied (with his Grace of Leinster at their tail) for the purpose of escorting the track of his Royal wheels. Add to this, that the whole of the inhabitants of the South of Ireland from Bantry Bay, Cork, Cahir and the intermediate cities had assembled pêle-mêle on the Curragh to get a glimpse of the idol, where there was neither house nor tree to afford them shelter. The common labouring people had set off like mad beggars . . . leaving their harvest (crying out to be cut) to the mercy of the wind and rain.

" But lo ! the wherry-go-nimbles, which had so unreasonably attacked the Royal stomach, (for even Kings are subject to these unkingly complaints), gave his Majesty full employment at the Phœnix Park, and the Duke of Leinster arrived at the Curragh with this direful intelligence.

* Emilia, daughter of St. J. Jeffreys, of Blarney Castle, married 1st Earl. Her anecdotes were as broad as they were long.

" Lord Portarlington and the other Stewards, 12 in number, were assembled to receive this 2nd. St. Patrick. They had spent near £5,000 in erecting a glass house and providing a suitable banquet for the Royal party. When, therefore, they were informed of the complaint which detained their promised guest, their grief was audible, but they were in some measure comforted by the assurance, that if the Castor Oil (so liberally administered) was true to its office, he would come on Friday, the day but one after.

" One of the Stewards stood forth with great solemnity in the august assembly of Managers and said, ' Gentlemen, I fear one thing has been omitted, which it appears may be an essential *necessary*, I mean, a watercloset, and I humbly propose that Artists may be forthwith summoned from Dublin to erect one before his arrival.' . . . His Grace of Leinster volunteered to ride himself to town, 23 Irish miles, to bring down Mr. Simmons, the Bramah of Dublin. His Grace's offer was thankfully accepted, and he rode off ventre à terre, and returned accompanied by said Artist . . . Mr. Simmons only asked instructions as to the dimensions and size which the Stewards wished to have for the seat, and its appurtenances. Lord Mayo rose and observed that ' He conceived the usual dimensions would suffice as His Majesty tho' corpulent was finely turned.' The Earl of Meath who had the day before received the Blue Ribbon at His Majesty's hands said, ' That tho' his limbs were small the contour of his person was round, and that he proposed that Mr. Massey Dawson, the Member for Clonmell, should be measured as a certain criterion to go by.' Mr. Massey Dawson declared his willingness to contribute by any means in his power. . . . In 24 hours . . . the machine . . . &c. &c. were on the road to the Curragh, and a few hours more saw it placed in its niche. But lo ! when the pump was tried a trifling oversight was discovered—no water was forthcoming except only that which poured from the heavens.

" [Here my Lady becomes so very loose in her discourse for many sentences that you must excuse me. T. C.]

" The Debate had just arrived at this stage when distant shouts were heard, and the Stewards flew to receive the Royal Sufferer. A tall friend of ours preceded him upstairs, and the Doctor following close in his *rear*, took an opportunity of assuring the Stewards that nothing but his anxious wish to wait upon them could have induced His Majesty to journey so far under existing circumstances.

" All the ceremonies of the reception being gone thro', the Horses started, but before they could arrive at the Winning Post, His Majesty was obliged to bolt. His Grace of Leinster was called for, as he had undertaken to do the honors of the new erection—exeunt the Duke walking first with a white wand, then the King, and immediately behind the Doctor. ' How fortunate ' was immediately echoed round the room, nay round the course itself, and thanks were immediately voted to the Lord of Portarlington. . . .

" The above is REALLY true, every circumstance as related did really and positively take place, and was seriously related to me by one of the Stewards. . . ."

True or not, Creevey's blue pencil here proves too tolerant even for present-day standards.

Brougham to Creevey

"Hill Street, Oct. 3rd.

" I write this to let you know that Mrs. B.* was brought to bed to-day between 12 and 1 of a girl, and that she had a very good time (as it is called), and is quite well.   It is odd enough that the very same time this day last year, I was delivered of my speech in opening the Queen's case.   I hope to-day's offspring will be longer lived,† for that one, tho' praised at first as a promising child, was forgotten in 48 hours. . . ."

* Mrs. Brougham was formerly Mrs. Spalding, daughter of Thomas Eden.
† Eleanor, Brougham's second daughter, died at the age of 17.

CHAPTER VII

1822

THE sojourn in the wilderness was coming to be regarded by the Whigs as a life sentence. Place and power seemed as distant as ever in 1822, but Creevey was beginning to find in the ease and luxury of Whig country houses that even the wilderness could be Paradise enough. For him it was a carnival year; he clearly reveals the Party-man mellowing into the Man of Fashion. He bent his mind to the first principles of botany with charming young women, and found in English scenery and family history a restful substitute for the fever of party politics. If the day of the Whigs should ever come, he would be found ready. His reputation as a pamphleteer was rising. Meanwhile he was fifty-four, hale and hearty, with no encumbrances and with all his youthful enthusiasms as lively as ever, and the world was an enchanting place. This year Castlereagh—who had recently succeeded his father, Lord Londonderry—committed suicide on August 13, adding one more illustrious name to that sinister roll which numbered Paull, Whitbread and Romilly in quick succession.

In Castlereagh's place Wellington represented Great Britain at the Congress of Verona, and after weeks of speculation the appointment of " the adventurer," Canning, to the Foreign Office was officially confirmed. At the end of the summer, George IV paid his famous visit to Edinburgh under the ægis of Sir Walter Scott.

Mrs. Taylor to Creevey

" Cantley, Jany. 23rd.

" Mr. Ridgway is a most faithless bookseller, he never sent your pamphlet till the 16th. . . . Mr.

Taylor is quite delighted with it, more so than with any thing I ever saw him read ; even he thinks it must do good, tho' you know he seldom allows that any good is to be done. Sir Joseph Copley * highly approved of it. He told me he thought it most powerful and well written, and he is a good and not a partial judge. . . .

" You do not mention Sir B. Bloomfield.† Did you see him at Brighton ? I hear the King has given Lady Bloomfield the Rangership of one of the Parks, but however plausibly they may keep up appearances, I am quite sure from what Mr. Denison told me of things that happened in Ireland, that his reign is over, and that Lady C. is determined to get rid of him. . . ."

Creevey to Miss Ord

" Feb. 8th.

" . . . I went up with Lord Sefton and dined in Arlington Street, and was carried back by him to the House by nine. On our way he told me an anecdote of Lambton :—

" On 12th Night at Paris, the Lambtons being at a Party at Mad'e. Flaugh's,‡ there was a good deal of music, and eventually little lotteries for all kinds of bonbons, and other trifles. In an unguarded moment Mad'e. Flaugh asked Lambton if he would not join in the lottery, upon which he was pleased to observe that, ' Musick and Sugar-plums were his abhorrence.' ' Ah,' said Mad'e. Flaugh, ' I suppose it is beneath

---

* Of Sprotboro'.   The painter and his son, Lord Lyndhurst, derived from this family.

† General Sir Benjamin, afterwards Lord, Bloomfield.   Succeeded McMahon in 1817 as the Regent's Private Secretary.   Resigned 1822.

‡ Flahault.   Margaret Mercer Elphinstone, Baroness Keith, married, in 1817, Comte de Flahault, Napoleon's secretary, a natural son of Talleyrand.

your dignity to join in our nonsense,' upon which the Reformer instantly took his hat and retired in the greatest indignation. . . ."

Creevey to Earl of Sefton

"Tunbridge Wells, July 14th.

" I can't say I was ever more annoyed than by the damnable mess I am got into by the great indiscretion of Ly. Glengall. . . . I told her by way of news that Lord Hardwick * had been killed the day before by a cricket ball with the lord knows what stuff besides about his Daughter, Ly. Caledon.

" I leave you to judge of my surprise when I saw the last piece of intelligence formally denied in the London newspapers of last night, with a regular reference to myself as the author. Now I know full well it will be no justification to any one who does not know me that this story of Lord Hardwick's death was a wilful lie and joke—death is too serious a subject to be so dealt with. No person can be more seriously concerned than myself at any uneasiness Lord Hardwick's family or friends may have been occasioned by this stupid folly of mine. . . . but only think of Ly. Glengall's believing what I stated to have happened on Tuesday last, which she received on *Thursday* (*two* days after), and only 36 miles from London.

" . . . I rely on your sound and excellent discretion for using this communication as you shall think fit. *Publishing* anything as defence of myself is quite out of the question, but as you are in the habit of seeing all the world, I do wish, should any occasion present itself, you would protect me from the imputation of being a deliberate unfeeling savage. . . . I

* Philip, 3rd Earl of Hardwicke.

need not say it is high time for me to close my propensity for joking, if I am to pay so dearly for it as
I am now doing.   Take compassion on me. . . .''

Creevey to Miss Ord

" July 18th.

" Now for my own calamities. . . . The subject
is all duly arranged, and parties regularly formed.
The *Jerseys*, *Greys*, &c. &c. &c. are all decidedly of
opinion that it was *infamous* in Lady Glengall sending
the extract about Lord Hardwick and family to Lady
Hardwick's Sisters (The Lady Lindsays) without
sending the *whole note*.   That no one but an idiot on
reading the *whole* could doubt of its being all a hoax.
Nevertheless it was Sir Robt. Wilson who sent to Paris
to prepare poor Ly. Eliz'h. Stuart * for the terrible
event at Tunbridge. . . .
     " I dined at Sefton's yesterday at ½ past 8. . . .
Duncannon and Western were there.   When my
Lady † and two of her Daughters went to Almack's, my
Lord and Ly. Louisa and a younger Son and myself
went to Vauxhall, which was very beautiful but
thinly attended, and the Company damned *low*
indeed.
     " . . . When I came here (Brooks's) from Vaux-
hall, Thanet who was at his Whist made one of his
regular laughs when he saw me, and Kensington put
out his hand saying, ' How are you, old fellow, you
have been damned illused.'   I met Admiral Martin in
the street who said, ' My Dear Creevey, never write to
your friend Lady Glengall again ; when I heard Ly.
De Roos and others the other night talking of your
shocking letter, I said, Come, come, Creevey is any-

---

* Lord Hardwicke's third daughter.   † Maria, d. of 6th Lord Craven.

thing but an illnatured man, I will forfeit my life that the whole is some joke of his.' . . ."

" July 19th.

" . . . Both Lord Jersey and Duncannon told me after I had finished my letter to you yesterday that they had never witnessed such a scene as took place yesterday between Lady Glengall and Lady Jersey at the house of the latter. Ly. Jersey told her the *wickedness* of her conduct . . . was such that she would be served right if every one's door was shut against her in future. Both Jersey and Duncannon were present, and say the *Devil* had not a word to say for herself. In short, Countess as she is, she is play'd the Devil with if I am to judge by what all the world says to me.

" Pray get O'Meara's Book.* I have been at it these two hours, and won't quit it till I reach Cantley."

" Cantley, July 21st.

" Upon my soul this *Mrs.* Brougham is the most unaccountable person I have ever known. Her being by far the ugliest of her sex, she cannot help ; but how a Gentleman's Daughter can so strictly resemble the commonest Pot Girl in her manner, I cannot for the life of me make out. Then the necessity she evidently thinks there is of being always on the languishing tack instead of the cursing and swearing she is so distinctly made for, makes her as ridiculous. . . ."

" July 29th.

" This being a rainy day I have been in my room from 12 till ½ past 6, but then I was going over Nap a second time. In truth I am enchanted with him, and

---

* O'Meara's " Voice from St. Helena " ; a worthless book.

with the manner in which he hands down your real *legitimates*, both Kings and Ministers, to all posterity. He is very eloquent as all people with any talent are when really illused.   He cuts a great figure.   What would I have given to have seen him in his little room as described by O'Meara. . . .

" I was working four or five hours today in posting up Wellington at Brussels by way of memoir and companion to Nap, not in any way as disparaging the Beau,* but as history.   Nap, upon the whole, does the Beau no injustice. . . .

" . . . Auckland went today.   The Duke of Sussex comes on the 8th or 9th of next month."

" August 3rd.

" . . . In consequence of this book of O'Meara's, I have from memory and from notes I have, put down in one of my little books, all that passed between Wellington and myself from the time I first met him in Brussels in 1815 till after the Battle of Waterloo. His (Wellington's) opinion to me was from the first that there would be no *fighting*, that Carnot, Lucien Bonaparte &c. would set up a Republick, and that Nap would be disposed of.   I have most curious *notes* of his opinions on these subjects, and which all turned out to be very foolish ones.   When, however, he found that it was to end in blows, he cuts a great figure.   You will remember, no doubt, his conversation with me in the Park (at Brussels) in the presence of A. and yourself—then in the conversation with myself the day after the Battle.   Never conqueror cut a greater figure.   It was as much to his own honor as to that of the French Army, and of Nap's fidelity to truth in all he says of that Battle.   Then I have in my notes Wellington's own statement to me in 1818 when

* Wellington.

discussing Lowe's tyranny to Bonaparte that he, Wellington, was obliged to ask the Government to remove Lowe from his Army before the Battle of Waterloo on account of his being such a *troublesome, tormenting, damned* fool.

" My own opinion is, that accident has given me the best means perhaps of any one living of giving an accurate picture (as far as it goes) of our modern Marlborough on this occasion of Waterloo. All I have said or written of him is so much in his favor that I sometimes think of shewing it to him, but now you'll say I am stark staring mad. . . ."

" Cantley, August 19th.

" I send you a letter I had this morning from Brougham. It is one of his masterpieces in force, spirit and talent. It is a very curious portrait of himself, and his resources. You will, of course, either insert it in the ' *History of Our Own Times* ' or else preserve the original for me. . . .

" *Philpots* * is you know a prebend of Durham, a pamphleteer, and wholesale libeller. He has got upwards of £6,000 a year in the Church, and got it too expressly as his reward for having calumniated Lord Grey, Lambton &c. in his different works. A pleasant Prosecutor to come to the King's Bench for vengeance against the Durham Printer. . . ."

Brougham to Creevey

" Aug. 16th.

" . . . I am very glad you regard the Durham fight as important agt. the villains, which I assure you

---

* Henry Phillpots, afterwards Bishop of Exeter. The reference is to the prosecution of John Ambrose Williams for libel of the Durham Cathedral clergy. Creevey's details are inaccurate.

I do too, and I think that *if the advantage is improved*
much real good will be done. . . . I assure you I felt
the full importance of the occasion, and bestirred
myself in proportion.   I never exerted myself more
in the Queen's business, being quite sensible that
besides the local villainy the *Church abuses generally*
were the very question.   I told you at Cantley that I
was resolved to bring them to a regular engagement,
and I had all my ammunition prepared, and my plan
of operations well considered, but I felt beforehand
much difficulty how I was to get into the thick of it.
I saw little chance of so skillful an adversary as
Scarlett leaving any opening in his line, and you know
the evils of trying out things head and shoulders,
without the lively interest and effect of them being
applicable to the moment, and in a great degree off-
hand.   Mercifully Scarlett was alarmed from the first,
and fearful of losing the verdict.   This made him
labour his speech beyond any thing I ever saw him, or
any prosecutor, do.   It was as able as possible, but
from his overpains to secure the verdict he left me
two openings through which a waggon of abuse &c.
might be driven—the lamentation over the Church-
men not having the press at command, and above all,
their ' Suppressed grief and tenderness towards the
Queen.'   When I reconnoitred and spied the last, I
really could hardly keep my seat and was almost
overset.   It was as when I first heard Majocchi say,
' *Non mi ricordo,*' which gave one a bird's eye view of
all that was to follow.   This is the real history of it.
Scarlett . . . did his uttermost, and even canted
plentifully, but I must say no man in Court enjoyed
the thing afterwards more heartily and I really think
he sat in a state of pure delight while the ceremony
was performing of baptizing the Clergy with fire.

12

" As to the Speech ; as a speech—of course it was
no great thing, being necessarily slight, but *I* certainly
can't do any better than the Scotch Progress (much of
which is omitted), and the Roar about hypocrisy—at
least for effect, and they succeeded extremely, and I
am only sorry I had not to give them those matters in
a higher place, but the time may come there too."

Enclosure
Marquis of Lansdowne to Brougham

"Bowood, August 18th.

" . . . The melancholy termination of poor
Londonderry's life is certainly one of the most extraordinary events I remember, if not one of the most
important.   It is difficult to foresee what will be the
political consequences, as the Ministers are understood
to be in a state of indecision at present as to the new
appointment, and nothing will be settled till the K.
returns from Scotland.   The conjecture is that no
offer will be made to C'g., and that the experiment of
Peel alone supported by the Chan'lr. . . . will be tried.
Can this succeed ?   If it does, we must be Tory and
church ridden for ever and ever. . . ."

Creevey to Miss Ord

"Cantley, August 20th.

" Our Royal visitor * comes tomorrow.   I send
you a letter I had from Brougham upon Castlereagh's
death . . . and now you may like to know what
an eye-witness of the passing scenes at Edinbro' says
of our Sovereign. . . .

" . . . ' There has been no attempt at familiarity
or instance of servile adulation, even the cheering has

* Duke of Sussex.

not been overdone. A party of 50 of us, Ladies and
Gentlemen, went out in the Queensferry Steamboat to
meet him off Abercaldy, (15 miles from Edinbro'), and
were along side the Yatch for some time. The whole
party sung " God save the King " which seemed to
delight him, and had a fine effect in a beautiful still
morning.

" ' . . . The carriages were astonishingly numerous,
but a vast falling off in their appearance from a
London Levée. The illumination was more general
than ever known here. The crowds immense, but
there was no want of order. The King is said to be
quite satisfied with his reception and to admire the
Town, and the good conduct of the people in the
procession. . . .'

" Who should come in just as I was writing this,
but Mr. Ferguson of Raith. He has not seen the King
because no one was received in mourning, and he w'd
not put off his. He says the King is charmed with the
orderly conduct of his Scotch subjects, says that there
is no nonsense, that they are all Gentlemen, meaning of
course that his Irish ones were all *fools* and *black-
guards.*"

*Lord Roslyn's * account of the Levee at Edinbro'*
" August 1822.

" The Levee on Saturday was delightful. The
King was placed so near the door that many passed
without noticing him. One person was asked how he
thought the King looked, and how he liked his dress
(which as you know was full Highland costume). The
answer was, he looked very well and young, and that

* 2nd Earl of Rosslyn. Councillor of State to the King in Scotland.
Held office between 1829 and 1835 as Privy Seal and President of the
Council. Died 1837.

the Major General's uniform he wore was very becoming.   Lord Graves who was in waiting told all the men as they entered that they must *kiss hands.* Some who had had the benefit of a Grammar School made violent attempts to kiss both in letter'd obedience, others who were more elegant and dégagés in their manner, kissed their own hands to the King as they passed him bowing, and at last the King was obliged to order Graves to say ' *Kiss the King's hand.'* . . ."

Creevey to Miss Ord

"Cantley, Sept. 3rd.

" Sir Joseph Copley and his Daughters have been here since Sunday.   As he is one of Canning's oldest personal friends, and his Daughters are good Cronies of Miss Canning, I lost no time in examining them. . . . Maria Copley * says the King is so inveterate in his hatred of Canning, and that he not only won't invite Mrs. and Miss Canning to his house when all the other Ministers' wives are invited, but he won't speak to them when he sees them, and behaves to them with most marked rudeness.   Copley told me last night he had no doubt Canning would go to India, and added, he *must* do so for he was over head and ears in debt. . . .

" . . . I am afraid your paper gives no account of Lambton's † magnificence in receiving little Sussex. A Coach and six with *seven* out-riders, and two standing footmen, from 600 to 700 Tenants and others on horseback, with the contents of Collieries and Cottages by thousands upon thousands on foot."

* She later married Lord Howick, 3rd Earl Grey.

† J. G. Lambton, afterwards created Earl of Durham. " King Jog " and " The Monarch."

"Sept. 11th.

" . . . I think the wind is changing in favor of Canning's staying in England, and leading the House of Commons.   I send you a note I had yesterday from Brougham in which it may plainly be seen, through the bluster of his continued belief in Canning's going, that he not only thinks in his heart he is to remain here, but that he is damnably annoyed at its being so. In confirmation of the fact of Canning's remaining Maria Copley in a note I had from her about some books in her Father's Library says, ' It appears that Canning is to be the man very decidedly for the simple reason that Mr. Peel refuses to undertake the business of leading.' . . .

" King Jog arrived here yesterday having only brought with him *nine* race horses.   What they may be good for remains to be proved, but I saw them all take their gallop yesterday and beautiful they looked.

" The *Monarch* is in the greatest possible feather, and does not in the least disguise from one that it is *he* and not the Duke of Sussex who has received the universal adulation of the North.   I have examined Lady Louisa * who is also here, and who was herself present both at Sunderland and Newcastle, and she describes the scenes at both places as the most extraordinary and striking ones she ever beheld from the enormous masses of people of all ranks, and their marked good conduct and enthusiasm united.   I don't wonder at little Sussex being delighted, he has beat dear Prinney easily, and according to Lambton's report, he is in perfect ecstasies with his Tour.   I presume Howick will be an exception to his rapturous reminiscences, for, according to Lambton, Lord Grey had nobody to meet him, and has written word that he was

* Lambton's 2nd wife ; daughter of 2nd Earl Grey.

bored to death with him. It seems one of his constant subjects of reference during his Tour has been
' the great force he left Creevey in at Cantley.' . . .

" King Jog was so condescending as to come to my
room while I was shaving this morning, and amused
himself with various criticisms upon the component
parts of my toilette. He is evidently deeply affected
at this probability of Canning staying at home, which
he is pleased to consider as *fatal*. His observations
upon the King's conduct are highly judicious—' What
folly (as he truly says) it is for this man to trouble
himself in his old age in fighting for and supporting an
administration that is so palpably upon its last legs
as never to be worth four and twenty hours' purchase,
whereas, was he to send for Lord Grey to make a
Government, he would never encounter the least
further opposition for the remainder of his life. Not
that he (Lambton) wishes, God knows, to see Lord
Grey take office ; *quite the contrary*, he believes it would
be a very bad thing for him and his friends.' Upon
your soul ! ! Was there ever ? I asked Lambton
if Sussex had cost him a thousand pounds. He said
he should consider it cheap, if he got off for that.
Sussex comes on Saturday and stays through the
races."

" September 14th.

" I send you a note I had from Our Wicked-shifts *
this morning. You see he is terribly low about
Canning, having quite made up his mind to swallow
Peel in a couple of mouthfulls.

" Apropos to Canning. My latest intelligence was
from the Copleys on Thursday, having spent two
hours most agreeably with the girls that day. There

* Brougham.

were two letters, one from Lord Geo: Bentinck, (the
Duke's Son) who was going out with Canning as
Military Secretary to India.   He writes from Stafford-
shire last *Sunday*, being then with Canning, and up to
that hour no offer had been made, tho' they knew
something was coming, but the young one mentions
Canning being very *indignant* at the *shameful treatment* he is receiving.   In what this consists he does not
say, nor can I imagine.   The other Sprotbro' letter
was from Chas. Greville of last Tuesday's date from
London.   He mentions that Canning was to arrive
that day, and that in the meantime an offer had been
sent to him. . . .

" Our present party are Lambton, and Ly. Louisa,
Geo: Baker, Dicky Kirton, and myself—for dinner
today—Little Sussex, Stephenson,* Keppel and Gore.
. . ."

Enclosure.   Brougham to Creevey

" I agree with your inferences from Lady C.
Greville's ignorance, and I retain my opinion, that
they won't be able to make it up with C., and that they
don't expect it, and don't indeed generally wish it.
But *he expects* an offer, and has as you see been most
forwardly advertising for it.   Indeed I never saw a
baser or more silly proceeding, and now I can give
you *a fact*.   C. was to have sailed the middle of this
month.   He has notified to the Captain of the
Jupiter that he shall not be ready before the middle of
October. . . . Meanwhile, if he does not come into
office, it is no fault of our beastly friends in certain
quarters. . . .

" Pray let little Cop.† know that the tone at

* Henry Stephenson, private secretary to Duke of Sussex.   Married
Mary, daughter of 4th Earl of Albemarle.
† Miss Copley.

Lowther is to treat him (Canning) with the utmost contempt, and there would be no harm in this getting round. . . ."

Creevey to Miss Ord

"Cantley, Sept. 16th.

"Don't let me mix up Politicks and racing together, so before we go to 'The Ledger' let me mention that I had some jaw with the Tories on the Race Ground yesterday. Canning is to be sworn in *this day*, as Castlereagh's successor, but not a single other change is to be made, so, as Copley justly says, never man rode his race so ill. The offer once made to him by the Governm't, he had the game in his own hands, and might have commanded what terms he pleased. . . . Lambton, however, continues to growl against this cursed blow, and he predicts that Canning will carry all before him in the House of Commons, and that the unhappy Whigs are once more removed for ages from their favorite object. . . .

"Liverpool is Canning's only friend, every one else is against him. What a charming Cabinet for the great performer to sit in. The letters of mine which Bennet refers to, are those I wrote to him from Brussels about the time of the Battle of Waterloo, and which I desired him to send me that I might correct my *narrative* by them. . . .

"Sussex kept us waiting till 8 for our dinner on Saturday, and nearly drove Taylor mad. He behaved very well when he *did* come, and has continued to do so since. I had two hours of him yesterday. . . ."

Enclosure. Hon. H. G. Bennet to Creevey

" . . . Are you not pleased at the thought of yet having a shot at your friend Canning ? For my part

I rejoice at his taking office, as it is another blow to his reputation, and tho' he is the very man for the House of Commons yet he will give no strength to the Government in the eyes of the people. . . . I begin to be very anxious for the meeting and long to come to blows.   I believe it is quite settled that Canning is to succeed to Lord Londonderry's office.   Lord Liverpool bullied the King by menacing a resignation, and at the same time bullied his colleagues by the same threat as they were all hostile to the Adventurer ; the Duke of York said, complaining of the weakness of the King, that he might as well have sent for the Whigs at once, and that he considered his accession as a dissolution of the Government. . . .

" I have got all your letters, where shall I send them to you ?   I rely on your returning them, they are too valuable to be given up, and I weep daily over the burning of your letter about Old Cole.   It was so true a picture. . . ."

Brougham to Creevey

" . . . This insanity of C. taking place alone, is hardly credible.   He must have been in woeful despair at being banished to India.   Indeed it reminds me of Denman's remark on his Liverpool Speech—' That it was like a man taking leave (and lingering) at the foot of the gallows,' and so he jumps at a reprieve, or even a respite.   Bennet's account of the D. of Y. is exactly consistent with the language of the rest of the family, as to this being a slap at the D. of Y.'s party. . . ."

Creevey to Miss Ord

"Sept. 17th.

" I have sent you yesterday's *official return*.   The day was perhaps the most famous in all the annals of racing villainy. *Rhodes Mills*, if possible, outdid himself. He has the management of ' Dear Eddard's ' * Stables, and so perfectly humbugged poor Petre to the last about the badness of his horse that within half an hour of the race, he bet Lambton a gin: that he w'd. not even start, and he (Petre) gave Wyvill (Mills' Brother in law) £200 to take his bets off his hands, by which Wyvill told me himself he got £5,000, and Rhodes Mills has won as much. I hear Lord Foley favor'd Rhodes Mills with his own view of his character in full Club yesterday after dinner. Lambton was a considerable loser by the day, tho' Wyvill gave him some kind of hint as to the real character of the horse, which induced him to take £2,000 to 100 just before the race began, which of course he wins. ' Dear Eddard ' was at the Ball last night in perfect ecstacies at his *fame* at having won the St. Ledger. . . .

"Oh, if you had but seen Our Mayor and his deputation from Doncaster an hour ago, they came in three *hack chaises and four*, all in full rig—the sword bearer in a Dicky of the first chaise, cock'd hat, laced cloak, and great Mace over his shoulder. We were all present at the Speeches, and ogled poor Lady Augusta Milbanke into a good burst of laughing, and some profuse blushing for so doing."

" Sept. 19th.

" This Racing and Royalty and Politicks make a rare jumble, but as they amuse you, we must separate them .as well as we can.

" Our Duke † was evidently mortified at not being sufficiently attended to at the Race on Monday by the Stewards when he was in the Stand. The

* Hon. Robert Edward Petre.   † Sussex.

Stewards are Lascelles, (a Son of Lord Harewood's
and M.P. of the most Tory Cast), the other Tom
Duncombe (a good temper'd young one as possible
and a Whig).   It was the latter who would not shew
the Duke any attention as Steward, and when
Lambton remonstrated with him, and pressed him to
do so, he laughed and said, he would see him (the D.)
damned first. . . . It seems that one day at dinner
at Lambton, the Duke and Lambton begun to play
off their jokes upon Tom ; Tom saw what they were at,
and as Milbanke * says ' being a fellow of spirit determined to resent it the first opportunity, and I think
he has served them both quite right.'   As this continued hostility, however, w'd have been quite fatal
to Sussex, Jack Vane interfered, and Tom struck in
an instant upon *such* an application and made
Lascelles do the same, and no two young men could
possibly do the thing better than they did the whole
of yesterday.   They w'd not let the Racing in the
morning, nor the dancing in the evening begin, till
the D. arrived.   At both places they received him at
his carriage door, and never left him &c. &c.   In
short, he left the Ball-room about 2 ' quite delighted,'
as well he might be, but he could not have stir'd a step
if Tom had not struck, which he never w'd have done
at Lambton's suit.   So much for the influence of
King Jog's Crown.   Milbanke said to me ' What a
touchy fellow Lambton is ; he came to my house last
winter with Ld. Darlington, and the first day we had
very bad sport indeed, so Lambton was affronted,
and said he supposed if we *had* anything of a run,
there was nobody in that country who could follow
the hounds.   So, as he got more impudent, I told

* Mark Milbank, of Thorp Perrow, married Augusta, daughter of
3rd Earl of Darlington (1st Duke of Cleveland).

him at last I knew of one that w'd keep up with the hounds, and break his (Lambton's) neck into the bargain if he would follow him.   So he asked who it was, and I said it was myself, and he never spoke to me all the night afterwards.'   Mark, you must know, is a perfect Nimrod.   Lambton has been terribly pounded this week, and no wonder according to Geo. Baker who says : Mr. Lambton, *you see* Sir, runs his horses till their legs are no better than burnt sticks. . . .'

" I have had a good deal more conversation with Sir Joseph, who still adheres to his first opinion, that Canning has played his game ill.   The King received him most graciously, which he was sure to do, and which of course proves nothing, but the quantity and universality of personal hostility to Canning is a damnable thing for him. . . . A Leader of the H. of Commons with his sole capital comprised of jokes and rhetoric, without any possessions in land or money, is ill suited to the pride and feelings of the English Aristocracy and Gentry.   Then a man once convicted of foul play in a personal matter between man and man, has a perpetual mill-stone about his neck. . . ."

" Sept. 25th.

" . . . What a singular paragraph there was in ' Courier ' last night about the Beau being ill, and bled at Beauvais.   I believe I have a kinder feeling towards the poor Beau than an immense majority of his countrymen has. . . ."

" Farnley, Oct. 7th.

" Yesterday was a proud day indeed, such a day for scenery as I never saw before.   It was at Bolton Abbey which we could not reach sooner from the rain, but first let me say that my faithful guide, Miss Maria

Fawkes, conducted me on Friday to Harewood in which expedition we both got drenched to the skin. Harewood you know, makes one of the ends of our valley. If you stand upon our steps looking over the Wharf, upon the hills opposite—the high grounds in Harewood Park form the extreme left, about 8 miles off. Would you believe under these circumstances that the monsters who built the modern house have turned their backs upon the valley, that they have pitched their tent on the other side of the hill, with nothing to see from it but a mere common place park with an ordinary duck pond in the centre as a substitute for the Wharf. . . . The house is a great modern, handsome structure, and full, I am told, of gold and silver. . . .

" We four, the three girls and I, went in our coach and four by nine. . . . A mile of the road and more from this house is in our own park, sloping down to, and bounded by, the Wharf. The opposite hills or almost mountains with a great deal of ornamental wood on them, make our deer park . . . Crossing the Wharf at Otley we go by the other side of it, keeping always close to it, having the antient seat of Vavasour just opposite, buried in and surrounded on all sides by antient trees with great green pastures sloping to the Wharf, covered with cattle and bounded above (as are both sides of the Valley) with hills or mountains of heather, and moor, and stone. To Vavasour succeeds Sir Henry Ibbetson in a modern house of large dimensions and very fine grounds . . . and so you go on for about seven miles the other side of Otley, when our Wharf makes a sudden turn . . . We come up with him at a bridge called Bolton Bridge, and near this is an excellent Inn called the Devonshire Arms, and now if you please you may as well get out of the

Coach, and just come into this great spacious pasture behind the Inn. . . . When half across the pasture you come to a dip in it, and there stands the Abbey in the further corner ; its side facing you, its great window at the end facing a perpendicular rock or rocks, and wood of very great height ; the Wharf playing round the Abbey, and leaving it on placing it in very nearly an island gently sloping to the river side. . . .

" . . . Turning your eye from the Abbey and moving forward you may chuse which of two great terraces you please to walk thro', both of rich pasture covered with beautiful cattle, the lower one, 20 feet perhaps below the other, bounded by the Wharf. Beautiful wood above, and the magnificent and mountainous blue *Park* above all. . . .

" . . . Just imagine all this in the finest Autumn day imaginable, with every possible colour in the woods, but there is an object at *three* different turns of the river presents itself to your view, and which beggars all description from me ; it is called Barden *Tower*, but ought to be called Barden *Castle*, for such it is. It is, as it were, suspended in woods, *framed* like a picture at about a third of the rise of the woods from the Wharf, and looking you full in the face. . . .

" . . . I never received anything like the pleasure from scenery in all my life before. . . .

" Skipton Castle as well as those of Appleby, Brougham, &c. &c., Naisden, Bolton, were originally all one property, and were all given by William at the Conquest to one of his Norman Companions, Robert de Romille, or a Gabriel de Moutin. . . .

" Well, it was *Cecilia Romilly*,* the only daughter of

* See Wordsworth.

Robert, who founded Bolton Abbey—is not this
curious ?   From her and her issue these possessions
came all in a very short time into the family of the
Cliffords (Lord Clifford) and with them they remained
full five hundred years.   Skipton Castle was always
the principal residence of the family, tho' all the others
appear to have been lived in.   *Barden* was built or
used by one of his family as a hunting box. . . . In
the reign of Henry 8th these Baron Cliffords were
promoted to be Earls of Cumberland, and it was
from an only Daughter of the third Earl of Cumberland, Lady Ann Clifford, that *I* derive my title to
represent these antient Castles.   You who know so
much more about these things than I do, are acquainted, I dare say, with this extraordinary woman,
for such she was, but I, who never heard of her
before, am quite delighted with her.   She was born
in 1588 (her Mother being Lady Margaret Russell,
Lord Bedford's daughter) and she lived to 1675, 13
years only before our revolution, and aged 87.   She
married first the Earl of Dorset, and 2ndly the Earl
of Pembroke.   By her first marriage she had two
daughters, the eldest of which married the *Earl of
Thanet*, the 2nd. the Earl of Northampton.   Having
survived both her husbands, and having *Knole* and
Wilton both in dower, she came here and defended her
Castles for three whole years against the Parliament.
Her Father's titles went to a brother of his, who
fought for many a year with his niece for the estate,
as did his son the last Earl of Cumberland, who likewise left an only daughter.   The whole was at length
arranged before Lady Pembroke's death, she keeping
Skipton, Appleby, and by far the greatest part of the
property, and her cousin having Bolton &c. &c.   The
Cousin married Lord Burlington, whose daughter

married Lord Devonshire, and thus the present Duke's title to Bolton Abbey. . . .

" Old Dow: Pembroke seems never to have forgotten the protection of her property or respect for the memory of her Mother, but here I am tumbling over Whittaker to find the pillar she erected in the publick road near Appleby to her Mother's memory. . . .

" What a damned fool I must be, but *occupation*, I have often heard you say, is an excellent thing, and so I have found it, for this pretty valley and all the interesting objects which surround it, operate like a charm upon me. . . ."

" Oct. 24th.

" . . . I send you . . . a note from another flirt of mine (Lady Caroline Pawlet), not on account of the composition, but because to be written at all from a *Lowther to me* is funny enough. . . .

" I am sorry to see the account in the papers of the poor Beau's illness at Vienna. If he does not get over it there is something very unfortunate in a person who has faced death so often as he has, at last losing his life from so apparently trifling a cause.

" Yesterday Maria Fawkes and I rode three or four miles to a wood of her Father's to see Lord Harewood's Hounds turn off, and a most delightful day we had. Old Pompous Humbug, Mylord, was all attention to Maria, and civility to me. She had never hunted before. I was much pleased with the particular propriety and good manners she shewed to this Neighbouring Grandee. A smoother or prettier run it was impossible to have, the only cross event, which however was amusing to all but myself, was my having a fall in leaping a ragged stone wall, and having to present a countryman with 3/– for catching my horse. . . ."

Lady C. Powlett * to Creevey
"Cantley, Oct. 18th.

" . . . We intended to pay our respects to *you* here in your character of Master of the Mansion ; I had promised myself to make much progress in Botany by instructing you in what I have already learnt, and by studying with you the most approved authors, some of whom I brought with me for the sole object of our mutual instruction.

" News is scarce just now. I have heard but of one intended marriage, that of Dow: Cowper aged 70 to a young Apothecary at Florence. She has long excluded herself from all observation on account of the absence of youth, beauty and lovers. I wonder if the latter has persuaded her she was mistaken in supposing the loss of the other advantages.

" Ld. Bessboro' has been at Cowes for the last six weeks. The Duncannons at Ld. Spencer's House at Ryde. Ld. D. goes daily to see Ld. Bessboro', and sends me word he has benefitted amazingly by the sea air, and change of scene.

" Miss Sparrow, you know, is married to Ld. Mandeville. Ly. Olivia on being introduced to the D. of Manchester complimented him, and said something gracious and favourable of Ld. M. The Duke's answer was, ' that he knew little or nothing of the Young Man. . . .' "

Miss Maria Copley to Creevey
"Sprotboro', October 24th.

" . . . I have rummaged over all sorts of old books of the times, and am become so interested about the

* Afterwards Duchess of Cleveland, daughter of 1st Earl of Lonsdale.

13

Dear Dow:* that I beg to be employed on the subject. It appears that there is certainly no memoir of her published. So Papa says, 'Pray prosecute your enquiries.' Tell me what books you have not about you that I may, to the best of my abilities, give you all the information you may wish to have out of them. Don't fancy that it will be a trouble to me, for there is no occupation I like so well as *bookworming*. . . .

" I have got here Lord and Lady F. Leveson, and Ly. Charlotte Greville and Sons, so fancy to yourself my happiness. They have been here a week, and stay some time longer.

" It is a very old story to tell you how frantic I was at your not coming here in Sept. tho' I did not expect you would be allowed. Pray let me have it in yr. handwriting that you will come here in Dec'r.

" The hounds were on the hill opposite to-day, and I saw a horse without a rider following them. It was a most touching remembrance of you—quite affecting. Don't do anything so rash again unless you have got a 25 yr. old colt to ride upon. . . ."

General Ferguson to Creevey

" Raith, 28th Oct.

" . . . I hear you are turned botanist. Is this to please yourself, or little Cop's formidable rival?

" . . . I wish you had condescended to come to Scotland, tho' we cannot boast of such attractions as you have in the South. . . .

" I am happy to say that poverty and ill paid rents are working a change *even* in the Scotch Lairds. They will not be thoroughly honest till they are reduced to beggary. . . ."

* Pembroke.

Creevey to Miss Ord

"Croxteth, Nov. 26th.

" . . . The Company here besides their own family are, the Frazers, Hopwoods, and Arthur Heywood.

" Saturday we shot all day about the house, and bagged about 100 head. Sunday I went with the Ladies to Church. Yesterday we shot about 4 miles off at Kirby Rough, and bagged about 140 head. Mrs. Hopwood, Ly. Louisa and Ly. Caroline and I danced a reel in a field to keep ourselves warm. Today we have hunted. I rode a new horse, ' Merryman,' but was very prudent, and confined myself to galloping and getting wet to the skin. . . ."

R. Bowyer to Creevey

" 6th Dec.

" The picture which Mr. Stephanoff is painting for me of the interior of the House of Commons being now in a state of great forwardness, I am very anxious that the space which is left for your portrait should be filled up as soon as possible, and I shall therefore esteem it a peculiar favor if you will have the goodness to oblige me with the loan of any Miniature or other drawing or picture you may chance to possess which is deemed a good likeness, or if you should not possess one, that you will do me the favor to sit to Mr. Wivell * who has made drawings of more than one hundred of the Members for the purpose of this picture. . . ."

Creevey to Miss Ord

" Croxteth, Dec. 15th.

" . . . We are now quite a domestic party, five Daughters, four Sons and Grenfell. I must say, I

* Abraham Wivell, portrait-painter, 1786–1849.

never saw man or woman live more happily with nine grown up children.*   It is my Lord who is the great moving principle.   He has a great deal of talent, and of various kinds, and has been in the greatest possible force and spirits and the greatest source of amusement and agreeableness to me ever since I came. What a contrast to that poor victim of temper who left us last week ! " †

* Only child of the 1st Earl, the 2nd Earl of Sefton married Maria, daughter of 6th Lord Craven. Their family was : Lord Molyneux, Berkeley, Henry and Francis ; Georgiana (now married to Charles Pascoe Grenfell), Maria, Louisa, Caroline and Katherine.

† Mr. Lambton.

CHAPTER VIII

1823

THE doings of the fashionable world and the events of the London Season claimed the bulk of Creevey's interest in 1823.

Creevey to Miss Ord

"March 17th.

" On Thursday I dined with Mrs. Taylor at 5, and went to Drury Lane to see ' Figaro,' ' Stone Deaf,' and ' Old and Young.' The House itself is very well worth seeing, it has been much contracted in its apparent size, and made a much better shape, and altogether from its beautiful decorations is a very handsome Theatre. We were in a Private Box, and opposite to us, in the D. of Devonshire's, sat Lord and Ly. Granville, two little girls and a boy, and a Governess, and I must say they contributed much to my amusement from the happiness of the whole party. . . .

" Did I mention to you that I played 5 rubbers at Whist with Ly. Glengall at Whitehall a few nights ago? She asked me to play, but I never spoke to her. I must however relax as I am entreated to do, and as she is in ruin as to her finances. Bailiffs are in her house, her coach is seized, and she actually *walks* to Whitehall at night with her maid. . . .

" . . . Barnes (of ' The Times ') who in the absence of Brougham always sends for me, tells me that the ' Constitutional,' which is the leading Opposition paper of France, has a sale of from 17,000 to 18,000 papers per day, whilst ' The Times,' which has the greatest of our English Papers, amounts only to 7,000 per day.   Vilette writes all the political articles in the ' Journal des Debats,' and Chateaubriand is one of its proprietors, and this has the next best sale. . . .

" Sefton had some talk with Esterhazy at the Opera on Saturday, who in answer to a question from Sefton, whether it w'd. be War or no War between France and Spain said, his *feeling* led him to think it would be *War*, tho' his judgement taught him to think it ought to be peace ; so Sefton said laughing, it was all the better for a certain young boy * he could mention.   ' Ah ! ' said Esterhazy, ' that is a subject I cannot talk upon.' So Sefton asked what kind of boy he was, and the other said, a remarkably fine one ; that he had just gone into the Army much against the Emperor's wishes, but that he would be a soldier, and that he was now an Officer in the Emperor's Own Regiment. . . .

" I have sat three times to the Artist, Wivell, he says the likeness will be as strong as any he has done."

" April 15th.

" As to our public concerns last night, nothing I think could be worse than Canning's † case ; it was a great deal more so than I had any notion of.   He has been made the dupe of these French devils, and his speech amounted to little more than an admission of that fact.   To think of Wellington learning for the first time at Paris on his way to Verona, that the affairs of Spain were to be the subject of discussion there.   As the friend of Spain he ought instantly to have taken himself off, when he found that without

* Duc de Reichstadt.   Esterhazy was Austrian Ambassador.
† Canning's policy at the Congress should have appealed to Creevey as both anti-French and liberal.

notice to Spain and in the absence of representatives
of that Nation, her concerns were to be interfered with.
In short, I think for the first time in the history of this
Kingdom, we have played a low, truckling, cowardly
part, and that we may prepare ourselves for every
kind of impudence and insolence from France.

" As to Our *Brougham* I consider his speech of last
night as one of the greatest specimens of the marvellous resources of this artist.   He literally arrived after
Canning had begun, and a more lively and successful
licking of the Minister and his case, and of the French
villains altogether, could not possibly have been
produced by any length of preparation.   In short, I
was delighted with him and kept pushing him on (as
he stated to me this morning) by my repeated shouts
in his rear of ' go on.' . . ."

" April 21st.

" . . . After winning two rubbers at Whist at
Whitehall I called in here (Brooks's) and as soon as I
entered Sefton said he wanted to speak to me ; that
he had been dining at Holland House with a large
party, and before his departure Ly. Holland had
requested a private conference with him.   She then
proceeded to state the united regrets of herself and
Lord Holland at having lost for nearly a year the society
of Mr. Creevey ; that they both considered this a real
loss, and *had often conversed together* upon what was its
foundation.   It might be owing to Mr. and Mrs. ——
going there, and sometimes they fancied something
else, but at all events the result of the conference
was to impress Lord Sefton with the feeling that he
alone was the person to terminate this melancholy
affair by inducing me to come again to see them, and
she flung herself upon his charity for this object so dear

to her ! Was there ever ? To say the truth I was
by no means sorry for this formal diplomatic approach
to a re-union as I thought my resentment had been
long enough shewn. . . . So it's all very well.
Sefton wanted to take me there yesterday, but I
thought that was too *hot* : in the course of the week
will do.

"Yesterday I dined at Taylor's. Brougham and
dear Mrs. Brougham came for a short time in the
evening ; his apology for hurrying away being that he
had to set Mrs. B. home in order that the carriage
might take *Him* out to Holland House where he was
going *to sleep*. He is in great force and very much *up*
after last week's campaign. . . ."

"April 23rd.

"Certainly last night was one of the most curious
I have known in Parliament, and its result MAY be
one of the most important. At the beginning of this
Session who would have thought that an open and
public enquiry would be instituted by the House of
Commons into the administration of the laws in
Ireland, and still more, who would have thought that
Burdett would effect this in opposition to the Government ? His having succeeded in having the Sheriff of
Dublin called to the Bar to account for his conduct
in the late trials is neither more nor less (in its consequences) than an enquiry into the general administration of justice. . . . Nothing could be more
wretched than Plunket, nor more feeble than Canning,
and then you see the result—a majority over them
of 130.

"What think you of seeing all our fine ladies rattling down this street today in their feathers and paint
to see their dear Sovereign, when lo and behold poor

ST. JAMES'S STREET, ABOUT THE TIME OF CREEVEY.
From an old print.

[To face p. 178.

dear Prinney was not to be seen, and the ladies were all turned back. The King had got the gout, and the Birthday Drawing Room was put off. Was this to save the blushes of his Ministers and himself, or was it real ? . . ."

" May 2nd.

" . . . I forget whether I told you of De Stael's letter to Brougham, saying every person of any property whatsoever had uniformly retreated from the presence of the conciliatory Bourbons, and every account by letter or from travellers fully confirms this. This is the best thing that can happen in the present state of things.

" I dined yesterday at Lambton's, being expressly asked to try a new *confectioner*. The party were the Seftons, Normanbys, Ld. Grey, Ld. Duncannon, Ld. Fitzwilliam, Althorp, *Mrs.* Brougham, Luttrell and myself. I arrived after they had been at dinner nearly a quarter of an hour, and as it struck me that the appearance of things was triste enough I was pleased to think I put these Grandees in motion, and it turned out a very pleasant meeting. Grey was capital, and even old Fitzwilliam at last was playful.

" Today I dine at Hughes's. Saturday at Sam Whitbread's Brewery, and Sunday at Sefton's. . . ."

" May 9th.

" . . . Our dinner at Roslyn's was all very well as it always is there. Wednesday at Ellice's to meet ' Brother Sussex,' Lambton, Ferguson, Ridley, Colborne, and various others. ' Brother Sussex ' complained after dinner of his picture at the exhibition not being put in the principal room, ' nay I believe indeed it was on the ground floor ! ' So I told him he ought to have canvassed Colborne who was the

Tip Top Virtuoso of the Town and settled all the places of all the pictures, and *Nic* entered into a regular defence giving the inferiority of the artist as the ground of this slight put upon the Duke, but he did it very pertly and like a presumptuous Prig of a savant, and with very bad manners and taste towards a person of Our Sussex's rank, so I shewed him up well, and kept a running fire upon him for some time to Sussex's great content. . . .

" . . . ' Sally ' * *shook hands* with me at Lady Derby's, and desired me always to come to her on Mondays when I could. . . ."

                                       " **May 10th.**

" . . . As I have nothing but nonsense to write to you about, allow me to state that Our fashionable *Whig* Haut Ton has been much convulsed of late by two events—The first is that at a dinner at Prince Esterhazy's the latter handed *Mrs. Canning* out of the room first, altho' the Countess of Tankerville was the lady of the highest rank in the room. This proceeding was therefore immediately resented by a spirited remonstrance against so palpable a violation of English Etiquette. Poor Esterhazy defended himself by stating that he had asked for and acted upon the counsel of Madame Lieven,† so a conference was appointed between the latter and Lady Jersey to settle this point. Lady Jersey began by saying that she had Lord Tankerville's authority for stating that as far as related to himself and Ly. Tankerville per-

* Lady Jersey.

† Princess Lieven, born a Benckendorff, was the wife of the Russian Ambassador in London from 1811. She held a unique position in London Society. She inspired fear but gained the confidence of the leading statesmen of Europe, notably Metternich, Guizot, Grey and Palmerston. Her aim was omniscience; her abilities high. She affected ennui and introduced waltzing at Almack's. She died in Paris in 1857.

sonally—*rank* was an object of the most perfect indifference, but it was upon national grounds and
customs that the claim was made.   Madame Lieven,
having disclaimed all intention of offence by the
advice she had given, contended that *abroad* Diplomatic and Ministerial Rank always preceded personal
rank, but here Our Countess had such a collection of
cases, and authorities of all description, even *books*,
that Mad'e. Lieven was brought upon her marrow-
bones and has solemnly promised that the outrage to
our British Nobility shall never be repeated.   The
second fracas relates to Mad'e. Lieven, as a Patroness
of Almack's, having refused tickets to San Lorenzo,
Spanish Ambassador, his Wife and Friends, and
being asked the reason she replied, that they had so
many more friends in England than she had that
they could never want tickets from her, and this
observation being made to the other Lady Patroness
with some tone of impertinence, she was informed
that the only ground of her being a Patroness was, to
give tickets to all Foreigners of Distinction, without
any distinction arising from Politicks, and it is
even said that the word *Cossack* was mentioned as
description of a person by whom English Ladies were
not to be taught manners.   I assure you all this is as
nearly and literally true as possible.

" Charles Brandling * and I have been lounging
about the streets together all the morning, and he
enjoyed very much, I think, picking up various of
my Whig *Comrogues*, particularly Brougham. Apropos
to the latter, Old St. Vincent has left him all his
papers, letters, &c., which are supposed to be very
curious, and Brougham offered me in Charles's
presence to have the compleat ransacking of them."

* Creevey's brother-in-law.

"May 15th.

"Our Beloved is better to-day—that marvellous stomach of his has saved him. . . . Prinney whose inflammation had reached from his toe nearly to the top of his thigh, and who was already partially affected with delirium from the great irritability, upon his stomach being literally soused with Opium and Bark Brandy and Wine, sucks in his cordial like mother's milk, recovers his senses, sleeps soundly, and shakes off his mortal enemy at a blow. His danger was extreem, but I presume he will now do again. . . ."

"June 3rd.

"My visit to Stoke Farm.* . . . I was taken down in the family open carriage, and the day was beautiful, but Sunday was the day of days, not only on account of its more than common splendor and gaiety, but I was taken to my beloved haunts, Windsor Castle and Eton. The feelings with which I went over the same ground three and thirty years ago were much stronger now. Then Molyneux took me through the schools, the Dormitory and Play Grounds where I had never been before, and I was planted in the proper place to see all the Boys come out of Church, and in short, from beauties *without* and associations and reminiscences *within*, my repast was a tip top rich one, and I came back delighted. . . ."

"June 24th.

". . . The Spanish Fête is to be at Covent Garden Theatre on the 4th. Ebers only asked £2,000 for the Opera House whilst Covent Garden is given to them, and Willis undertakes to light it &c. for £500. This

* Lord Sefton's house near Windsor.

fête has produced the greatest schism in the ranks of the *Tories*, but Lady Sandwich leads the seceders from the Govern't, and is as firm as a rock.

" Wellington has been violently assailed by Lady Jersey and all the Whig Ladies as well as by Lady Sandwich to sanction the fête by his presence, but he jokes and says he sh'd: be hanged if he was found there, but if they would make it a masquerade he would still go incog:. Duncannon, however, who is always the safest authority on all subjects he thinks about, says the Government click will eventually be dead beat on this point, and that every ticket will be sold. Indeed, I believe, that is very nearly the case already ; my only fear is there will be no Spanish Patriots left to use the money, for every thing looks infernally ill, at least according to the French accounts.

" Yesterday I dined at Whitehall, and went with Mrs. Taylor in the evening to the Opera, where she and Mrs. George Lamb have a box the alternate weeks. I could not help thinking as I sat between these two ladies, what the devil could make them spend their money in this way—for the devil a bit did they understand or care for the music, and almost as little for the dancing, and not a single visitor was there to pay his respects to either Lady.

" . . . I am invited to make the said Stoke my Country House till Sept'r., and then go to Croxteth, but then how am I to manage with Newport's invitation to me to come over to *Ireland,* and how am I to keep the promise which Milton says I have made, to spend Nov'r: and Dec'r: with him and Lord Fitzwilliam at Milton. *King Jog* has jilted me to-day, he was to have called upon me at my lodgings to take me to give *my opinion* of some pictures he has bought.

This is his 2nd. piece of patronage of the same kind, but still I *cannot* trust him enough to go and see him at Lambton."

"July 5th.

"I dined yesterday at Sefton's, Lord Grey was there, and he said in his most pathetic strain, 'When do you come to Tunbridge, Creevey?' so I said, 'In a month perhaps.'—'Not for a month!' he said, and then I found he had just taken the Bowling Green House for two months. . . . We dined rather earlier than usual that the Ladies might be dressed in time for the Ball, so of course I staid to see them all rigg'd and off, and very well indeed they looked. Lady Sefton and Ly. Georgina in White profusely set with gold stars of the first magnitude, and two very handsome gold flounces, gold bouquets and feathers without end in the head. Ladies Maria, Louisa and Caroline, who were three of a Quadrille, were excellently dressed, and I never saw them look half so well. The costume was the exclusive production of the Count St. Antonio—who was himself one of the Quadrille. Large black Spanish hats, one white feather coming over the front of the hat, all the others playing themselves behind the hat in all directions. The dress, white muslin, blue satin triangular trimming with tags, blue satin stomacher &c. &c. I have examined every one I have seen today as to the *real merits* of the concern, and there is no difference of opinion as to its having been the best Ball and the most beautiful sight that London has witnessed for years. . . . In short, the concern is clearly in port, which after all the villainy of 'John Bull,' and all the blackguard conduct of the Tories, is a very great triumph. . . . Since writing the above I have seen the fastidious Grey, Sefton, Tankerville and Thanet, who report it to have been in every respect *perfect*. The dresses of Lady Jersey and Lady Cowper are said to have been brilliant in the extreme. The former was dressed under the immediate inspection of the Duchess San Lorenzo, so of course she was *Spanish* to the back bone. Lord *Dudley* says he went to be present at a *failure*, but that he never laid out two pounds to such advantage in his life. . . ."

" July 9th.

" Sunday was a terrible day of blunders with me. You know I was to go to Stoke, so having had no communication from Sefton, I sent my cloaths to Arlington Street to go down in their carriage, and a note saying I sh'd. turn up at dinner time. So off I set down the Hounslow road meaning to walk till I was picked up by some coach—not a coach however passed me but what was full ; finding myself at Kew Bridge and the evening advancing I retired into a publick house, and dined, and then retraced my steps to London. . . . On Monday, the Ladies from Stoke came up for Mrs. Byng's Ball leaving my Lord at Stoke, and asking me to go back there yesterday, but devil a bit of my bag had they brought, in which was my only coat for going to Mrs. Byng's, to say nothing of powder box, razors, &c. &c., so of course I could not go to Mrs. Byng's, nor yet did I return to Stoke, and here is Sefton abusing me like a pickpocket, being just arrived, and, what is better still, having brought my bag.

" I am to meet the Taylors at dinner on Friday at Denison's, and tomorrow week they are to take me in their carriage to dine at Lord Duncannon's at Roehampton. Saturday we have a great turtle dinner at Sefton's. Monday I dine at 'Comical Bob.' * I have partly promised Lord King to go to Ockham † Friday week to stay a few days, and if you come to that I have just promised Lauderdale to give him a week at Dunbar if I go into Northumberland, and Brougham last night in the House of Commons pressed me much to come to him at Brougham, and he would take me into Scotland to meet the Jerseys at Drummond Castle, and to see Edinbro' and other lions without end. So pray tell me what the devil I am to do."

" July 18th.

" . . . I did not go to the Ball, it is said to have been dull, but very fine. Taylor who went as a Jew Pedlar and Knife Seller was smoaked instantly as I told him he would be, and got most infernally hustled, tho' he won't allow it. The most entertaining persons appear to have been Arthur Hill, Alvanley and Glengall as Lady Patronesses of Almack's, and of course giving themselves the greatest airs. They played off their tyranny and excluding system upon poor Dow: Richmond with such success that she was reduced to tears. They were furnished with tickets, and their humour was in examining the titles of such persons as presumed to ask for them. Lord Molyneux who did capitally as a French Postilion finally drank too much wine, and was too boisterous."

" July 30th.

" The weather was so atrocious yesterday that we abandoned the country for the Opera to hear Ricciado from beginning to end. . . . I wished to sleep at my lodgings, which I knew were empty, (as you know how I value my liberty), but by Ly. Sefton however the proposition was quite scouted, and so I slept in

* Lord R. Spencer.   † Ockham Park, Ripley.

Cap'n. Berk'y. Molyneux's room in Arlington Street, and I never saw Lady Sefton and her Daughter to greater advantage when my Lord was confined to his room with one of his headaches.   We return to Stoke at ½ past 3.—the Ladies having just walked to Howell & James's, about whom Ly. Louisa said rather a funny thing.   She said she sh'd. tell them what her allowance was, and then ask them whether they w'd. contract to *dress* her, and at what *rate*.

" Do you know that Lady Anne Harley is either married or to be married to Col. Fabvier, A.D.C. that was to Marmont, and one of the French Officers who put himself at the head of the Spanish Troops crying ' Vive Napoléon ' when the French first crossed the ' Biddy-Ossy.'   It is this connection which has banished Ly. Oxford from Paris.   The Col:'s letters to her and her Daughter were intercepted and were full of Jacobinism &c. &c.   Kinnaird told me her folly had become such that no Englishman w'd. or could go near her house.

" *Ten* of us got a pretty good ride in spite of the atrocious weather on Sunday, and 13 of us on Monday. We were obliged to run for it, and wait till after for a fair start.   My Lady and her three Daughters and myself rode 18 miles after 3 o'clock the other day. She (my Lady) is certainly the strongest woman I ever saw—neither riding nor *eating* ever makes her sleepy. If you had seen the plates of venison she eat yesterday, and by her allusions to the hashed edition we are to have of it today, I conclude she will be equally active."

Mrs. Taylor to Creevey

" Cantley, Aug. 13.

" . . . Now, My Dear Mr. Creevey, I am going to tell you what I promised never to mention, but as I

14

know you like to communicate every thing to your Daughters, and that they will see the necessity of secrecy. . . . When the Darlingtons were here last week my Lady and I were talking over our *sincere friend*, Brougham, and Appleby, and so forth, and your not being secure of a seat.* She said that I had done very wrong in not having mentioned it earlier to Ld. Darlington, but that she believed he had still a seat not engaged, and that tho' *she had never interfered* in matters of this kind (pretty well I thank you), she should certainly use her influence to secure it for you. . . .

" It will give me sincere pleasure if this succeeds, and meets your wishes, for Brougham told me on his way to Town a few days before my conversation with Ly. Darlington, that you had lost all chance of coming into Parliament, not only by the line you took on the Catholic Question yourself, but also by the way you influenced Mr. Lambton and others. . . .

" Miss Copley, the only one of the family at Sprotbro' at present, is in a state of excitement not to be described, by the expectation of having the Duke of Devonshire, Ld. and Ly. Exeter, and I cannot tell you what other fine people at the Show. . . ."

Earl of Sefton to Creevey

" August 19th.

" . . . We dined with Duncannon on Friday, and met that Arch Bore, the D. of Sussex ; he staid there till 12, and was quite himself. I am sure the enclosed paragraph from the ' Windsor Express ' will interest you, and every friend of the descendants of the Electress Sophia. Mr. Bannister, the Orator, is

* Lord Thanet's health was giving anxiety to Creevey. He died not long afterwards, when Creevey lost his seat.

our butcher at Windsor, and his sentiments were of course of the most disinterested kind."

Copy of paper cutting referred to

" . . . On Tuesday, being the anniversary of the King's Birth Day, his Majesty had a select party to dinner, amongst whom were the Duke of York, the Duke of Dorset, Count Lieven, the Marquis and Lord Francis Conyngham, Sir W. Knighton, Sir W. Keppel, Sir Edmund Nagle, Sir Herbert Taylor, and Col. Thornton.

" His Majesty, with that considerate kindness by which he is so peculiarly characterised, on Tuesday bestowed a signal honour and gratification on his Tradesmen at Windsor and the neighbourhood, by commanding them to be invited to join his pages and other principal persons of his household, at a Ball at Cumberland Lodge. The preparations on this occasion were on a scale of princely magnificence. The Ball commenced about 9 o'clock, with Country Dances and Quadrilles alternately; the band was excellent, and dancing was continued with great spirit till the hour of supper. At that time a grand suite of rooms was thrown open, and the company, consisting of about 130, sat down to a supper consisting of every delicacy that the season could produce, or art could devise. His Majesty's health was drunk with thunders of applause and soon afterwards Mr. Bannister took occasion to express with great feeling and propriety, the sentiments which his Majesty's Tradesmen, and the inhabitants of Windsor generally, felt at this gracious mark of his Majesty's patronage and approbation. Dancing was afterwards resumed, and the company did not separate till the sun was gilding the surrounding scenery with his morning hues. . . ."

Earl Grey to Creevey

"Sept. 6th.

" Beaumont * came as far as Ferry Bridge, with the intention of fighting me, but was stopped there by Wm. Lambton, to whom he had written to be his second.   Upon seeing the correspondence W. L. told him at once that he must be mad, that no man of honour or common sense could be induced to act for him in such an affair, and at last persuaded him instead of coming on to town, to go to Scarborough, with the intention of going abroad, after a short residence there.   His conversation with W. L. was very long, and exhibited full proofs of insanity.   His family ought really to look after him. . . ."

* M.P. for the County of Northumberland.   Lord Grey was considering putting his son up as a candidate.

CHAPTER IX

1824

By the year 1824 the evolution of the Man-of-Fashion was complete. The Party-man had become the house-party man, and the splendours of the London Season and the tittle-tattle of the country-house claimed all the interest and energy which in earlier and more hopeful days he had given so freely to party tactics. He was very much in his element among his Whig hosts and their womenfolk. The little impudences and the defiance of apprenticeship were done with. He was accepted on his merits and almost at his own valuation, for the social gifts he had to bestow, and henceforward his conduct was as assured and his manners as serene as any in his charmed circle.

He had the ladies on his side from the first ; he was born with a knowledge of how to deal with them, and (a small but significant point) was perfectly at home in the intricate technique of aristocratic conventions, of courtesy titles and methods of address, to which much meticulous attention was paid in those days. Creevey steered through these difficult shoals with faultless certainty. His sister, as we shall see, remained obstinately, ultra-respectably, incorrigibly, middle class. Mr. Creevey was at last in his proper element and he drank it in in delicious sips. He rejoiced in every new instance of the luxury and ease and security of life in the privileged class, and recorded its splendours and frailties with impartial frankness and a fine sense of humour.

Creevey to Miss Ord

" April 2nd, 1824.

" . . . Nothing could answer better than my Saturday's dinner at the Mansion House. The Greeks

were a most unexpected Godsend. The contrast
between the vivacity of their faces and those of the
Spaniards was particularly striking. Reerorgo is a
regular *Boss*, and Mina truly British, but there is
something peculiarly striking in the intelligence of
the latter's eye, and in the honesty, heartiness, and yet
modesty, of his manner. The handsome Greek who
wore his native costume is a merchant of fortune, who
has fought in one of his own ships against the Turks,
and has given his ships and everything else to the
Greek Cause. I should say he was from 35 to 40
years of age, incomparably handsome, a perfect
Dandy in his dress and neatness, and with excellent
manners for a *jolly fellow* which he evidently is. . . .
Tho' last, not least, let me observe the Waithman *
Family, both male and female, were in all their glory.
I could not help thinking when I looked at them, what
they must think of their *Shop*, poor things, when they
return to it after all their finery. There were at least
8 or 10 Livery Servants covered with lace, in silk
stockings and buckles, to say nothing of my lord
Mayor's State *Postillion* who stood behind his lordship's back all the time, in full costume, booted and
spurred, and wearing his cap *on*, which evidently must
have been made at the silversmith's, and mounting at
least two feet above his head. Mylord and Mylady
sat ' jig by jole ' (is that right) occupying the head of
the table to their noble selves. The Chaplain at the
bottom in full Canonicals—the Duke of Sussex, and at
least 30 more of us ranged down the sides. There
were two ceremonies after dinner that were highly
touching. One was that mylord's Secretary, standing
behind him in a Civic gown, demanded silence, and
then producing a paper he called over the names of

* Robert Waithman was elected Lord Mayor, Oct. 1823.

the gens distingués who were present (in which of course I was included), and then concluded by shouting out, ' Your Royal Highness, and mylords and gentlemen present. This *loving couple,** the Lord and Lady Mayoress drink to all your good healths, and bid you a hearty welcome to the City of London.' The 2nd. Ceremony was placing before mylord and mylady two immense and splendid gold dishes, each filled with rose water, and after these distinguished personages had dabbed their napkins in this perfume, and washed their precious muzzles, the Royal Visitor was treated with a secondhand dip, and the two vessels sailed down, one on each side to the bottom of the table, so that we of the tiers-état, Radicals and all, had the honor of being washed with mylord and Lady's identical own water.

" I ought to observe that before dinner mylady occupied one sofa by the fire side herself—evidently intending the Frère du Roi for her companion. The two Demoiselles Waithman occupied the opposite sofa, where I was aspiring enough to plant myself by their side, and so availing myself of a former Brighton acquaintance I gained without loss of time their entire confidence. Their occupation appeared to me both natural and ingenious. They each held in one hand (concealed) a paper with the names of the company invited, the other fair hand contained a *pin*, so as each visitor was announced smack went the Ladies' pins thro' his body as answering his invitation. . . . Little Sussex was so good as to carry me to the Opera House afterwards.

"Tuesday, as I told you, I dined at Kensington,†

---

* Creevey's deafness troubled him much towards the end of his life. He misheard " loving cup."
† The Duke of Sussex had rooms in the Palace.

and was taken there and brought back to Brooks's by Stephenson in the Duke's Coach. Our Party were the D. of Norfolk, Archy: Hamilton, Ld. Nugent, Ld. Arundel, Brougham, Ellice, some gentlemen of the Scotch Bar, the Duke's Son (D'Este) * &c. Sussex's affectionate deportment to me was ' *beyond* ' and nothing could be more natural or better done than his calling to me at dinner, and sending his love and sweet things to little Hamilton, and asking how the Ladies were, and hoping they were agreeably settled in Essex.† . . .

" Tomorrow I dine with Jockey of Norfolk,‡ and on Friday with Brougham at 5 o'clock for the purpose of attending an evening Lecture upon *Mechanics* to the rising young world of the lower orders. A job of Brougham's own, for what purpose, he knows best.

" . . . Apropos to Sussex. Stephenson told me on Sunday that when he came into his service he owed £100,000, that £50,000 has been since paid off, and that the other half is in rapid liquidation. This is something for a Prince, is it not ? "

" May 12th.

" Miss Lemon marries old De Dunstanville aged 68 or 9. He has already settled upon her £1,000 a year, lest he sh'd. die before the time expires, when according to rule he can marry again, the dear late Lady De Dunstanville being only deceased about 6 months. This is exclusive of clothes, pearls and diamonds, which are daily pouring in. It is an old passion on *his* part. He is as rich as a jew, and will endow her, I take for granted, accordingly. His only

* Sir Augustus D'Este, H.R.H.'s son by his first wife, Lady Augusta Murray.
† At Rivenhall Place.
‡ The nickname of the 11th Duke, who died in 1815, is sometimes applied to the 12th Duke.

issue at present is one Daughter of Miss Lemon's age, ugly as sin, cross as the devil, and a Baroness that is to be in her own right.* Another Barony, however, is still reserved for Miss Lemon's *Son*, so the Lord send her a safe delivery. . . .

" Today I dine at Ferguson's. The express object being to try a man cook for his Brother, the two leading men on the Jury being Lord Sefton and Ld. Robt. Spencer. Mr. and Mrs. Ferguson, the Taylors, Ld. Roslyn, Auckland and myself.

" On Monday I propose going to Newmarket. The Seftons have a house there, so after taking the races on Tuesday and Wednesday, we are to live Thursday at Cambridge, where their Son Francis is at present, and be in Town again on Friday."

" June 4th.

" . . . You may suppose I was punctual to my time in Arlington Street yesterday morning to accompany the Ladies to Epsom. The scene altogether *in and out* is the most extraordinary England can produce. Sefton was stationed at the entrance of the Course to meet his family, and conducted us to the best spot for seeing the Races, and everything else. He took me afterwards to see the *Lions*, a Paddock where you enter on foot *only*, and on paying a shilling, and where all the Horses for the *Derby* are led round before the Race and then saddled. You would have supposed on looking around you that both Houses of Parliament were there ; be that however as it may, Sefton and I were standing close together, and in a considerable crowd, to make our observations upon ' Reformer ' and ' Cedric ' &c., Lord Jersey was just opposite to me, and near me Lord Derby, Edward

* Frances, in remainder to the Barony of Basset.

Stanley, Duke of York, D. of Grafton, Duke of Rutland &c. &c. Nevertheless highly distinguished as my Company was, I felt (as I imagined) some Gentleman's hand playing itself in my pocket, and on suddenly clapping my own hand down there I felt quite as sure that the other slipped away. I found my four sovereigns and watch quite safe, but on turning suddenly to Sefton and mentioning this fact to him, he felt his own pocket and observed he was ' not so lucky ' for his purse was gone with 15 Sover'ns in it, and the pocket turned inside out. . . . I saw all the world there as you may suppose—the Derby was an indifferent race, Sir John Shelley's horse, ' Cedric ' winning quite easy. Shelley won £5,000, which I am not sorry for. We got back about ½ past seven covered with dust, and having got well washed and brushed sat down to dinner about 8, and in the evening (as the night before) I played Whist at Whitehall till ½ past one."

" June 18th.

" . . . Our Party * was the Taylors, Lord and Ly. Duncannon, Lord Arthur Hill, *Fergy*, Mills, with the Grenfells, Ld. Molyneux, two of his Brothers, Brougham (yesterday), and myself. I must say never thing was done better than on the part of Mylord, and indeed Mylady too. A party of 18 was conveyed three succeeding days in four of Mylord's carriages of one kind or other these eleven miles and back again, and then *two* turtles, venison, &c. &c. There is certainly nothing more perfect in England than this drive through Eton and Windsor Park, concluding with the course at Ascot, and the promenade upon it between the Races. . . .

* For Ascot at Stoke Farm (Lord Sefton's).

" Arthur Hill is gone to live in Arlington Street with his Aunt, Lady Salisbury. She has set up a table for him, and another Nephew, and son of Lord Talbot's, a clergyman, and says they must provide her with young people for company, which at 72 is being very gay, is it not ?

" Atty * is as good as any Play in his description of a late dinner at Little Sussex's. He was invited for the express purpose of destroying all formality in the other visitors, who were exclusively Royal, such as Duke and Duchess of Gloucester, Princess Augusta, Duchesses of Clarence and Kent, and the Daughter of the latter,† Princess Sophia of Gloucester, and in the evening Princess Sophia. Sussex seems to have distinguished himself greatly in the familiar line by calling ' Slice ' ' most Noble Duke of Gloucester,' and asking if his dinner was suited to his Royal stomach, then calling Leopold ' Nephew of mine,' and Princess Sophia of G. ' Dear Coz of Gloucester.' Added to this he gave a very humorous account of his own Military Services as Col. of the *London Artillery Company* in surpressing a riot some time since. The Royal Ladies were quite enchanted with this *fun*, but not so the *Gentlemen*. Slice evidently considered it as a profane attack both upon Royalty and the Army, and the sleek Leopold observed to Atty in private, that ' His R.H. was in very great spirits.' The Duchess of Gloucester and Princess Augusta sat on each side of Sussex, and according to Atty nearly burst their sides with laughing. . . .

" I shook hands with the Beau on the Course at Ascot. I never beheld such a spectre as he is become. . . ."

* Lord Arthur Hill.   † Princess Féodore of Leiningen.

" June 25th.

" . . . Yesterday I had a busy day. I was in the *New* Bedlam four or five hours. I did not know before that the old one had been pulled down. *This* one is a little way over Westminster Bridge, a most magnificent building, and most magnificently supported—I think, *almost* too much so. There are 214 in it, all of whom I saw, and only one under coercion, as handsome and fine a man as ever I saw. He was fastened by one wrist to his bed, but talked perfectly reasonably. He had been tried for a murder, and pardoned only upon the plea of insanity, and in coming up to this new habitation on top of a coach he contrived to murder another. I had the pleasure of an interview with Margaret Nicholson,* aged 86, and whose forte is playing at *Whist*. She is a capital player. Hatfield † too I conversed with. I saw the girl who lived with the present Lord Chandos (who gave her a Bond under a great penalty as a Judge that he would marry her), and she went mad upon the family getting the Bond from her by force, and making Lord Chandos leave her. Her face was one of the most perfect melancholy, her eyes beautiful, but we could not prevail upon her to utter.

" Lord Robt. Seymour, who is the most active Governor, was one of our chaperons. . . ."

" June 30th.

" I have been sitting a long time this morning with the Copleys at their Hotel—a shorter time with Lady Robt. Spencer, and when I was so near, it was impossible not to look in at the Seftons, to see how they all were after their Ball. . . . I found the whole family and Mylord, and I have settled to go together

* She attempted to stab George III with a paper-knife in 1796.
† He shot at George III in Drury Lane Theatre in 1800.

to Almack's tonight, our object being to see the two
Grand Quadrilles who so nearly came to blows at the
Caledonian Ball.   They are to be in the same costume,
and we are not without hopes that on the appearance
of these Rival troops in their proper colour again,
hostilities may be renewed.   Lady Mansfield and
Lady Huntley lead for the Scotch Quadrille, Lady
Morley and I forget who else, for the English. . . .

" I wish you had seen Sefton's Aunt, the Dow
Duchess of Newcastle, last night, in a little black hat
tied under her chin with a little powder puff black
feather standing bolt upright in it.   The image of her
Brother, Lord Harrington, and yet also the image of
Ladies in riding habits in old pictures, or rather in old
paper hangings. . . ."

" July 9th.

" The other night at Lady Sefton's Ball I was of
great use to Mrs. Tom Sheridan * in getting three different partners for her Daughter.   Whilst the young one
was dancing I was privy to a conversation between the
Mother and *Young Lady Londonderry*,† who it seems
are Cousins, at least Ly. Antrim and Mrs. Tom are.
Lady Londonderry had a necklace and earrings of
pearls on, which produced the same effect on Mrs
Tom's eyes as they did on mine—for they were literally as big as the eggs of small birds, and perfectly
beautiful—so Mrs. Tom very naturally asked what
they cost, so says the Marchioness in reply, ' Why
Lord Stewart bought them very *cheap*, they were
Madame Murat's who was obliged to sell them at
Vienna, so Lord Stewart got them for *ten thousand*

* Born a Callander. Daughter-in-law of R. B. Sheridan and mother
of Mrs. Norton, Lady Dufferin and the Duchess of Somerset.
† Frances, daughter of Sir H. Vane Tempest ; 2nd wife of 3rd
Marquis.

pounds which every one knows is much less than they were worth.' Upon your soul! What a fortune for poor Mrs. Tom if she could have got them!

" The De Guiches * were there of course. I don't think Mad'e. De Guiche *very* pretty—it is a good tempered merry French face. I think you asked me if she was a flirt, which puts me in mind of a story Sefton told me in driving me to Hampton Court last Sunday : It seems that Mad. De Guiche came over here two years ago, principally to see the Lambtons. It was an old connection of the 10th between Lambton and Grammont, pure friendship of two ' ancient comrades,' so everything Lambton had, his houses, opera box, horses, carriages &c. &c. were at their service, and the London campaign was to close with their going to Lambton, there to stay for months. One fine day, however, they had a party on the water to Richmond, and a junketery dinner at the Castle—the Seftons were of the party, as they most commonly were —as they were walking up Richmond Hill Mad'e. Guiche, having very abruptly quitted Lambton's arm, begged Lord Sefton in a very grave manner to let her lean on him. The *result* is, Lambton had made violent love to Mad'e De Guiche, which she told her Husband. He consulted Ossulston whether he should not take a shot at his ' ancient comrade,' but it was wisely determined to have no jaw or exposure, but to return to Paris instead of going to Lambton. . . .''

" Cantley, Doncaster, Sept. 20th.

" The Races began yesterday with a moderate show of company, the only Ladies on the Stand being the Duchess of Leeds, and her pretty Daughter, Lady *Londonderry*, Ly. Normanby, Ly. A. Milbanke, Ly. C.

* Son of Antoine, Duc de Grammont, and brother of Corise, afterwards Lady Tankerville.

Powlett, Ly. Cooke and Mrs. Taylor. . . . With
Mrs. Taylor's permission I had asked George Payne,*
but after accepting the invitation he has excused
himself on account of his being so busy with his *Bets*
for tomorrow. This breaking down of ' Swiss ' in his
gallop yesterday has played the devil with George
amongst many others. He *may lose* £10,000, he told
me he *must* lose at least between £3,000 and £4,000.
This ill-fated ill-conditioned Lambton looks like the
devil, and well he may, he has got into another fighting scrape. ' *Dear Eddard* ' had his house full at his
Races last week, Lambton and his friend *Dandy* Mills
being two of the party. Some difference of opinion
about a race arising between these friends, Mills
accounted for it by some insinuation that Lambton
had an interest, in his opinion, which the other replied
to by saying he was a lyar. Mills' first impression, it
is said, was evidently to floor him, but then correcting
himself, he said, ' I presume, Sir, you know the penalty
of applying to me the expression you have just used,
and I call upon you to prepare yourself immediately.'
A Surgeon was immediately sent for from Pontefract,
pistols, seconds, &c. prepared, but in the meantime
Tom Duncombe had persuaded Lambton to make the
most unqualified apology to Mills. There were not
less than 20 people present at this scene. Dear
Eddard is a Magistrate, so he insisted they sh'd. not
fight on his property. . . . He asked me with great
seriousness if he had not been very much abused. . . .

" You have seen by the papers that Old Trevor
after having become Lord Hampden lived three weeks
and died. During this short time, however, he made
a will, by which he has left our Brussels friend Genl.

---

* Of Sulby Hall. Patron of the Turf and gambler. He lived till
1878. Edward VII, as Prince of Wales, attended his funeral.

Brand * an estate of £8,000 per annum clear, and £60,000 in money, so Sam Whitbread will pick up something with his Wife still. . . .

" Our Hostess never shines so much as with her house full.   Her table is perfect, the outside of hospitality of the best kind, and all clock work as to regularity without a particle of fuss.

" To be sure the contributions for the week are not amiss.   A whole Buck from Chillingham, and half a one from Lord Darlington.   There are sixteen brace of black game and grouse in the house from Ferguson, Roslyn and Maule, and Lady Augusta Milbanke brought a stock of Pineapples with her, that for size and goodness I have scarcely seen equalled."

" Lambton, Sept. 23rd.

" . . . Well, the first event that was buzzed about yesterday was, that Sir Roger Gresley had found Lady Londonderry's page in Lady Sophia Gresley's † Dressing Room combing his hair and perfuming himself with her combs and smelling bottles.   This, you may suppose, was not less favourably received from Lady Sophia being a *Coventry Filly*.   However, be that as it may, upon the Race Ground, Lady Augusta Milbanke being in Lady Londonderry's Coach, and the Page on the box, Sir Roger came up to make his complaint in form, and the Page was ordered to descend, and he denied the fact, but he was severely reprimanded, and told if he was ever found again in a Lady's Dressing Room he would be instantly dismissed. Observe he is quite a fully grown young man, and good looking, *altho'* My Lady does frequently beat him, or gets My Lord to do so for her. . . ."

* General Brand became 21st Lord Dacre. His daughter Julia married S. C. Whitbread.
† Daughter of 7th Earl of Coventry. Married Sir R. Gresley in 1821.

"Lambton, Oct. 24th.

"Well, things are coming to a crisis here. We were only the family and Earl Grey, Wilton and Milbanke at breakfast today, and in an hour or two, I believe, all will be gone. The Londonderrys left yesterday after the Races, which were particularly good. But the *Monarch* is infernally damaged in publick opinion by his Races. *He wins a great deal too much.* His horses have a great advantage in being at home, and in their own stables, whilst the others come from distances, and are kept in strange stables. He has also a most decided advantage in his Jockey, Cap'n White, who rides *much* better than any one here. You can't imagine how delighted every one was at his horse 'Mirth' being beat by Mills' horse 'Squirrel' yesterday. On Grey saying to me how delighted he was, I said, 'Mirth' is Lambton's, is she not?' 'Yes, but *damn* "Mirth," she has won a great deal too much already.' . . ."

". . . There are two persons in the house I have never mentioned yet, Mrs. Henry Cavendish, and Mrs. Wm. Lambton. The former keeps herself very much to herself, and I have never happened to be next her, but she has a regularly beautiful face, a very pretty countenance (tho' like her Brother, Wm. Lambton) and dresses to admiration. Mrs. W. Lambton seems highly pleased with her face and the child *or children* she is going to produce. In your days you never saw such a size or such a display of it. However, it is but justice to say she seems as good natured as she is big, and quite as happy. She told me that Lady Londonderry begged to speak with her before she went yesterday, and it was to ask her if she had not seen her French Maid lying crying in the passage, and on her answering, 'Yes,' the Marchioness said it was

15

very odd, and she rather thought she must have been *tipsy, for she had never said nor done anything harsh to her.* Was there ever ?   If the Maid wanted any proof of what she said being true, her Mistress furnished it herself, and by all accounts it produced a devil of a sensation amongst the other servants who were all full of it to their Masters and Mistresses as well as of Lambton's affair with his man, and all equally indignant against both parties.   Is it not almost incredible that these Grandees should make themselves such idiots ? . . . .

" Knowsley, Nov. 21st.

" . . . The Party here are Ebrington,* and his Brother George,† and two Sisters, and Wilbraham,‡ the Husband of one of them ; Lord Sefton and one Daughter and Son, Mr. Stopford, Mr. Legge and two Sisters, Mr. Sneyd (the wit and dandy), Lord Stanley and his two Daughters, and a large assortment of Hornbys.

" The whole party are now gone to Church for the 2nd time. There were two coaches, full inside and out, my Lord's phaeton, a gig, and saddle horses, and last and by no means least in the procession, the caravan which carries the *fighting cocks* to Preston with 12 maids and three men in it. . . ."

" Knowsley, November 23rd.

" . . . In the evening Lord Derby read prayers from the furthest end of the Library, the doors being open ; that room was filled with company, the Hall was filled with servants kneeling round the Billiard

---

* Afterwards 2nd Earl Fortescue.

† Born 1791. His widow, a daughter of 1st Earl of Harrowby, lived till 1899.

‡ Geo. Wilbraham, married Lady Anne Fortescue.

Table, some six or eight of us behind them in the
Drawing Room, the doors of which were likewise open.
After the ceremony my Lady joined me again in the
Gallery, and I was remarking how well Lord Derby
read, and how distinctly I heard every word he said at
that distance. ' Yes,' said she, ' he likes it extremely
and is a great stickler for doing the thing all himself.
When the Archbishop of York was here the other day,
he wanted to read the prayers, but Ld. Derby would
not hear of it, he w'd. not even let him say Grace,
but always contrived to get the start of him, so that
the Archbishop at last said, ' Come let us settle this
matter, we are Brother Directors of the Ancient Music,
so let us sing a Grace together as a Duet.' . . ."

" Kinmel,* December 18th.

" Yesterday was our day at the Dean of St.
Asaph's.†   I must account for the interest I felt in this
visit by telling you that it is just 40 years since Newcome ‡ gave me to learn as an exercise poor Erskine's
speech (then in the Newspapers) in defence of the
Dean of St. Asaph then tried for a libel.§   During my
subsequent acquaintance with Erskine this circumstance was constantly in my mind, and it was a kind
of completion of this reminiscence to see the old fellow
himself, to the defence of whom Erskine owed so much
of his fame. . . .   We found the old fellow in an
admirable old fashioned house, and a very nice place.
He is in his 80th year as fresh in intellectual faculties
of every kind as if he was 20.   In appearance and in
manners the image of Lord Derby, but not so infirm,

* Col. Hughes'.
† William Shipley, born 1745, son of Bishop of St. Asaph's.
‡ Creevey's headmaster at Hackney.
§ In this celebrated trial the question was mooted whether "libel or
10 libel ? " was for the decision of judge or jury.

and a little more grave.   In about an hour, the weather becoming rather clearer, we all sallied out to the shooting ground about a mile off.   He went in his gig and then mounted his shooting poney, and tho' the rain set in again and continued all day, there he remained till it was dark, with no other covering than his little black velvet shooting jacket.   The pheasants were much more numerous, and the shooting altogether much better than 'either here, Croxteth, or Knowsley, and the Old Buck shot the birds from his poney as well as any younger man could have done on foot. . . .

" I spent a very agreeable day altogether, indeed the Dean is very wealthy, and lives extremely well. Nothing could be more agreeable, natural and polite than he was.   He gave us plenty of the best wines of all kinds, and after tea I played three rubbers at Whist with him, and after that three games of Ecarté with his Grand-daughter, Miss Shipley, and we got back here before 12."

CHAPTER X

1825-6

THE letters of 1825 require no explanatory introduction.

Creevey to Miss Ord

" Newcastle, Jan. 3rd, 1825.

". . . As I have taken liberties occasionally with my Sister's conduct, allow me on this occasion to do her justice. The night before I left her, she held forth upon a very favorite subject of hers, her *will*, how she had left me what she had for my life, and then divided it into various ducks and drakes to our cousins, so I let her have the sole possession of the subject without uttering a word myself. I thought, however, afterwards that I ought to put her in possession of my feelings and intentions on this subject, and accordingly I took some pains with a note which I wrote to her from Kinmel, and which I requested her to preserve as a record of my views. I stated to her the precise nature of my situation ; I told her that some time or other about £400 would be to be raised out of my moiety of Uncle Eaton's property, to pay debt to that amount principally to Vizard, but that I should never be called upon myself to sell for that purpose, and that I hoped to be able to avoid selling altogether.

" That in such case my intention was that she should have it subject to this debt for her life, and afterwards that it should go to you three, and I added as to this last disposition, that I did not feel myself called upon for any justification to my own relations in paying this piece of attention to those to whom all my obligations were due.* . . . I . . . received a most excellent answer from her, approving most cordially of my opinions. . . . "

Earl of Sefton to Creevey

"Paris, Jan. 24th.

" Thanet† died this morning of a complication of disorders—mortification in the leg, erisipelas, cholera morbus, fever and gout. His own imprudence had been extreme. To see such a person die at a wretched Hotel without connexion or comfort about him, was really a most deplorable sight. . . . "

Creevey to Miss Ord

"Feb. 1/2nd.

" I need not add that having been Thanet's Member, under all the circumstances of the case, will be a very agreeable reminiscence to me as long as I live, and I can't discover at this time that my happiness is affected to the amount of a pin's head at the loss of my seat ; my belief is that such will continue to be the case. . . . "

"Raby Castle, Feby. 16th.

" I can't go to bed, tho' in my room for that purpose, without having a word with you. First of all because I *hunt* tomorrow, and shall have no opportunity. Don't be alarmed at my talking of hunting, for Lady Darlington ‡ insists on my riding her own horse

---

* His will, made in 1835, was in very different terms.

† Creevey's patron, Sackville Tufton, 9th Earl of Thanet, took little part in politics, but supported the advanced Whigs and suffered in youth for the cause. He died at Châlons.

‡ Elizabeth Russell, second wife of 3rd Earl of Darlington, afterwards 1st Duke of Cleveland, K.G. At the time of their marriage, July 27th, 1813, Lady Holland described her as Lord Darlington's " bonne amie, Mrs. Russell, alias Funnereau."

' Raby,' the safest and quickest horse possible, and her own groom is to accompany me. . . . Was there ever ? . . .

"We dined about 20. I took out Ly. Augusta* leaving the Cyprian Countess to Taylor, but she called to me to come and sit next her. From her conversation I could find that little Sussex had given her a very favorable impression of me ; however, be that as it may, nothing can exceed the civility of both her and My Lord ever since I entered the house. . . ."

" Raby, Feby. 17th.

"We continue all sunshine. I was next Mylady at breakfast, and very pretty company we were, and she would have me take a crust of bread properly done up in paper in my pocket. Then the Ladies being present in the great hall when we mounted, I complained of having no *professional whip*, so Mylady sent for her own, and presented it to me. Well, then Mylord and I had a very agreeable ride of about 5 miles to cover, where I found ' Raby,' and such a horse, and such a chaperon of a groom or whipper-in to take care of me, and such a day, and such a scene for beauty and animation I never beheld. Our ground was on the high banks of the Tees where we found, and after a run of about an hour and a half or more killed, I going over every leap that any one else did, and being in at the death, but then these leaps are no great things, and such a horse, and guide made them really nothing. We afterwards went to another cover where we found again, but then I parted convoy having had a pretty good supply of exercise. My Whipper-in conducted me home. I then joined the Ladies in the garden, and damned agreeable we are,

* Lord Darlington's daughter.   Wife of Mark Milbank.

but as *Duets* are always the most agreeable, Mylady and I soon separated from the rest. . . . Then she would take me and shew me the stables, and she petted the horses, and had the cloaths taken off one or two to shew me their beautiful shapes, and she was *Myladied* up and down through every stable, and with faces as grave, and *hearts as devoted* as if she had been an hereditary Countess of Darlington every bit. . . . Yet from any thing that has passed her lips, as yet, I defy any one who did not know her, to discover her former vocation, or even her birth, parentage, and education. She puts me perpetually in mind of Ly. Dacre both in looks and voice, particularly the latter, tho' not in age, for she is as fresh as a four year old, and made for ' de laugh.' I never saw two females laugh more heartily than she and Mrs. Shaftoe at the story of Mrs. *Borch* and the potato.

" The concern altogether is a very agreeable one. *He*, you know, is a very clever man, and his civility and attention to me are unbounded. He is now waiting to shew me the Baron's Hall."

" Cantley, Feb. 21st.

" Don't you think we are very pretty Travellers ? We left Raby at a ¼ past 10 this morning, we have come 90 miles ; we ate mutton chops at Boroughbridge, we broke our axletree, and by some miracle escaped an overturn at the entrance of Doncaster. Michael, Mrs. Taylor and I came on in a hack chaise, and we were all at dinner here by 8 o'clock. Every thing ended at Raby as well as it had begun.

" It is quite clear to me that Mrs. Taylor and Michael without saying a word to *me* are at work for a seat for me. . . ."

" London, March 7th.

" . . . Old Dow: Richmond upon the marriage that is about to take place between Mrs. Tighe's eldest Son, and a young Ly. Lennox: The Dow: had fixed . . . upon . . . Lord Harvey . . . The Duke took Tighe to his Mother's, and leaving him belowstairs, went up to announce the fact to her himself. She began with saying, ' Can't see Mr. Tighe—Lord Harvey—to be sure Ld. Bristol wrote an uncommonly handsome letter in favor of Mr. Tighe, but can't possibly see him—Lord Harvey.' So the Duke said it was quite impossible to resist the thing any longer, and he would step down and bring Mr. Tighe up, to which she kept going on, ' Can't possibly see Mr. Tighe, Lord Harvey,' and when the two Gentlemen came in they found her in the middle of the room *with her eyes shut*, and after some pause she said, ' Duke of Richmond, leave the room,' and then I suppose it was settled, but she goes on still. ' Never can go to Ireland after this connection with Mr. Tighe,' * and some one having asked her how the first family dinner had gone off, which consisted of the Bedfords, *Bathursts* &c. &c. to meet Mr. Tighe, she said, ' Quite shocking. Mr. Tighe talked such horrid politicks, Lord Bathurst very near leaving the room.' "

" March 16th.

" . . . There are all kinds of reports about the state of the King's health. From the *Apothecary* department it is said there is a general regular declining in strength and flesh, the symptoms in short of a general breaking up. From Halford's shop it is said he is better than he has been these two years *but* that

* Lady Louisa married Mr. W. F. Tighe, of Woodstock, Co. Kilkenny, in April. After the marriage the Duchess on one occasion stayed some time there but never spoke to her son-in-law.

his present extreme inactivity is very unfavourable to the continuance of his health. In the mean time Our *York* is all alive O ! He dined at Sefton's this day week as gay as a lark, and gave them a description of a new house he (York) is going to build upon site of his present one, which is to be pulled down forthwith, and he has taken Ly. Ellenbro's house (Queen Caroline's that was) in South Audley Street for two years whilst his own is building. You may suppose the scale of his operations when I tell you that his principal apartment is to be 82 feet long. This I think for a gentleman in his 62nd. year without a sou in the world, and owing it is said at least a million of money, is pretty well, but it shews clearly that those who raise the money for him are confident he will get the Throne. . . ."

" Stoke Farm, June 3rd.

" Well, we had a most prosperous day yesterday, got to Ascot quite in time for everything, and saw the finest Race that according to all the critics ever was seen between ' Bizarre ' and ' Longwaist ' for the Cup. We saw your old acquaintance *Prinney* looking quite as well, and nearly as merry as we have seen him in his best days. Contrary to his former practice, he drove up the Course to his stand, in the presence of everybody—himself in the first coach and four, the Duke of Wellington sitting by his side. There were three other carriages and four, and a phaeton after him, and I sh'd. think 20 servants in scarlet on horseback, and as all his horses are of the greatest beauty, the whole thing looked very splendid ; in short, quite as it should be. Ly. Conyngham and Ly. Eliz'th., Ly. Mountcharles, Ly. Bathurst, . . . Ly. Cowper &c. &c. were the Ladies about him, but the *beauty* of

the day out and out was Mrs. Hughes Ball ci-devant
Mercandotti ; she was in the D. of York's stand, and
surrounded by all the dandys.

" . . . This is one of the finest days possible, so
Mylord drives the Ladies to Ascot, and Francis and I
ride.   What strength the women of this family have !
Mylady and two of her Daughters were at Almack's
till late yesterday morning, and Ly. Maria was with
the Greys at Ld. Hertford's *Opera* till 3, and the same
Lady Maria was off by 8 this morning with her
Brother on horseback to Taplow, 6 miles off, to see
her little Nephew Grenfell, and she was back again
to breakfast. . . . ."

" June 9th.

" . . . I have a card as large as life from the Earl
and Countess of Darlington to dine with them on the
22nd. to meet the Duke of Sussex, so I take it for
granted I must go, whatever may come of it, but, as
you say, I w'd. much rather belong to this dry Earl
of Thanet * than this bowing and scraping Earl of
Darlington. Apropos to the former, Lord Robt.
Spencer who is related to him, waited upon him in due
form, and requested him to name his own day for
dining, but which the Earl declined doing upon his
accustomed allegation that he did not like dining
out. . . ."

" June 23rd.

" . . . When I returned to my lodging I found
Mrs. Taylor had been there and left word she w'd. call
for me at ½ past 6, which she did, and we were the
first † ; little Sussex came about ten minutes after, but
we did not sit down to dinner till ½ past 7, which was

* The late peer's brother, Charles.   † At the Darlingtons'.

said to be the fault of a new cook. We were two or three and twenty I believe altogether. The Earl and Countess,* Ly. Arabella, Miss Taylor, Sussex, his son D'Este, and Stephenson, Mr. and Mrs. Taylor, Jack Vane, and Creevey, Mr. and Mrs. Brougham, and a Brother of Brougham's, Dr. and Mrs. Lushington, Mr. and Lady Louisa Lambton, Milbank, and Ly. Augusta, Earls Grey and Roslyn, and Ld. Duncannon. The *humour* of the day was Mrs. Brougham. She came in more languishing than ever. I announced to my different female friends my conviction that at length she would accomplish her favorite project of fainting, before she left the house. I handed Ly. Arabella down stairs, and sat between her and Lambton. We had Mrs. Brougham nearly opposite. She was going her lengths the whole of dinner, so that I made Ly. Arabella nearly die with laughing at her. At last, however, her colour did really desert her face, and she actually bolted. Ld. Darlington left his seat and handed her out, but not a single Lady of the family either went with her or followed her. When Mylord returned, we told him we thought he ought to tell Brougham of it, who sat about 8 or 9 from her on the same side of the table, and so mylord did, but all the return he got for it was a twitch or two of the nose, and he kept his place as steadily as everybody else, and what became of Dear Mrs. Brougham I know not, for I neither heard nor saw anything more of her afterwards. The Raby Cook beat the new one easy. I wish you had seen the servants. I called them to Ly. Arabella the New and Old Imperial Guard. They were one and all in bags and bouquets, the four servants out of livery had brown coats with gold embroidery, and *frogs* exactly

* Of Darlington.

the same as the King's dress uniform, the six or seven
Livery servants were in bright yellow dress coats.
One end of the table was very very merry, which is
more than I suspect the other was. *King Jog* was as
amiable as be damned, and nothing will serve him but
I must come and occupy my *own* room again at
Lambton. Poor Ld. Grey looked terribly ill I thought,
but it is said he is greatly improved. . . .

" I am much amused with Ly. Holland having set
up a hue and cry after me. Duncannon said yesterday
that in her different notes to people to come to her,
she always ends, ' And pray if you have any influence
with Mr. Creevey, do bring him.' . . ."

" Stoke Farm, August 24th.

" I found here our Aunt, the Duchess of Newcastle,* the Frazers, and Billy Churchill (who was a
great croney of Ld. Craven's) ; Dow: Salisbury † had
left that morning, which I was sorry for, as Ly. Louisa
says it was very good fun to hear her and the Duchess
of Newcastle together. The latter of these young
people considers herself as entirely out of the World,
so she asked the other for information upon all subjects which was very graciously supplied by her. I
was very sorry the Duchess herself went away yesterday, for I took to her much, and to her *dress* still more.
She came from Frogmore where she had been staying
a week with Princess Augusta. . . ."

" Cantley, Septr. 16th.

" . . . The Countess of Tankerville ‡ and Ly.
Emma came here yesterday to dinner, and are to be

---

* Anna Maria, daughter of 2nd Earl of Harrington.
 † Emily Mary, daughter of 1st Marquis of Downshire ; wife of 1st
Marquis of Salisbury. She was burned to death at Hatfield in 1835.
 ‡ Corise de Grammont, brought up at Devonshire House. Her
daughter, Emma, married the 3rd Earl of Malmesbury.

off this morning for Chillingham.   This alteration in
her Ladyship's plans she accounts for, from her fear
of Ld. Tankerville's anger if she stays, as he has
written to her that he shall be at home from Scotland
this week, and fully expects her to be so too.

" This Mrs. Taylor and I consider as *fudge*, that
her object in proposing her visit here was the D. of
Devonshire, and he being off, she is so too.   You
know he gave a fête this year upon Ly. Emma's
coming out ; the fireworks and lamps having the
word ' Emma ' in every shape and colour.   I cannot
say much of the beauty of the young lady, she is very
like the old Lady Tankerville, only 20 times more
near sighted.   As for the Mother, she is really beyond
everything for *fun*.   She has been making me laugh
for hours, and I have made her tell her stories over
and over again.   I think she shines most about Mrs.
Coutts,* with whom she has lately become acquainted
at Worthing.   It is impossible by letter to do justice
to her *acting*, and her broken English.   ' A Play being
to be acted at Worthing . . . Mrs. Coutts . . . left
her own box, and came to ours, and sat herself upon
an empty bench, just behind us, and almost directly
she began, " I am sure, Ly. Tankerville, you must find
this a very wicked and illnatured world, I know I find
it so to myself.   I dare say you have heard all the
stories they tell of me going to be married to Lord
Burford.†   Good God how can you think I wd. marry
a boy.   He is quite a child as compared with me ;
then when I think of my dear Mr. Coutts, how is it
possible ?   To be sure Ld. Burford is quite charming ;
it is impossible to live with him, and not quite to love
him ; then his Sisters are so charming.   It is so

---

* Harriet Mellon, widow of the banker.
† 9th Duke of St. Albans.   She married him in 1827.

delightful to me after spending a morning with those vulgar people at my Bank to enjoy the society of these enlightened girls. . . . I have not . . . a friend in the world, every body cheats me ; I pay three times as much as any body else for every thing ; then I can't manage my accounts, and tho' dear Mr. Coutts left me so much, I am very often short of money. Illnatured people say I married Mr. Coutts for money, how can that be when I give his Daughter £35,000 a year. . . ." ' So I said, 'My dear Mrs. Coutts, surely you might get somebody who is poor to take care of your concerns for £200 or £300 per year—for instance Poodle Byng.' . . ."

" Septr. 24th.

" . . . I am just out of the Dining room at 10, and up to the chin (not in wine) but in *Ecarté* engagements for the rest of the evening.

" Well, NO *dissolution*, we have it from official quarters in all directions, and with details. In short, it is settled, and *I am good* for July, or I shd. say October 1826. So ' its all mighty well, my Dears,' and I can say with great truth, that my principal gratification at this result is, that I think it is agreeable to you all, and that we can go on defrauding the public by not paying for any letters we write. . . .

" We have had a capital week ; the Seftons old and young have been delighted, and the *poor sufferer* Lambton has conducted himself with a philosophy, and even an amiability that his warmest admirers could never have expected. Only think, poor Fellow, of his giving 2,500 Guis. for dear ' Cedric,' who never lost a Race (having run 12) when he was Shelley's Horse, and travels down to Doncaster for the honor of being 4th. . . . The mob actually convulsed with joy at the Wentworth triumph over him. To conclude, he that very night buys a horse of Ld. Sligo, ' Canteen,' for 1,000 Guis. for the purpose of next day repairing his misfortune, when lo and behold *one George Payne* with an unknown horse ' Barytes,' which he likewise had just purchased, beats the great ' Canteen ' in the cleverest way possible. . . .

" (In my bedroom, two o'clock in the morning) Mrs. Taylor and I having done Mylord and Mylady out of £3. apiece at Ecarté, so it's all mighty well, and nobody can afford it better.

" . . . There were *two* dancing rooms, so . . . Ly. Londonderry * comes to Mrs. Taylor, in my hearing, . . . ' Don't you think, Mrs. Taylor, it w'd. be a good thing to have a Country Dance, and for me to begin it ? ' ' Oh ! *my dear Child* it is exactly what I could wish you to do,' and so of course, being done by the Marchioness of Londonderry, all the Grandees, Duke of Devonshire (who was here after all), the Princes † of Brunswick, Ditto of Wowsk (Russian) were all at right hand and left in no time ; the Molyneux Ladies had partners without end, Princes and Nobles, British and Foreign, and they have been quite delighted with their week, not omitting what they have done their Father out of at Hepper's."

" Sept. 29th.

" . . . Monday I went with all the Ladies to the Ball. Tuesday we staid at home. Wednesday, Ball again. Thursday, the Ladies went to the Ball, and I staid at home and won a pound or two of Little Sussex at Ecarté.

" What think you of the impertinence of the

* Frances Vane-Tempest, second wife of 3rd Marquis of Londonderry. Mrs. Taylor's niece.

† Sons of the Duke of Brunswick, who was killed at Quatre Bras.

Copley Girls that night ?   Altho' Lady Londonderry
had told them that she meant to get up a Ball, with
which they professed to be ' highly delighted ' and said
of course they would be there, and altho' the Duke of
Devonshire had engaged Ly. Londonderry to dance
with him, the said Copleys got up a musick party at
Sprotbro' of the Mansfields, Vernons &c. &c., and
not one of them came to the Ball, not even the D.
of Devonshire.   The latter, I believe, sent the *next
morning* some kind of apology to Ly. Londonderry,
saying his carriage was actually at the door, but that
he was too unwell to venture out, and he returned that
day to Chatsworth.   Our Niece mentioned all this to
her Aunt as a piece of great incivility, but without
any anger, not so however her fiery little Marquis who
talked about ' *a* Sir *John* * Copley that lives in this
neighbourhood ' in a manner that it was thought w'd.
find its way to Sprotbro.' . . .

" I am somehow much convinced of the sincerity
of Ly. Darlington.   She said, ' I have asked it of Ld.
Darlington as a personal favor to myself, and as the
greatest he can do me.   I feel Mrs. Taylor, that I owe
it to you, and I am sure it will be accomplished.'
Then she again talked of there being one seat that
might still be vacant, but she w'd. not dwell upon it
without a greater certainty. . . .

" It is a curious thing, but it is not less true on
that account, that altho' I really think I sh'd. not
have minded being turned out of Parliament at
present the least bit, *yet* I am really very much pleased
to remain in, and to have the probability of another
year to turn ourselves in.   It is a funny thing, if after
all, my conduct about the Catholics, which according to Brougham played the devil with my Parlia-

* Sir *John* Copley.   His name was Joseph.

16

mentary prospects, is in some measure connected with my stealing another year out of poor dear old Appleby. . . .

"Dear Dow Bland has just been going over Devonshire House with me, as we drank our Coffee together. She was a friend of the first Duchess, and says she was a real good one if she had not been spoilt. She adds that Ly. Melbourne was the real original devil of all that click, and that she extended her amours so late in life as to entrap Ld. Byron. The last fact I never heard before, but true or not I doat upon old Bland. . . ."

"October 4th.

". . . I still delight in our Blands. My only regret is that their *two* maids are not of the party. One of them is quite as much *rouged* as her Mistress, she has only lived with them 23 years. . . . Old Bland is very great upon maid servants. She says, manufactures and *education* have destroyed the race. The time was when she could have respectable young women—farmer's daughters—to be either dairymaids, housemaids, or even kitchen maids, but that now she can't pick up an article worth a farthing for love or money. . . . The only *weakness* I have as yet discovered in my friend's character is a propensity to claim an odd trick or an honor without the slightest pretensions to either. . . .

". . . I am sorry to say her fraudulent activity at cards last night was redoubled, probably because it was her last go—for in addition to claims upon honors and tricks without foundation, she took to scoring up points that had never been gained, and this so palpably that her partner, Capt. Bouverie of the Blues, Lady Robert's grandson, and a capital player, and

most gentlemanlike little fellow, was obliged to give
her up in every one of her depredations. . . . ''

'' Oct. 6th.

'' The most interesting to me since I wrote last has
been reading our Jaffa's* Memoir of the Russian
Campaign. . . .

'' Jaffa told Mrs. Taylor and myself a curious
thing yesterday, whilst we were riding. ' There,'
says he, ' it was just about the length of that village
that I rode after Murat, with my pistol cocked, quite
within reach of him, but I could not find it in my heart
to fire at him, and no reflection has gratified me more
since than my not doing so.' This was in Russia in
1812, and in 1814 Jaff was sent on some mission to
Murat's Army or Head Quarters or Court, when he
was presented to Murat who instantly put out his
hand to him, and said he had always wished to see him,
and thank him for his noble conduct, for that he fully
expected his death from him. Now I must believe
this to be *true*, and *if it is* I think you must admit it is
a very curious historical *pint*.

'' Well, Mrs. Taylor has an answer from the Countess,
and it's all mighty well as to my not going to Raby
now. She then writes, ' Mr. Creevey's amusing and
kind letter I received with infinite pleasure, and
indeed whatever he either writes or says must always
be entertaining.' Upon your soul ! ! ! . . .

'' I saw Copley today in Doncaster, and heard from
him that Lord Charles Fitzroy is going to be married
to Miss Cavendish. They are but a dry couple. Ld.
George gives his Daughter £40,000. I asked Copley
how he managed with his deaf Duke† during the Race
Week, and he said he was perfectly sure the said Duke
never heard one word he said during the whole time.

* Gen. Sir Robert Wilson.   † Of Devonshire.

He mentions one trait of his friend that was not amiss. There is a Mrs. Lumley in this neighbourhood, a little, pretty, flirting, Irish woman, that all the men make up to, so the Duke to be in the fashion desired to be introduced to her, and the next time she saw him she presumed to *nod* at him, a liberty which he instantly resented by declaiming her to be a very vulgar woman, and that he never sh'd. take any further notice of her. . . . "

"October 16th.

" . . . After Lambton Races we go to Newton House, where we shall stay about a week, and then we go on to Thorp* (Milbank's) where we are to remain ten days or a fortnight, so it will be the latter end of November before *this* set of engagements end. . . .

" . . . I have just finished the 1st. of my ' Letters to Lord John Russell upon his notice of a motion for Parliamentary Reform.' I am extremely pleased with my work, and if an author is allowed to be a Judge of his own offspring, I think it will have great success, and produce no small effect. *Brougham* comes on Tuesday on his way to Town, whom of course I must consult as *Reviewer*, and if he approves, I shall give it him to take to Town, and let it go to press out of hand. I don't put my name to it at present. . . . I hit damned hard in my work, and yet am as mild as milk.

" Moore's Life of Sheridan, what I have seen of it, is damnable."

"Lambton, Oct. 23rd.

" Just arrived, and if there is time before this Bell rings, I may as well open the campaign by giving a list, as far as I can see, of the Company—the Normanbys, Sir James and Lady Graham, Lady Tankerville

* Thorp Perrow.

and Lady Emma, Mr. and Mrs. Wm. Lambton, Mr. and Mrs. Taylor, Mr. and Mrs. Wyrvill, Lord Wilton, Bob Grosvenor, Frank Russell, Mr. Russell of this County, Sir Robt. Wilson and his Daughter, Milbank, General and Mrs. Grey, Lord Howick, Sir Alex'r. Don, Geo. Payne, Mr. Holyoak, Sir Hedworth Williamson, John Mills, Cap'n. Berkeley, Hedworth Lambton, 'Dear Eddard,' Captn. Wyrvill, Major Healey, Captn. White, Mr. Creevey, Tom Duncombe, and others I must have omitted, but I know we are to be 37 at dinner, and Mills tells me there is a great improvement in the concern. A new cook and a very good one, and the victuals much more plentiful.

" Our Jog was graciosity to me to the outside, and nothing could be better than Lady Louisa—so it's all mighty well."

" Lambton, Oct. 25th.

" Let me see. Events of yesterday. . . . The party at night at its different avocations, i.e., a noisy hazard table at one side of the hall, a match at Billiards at the other, Lady Tankerville, Mrs. Taylor, Lord Howick and myself at an animated rubber of whist in one part of the Drawing Room, Lady Normanby enchanting her ravished audience with her vocal and instrumental musick in another ; when lo and behold out went the *gas* from the top of the house to the bottom. No, nothing can do justice to the scene, and the confusion it produced, for you must know the house is literally lighted by gas, there is not a candle to be had for love or money. . . .

" Our Milbank, having looked in vain for a candle stick last night, took a little Ormolu one from the Library table, and when it had served its purpose in lighting his candle in his bed room, he flung it out of his window that it might not be found in his room."

The last full year of Lord Liverpool's long administration was a gloomy one. It was a time of grave industrial depression and acute distress which the Government endeavoured to relieve by a measure permitting a limited importation of corn. Liverpool's own health was breaking up under the strain of these anxieties and the ever-present Catholic question, and he was conscious that the life of his government and his own alike hung by a thread.

By contrast with the two preceding years of carnival, the first half of 1826 was, for Creevey also, tinged with disappointment and sadness.

Mrs. Creevey's brother, Charles Brandling, died in January.

At the end of May Creevey was led to believe, through a mistake of Mrs. Taylor's, that Lord Darlington had offered him a safe seat at Winchelsea, a borough of eleven electors. It turned out, however, that Lord Darlington wanted Creevey to represent his chosen candidate, Lord Howick, at the election, and Creevey found himself committed to this exercise in altruism—and he carried it off, despite his bitter disappointment, with dignity and good humour. Then, at the end of June, Sefton's daughter Georgiana, the wife of Charles Pascoe Grenfell, died suddenly, leaving a family of young children. Sefton was for a time inconsolable, and Creevey, who was fast becoming almost a member of the family, shared its sorrow and proved a very present help in trouble. From this year the real intimacy between him and Sefton began, and (if indeed they were sons of the same father and Sefton had been aware of the fact all along) it must have been about this time that Creevey was informed of it. For if certain allusions which occur in the correspondence from this time onwards bear a construction which may be put on them, the legend clearly became henceforth a secret known to the whole family, including the illegitimate member. At the end of the year, Creevey went to live with his friends, the Taylors, at their house in Whitehall.

Creevey to Miss Ord

"Feb. 4th., 1826.

" . . . I thank you for your letter of last night as being most agreeable and satisfactory to a feverish Author, because I may say without *muggery* I have the most perfect reliance on your combined judgements, and then in return you have some reason to be satisfied in seeing *your own* view of the case compleatly adopted by the ' Times ' newspaper, which I am happy to say is not only the best written paper at present in the press, and the most sold, but its principles are notorious for *following* rather than leading public opinion, so I ought to conclude my case with the public is good.   I say nothing now of those contingent sacrifices you allude to of being out of Parliament.   I shall be 58 next month, poor Charles Brandling* would only have been 57 today, and who would have supposed I should have outlived him ?   It is very cheap being honest at such an age.   I don't care a farthing for anything in the world but you three and Anne's two children. . . ."

Lord John Russell to Creevey

"Feby. 20th.

" I should have thanked you before for your pamphlet, had I not been at Paris when your letter arrived.   I think it excellent, and calculated to do good when money ceases to be uppermost in every one's thoughts.   I fear, however, there are *very few* cases in which Election Committees restore the right of voting to householders.

" We have not yet done with bank and bullion. When you come to Town we will see what I can do about Reform this session."

* Mrs. Creevey's brother had recently died.

Creevey to Miss Ord

"Stoke, August 11th.

" . . . I am sure you'll be glad to know that we are looking *better* here. The young Ladies are getting round to their old manners with me, to let me try to amuse them, and in truth to be amused. *He* too has had some better nights, and by Lady Sefton's assistance in telling me when and where I am to fling myself in his way, we go thro' the day very well. These two little boys of Lady Georgiana's are quite charming, one turned 3 and the other 2. The eldest the image of its Mother—the same pale complexion, the same gentle and composed manner. The other is a more riotous chap, but both as *good* and tractable as ever they can be, and most companionable. They are on the lawn here with their Aunts and Grandmama for several hours every day, during some part of which Sefton has always some play with them, but it never fails to nearly overpower him when it is over, and it is one of the occasions when I am always upon the watch for him. . . . He and she and Lady Maria and I went in the carriage yesterday to see all that is going on at Windsor, and Mr. Wyatt-*Ville* himself did us the honor of conducting us thro' all the new apartments and showing us all the projected improvements. All the New Living Rooms make a very good Gentleman's or Nobleman's house, nothing more. Indeed I dare say Woburn is a better house, but then the situation you know is such a thing, and there is one part of the house newly created, which, with my propensities, is above all price, and that is a corridor 16 feet wide and 560 in length—a gallery connected with every living room, and which is to be filled with pictures. My eye, what a spot for a ' *walky, walky.*' . . .

" Sefton is gone to Town today, and I flatter my-self he is going to bring me a compliment of a new pair of spectacles, ones that will stick faster on one's head than my present ones. I only guess this from his *manner* last night in making me try *his*, and how the glasses suited. At all events he is pledged to bring me back some *Rhubarb Pills*.

" Lady Sefton is gone to Taplow (Old Grenfell's) 7 miles off to see Lady Georgiana's baby, and another little girl between 1 and 2 years old, for she has left 5 children. . . ."

" Stoke, August 20th.

" . . . Sir John Lade * has undertaken to my Lord to place us all some day next week in a position from which we can see unobserved our beloved Sovereign enjoying the innocent recreation of fishing in the Virginia Water, and if this is once accomplished, it must afford matter for writing about. . . . Old Salisbury † arrived yesterday. . . . *In* the phaeton were a spaniel and a pug dog as her ladyship's only companions. . . .

" We play cards together each night, but before that Sefton had put us afloat at our tea table out of doors, and we are doing extremely well, I thank you. It is true she speaks if possible more slowly and more awfully than Lady Sefton, but she has evidently a very quick ear for a joke, however guarded her merriment may be.

" I have only heard her as yet mention one of her Court Nannygoats. Before dinner was announced ‡ she perceived a Royal whisper from the Monarch to

* Famous Whip and Corinthian and crony of the Regent. *Vide* Doyle's *Rodney Stone*. Died in poverty on a pension continued by Queen Victoria.

† Lady Salisbury. ‡ At the royal cottage.

Lady Conyngham, but God forbid she should even have guessed what it was about, but upon going out to dinner, altho' the Duchess of Gloucester was present, and it is unalterable law that one Royalty always takes out another, to the great horror of our old Sally, the King said, 'Come, my dear Salisbury, you must come with me. Mary (meaning the Duchess of Gloucester), the Duke of Dorset will take you out,' and the said Duchess knowing full well what this meant, took up a position *opposite* her Brother, thus leaving the young man to enjoy his device of sitting between the dear Marchioness of Salisbury, and *Conyngham*. Now was there ever ? Only 64 years old yesterday week and can't be separated a couple of yards from his large Angel even at dinner. In the evenings he plays at *shilling* whist, and likes it much. . . ."

"Stoke, Tuesday, August 22nd.

" . . . We have just lost our *Sally*, and I only wish you could have seen her four long tails with white reins, and huge tassells on each horse, and herself driving her dogs 20 miles to London.

" Saturday and Sunday were so hot that none of us were able to ride, but yesterday my Lady with her four Daughters, and two Sons, and old *Sally* and I took the field to Bulstrode, and its environs—*Sall* * being the only one who mounted her horse like an arrow from the hand of her groom, the horse too being an uncommonly high one, milk white, dressed in a net, and a present (as she informed me) from her Son Salisbury who had given 200 Guineas for it. It seems the old girl has a jointure of £5,000 a year, and the house in Arlington Street, but Sefton says, runs out infernally. . . . I had a good deal of jaw with her

* She was now 76 years old.

yesterday in our ride, and tho' I did not discover any of the talent Sefton gives her credit for, her *opinions* upon different matters were very amusing.   By way of an outing for her, we have driven out the last two nights after coffee, about ten o'clock in two open carriages, taking the road to Salt Hill, and so seeing *the London Mails to the West of England arrive and change horses &c.*, and *poor* as such amusement may appear to be for persons of our rank and age, I assure you it gave very great and general satisfaction, and so after a cool drive of ten miles about, we returned to our tea, and as near 12 as might be each night, we have made up a rubber for *Sally* at crown points, and about ½ past one and after finishing 3 or 4 rubbers, she has retired to her *couché*. . . ."

" August 25th.

" . . . Only think of our going yesterday in pursuit of Virginia Water, and absolutely springing the King Fisher himself, not fishing however, but in a little phaeton with Lady Conyngham, and what think you of his *hiding* himself, and our waiting to see him fairly unkennelled again.   It is all true, upon my soul. . . ."

" Croxteth, October 9th.

" I left London on Friday, and to my great delight had the coach all to myself.   After travelling all night arrived at Prescot a little after five on Saturday evening, and as I was just going to order a chaise *two* ostlers came running up to say, ' My Lord's carriage is waiting for you, Sir,' and so in the family coach, and with My Lady's footman to take care of me, I came here. I found Sefton better than I expected. . . ."

"November 1st.

"When Lady Sefton and I were left alone yesterday, I said, ' Well, really, Lady Sefton, I think I may now congratulate you upon Lord Sefton having at length got the better of his misery,' and she answered, ' Oh yes, Mr. Creevey, it is so, and it is all your own doing, and you are the only person who knows how and when to amuse him. Everybody else has failed. Poor Victor de L'Aigle who is the kindest and most attached creature in the world, came from France on purpose to see us, but instead of amusing Lord Sefton, his own eyes were always filling with tears when he looked at him. Then Mrs. —— used to amuse Lord Sefton extremely, but her manner is so daring that he took quite a horror at her. In short, you are the only person who understands him, and cleverness and jokes are the only things he will attend to.' Curious enough, is it not, and very satisfactory ? . . .

"Sefton is gone to Liverpool upon a *new* brush with the Corporation about some land *they* say he conveyed to them 20 years ago, and which *I* say he never did. You know I rather pride myself upon my ancient *conveyancing* knowledge. His own Attorney would evidently have struck, but the thing is as clear as day, and so they are all beginning to see, and by which he will get some thousands of pounds."

"Novr. 18th.

"I am sure you would not wish me to miss Lady Foley.* It is very nearly the direct road to London. Then to see a Noble Novel Writer who has never been known in the midst of all their ruin to degrade herself by putting on either a pair of gloves or a ribbon a *second time*, and who has always 4 *Ponies* ready

* Daughter of 2nd Duke of Leinster and wife of 3rd Lord Foley.

CROXTETH, LIVERPOOL. (QUEEN ANNE FRONT).

By courtesy of Helena, Countess of Sefton.

To face p. 230.

saddled and bridled for any enterprise or excursion that may come into her head, is surely worth seeing, to say nothing of Foley, who without a halfp'orth of income keeps the best house,* has planted more oak trees than any man in England, and by the influence of his name and personal popularity returns two members for Droitwich and one for the County. Then he would get his next neighbour, Ld. Dudley,† to meet me, so we should have ' Jean qui pluert et Jean qui ris,' ‡ Ward being in a state of lingering existence under the frightful pressure of £120,000 a year. . . .

" The Duke of York's case seems a marvellous one. Sefton hears constantly of him from Head Quarters, and his first favorable report was from a curious quarter. *Ude*, the cook of all cooks in the great world, who lived for years with Sefton, and who now lives with the Duke, both as cook and friend, writes to Sefton begging him not to mind what the Papers say, for that his appetite is returned, and that he will do. This is confirmed by letters from Greville and Armstrong both in the household. . . ."

" Whitehall, London, Decr. 21st.

" Well, I must say that no man ever had a better *hotel* than I have, and I am equally certain that Mrs. Taylor is perfectly sincere when she expresses her hope that I will always use it as my own in future . . . and here our Taylor has just put his head into the room saying, ' My dear creature I beg you will ask whoever you like to dine here,' in which too, I am sure he is likewise quite sincere, so that really in *my* circle I know of no such shop or such people. . . ."

* At Witley Court, Worcestershire.
† John 9th Lord Ward. Created Earl of Dudley. He bought Witley from Lord Foley.
‡ Creevey was not strong at French.

CHAPTER XI

1827

THE political events and constant reshufflings in the Government which followed Lord Liverpool's long administration have lost much of the interest which they still afforded thirty years ago. The scheme of the present volume of Creevey Papers relegates them —especially since Sir Herbert Maxwell gave them considerable prominence—to the background of the scene in which Creevey and his circle play out their comedy of manners. A brief summary of the changes in the administration during the years 1827–8 will serve to explain some of the allusions in the letters which follow. Without it, the undercurrent of excitement which runs through them would be inexplicable to a generation to whom changes of governments, of dynasties, of constitutions, of national policies, are everyday affairs which evoke no unusual interest.

In February 1827 Liverpool* made way for Canning, who had long been preparing for that day. Though the King distrusted his Catholic policy, Canning had secured the favour of the Court. But he, like Brougham, was suspect to politicians of all parties, an adventurer and opportunist for all his brilliant gifts. He failed to form a Tory Government, among others Wellington, Eldon and Peel resigning on his appointment. He was thrown back on a coalition, and his negotiations with Lord Lansdowne (Henry Petty) kept excitement at fever heat for many weeks.

His Government was formed in April and included Lyndhurst, Goderich, Huskisson, Palmerston and the Duke of Clarence. But Canning died in August and all was to do again. Both parties were split up into factions, and Creevey's " Mountain " was reft in twain.

* An apoplectic seizure compelled him to resign.

Lansdowne was a traitor confessed; Brougham, too shifty to be nailed down, was credited with every kind of infamy.

Canning was succeeded by Goderich (with Palmerston, Lansdowne, and Huskisson in his cabinet). Goderich gave place in January 1828 to the Duke of Wellington, and the Duke saw George IV out.

Mr. Creevey enjoyed these historical events rather as an observer and student of politics than as a participator. He still found in the wilderness Paradise enow, and he poured out his wit and malice on all and sundry in public life with less earnestness and more vivacity than of old. The Man-of-fashion still dominated the Party-man, but the future historian of his own times was not idle, and among the papers of this year are copies of Wellington's correspondence with the King and Goderich respecting his resignation and resumption of the office of Commander-in-Chief, sent by him to Lord Lonsdale in explanation of his conduct.

Creevey to Miss Ord

"Brooks's, Feby. 6th, 1827.

" . . . I went to Arlington Street, and found Lady Sefton as good as good, and quite merry; the young ones too quite alive, and all most anxious for my coming to tell of Papa having invited *Lady Holland* to dine there Sunday week after all his abuse of her, and all his vows that he never would again go near her. . . .

" Sefton made me come into his own room after I had had my coze with the Ladies. I promised to dine there tomorrow to meet Sir Charles Stuart. As Little Sussex was prevented from dining with the Hollands from illness, I went from Arlington Street to Kensington, and wrote my name there. It seems he (Sussex) has been one of the many victims of the Duke of York's funeral, by catching cold in the Chapel. The

Duke of Montrose has been at death's door from it, Roslyn is still confined, Wellington was very severely hit, and Canning's illness is from the same cause. By all the accounts Mrs. Taylor has from Stephenson * about *Billy Clarence's* conduct at the funeral, it must have been perfect. What think you to begin with of these Princes being kept waiting in the cold Chapel an hour and a half before every thing was ready, during which period various peers made the most marked homage to *Billy*, and as Stephenson was the Duke of Sussex's train bearer, he was privy to all that passed. . . . Whenever there was an interval he turned to Sussex with the same observation, ' We shall be treated *now*, Brother Augustus, very differently from what we have been.' . . . I quite long to hear our Sussex about it, and they say *Mrs. Kent* quite belongs to this click, so there ought to be some fun. The Duke of York's debts don't exceed £150,000, the new house included. He owes about £50,000 of it to his Sister Sophia.

" It is said Prinney fell over head and ears in love with *Miss Chester*, the actress, the two nights he was at the play, and that Lady Conyngham has been made very uneasy, which of course is all my eye. . . .''

" Feby. 20th.

" . . . The Duke of Cumberland cannot be dead, as Lord Sefton has just left the Duke of Sussex who ' had not *hard* of it.'

" Every one in the dark as to Liverpool's successor, tho' the general feeling is in favor of Canning being the man. . . .

" . . . I have been called out by Barnes of the ' Times ' who told me he had had a direct application

* See note, p. 161. He was not a son of the Duke of York (*Creevey Papers*) or of any other royal duke.

if not *from* at least *on behalf* of the King to give no
more account of his private life at Brighton. . . ."

" Feby. 22nd.

" . . . Tankerville keeps to his text that Peel went
to Brighton to propose himself as Liverpool's successor, and he adds to it now, that the King's answer was,
he was too ill to attend to business, but that he would
think of it. . . . Kensington, on the other hand, says
that not a word has been said to the King about a
successor to Liverpool. . . . From all I hear my belief
is that Liverpool is not going to die, and it seems to
follow of course in the present state of the Cabinet
that they will do nothing till he is sufficiently recovered
to be consulted upon this subject.   In the meantime
by Kensington's account Huskisson must be infernally
ill, so how these victims of the funeral will go on with
their Corn Laws and Free Trade and Catholics one
can't make out. . . ."

" March 15th.

" . . . Well, now for Sally's benefit yesterday, or
rather mine at Sally's House, and I assure you it was
perfect.   Being told by Lord Arthur to be very punctual to a quarter past seven, I was so, and found in
addition to Sally, My Lord and Lady Sefton, Ladies
Maria and Caroline Molyneux, their Brothers Henry
and Francis, Lord Arthur and Lord Marcus Hill and
Montgomery, and afterwards arrived Jack Fremantle. . . .
" . . . Our dinner was of the very best order in
quantity and quality, and our establishment was three
gentlemen out of livery, three sky blue footmen, and
a page.   Upon beginning my fish, a gentleman, without my asking for it, presented me with a large bottle

17

of *ketchup*, and upon looking with some suspicion towards Sefton, the old girl who was next to him, had her eye glass fixed upon me, and in her solemn low toned voice said, ' You are very fond, Mr. Creevey, of ketchup, I understand, and so am I,' so this of course had been got up by Sefton and Atty, and we went on in the same playful way the whole time. To conclude, when we left the Dining Room for the Drawing Room (one opening into the other), in their all combining against me to push me first into the Drawing Room, which they accomplished by sheer force, the operation being so noisy that Lady Salisbury observed to Lady Sefton, ' What a row they are making, I wish I was there.' . . . We left at eleven, and in the passage passed her two cock'd-hat chairmen waiting to take her a-visiting to Emily, Marchioness of Londonderry, and Sefton said that upon her return, she would have, as she always had, a little hot supper of chicken or something else for her own private eating. . . ."

"March 26th.

" Let me see, where did I leave off, and where am I to begin ? Saturday was a considerable field day in Arlington Street, the Duncannons and the Jerseys, Geo. and Mrs. Lamb, Lord Foley, Punch Greville, and Genl. McDonald, and a very merry jolly dinner and evening we had. What remarkably fresh, clean looking creatures the sisters—Ladies Jersey and Duncannon are. . . .

" . . . What a handsome, spanking creature Lady Erroll* is, and how like her Mother, particularly when she used to be acting *Nell*. She looks as if she was quite uncomfortable in her fine cloaths and wanted to have them off. . . . I shall of course dine at the

* Elizabeth Fitzclarence, daughter of William IV and Mrs. Jordan, married 18th Earl of Erroll.

Hollands' on Sunday week ; the Jerseys I know dine there as well as the Seftons. I think I can't be reckoned amongst the *Slaves* of Holland House in accepting this invitation. You know what a sensitive, fanciful devil I am. ' Oh! thoughtless mortals, &c. &c.' I have now taken it into my head, right or wrong I know not, that there is rather a particular civility shown me on all hands, and then again I fancy it has something to do with my *work*, tho' I never *hard* of it till yesterday. . . ."

                              " Brooks's, April 10th.

" Rum enough this, to be weather-bound at Brooks's so early in the day as 12 o'clock, but the fact My Dear you see is this. Our Young Ladies in Arlington Street asked me yesterday to come and breakfast with them today at ten, and so to walk with them at ½ before eleven down to St. James' Palace, to see the guard changed, and I kept my appointment accordingly, and a very good breakfast we young people had in the absence of Papa and Mama, but when the time for walking came, down came the rain, and it has poured ever since. . . .

" No Premier yet. It is now universally considered as true that the hitch is entirely between Canning and *Prinney*, and not between the former and his colleagues. The Sovereign is a true Protestant, and demands securities from Canning before he gives him supreme power that he will not use this new power in favor of the Pope. . . .

" My Lord and My Lady Sefton, Lady Katherine and myself in the carriage, and the other three young Ladies and Francis on horseback made a charming tour after I finished yesterday's letter. Thro' Dulwich, Herne Hill &c. &c. . . ."

"Brooks's again.

"You see I thought it best to step out and take my place in the *Fakenham* Coach for Thursday, which I have done, price £2, and Fakenham is 9 miles from Holkham, and 110 from London, so I presume I will have to lodge there that night. . . ."

"Holkham, April 14th.

". . . I got to Fakenham (10 miles off on Thursday about 9) the coach coming no further, so I dined very comfortably, went to bed, and came over yesterday morning in a CHAY before Church to which I went. My journey down was delightful, independent of the finish of the day. No tract of 100 miles is so full of associations to the Humble Individual who has now the honor to address you. I begin with my first entrance into life at Hackney, and then thro' my academical residence amongst all the Royal Male and Female Founders of Colleges at Cambridge to whom I am passionately attached with all their sins, and in defiance of Bruffam and the enlightened moderns who are now founding Stinkomiles College at the end of Gower Street in London.* Newmarket too was not without its reminiscences, and then I entered upon the County, one of whose towns I represented in Parliament sixteen years of my life, and on one side of me I had that house of Lord Bradford's where we once were at a Ball, and on the other side old Buckenham, and then again for political reminiscences, I had Rainham before me, and Houghton, hard by, the Townshends and the Walpoles, and to sum up the whole, I was coming to the birthplace and the property of much the best politician that England has

* Brougham was largely responsible for the founding of London University.

ever known, Old Chief Justice Coke. Such, My
Dears, were the thoughts which accompanied me in
my stage coach, and however feeble they may appear
to others, I assure you I found them very agreeable
companions. . . .

" Digby and Lady Andover are both speechless,
[*erased*] Stanhope and Mrs. Stanhope are worthy,
honest, absent, lackadaisical bodies that don't seem
to know where they are, or who they are with, and
this is our present stock except a young British Museum
Artist, who is classing manuscripts, and a silent par-
son without a name ; but then what have we not in
reserve ? Do not we expect *Lord John Russell*, the
Knight of Kerry, *Spring Rice*, and various other great
and publick characters? We do indeed, tho' during
the different times I have been here I have known
many expected who never came . . ."

Earl of Sefton to Creevey

" April 13th.

". . . The D. of Wellington . . . says, nothing
shall induce him to connect himself with *that man*.*
That he sh'ld. be liable to such impertinence, he could
not put up with it. . . .

" Granville is Secy. for Foreign ; Warde, Privy
Seal ; Robinson, Colonies.

" It is reported that Huskisson is to be Home
Secy. The Great Seal to be in commission. . . ."

Creevey to Miss Ord

" Holkham, April 17th.

". . . The more one thinks of the whole smash,
the more astonishing it is. How right poor Alava
was when he told me at Brussels the morning after

* *i.e.* Canning.

we knew Wellington was Master of the Ordnance, that
he (Alava) was horrified. That Wellington ought
never to have become a *politician*, but to remain the
soldier of England, aye the soldier of Europe, in case
he should ever again be wanted. Such were Alava's
precise and honest sentiments, and wise and much
happier would the *Beau* have been had he acted upon
these, instead of which, here he is, having extinguished
Bonaparte and all the world in battle, at last
floor'd himself by the very man he prevailed upon
not to go to India but to stay and go halves with
him in the Government at home. By God, it is too
much . . .

". . . Our only accessor today has been Lord
John."

" April 21st.

" Well, so Lansdowne won't touch office. Canning
and he met by appointment yesterday when the
latter refused coming into the New Administration,
but the meeting and termination of it were highly
amicable. . . .

" Lord Dudley has refused the offer of the Privy
Seal. In short, I think Canning in the greatest
danger of failing in his project, and if he does so he
falls ten thousand fathoms. . . .''

" Whitehall, June 18th.

". . . I was an hour at least in Berkely Square
[Lord Grey's], about half the time with her, and then
came in My Lord. You never saw two poor creatures
more sore than they are at all the abuse he meets with
from the *Whigs*. . . . Lady Grey said to me, ' Now,
Mr. Creevey, having been here a week, is your opinion
of Lord Grey's conduct as favorable as when you
came ? ' Only think of their being driven to this,

and only from his having acted an honest part, whilst the rest of his party have been mean knaves. He was much more instructive than any one I have met yet about the formation of Canning's Government, and his facts are all from the parties concerned. When the King had given Canning his commands, he *sent for* the Archbishop of Canterbury, and Bishop of London, and had them with him *five hours* ; during which time he told them again and again, that Canning was to form a Cabinet upon precisely the same model as the last, that is to say, with a preponderance of one *against* the Catholics. It was known soon after this interview that Canning had been in the Palace, all the time of it, and as the King left the room once for about 20 minutes, the Bishops concluded it was to state to Canning what the King was communicating to them. And when Canning wrote a letter to the Speaker,* which he did, pressing him most strongly to become Peel's successor in the Home Department, he begged him not to return an answer *till he had seen his Father, the Archbishop.* This insinuation, however, that the Cabinet was still to be Anti-catholic would not do, and the Speaker returned an unqualified refusal. Canning then made the same offer, first to Wallace, and then to Lord Colchester,† both thorough-stitch *Anti*-Catholics, but they were alike—inaccessible, and then it was that Canning stated his difficulties to the King, and produced Brougham's letter to Wilson ; when it was agreed between the King and Canning to take Brougham at his word, and Lord Lansdowne was sounded upon what terms he would join the Government. A meeting of *friends* at Lansdowne House

---

* Charles Manners-Sutton, 1st Viscount Canterbury, son of the Archbishop.

† Charles Abbot, former Speaker.

drew up *the terms*, which were—that the Lord
Lieutenancy, Lord Chancellor, and Secretary for
Ireland should be friends to the Catholics, and
Lansdowne to be Secretary of State for the Home
Department, and to lead the House of Lords. This
proposal, however, was immediately rejected by
Canning, and the whole thing was off, and then came
the meeting in the rump of the Whigs headed by
Brougham which led to the surrender of Lansdowne
and his followers into the hands of Canning upon any
terms he might be pleased to grant them. . . . To
continue my narrative of our beloved Sovereign, I
went from Lord Grey's yesterday to Lord Darlington's,
when Lady Darlington told me the following story.
As I observed in a former letter, the King has taken to
coming upon the course at Ascot before the Races to
see the horses take their gallops and trials, so the day
when Lord Darlington's horse, ' Memnon,' was to run,
and one of the King's was in the same race, upon
coming on the course in his phaeton with Lord
Conyngham by his side, he met or passed Lord
Darlington's top Jockey, Chiffney, upon one of Lord
Darlington's horses, so the Monarch pulling up said,
' Well, Sam, so you are going to beat me today.'
' I don't know that, please your Majesty,' says
Sam, ' but My Lord's is a good horse.'   ' Aye,
aye,' says Prinney, ' I know that, and I know that
he'll beat me, but I don't care.   I was always
fond of racing, you know, Sam, and it makes me
quite happy to take to it again.'   And just at this
time one of the King's race horses passed, and he
observed to Chiffney ' There, Sam, now that's an
Irish horse and this is an Irish*man* sitting by my side,
and one can run about as well as the other.   They
have both been brought up, you see, Sam, upon

potatoes, and can make no play at all.' Now was there ever ? . . ."

" June 19th.

". . . Let me correct an error in our Biography of George 4th. It was *Bill* Chiffney, Ld. Darlington's *trainer*, and not *Sam* Chiffney the *jockey*, that the Monarch honor'd with his conversation, always calling him Bill.

" The King seeing the Duke of Dorset on the course at the races sent for him into the stand. The Duke, you know, *struck* as Master of the Horse, avowing to the King his decided hostility to Canning, and accordingly was one of the majority with Wellington. As soon as he appeared, the King put out both his hands to him saying, ' My Dear Little *Sack*, how are you, and why did not you come to me before?' You know he was Lord Sackville before he was Duke. Very gratifying to Canning to see Opposition Peers treated in this manner, . . ."

" Barningham (Mr. M. Milbank's), August 19th.

". . . You must have been struck I think with the long article from the ' Moniteur ' upon Canning's death. I was, so much so that I could not resist flying a kite to Lord Grey by that post, . . . in exposing that universal Humbug, now so fashionable, . . . that Canning was the author of any *new* National Policy for the country. Never since I was born have I witnessed such delusions or such barefaced villainy. Nevertheless, as I have observed to Grey, I think France was ' *cowed* ' by the swaggering of Canning, and that she is going to be damned impertinent with the feeble devils who are to be Canning's successors . . ."

Earl Grey to Creevey

". . . I . . . missed the article in the 'Moniteur,' . . . I saw an allusion to it, however, . . . and from what you say I form the same opinion of it that you do. The Apostolical Party in France and throughout Europe, I have no doubt, detested Canning, and rejoiced in his death, and this is perhaps the best thing that can be said in his favour. But I am far from believing that his policy w'd. ultimately have been found so prejudicial to their interests as they may have apprehended, and what I think most to be regretted in his death, is that it took place before his character and conduct were fully developed. . . .

" I can tell you little more of the changes that Canning's death has made necessary, than you will see in the papers. I have heard, and I believe, that the King declared, almost immediately, that he w'd. have no more Whigs ; and every thing that we have hitherto seen is entirely in the spirit of such a determination. Huskisson . . . has been offered the Colonial Office, and the head of the House of Commons. I suppose the appointment of Herries is deferred till Huskisson's answer can be received, which seems probable from his having been at Windsor and sworn as a Member of the Privy Council. By others it is said that he hesitates about accepting in any case, and again that strong remonstrances against his appointment have been made by our old friends. If his appointment does not take place, it is said Palmerston is to be Chan'r. of the Ex :, but who in that case is to be Sec'y. at War ? I have not heard ; probably not a Whig.

" The Duke of Wellington was offered the Army in

such a way, that he could not refuse it, and his acceptance, together with the other changes, will necessarily
give strength to the Govt.   The Tory Opposition
will be divided, if not annihilated then.   Peel will
probably look to a return to power by conciliatory
rather than by fertile measures, and it seems to me
most likely that the administration will, at no distant
period, be re-established on its old principles, and
almost its old form, by the ecstacies of our old friends,
who after submitting to indignities which will have
rendered them helpless, will at last find themselves
compelled to retire. . . ."

Creevey to Miss Ord
" Lowther Castle, August 27th.

" . . . I think I am settled here for life.   I don't
know where to begin, and before I do begin I shall
have to end, as Lady Caroline, Mrs. Taylor and I are
going an airing, and at present I am rather *bosky* after
luncheon. . . . There is nothing like an *impression*.
At five o'clock yesterday evening, I thought I was
entering the most formal house in England, and at
half past six dear Lady Lonsdale and I were going out
arm in arm to dinner, three boys of Colonel Lowther's
pulling with all their might and main at my coat flaps
to make me stay and play with them, and in the
evening, as we could have no cards from its being
Sunday, Lord Pollington was kind enough to entertain
us with his excellent imitations of squeaking pigs,
Guinea Fowls, dialogues between crying children, and
the devil knows what besides. . . ."

" Lowther, August 28th.

" A line merely to say how very cosy and comfortable we continue to be, tho' now reduced to a
family party. . . .

" I ought to mention that our last day at Barningham went off to admiration, we being all alone, and
Milbank toiled all morning in the Greta to catch me a
dish of trout for dinner which he accomplished, and
our evening concluded with a very severe batch at
whist, which was enlivened by the following circumstance :

" The day before, the Clergyman of the Parish
dined with us, and his Wife, the latter being a fortune
from *seeds*, good for £15,000 ; such a devil for ugliness
and dress as you never beheld—a regular strolling
player in a barn, a cap bolt upright of a yard's length,
her hair behind nearly pulled up to the roots to be
got into the cap, and in the front an amethyst star
half mast high ; so I did nothing but rave about her,
and at our Whist, Lady Augusta entertained, ' Well, I
believe after all that Mrs. Callings is a very good kind
of woman at bottom,' so, says I, ' I know nothing of
her bottom, but she is a deuced comical one at top,'
which soon made for our Mark, and Gusty blushed
and roared, and laid down her cards, ever and anon
bawling out ' L-o-r-d, Mr. Creevey, what a droll man
you are. Nobody but you could have said such a
thing.' But I must leave you, my dears, being called
away for a laking excursion."

" Doncaster, Sept. 20th.

" . . . Charles Greville and Lord Warncliffe
(Stuart Wortley) *and I* were very merry together last
night upon the subject of a leading article in yesterday's ' *Times* ' *newspaper*—a puff of Brougham by
himself, claiming the Solicitor Generalship for him
as the one remaining man of talent in the country,
and treating his competitor, *Shadwell*, as so low a
concern ' that no parish would elect him as their vestry
clerk.' . . .

" Mrs. William* asked me to chaperon her and young Mary to the Ball, (Billy being disabled) which I did, and walked by her about the room a good deal, and you can't imagine what enquiries were made by the *quality* from me, who my pretty friend was. . . .

" All your race was at the Ball tonight, young Mrs. James Ord keeping up her improved looks. . . . Sir *Tho. Lawrence* came up to Mrs. Willm. . . . as a patroness no doubt of himself and his art, and he condescended to express his admiration of young Mary's countenance. . . ."

" Wentworth, September 24th.

" . . . On our arrival here on Saturday we found Milton and his eldest Son without their coats playing at cricket with the servants just in front of the house. The party was then surely domestic. The dear amiable old man,† his Sister, Ly. Frances Fitzwilliam, Milton and Ly. Milton,‡ their two grown up Daughters and Son, Fred Ponsonby, a young Mr. Spears and a Mr. Duberly ; afterwards came the Cowpers, and tho' last, not least, Princess Lieven. I have always heard a great deal of the talents of Madame Lieven, and I think I have heard she is considerably afflicted with *ennui*. . . . I used to have some hold on Ly. Milton for a laugh, and with Cowper for an ally we did great things, so much so that Mad'e. Lieven more than once stretched her *snipe* face towards my corner with something like an expression of a wish in it to be of our party, and so when we went to Coffee, and I was standing by the table, she got up from her chair,

* Brandling.
† 4th Earl Fitzwilliam. He married first Lady Charlotte Ponsonby, daughter of 2nd Earl of Bessborough, and secondly the widow of 1st Lord Ponsonby.
‡ Daughter of 1st Lord Dundas.

came up to me and began talking immediately, and
our intercourse was from that moment so prosperous,
that at parting just now she was pleased to express her
regret that I was not going to Chatsworth (where they
are going), but to hope, at all events, it would not
be long before we met in London, and if you come to
that, Prince Lieven, who arrived here to dinner
yesterday from London, was pleased likewise to say
when he squeezed my hand at parting, that he was
very happy to have the pleasure of making my
acquaintance. Was there ever? The Snipe considered me all the time as being in Parliament, and I
thought it quite unnecessary to undeceive her, so it
was ' all mighty well.' . . . I had a great deal of
conversation with her, and very agreeable she was.
Afterwards at the request of Ly. Cowper's Daughter,
she sat down with great good humour to the piano-
forte, and played most beautifully, and I am sure most
skilfully, and I was the only man who attended.   She
asked, ' *Monsieur Creevey aimez de musique?* ' * and
when she had finished she came to me and said in the
French language, how very few men in England were
fond of musick, and when we were going thro' the
Stables this morning, and poor Old Billy was shewing
her all his horses, which are beautiful and most
numerous, she slipt from under his arm to come and
say to me, ' I have just as much pleasure in looking at
these horses as you Englishmen have in hearing
musick.' . . ."

" Raby, Oct. 6th.

" . . . The *Pop* was not forthcoming at dinner
yesterday. . . . Mrs. Taylor says there is a rumour in
the family that there has been the devil of a blow up

* Creevey's French !

between her and her *maid*. . . . The Marquis * seems
absorbed in thought. . . . The King . . . has given
him permission to quarter the Royal Arms with his
own, in compliment to his descent in the female line
from Charles the 2nd. and Miss Villiers, in the person
of the first Duke of Cleveland. This accession
of dignity gives him *two crests*, the Royal Lion and his
own crest, and both are to find their way upon the
servants' buttons, and the question is which is to have
the place of honor. And here, I must say, I think
the Marquis reasons with very logical accuracy—'*If,*'
says he, ' I had the same rank with my Royal
Ancestor, the *Duke* of Cleveland, spurious as that
descent is, I should prefer it to my own, and place the
Lion before my own crest, but as the *Marquis* of
Cleveland is not a Royal title, and still is equally
spurious, I shall prefer my own title, and place my
crest before the Royal Lion.' *Upon your soul!*
Now ' r-a-a-lly ' was there ever ? Is it not *too* ? . . .
I must go and tender my homage to the *Haradan*.†
. . . The first day after I came she walked me down
to Staindrop with her, the neighbouring town about a
mile off, and we paid visits to the Apothecary's
family, the Steward's Lady, and shopped a little. In
the course of our walk she abused *James* Brougham
without reserve, and I thought was coming rather
near the Brother, so I said, ' I wonder whether he will
be Solicitor-General ? ' ' Impossible,' said she, ' he
is pledged you know to support Government without
taking office ' ; ' and yet,' says I, ' he complains of
being excluded. I have seen it under his own hand.'
' That's very odd,' says she, ' I am sure Lord Darlington considers him as pledged not to take office from

* Lord Darlington had just been created Marquis of Cleveland.
† Lady Cleveland. Also known as " The Poplolly."

all he has said and written to him, and I should think would have a very different opinion of him if he did so. I am sure, at least, *I* should, but Lord Darlington has a letter from him this morning proposing to come here next Tuesday, but he never mentions the Solicitor Generalship, nor anything of the kind.' Was there ever such a double-faced villain ?

"Old Sussex comes here on Monday, and Cis Buggin* too. Was there ever such a low lived concern ? and Brougham comes to meet them, so they will have it all their own way in politicks. . . ."

"Howick, October 13th.

"We were all Monday at Durham, and got here on Tuesday which you will be glad to hear was time enough to catch our old friends the *Bathursts* † tho' it was only for a day. . . . Lady Bathurst was so entrenched in hat and feathers, and gave me so little encouragement (as I thought) to bring my bad ear into action, that for the first quarter of an hour I thought my prospects very gloomy indeed, but I presently broke the line with dear old Dow: Julia Lady Petre, *souverin* her happy ' *Blind Man's Buff* ' days with Lord Grey when she lost her gown and one shoe, and I never looked behind me afterwards. You may suppose how well I stood before the dinner was over, when Grey said, ' Let me send you a piece of this red herring, Creevey, I know you will like it,' and Lady Bathurst added, ' And let me, Mr. Creevey,

* Lady Cecilia's surnames are confusing. Born a Gore, daughter of 2nd Earl of Arran, she married first Sir George Buggin. Reverting on widowhood to her mother's maiden name of Underwood, she married secondly, as his second wife, H.R.H. the Duke of Sussex in 1832. Queen Victoria created her Duchess of Inverness in 1840. She died without issue in 1873.

† 3rd Earl, married Georgina, sister of 4th Duke of Richmond. He held office in several Tory Administrations.

recommend you to eat some of the cream cheese with it, you can't imagine how well they eat together,' and so of course I did, and having done so I said, ' Bless me, what *a pretty coalition*,' and Grey blushed and laughed with his face downwards, and she laughed too.   She is a palavering, perfidious, decayed flatterer with no talents to begin with, and very scanty remains of good looks to end with. . . .

" What think you of Lady Londonderry when she slept at the Bishop of Durham's, asking if there were *no cambric* sheets ? . . ."

Mrs. Taylor to Creevey

" Whitehall, Nov. 12th.

" . . . I write to announce Mr. Brougham's first visit to me last night.   He was visibly in very bad temper, and talked at and against every body I liked. Poor Ld. Grey came in for a large share of his abuse for having changed his opinions so far as to receive Ld. Bathurst into his house. . . .

" . . . I told him what an agreeable summer I had spent going about with you, and how well we had found *Ld. and Ly. Grey*, that he was grown twenty years younger since he left London, and what an agreeable party we had there. . . .

" The Government people are visibly sore and frightened to death of Ld. Grey, and really scarcely seem to think they can go on.

" I hope you will be able to come to us as soon as Miss Ord is settled at Rivenhall.   I shall be curious to hear how you got on at Croxteth. . . ."

Creevey to Miss Ord

" Croxteth, Nov. 21st.

" . . . I arrived . . . yesterday. . . . After My Lord had *insisted* upon my having a mutton chop

18

dressed for me, I pottered about over my old haunts, and upon my returning found Mr. and Mrs. Hopwood, their son, the Captain, and Miss, arrived from Hopwood and Count Montrond * and Tommy Duncombe from London. . . . One of the young ladies said, ' We have seen a good deal of Mr. Brougham lately, he went to the play with us 3 or 4 times, and you never saw such a figure as he is. He wears a black stock or collar round his neck, it is so wide that you can see a dirty coloured handkerchief under tied tight round his neck. You never saw such an object, or anything half so dirty.' This is all that has passed hitherto respecting the ' Archfiend.' . . . Mull † was pleased to express his great satisfaction at my restoration *to the bosom of my family*. So . . . it's all mighty well. But I have scarcely time to tell you more, for Sefton made me go out with them to their shooting ground, and our post for Prescot goes at four, it being now very near that hour. . . .''

" Nov. 22nd.

'' . . . The *Pet* continues to be every thing I could wish, and I cannot help flattering myself is as near upon the *Rat* as possible from his new Allies. He said to me last night over our tea, ' You know, Brougham had the offer made him of being Chief Baron ? ' ' Yes,' said I, ' from Canning, and for the purpose of getting rid of him.' ' Yes,' said Sefton, ' just so ; ' but this morning after breakfast he has been as good as a play. He lays it down as a fact known to all that Lord Dudley and Lady Copley or Lyndhurst are *one*, and that he never thinks of the Foreign Office or any-

* Count Montrond, roué and gambler, witty, sly and dangerous, escaped the guillotine to be distrusted and employed both by Bonaparte and Talleyrand.

† Lord Molyneux.

thing else but her, whilst Copley himself never thinks
of the Court of Chancery or any thing else but his
parties at Roehampton, and his pleasure generally.
' So,' says Sefton, ' I took an occasion the other day
at Brooks's to tell Abercromby at some length what a
damned fool Copley was making of himself, and how
sure he was of being deceived in all ways, and very
soon too, and so,' added Sefton, ' Abercromby took
to profound silence for some time, and at last said
with his peculiar solemnity, " It is a subject that has
given me great uneasiness for some time past and I
have always been afraid of hearing the observations
you have just made." ' After this conversation, and
a little more upon our new subject—our victory at
Navarino, in which we are both so united in opinion—
Sefton said, ' I think I'll write to Grey today and
congratulate him upon his Boy being safe,' and of
course I encouraged him so to do, and then we all
went to the stables, and Joss was bid to strip Mr.
Creevey's new horse, and to turn him round in the
stall. I had been told more than once before of his
beauty, and of his being quite made for me, and
certainly to my mind I never saw a handsomer horse.
Was there ever ? . . .

" Permit me to mention an alteration *in* our breakfasts. I observed yesterday four silver covers, top,
bottom and sides, and upon their being taken up they
were all hot dishes—kidneys at top, mashed potatoes
at bottom, 3 partridges at one side with bread sauce,
crums &c. &c., Pattys at the other. Today Mutton
cutlets at top, mashed pots: at bottom, omlet at one
side, and a pheasant the other. Now *r-a-ally* as Mrs.
Taylor would say, ' I think that is *trop*, is it not ? ' . . .

" Permit me to conclude with a piece of muggery
I have just received, and which we old chaps are

mighty fond of. Lady Louisa showed me a letter
from Lady Georgina Grey in which she is pleased to
say, of all their visitors at Howick this year, the one
they were the most sorry to part with was Mr. Creevey
&c. &c. &c.   Upon your soul!   Old School Lane! and
am for ever."

" Croxteth, Nov. 25th.

" . . . Yesterday was beautiful, tho' the ground
was covered with snow, so it was settled to shoot in
Craven Wood, and as the ladies' cottage is there, they
always give a kind of jollification upon such occasion,
and much dissatisfaction was expressed, when it was
reported that Mr. Creevey was going to Liverpool, but
Lady Sefton said, ' Mr. Creevey is going to see his
Sister, and he always does what is right.   Would you
have any game sent to your Sister, Mr. Creevey ? '
' Not *yet*, thank you, Lady Sefton,' says I.   ' You have
had but one battue yet, and it is a bad pheasant year
(which is the case), besides I am going to draw upon
Lord Sefton for my Grand-daughter's birthday.'   So
off I walked to Liverpool, and as I was sitting cozing
with my Sister, up drove my Lord's gig and groom in
it, and so, thinks I, what is this for, when a card comes
in, 2 pheasants and one hare with Lady Sefton's
compliments to Miss Creevey, and a message from
Lady Sefton to Mr. Creevey, that she has sent the gig
for him, it must be uncomfortable walking.   Now,
r-a-ally was not all this pretty attention *too* ?   However, having no great coat, and being wet in the feet, I
preferred trudging it back to an open carriage.   I
found my Sister in the most perfect preservation in
all ways, and looking better than ever I saw her in
my life.   I got back here about half past five, and as
the birds were all flown, I flew too to my own bedroom
where having discarded all my cloaths but my shirt

and banyan, my Lord came and made me a visit in
his banyan and slippers, and a very agreeable half an
hour jaw we had.   When he talks politicks with me,
I am always thinking whether he is withholding any
thing from me, as he has been so much in Brougham's
and the new Whig camp, but still I don't think that is
his character ; I mean concealment. . . .

"In the meantime what an age it is before one
learns how the Turk takes this Navarino touch. . . .

"My new Horse is quite charming, was bought
on purpose, and only cost 120 gns.   Joss always calls
him Mr. Creevey's horse."

". . . Croxteth, Saturday morning Dec. 15th, 10
o'clock and not a soul come down yet, and such a
morning for rain, but my own great coat, and our
Mary's umbrella were quite sufficient protection in
the gig.

"Miss Creevey's drum went off to admiration last
night and my Lord's pheasant and hare with Hannah
Rickman's cakes and Miss Creevey's Port and *Madeira*
made the ladies as well as gentlemen very gay and
merry.   Before I left him for Liverpool my Lord had
two letters, the first from De Ros, and the second
from Punch Greville, both overflowing with matter
and jokes against the Government, and which My Lord
read aloud with great apparent satisfaction.   De Ros
says, 'Nothing can equal the consternation of the
Ministers, that they have Cabinet Councils every other
hour, that the Ambassadors are at one another's doors
all day long, that Esterhazy runs about the Town like
a wild cat, and that Dudley's *frame* is so diminished
from the united impression made upon it by the *Turk*,
and the *tender* passion, and with the fear of Earl
Grey always before his eyes, that his face is scarcely

visible to the naked eye.   With a great deal more of
very pretty fun. . . ."

Mrs. Taylor to Creevey

" I have sent you a ' Times ' of today, which I
think shows by the abuse in it of Ld. Grey the fear
the Government, or the Archfiend, have of him.   The
mess thickens, beautiful Ld. Goderich resigns, nomi-
nally on account of domestic illness, but in truth the
Finance and every thing else is in such a state, and
with the King quite beyond his power to controul
(*wanting restraint* more than his Father did) that he
cannot go on. . . .

" Lansdowne fails to make any communication as
to his successor to Sir Knighton.   Nobody seems to
have an idea what is to be done.   Lambton and the
others, it is supposed, will not get their peerages.   It
is really quite delightful to see the wretched supporters
of this miserable Government, for they are at a loss
what to say, having committed themselves as they
have done. . . .

" What a situation Ld. Grey is placed in, everything turns up to support his opinions, and all they
have to say of him—that he has had Ld. Bathurst
at his house ! . . ."

CHAPTER XII

1828

OVER the serene waters of Privilege Mr. Creevey's bark floated, undisturbed by political storms and changes of Government. When occasion demanded, he was politely political and sympathetically partisan, but his mind was fixed on writing social history, and in 1828 his Sussex fortnight and his autumn tour in Ireland documented domestic life of a century ago in a score of famous Whig country houses in West Sussex and Southern Ireland.

One of the little girls at Bessborough whom Creevey praises in the letters which follow, more than once referred at the end of her long life to that visit and to the wit and charm and kindness of " dear Mr. Creevey," and the present editor, who heard her, has a clear recollection of her words which bridge 106 years.

For Creevey himself it was a memorable visit, marked in his records with a white chalk, and he who in an age of licence spared neither sex nor age in criticism, had nothing but reverence and admiration for Lady Jersey's sister, the angelic Lady Duncannon.

Earl of Sefton to Creevey

" Jan. 18th.

" It is confidently said, so I believe it, Huskisson, Dudley, Grant, Palmerston, the Chancellor and Herries, of the old Government, *remain*. Peel to be a Secretary of State *only* ; Grant, Chancellor of the Exchequer, and Herries some other office. Some say *Wellington*, some say Melbourne, Premier. Peel leader of H. of Commons.

" Navarino is to be *supported*.

257

" Althorp to be Chairman of the Finance Committee.

" Free Trade for ever also.

" Lambton, *Ld. Durham.*

" Headache till ½ past 5, so excuse scrawl."

Creevey to Miss Ord

" Feby. 11th.

" . . . As Taylor dined at the Speaker's yesterday, I had to do the honors to old Lord Robert Spencer, and really my tête-à-tête with old ' Comical ' was both curious and entertaining. He, aged 81, was just returned from a visit to his Sister, Dowr. Pembroke, in Richmond Park, aged 94 and quite well. In our unreserved moments his criticisms upon men were quite delightful. He considers the wit Sydney Smith as a ' boisterous Mountebank.' He is intent upon my becoming better acquainted with a contemporary of mine and his—the Earl of Egremont by name—aged 77, who, Bob says, is made for me.

" In my ramble through the Town yesterday, amongst various others whom I met was Billy Wingfield, the most successful humbug simpleton I have known in all my life, and who now in addition to all his other marvellous pieces of good fortune, is an Essex Squire of several thousands a year. So as he was pleased to gallop after me to dine with him next Friday, I mean to see what kind of dinner and company one meets with now-a-days at a Master-in-Chancery in Bloomsbury Square.

" My next messmate in the streets was Sir George Warrender, whom I was for passing with a ' How are you, Warrender ? ' but no such thing could be submitted to, I assure you, so off he went with, ' Well, Creevey, wonders will never cease ! ' I met Lord

Bathurst at the Duke of Buccleuch's in Scotland, who said he had met Mr. Creevey at Lord Grey's, and that altho' he had always entertained the strongest prejudice against him, he had found him the most agreeable fellow possible. . . ."

" Feby. 18th.

" We were 17 at dinner at Little Sussex's, the Clevelands, &c. Sussex you know is always very civil to me, but upon my soul! yesterday he was *beyond*. I never was so dozed in my life. ' You never come near me, Creevey.' ' I always come, Sir, when you do me the honor to invite me.' ' Yes, but why don't you come without inviting. You know I should always be delighted to see you, and the oftener the better. How is Mrs. Hamilton, and the Ladies, and young Hamilton ? ' All this *roaring* out during dinner ; then again with the Clevelands on each side, ' Are you coming into Parliament again, Creevey ? ' ' No, Sir.' ' I wish you were, and yet I don't know why I should, for it's a damned state of things. For myself I've done with politicks, but I'm always with *you*. . . .' "

" Feby. 28th.

" . . . I have been sitting with Sefton who has a headache. He is quite convinced that Wellington will turn out the greatest *Economical* Reformer the Country can produce, and he thinks that after he has proved himself to have such dispositions, Grey will come into office, but *I* say *not* without Ireland being set at rest, and even then at Grey's time of life, it is idle to speculate on such matters. Sefton was at me again about Lord Radnor bringing me into Parliament, which I would not touch."

" March 3rd.

" It is a pity I cannot accommodate the D. of Norfolk by dining with him, and eating some of his *six year old mutton.* I was rather sorry I could not accept this 2nd. invitation. When you read too the other *affectionate* invitation from Countess Grey, you must admit it was a proud day for old *School Lane.* . . .

" . . . After *such* an invitation, I could not be otherwise than well received by Mylady who was with her Lord and Roslyn and Rogers in one room, the young Ladies with others in the next. A visit there is always agreeable. In the midst of it Grey called me from the young ones, saying, ' Creevey, I want to shew you something,' and going to a retired table he put into my hand a letter he had received from Ld. Cleveland, enclosing one he, the Marquis, had received from Brougham. The object of both is peace and friendship between Grey and Brougham. . . .

" . . . Brougham's letter is the composition of the same tortuous villain as ever, and in folly and insanity by no means inferior to his former effusions. We both *roared* at it. He takes a merit to himself in never having denied the expressions imputed to him, but swears that no offensive meaning can be attached to them, and appeals to his known *devotion* to Lord Grey *now*, and for ever past, in support of this. In short, such a mean lyar never existed.

" I believe you are quite right in your notion of the kind of hold Brougham has over Sefton, it is that of a bottle conjuror over a man in *search* of excitement. Sefton thinks Brougham's talents will produce miracles for him at last. It is quite true that his (B's) late great law Speech has produced a perfect torrent of retainers, I mean general retainers from attorneys.* This quite turns his head, already on the swing before. He plays off his own importance, I have no doubt, most profusely on Sefton."

" March 5th.

" I was much struck with a fact stated by C. Calvert at dinner yesterday—that Barclay of the Borough, by far the greatest Brewer of *Ale and Beer* in England, in the last 3, 4, or 6 months *of* 1826 (I forget the precise number of months) sold 160,000 Barrells of Beer and Ale, and that in exactly the corresponding months of 1827 he sold only 90,000, being a falling off of 70,000 out of 160,000, or nearly half. This is entirely owing to Mr. Huskisson's policy in taking off the duty upon *Gin*, which is now so cheap that a whole family may and do get drunk with it for a shilling. Denison confirmed this by telling me that he and his Brother Magistrates in Surrey had been so struck and horrified with the increase of Gin drinking and *crime* during the last year, that they had procured the return of Gin imported for some years past, and that last year's importation was nearly as 40 to 20 or nearly double of the former ones. . . .

" Here is Wm. Ponsonby † asking me to do him and Ly. Barbara *the honor* of dining with them on Saturday, and George Ponsonby ‡ with a letter from Lord Robert Spencer urging him to secure Creevey to meet Ld. Grey at Woolbeding for a few days, which I will if I can. . . ."

---

* When Brougham, after refusing Canning's offer of the post of Chief Baron, reappeared " in silk," he regained for a short time his great practice.

† Third son of 3rd Earl of Bessborough. Married Barbara, daughter of 5th Earl of Shaftesbury. Created Lord de Mauley.

‡ Son of 1st Lord Ponsonby. His second wife was Diana Bouverie, daughter of Lady Robert Spencer. They succeeded to Woolbeding.

" March 6th.

" . . . Dumaresque told me that the Beau made him get into his cabriolet that he might have some conversation with him, and upon the Colonel expressing some fear that he was working himself to death, the other replied, ' I am damnably worked it's true, but nothing will kill me.' Sir Colin whom I met in the street yesterday, said, ' We'll be hard put to it, Mr. Creevey, to carry the Duke through all his trouble and fatigue.' So also said Earl Dudley in St. James's Park today. Not such was his opinion of me, vowing he never saw me look so fresh and well. ' Pretty well,' says I, ' for a man who was 60 yesterday.' ' How do you manage it ? ' says he. ' By never thinking of Turks, Russians, or English Politicians,' said I. . . ."

" Brooks's, March 8th.

" . . . On coming up here Stephenson overtook me. ' Well,' says I, ' what news of the Sovereign ? ' ' Why,' said he, ' the Duke of Sussex had an opportunity yesterday of knowing at least what his Sisters, the Princess Augusta and Duchess of Gloucester, thought, for being with them, some claim of the Duke of Clarence was discussed, and both the Sisters were for his waiving it, *as the King most probably would not live six months.*' . . . It is certainly true that Charles Greville as Clerk of the Council had to rouse him more than once on Wednesday at the Council from something like sleep, when people were to be presented. Lord Grey told me just now he had 17 leeches on one knee at the time. . . .

" In walking up this street with Stephenson, I saw Lord Dudley on the other side of it, just going to mount his horse, so never having seen him since his greatness, and happening to catch his eye, I telegraphed him, and having instantly abandoned his stirrup, he called out, ' I'll come over to you,' but as I justly observed, ' God forbid he should so demean himself,' and we met about half way, and very pretty company in the dirt the noble secretary * was, so of course amongst other things I said, ' Well, what shall you make of the Turk ? ' ' Why, I don't know. He is a *rum one* to deal with indeed,' and then he said, ' only think of Falke and me whom you used to feed so at Aix-la-Chapelle, having to meet every day to talk about this damned Turk,' and as he concluded with hollowing out from his horse when he had mounted to ask *where* I was, I flatter myself he may send me a *nottice* to dine with him.   Just after him I met Earl Grey, and Baron Durham † arm in arm, who seemed not a little surprised at my familiar separation from Earl Dudley, which they had witnessed, nor were they less so at his discourse, which I related. Lord Grey said, ' Do you dine at the Duke of Sussex's, Creevey, Sunday week ? ' ' Yes,' says I, ' it is a dinner you know purely for *you*, and in honor of your publick conduct, which,' says I, ' from little Sussex is not amiss,' and he, Grey, had not known it and was much amused and not displeased, nor yet I suppose was Baron Durham, for he said, in the most gracious manner, ' I hope, Creevey, you are not engaged on the 15th. as a card is on its way to you.' . . ."

" Stoke, June 3rd.

" . . . I found Earl Grey and his Daughter, Montrond, &c., &c.   I mention those two because I had a walk with each. . . .

* 1st Earl of Dudley.   Appointed Foreign Secretary by Canning, he remained under Wellington until May 1828.

† John Lambton, " King Jog," got his first step in the peerage in January of this year.

" My walk with Montrond was at his own request, during which he was pleased to observe that it was very foolish for a clever man ever to read ; that books only interfered with his understanding, and ought only to be read by foolish people to talk about, and to conceal their own poverty of matter. So much for old parlez-vous.

" Our dinner went off to perfect admiration, tho' we were *only* 23—Anson, Duncombe, and Shelley being kept by the House of Commons. De Ros not arrived, nor yet Henry Molyneux.

" I never saw My Lord in greater force, nor better trim, and all was perfect, and my Lady of course ditto, and she and I played at Ecarté for an hour and a half. . . ."

" June 4th.

" . . . Nothing could exceed yesterday in all ways. It was a pleasure too to see our beloved Sovereign enjoy it as he seemed to do, and I never saw him look better in all my life. He drove up the course with little George of Cumberland by his side, with 7 carriages and 31 outriders, besides footmen seated behind the carriages. Indeed if you come to that, I thought we were not amiss. My Lord turning out *four* of *his own* carriages, two with his own horses, and two with 4 posters in each. We passed George Payne driving his four in hand just before we reached Ascot, Lord Worcester by his side on the box, and Holyoak and others on the roof. It was a sincere pleasure to me to see George's horse ' Belzone ' beat the King's *two* horses. . . . Jersey went into the King's stand after the Race and found the Sovereign in high good humour about it, observing he had always said Mr. Payne's horse would be too much for his mare, and he added *he was a little nervous about*

Thursday ; i.e. when his Mare ' Fleur de Lys ' that he bought off our Mat Ridley, is to run for the Cup. Sefton had got a private stand prepared for his party, so all was charming.   I belonged to the same carriage with Lord Grey, and he was as pleased as Punch all the time.   In the evening, that is at dinner, we had 13 quarts of turtle from the London Tavern to console us, and there is to be a similar importation today. The dinner was sufficiently gay, and the night even *boisterous*, in as much as at our *Gallery* or low Whist Table, Mull, Jules and I sang a medley of French and English so loud and to tunes so charmingly popular that we broke up the *deep* whist table, and the Clerk of the Council, Greville, was so sulky, he would never utter afterwards ; Sefton, Grey, and all the Ladies being convulsed at our merits and success.   The campaign concluded by a game at sudden death, or single handed commerce, upon a considerable scale, and as the pool was won by Tom Duncombe, who had never played at this difficult game before, we thought it due to the Hon'ble. Member for Hertford to *chair* him, which we did with great effect. . . ."

" June 5th.

" . . . Old Dow: Salisbury was on the course yesterday, and went from thence with Downshire and Atty Hill to dine at the Christopher at Eton, and go down with Downshire's Tom Hillsbro' in a boat to Stanley Hall (4th of June), and Mull and Geo Anson who were there, saw her in the midst of the boats and boys."

" Whitehall, June 17th.

" . . . Frances* and I took the field at last, and arrived at Holly Lodge† about 5.   Somewhat late for a

* Mrs. Taylor.   † Duchess of St. Albans' (Mrs. Coutts).

breakfast you will say that was fixed for *one*, but Lord Chesterfield, Mrs. Fox Lane and Lady Radnor were in the carriage before us, and Lord Bristol and family in the one behind us, so that we were not singular, you see. The day must have thinned the party considerably, but there were quite enough to make it very pretty, and very gay. The ground too being well suited to the occasion in its own gaiety in flowers, walks, and lawns, &c. . . . In a short time we went into the house, every room of which was full of tables, and eatables, and having very soon fallen in with *Nell*, she would willingly have conducted us to the room where the Duchess was regaling the Dukes of Cumberland, Sussex, and Prince Leopold with *turtle*, but we preferred humble company and humbler food, so we took to the Chesterfield and Bristol party —*white* soup &c. When old Dow. Coutts made her rounds into the other room we fell in with her, and I was presented, and a more disgusting, frowsy, hairy old B. could not have been found in the Seven Dials. . . .

" You would have been pleased to see a group of our London young ladies shooting with bows and arrows at targets—the elegant attitudes they put themselves into were really *too*. We were there about 2 hours, and it answered extremely well. . . .

" Old Coutts asked Mrs. Taylor if she had seen the *basket*, and upon answering no, it was sent for, and a most beautiful silver one it was, and it had been presented yesterday morning to old Blowsy by her Duke, it being that day twelve month they were married, and there was a device of a *flitch* of Bacon in lard at the bottom of the basket, with four lines of poetry to accompany it, the termination of one being ' marriage vow,' and the next one ' Eleanor's and my

friend old " *Dunmow* ".'* Now to think of poor people
actually starving for want of vituals, and this prodigal
fool and devil to be alive and merry."

Earl of Sefton to Creevey

" August 1st.

" . . . We shall be delighted to see you Monday,
and are determined to make you go with us to Chichester the 11th, for Goodwood Races.   We go to the
Inn, and you will be much amused." . . .

" August 2nd.

" I forgot to tell you in my letter yesterday that we
shall only stay 2 or 3 days at Chichester, and then
go to Ld. Robert's.†   I think the whole of this will
suit you, as you will have quite enough of Michael
in your Northern trip, and I have often heard you say
you had a wish to go to Ld. R's."

Creevey to Miss Ord

" August 7th.

" . . . Sefton says that when Greville attended
the King the other day as Clerk of the Council then
held before him, the King said to him, ' Well, Charles,
you have got your place in Jamaica ‡ at last, do you
mean to leave us and resign your clerkship of the
Council ? ' and when Greville replied (in substance)
' *Du tout, du tout*,' Prinney said, ' Well, Charles, you
can't be better pleased at getting this place than I
am at my *mare " Maria " winning the Cup*. . . .'
Lord Jersey told Sefton there never was any thing like
him and the spirits he was in the day he gave the

* The Dunmow Flitch ceremony needs no particularisation.
† Lord R. Spencer's at Woolbeding, Midhurst.
‡ As Secretary for Jamaica, Greville never visited the Island, but he
advanced its interests at home.   He remained Chief Clerk until 1857.

19

dinner at *St. James's Palace* to his brother Jockeys of the Turf. . . . He would *handycap* all their horses, after dinner, for future matches, i.e., specifying the *weights* they should carry according to sex and age, and upon some general satisfaction being expressed at the result of his arrangement, he said, He was delighted and he did not think there was so good a hand in England at a *handycap* as himself. . . . The dinner was indifferent, and the champagne worse ; so much so that Prinney said, ' Jersey, that champagne is damned bad, is it not ; very odd that I never can get a good bottle of Sillery ? ' Jersey could not deny the fact, and so by way of parrying the observation, said, ' I never tasted finer Claret than Your Majesty's.' ' Ah ! ' said Prinney, ' there you are right, Jersey, I don't believe any man in England has better claret than I have.' Now was there r-a-a-lly ever ? A King aged 66, of such a country and in such times ! . . .''

                    " Dolphin Inn, Chichester, August 11th.

'' . . . The drive here of sixty miles,* is not, I think, to be surpassed for beauty in England for that extent. The men and maids were the advanced guard, and we followed in the shooting carriage. . . .

'' Our Hotel here we found really perfection, and the dinner not less so when it came. During its continuance, a note came from the Duchess of Richmond† to Lady Sefton, really an extremely pretty one, saying she could not bear to think of her being so near them and at an Inn, and saying also that owing to some excuses they had received, they could now take them in, and begging them to come. This being

* From Stoke, Windsor.
† Wife of 5th Duke. Daughter of Henry, Marquis of Anglesey.

declined, the Duke has sent my Lord half a Buck lest
we should starve here.   Sefton says he would not have
gone there upon any account.   I have been always in
error in thinking they were there before.   They never
were, they were *here* at this house upon a visit to
Berkeley with his Regiment, but both Sefton and my
Lady have been most intimate with the Duchess from
her childhood, and her note expressed her obligation
to both. . . .''

" August 13th.

" Our ' Bobadilla ' has won, and very easily too.

" This makes it impossible that I should go into
the North with the Taylors.

" Well, and so what shall I do with myself ?   Shall
I be off for France, or Ireland ?   Sefton swears I shall
stay a fortnight at *least* at Stoke, to which place we
shall get on Sunday.   On Saturday we go early to
Petworth, and stay all night.   Ld. Egremont* was in
the Stand today when this was settled.''

" Bedroom, Woolbeding, August 15th.

" . . . This corner of Sussex is as desirable for a
residence, if not more so, than any I know ; and
Goodwood is the choicest spot ; *dry* soil and *down* are
first rate ingredients with me ; then the Park is very
spacious, beautifully wooded, with every inequality
and variety of ground, and commanding beautiful
views of both *sea* and land.   The house is a handsome
one to look at tho' of an irregular shape, but the
interior, which I went over yesterday, is perfection.
. . . The Hall which you enter has very handsome
pillars in it, but they don't crowd it and darken it as

* George O'Brien, Earl of Egremont.   George Wyndham, adopted
heir of the 3rd Earl, was created Lord Leconfield and succeeded to
Petworth when the Egremont peerage died out.

they do at Lowther, Thorndon, Wentworth, and Raby. They are not in one's way, and it is a charming room or place to walk about in, as the Duke and I did without hats on. . . . The Duke took me about the house in a most good humoured, natural way, and I should have liked to have spent two or three hours more there. The Dining Room, Libraries, &c. &c. are all as good as possible, and there are some beautiful pictures scattered up and down in different rooms and staircases, that one ought to see collected in the picture gallery which is to be. Everybody belonging to the founder of the family, Charles the 2nd., is to be found there, as you may suppose, in original pictures by different masters. . . . An original one by Vandyke of your Charles the 2nd. as a boy, and as like as two p's. . . .

"There were quantities of visitors in the house, many of whom, of course, one knows as *brother dandys* or Turf Men and many I did not. They were scattered about in the Libraries, Billiard Room, Hall, and Drawing Room . . . and the whole seemed as gay and cheerful a concern as one could see anywhere, and I came away mighty pleased with both the Master and his house. What a contrast, we all said, to Arundel. That horrid, dismal *benighted* castle, with a gallery in it 190 feet long of the most dingy oak, and a window at the *top* of each end to light it, and everything else in the place equally dismal. Lady Sefton said really a good thing upon the subject. There are about a dozen enormous owls in the keep,* not of the old stock, but imported of late years from America, as large as eagles, and the same black brown colour, with enormous eyes set in large scarlet or orange coloured borders, the latter being parts of their eyes, so Lady

* I.e. at Arundel.

Sefton said, ' I have no patience with the Duke for keeping the poor things stretching their eyes in the *light* for people to look at, the gallery is quite the place for them to live in.' . . .

" Well, we left the Dolphin yesterday, exceedingly pleased with our *fare*, and the expense of which my Lord thought ' not out of the way,' £40, but £10 of that was for post horses, and as we brought away £700 that Bobadilla won us, it was all very well, you know. The Race Course is the prettiest possible just outside of the Park Wall, and a delightful, cheerful, commodious stand just the reverse of that at Chelmsford. Here, of course, we had the contents of Goodwood and the neighbourhood, which is well supplied with good company. Cowdray turned out a large party daily (Poyntzs), *Isabella Exeter* * (as the Copleys call her), his Daughter, Lord Exeter, Tom Manners &c. &c. Poyntz himself was damned affable with me, and as for Walter Burrell, and his rib, nothing will serve them but my coming to them on the 10th. of next month to meet her Brother, Edward Ellice, and *Ly. Hannah*.† Lord Charles Somerset from Goodwood was my constant play-fellow in the Stand, and tomorrow he meets us at Petworth. . . .

" Tell Annie there is a most beautiful old building at Chichester of a *Cross*, the centre of the four principal streets, built by a Bishop of Chichester in the reign of Edward the 4th., with which both Lady Sefton and I fell in love. . . .

" We found here‡ the Ponsonbys § of course, and

---

* Wife of 2nd Marquis and daughter of William Stephen Poyntz of Cowdray.

† Lady Hannah Ellice was a sister of Earl Grey. A note on Edward Ellice will be found at the beginning of Chapter XX.

‡ At Woolbeding.

§ George Ponsonbys.

Fan,* Sir Geo. Robinson, Rogers and Motteux. Poor Lord Robert is feeble in all ways I think except in *eating*. The place is very limited, the house likewise, the dining room excepted, which is excellent. The dinner inferior to no one's, and the wine aussi, but then all's told, for any thing more dull cannot possibly be conceived. . . .

" Poor Lady Sefton does not show today from having a terrible *headache* (as *he* says) but I never knew such a thing happen before. I suspect it is all a sham to escape the bore of the thing. She made all kinds of *quiet* signs to me last night of her despair, till we got to our Ecarté, which by the bye we had every night at the Dolphin. . . ."

" Woolbeding, August 16th.

" . . . The day is brilliant. . . . I had not a notion of seeing trees of such magnitude and of such modern growth. There are Cedars, Planes, Spanish Chesnuts, &c. all really monstrous trees,† one may say, and all of his planting. . . . I walked over to Cowdray and about its ruins yesterday, and a great place it must have been of Queen Elizabeth's time of building. Poyntz has built another modern moderate house in another part of the Park. He came over here to make a morning call yesterday at *half past six* accompanied by Lady Clinton (another of his Daughters), Lord Clinton, Miss Poyntz, William Bathurst, Pierpoint &c., and we walked by the fountain,‡ which is always the subject of admiration but Bob never mentioned where it came from of course in

---

* Frances, daughter of Lady Robert and the Hon. E. Bouverie.
† A giant Tulip-tree to-day takes pride of place.
‡ This famous fountain, ascribed to John of Bologna or to Benvenuto Cellini, stood at Cowdray until the fire.

the presence of the Montagues.* We had a much more jolly day yesterday than the one before. Sefton and I arranged ourselves better at dinner. I took Fan in hand, and he the Amazonian Di.,† and now I think I have done with Woolbeding. . . ."

"Stoke, August 18th.

" . . . After finishing my letter at Woolbeding on Saturday, we all took most beautiful and agreeable walks (all I mean except Lord Robert), and every thing ended as well as possible, and the old Man asked me if I could not come again before the winter. So it was all very well. We started about 3 for Petworth, which was only 7 miles off, Sefton's object being to see Lord Egremont's Racing Stud before dinner ; passed thro' Cowdray Park which tho' pretty enough is very inferior to all other parks and places in that district. It has one ornament, however, which I should fancy is not to be found through England besides, and that is a very considerable avenue of Spanish Chesnut Trees as large as the oldest oak trees one sees, and as fresh as the youngest. We were soon, as you may suppose, at Petworth, the outside of which was familiar to my recollection of 30 years past, when I rode from Chichester to look at it. A very long, modern white or grey building of two stories high without a wing or a portico or pillar or even a *door* except you call a window one ; for it is more like the latter than the former. I think there are 21 or 22 great windows in a line in front, but the length is immense. . . . I was much amused in going thro' one room, where I was lost in admiration of a portrait of

---

* Mr. Poyntz married the last Lord Montagu's heiress. Creevey later corrects a " canard " that Lord Robert " appropriated " the fountain in the confusion of fire.

† Mrs. Ponsonby.

Lord Strafford by Vandyke, and another of an Earl of
Northumberland by the same, to hear Lord Egremont
say as he was walking on, ' Lord Sefton there is your
Mother.' ' God, so there is,' said Sefton, ' and very
like too,' and shortly afterwards walking by the side
of one of the young Ladies he said, ' There's your
Grandmother,' and true enough there was the Mar-
gravine.   Now far be it from me to insinuate that
these two ladies belonged to my Lord's Seraglio, but
certain it is never persons were more worthy of it,
and in truth I dare say they were so.   What made this
the more funny to my own private thoughts was our
stopping shortly after in another room, at a modern
showy picture in which Lord Egremont was a principal figure, when the Royal and Foreign Grandees
were in England in 1814.   They spent a day and night
at Petworth, and as artists are always allowed to do
what they like there, one of them was upon the spot
to make a picture of this melting scene. . . . The
figures are the Emperor of Russia with his Sister the
Duchess of Oldenburgh upon his arm in the act of
being introduced by the Prince Regent to Lord
Egremont. . . . Lord Yarmouth behind the Prince,
Lord Charles Bentinck behind the King of Prussia
. . . Lord Egremont, Lady Burrell, and all her Sisters
in front, and her Brothers and others behind, and on
looking at this side of the picture Lord Egremont
said, ' Lady Sefton, don't you see anybody you know
there ? ' and sure enough there is Berkeley Craven as
like as life.   It was comical, was it not, to see him in
such company after what had just passed ? and I
should not at all wonder if he was one of old Egremont's very numerous Stud. . . .

    " . . . We formed in a very excellent habitable
library and drawing room united, our party being

nearly domestic—us five, Ld. Egremont and Misses
Wyndham, Mr. King and Mrs. who was one of the
Misses Wyndham, and a Brother of his, the eldest male
Wyndham, Lord Charles Somerset, and his Daughter,
Mrs. Wyndham, Lady Emily Marsham (sister to Lord
Romney and niece of Lord *Egremont*, and who lives at
Petworth) a Chaplain and another young Lady. . . .

  " The dinner was of the first order, turtle, venison,
moor game, &c. without stint. The servants, too,
very numerous tho' most of them very advanced in
years and tottered, and comical in their looks. The
wax candles too were sufficiently numerous to light
us all up well tho' we were at one end of a room sixty
feet long, the wainscoat of which was Gibbons' carving
in wood. . . . However, all went off extremely well,
and as a specimen of Egremont's *dryness*, let me mention that Sefton said, ' This is very good Claret, Lord
Egremont,' to which the other was pleased to reply in
his manner, ' Is it ? ' . . . By half past ten the Ladies
of the house were all gone to bed, leaving those of
this house to follow their own inventions, nor was this
the only proof of the early habits of the whole house,
for observing a footman bring in a glass of wine and
water to the Chaplain, Sefton said to me, ' You'd
better take this opportunity of getting some too, or
you'll be done,' so I went and asked him to bring me
a glass likewise, and the self same footman returned
in a very few minutes saying the Butler *was gone to
bed*. I thought Sefton would have burst at this, as
being much too good a thing to have ever happened.
. . . Mr. King's account of the servants was, that
there were more of them in that house of both sexes,
and in all departments, than in any house in England,
that they were all very good in their way, but that
they could not stand being put out of it, and were

never interfered with, that they were all bred upon the spot, and all related to each other. . . ."

". . . I was rather fidgetty in the morning to be about the house after the pictures, but my valet did not bring my cloaths till near nine, and then I started. In coming into the Hall, it is but justice to the servants to say, that if they like early hours to go to bed by, in the morning they are at their posts with the lark, for I found there two gentlemen out of livery, and *the* foot boy with coffee pots, tea pots, kettles, chafing dishes to keep rolls etc. hot, and everything in the eatable way, and I was directly asked whether I would breakfast *there*, and *where* I would have it. This, I was told afterwards, always lasts from 9 till 12. I declined their offer for the present, and I begged one of the gentlemen to conduct me . . . As my guide never left me I could only run over these pictures hastily, and come away . . . Fortunately in one of the rooms, old Egremont came *slouching* by me ; so says I, ' Pray, Lord Egremont, what is that curious picture of the coach and six . . . ? ' ' Ah ! ' says he, ' it is a devilish clever picture, is it not ? Let's go look at it,' and so we did, and it was a picture of Charles the 2nd. going an airing with *Ladies* just turning out of Whitehall. The present front of that building being part of the picture, and all in the calèche and out of it being portraits. Having observed upon the horses, and other things in it being so clever, he fixed his eyes upon a picture of a handsome woman, that was evidently being copied, and he said, ' Did you ever see a handsomer face than that ? ' ' Never,' says I, ' by whom was it done ? ' ' By Sir Joshua Reynolds,' says he. ' How long has it been painted ? ' ' 50 years,' said he, and as he still stood looking at it, I at length said, ' Whose picture is it,

Lord Egremont ? ' ' Oh ! ' he said, ' it was a lady not much known in the world,' and he turned away. . . . It is in vain to attempt anything like a detailed description of the *immensity* of pictures on the ground floor of the house, and, as I was informed, all the rooms above are full of them. Then they are all mixed up together, good and bad, . . . and he is perpetually changing their places. . . .

" Take a specimen of the style of the house from the sixty foot dining room. In the centre of one side stands Henry the 8th, a full length, the finest Holbein I ever saw, and an immense picture—upon his two shoulders are perched two heads by Sir Joshua, the late Ladies Carnarvon and Romney, Lord Egremont's two Sisters. At the top and bottom of the room are a Duke and Duchess of Somerset of James the First's time, great full lengths. On one side of Henry the 8th, the modern ' *Proud* ' Duke of Somerset (as he was called), and as he was the patron of Gibbons the Carver, his full length picture is set in carved flowers, festoons, baskets, &c. His Wife in another similar compartment by his side, and on the other side of Henry the 8th. two other females of his family in the same way. Immense as these pictures are with all their garniture there are still panels to spare, and as he always has artists ready in the house, in one of these compartments, you have Petworth Park by Turner, in another Lord Egremont taking a walk with nine dogs, that are his constant companions, by the same artist ; . . . The only room with any pretension to regularity in its pictures is what is called the breakfast room, a most beautifully proportioned white and gold modern room, with four splendid full length Vandyke Ladies in it. . . . In a party of Titian, Rembrandt, . . . Turner, Reynolds, . . . &c. he,

Lord E., said, ' You know that picture ? ' . . . I never saw it before, or heard of it. The Painter's name is Leslie,* the subject is Sancho Pancha . . . it is the cleverest and prettiest thing I ever saw. Was your *Sally Jennings*† (in lodge) done from Petworth ? She is there, but I could not see by what master. . . . There is no peerage here, and I can't remember how Sir Wm. Wyndham was connected with the Percys, as well as Somersets,‡ but of Earls of Northumberland and Lords Percy, there are pictures by Vandyke without end . . . But now I must have bored you to death, and so I leave Petworth, as I did on Sunday at half past eleven with infinite regret at not seeing more, for I never saw any place under a more agreeable or stronger excitement.

" Well, here is our old Duchess of Newcastle, and she and Lady Sefton and I had a real set to at Ecarté last night, and tonight I shall have old Sally Salisbury to play at whist with, and Greville and Giles and Lord and Lady Worcester. This day week, the Cowpers and Lievens come, and I am told I shall not stir till they are gone, . . . and now prepare yourself for a resolution I have come to of taking a trip to *Ireland*, when I leave this place. My mind is quite made up. . . ."

" Stoke, August 24th.

". . . I am greatly indebted to you for all your information, and learning about *Cellini*, which I shall put by in a safe corner, as well as for your trouble in

* Charles Robert Leslie's " Sancho and the Duchess." Among the pictures noticed by Creevey are : Nos. 311, 223, 382, 340, 268, 89, 135, 143, 137, 345, 344, 132, 34, and 197 in the Petworth Catalogue (1920).

† Wife of 1st Duke of Marlborough.

‡ The vast property of the 7th Duke of Somerset was on his death divided between Sir Hugh Smithson (afterwards created Duke of Northumberland) and Sir W. Wyndham.

extracting Lord Egremont's pedigree from the peerage.   Upon the first subject let me observe in justice
to Lord Robert, that Sefton heard him say, Poyntz
had given him the fountain, and more than that, that
he doubted his power to do so considering it as a heir-
loom.*   All that I can depose to is what ' the Comical '
told me himself, viz., that he saw it in a state of great
delapidation after the fire, and that it cost him £100
to remove it, repair it, and put it up at Woolbeding.
Lady Caroline Molyneux has made me a very pretty
drawing of it as well as of Petworth, which I shall bring
back with me.   There was a large silver [*obliterated*]
by Cellini in Lord Montague's possession, which was
sold with the rest of his plate.   Poyntz married the
only Sister of the Lord Montague who was drowned,
by whom he had Cowdray ; and their two and only
sons, you may remember, were drowned a few years
ago at Bognor by the upsetting of a sailing boat, in
which Poyntz himself was and most narrowly escaped
drowning too.   All in the presence of Mrs. Poyntz
who was on shore.   Cowdray is now settled after
Poyntz and Mrs. Poyntz's death upon their three
daughters equally, Lady Chester, Lady Exeter, and
Miss Poyntz. . . . Lord Egremont has a nephew † who
succeeds to the title, but succeeding to his property
depends almost entirely upon his own will and
pleasure, and thus I close my account with him and
Petworth for the present. . . .

    ". . . We have really had a very jolly week here,
the two old girls, Newcastle and Salisbury, staying all
the week, and being above even themselves, altho'
the Duchess considers Old Salisbury as the arrantest
old profligate the town can produce, and on the other

* The offer was made and accepted in the courtyard at Cowdray.
† George Francis, 4th and last Earl.

hand Sally holds the Duchess in the uttermost contempt as an unenlightened provincial. The voices
of these lovely females too are everything one could
wish. Sally's is that of Lord Thurlow, whilst I
know no pipe so slender as that of the Duchess, . . ."

" August 28th.

". . . Madame Lieven goes to call on Mrs.
Conyngham but she returns here. Nothing can equal
her graciousity except her playing upon the piano-
forte, which is real genius and inspiration. My Lord
and his Daughters were lost last night in astonishment
and admiration of her performance. Do you remember
my ever having been mixed up at Brussels with the
Prince—Pierre D'Aremberg ? I had, and now have,
some indistinct impression of it, but he, however,
brought it to a *pint* yesterday at dinner by calling
upon Monsieur Creevey to drink a verre de vin with
him as an old ami de Bruxelles, and then I heard him
telling all about him, how I succoured the Blessés
après la Bataille de Waterloo, and afterwards we had
such handshaking and pawing that r-a-ally I was
never more affraid of exposures in my life, and he has
been at it again this morning. He says Brussels is
increased by a third, and greatly beautified—the
ramparts being converted into Boulevards, and very
good houses built upon them. . . ."

" August 29th.

" What a *natural* Wag Alvanley is ; how different
from these artificial conversation makers Luttrell,
Rogers & Co. Never man was so improved as William
Lamb,* whether from gaining his title, or losing his
Wife I know not.

* Lord Melbourne.   His wife was Lady Caroline Lamb.

". . . Montrond too, is a natural and really a gay wag, always alive, and yet in the quietest way. We continue great cronies, and he is always a resource. Our Luttrell can't bear the sight of him, because he told him he could not for his life make out what was the advice he gave to Julia. Luttrell's poem, you know, of ' Advice to Julia,' . . .''

CHAPTER XIII

1828 (*continued*)

Creevey to Miss Ord

" Morrisons Hotel, *Dear* Dublin, Sept. 3rd.

" HAVING just dined in the Coffee Room of my Hotel here I may as well mention what I have done since I left Mr. Smythe Owen's * yesterday. It is utterly impossible to do justice to my drive of yesterday. . . . You go thro' the whole of Wales *in the air*. How you get there (it is so imperceptable) one can't tell, but there you are at the top of the mountain, with those beautiful valleys below you. Look out of the window and you think again and again the Rocks and woods *must* stop you, but round some corner or other you always go in a road just as good as Regent Street, and about half as wide, and with a wall on each side to protect you from falling into the valleys, of 80 miles in length . . . between Shrewsbury and Holyhead . . . Having started from the former place at 8 a.m. we did our 110 miles by 4 p.m. with the most perfect ease. . . .

" . . . Dublin tells its own story. The Aristocracy have sold their country to England ; they have left excellent streets and publick buildings to starve in, and to tumble down, and they have bribed in return England to make the most beautiful publick roads, by which they may come backwards and forwards to review the effects of their own infamy—but this is a digression produced by too much *filling*

* Condover Hall, Salop.

for my native land . . . A valet being ordered to carry my portmanteau up to my bedroom, I sallied out de suite to see the town, but another chap, genuine Irish, pursued me, with a ' Pray, your Honor will you give your name lest any gentleman should call upon you ? ' so says I, ' My name is upon my Portmanteau, but its so and so ; I suppose there is no letter for me,' and off he went, and out he and about three others came again, the Chief compris, with a letter in his hand ; . . . ' Sir,' said the Chief, ' Colonel Morrison has been here for you these three days. He has received a letter from Lord Melbourne, and he is *determined* to show you every *possible* civility in his power.' . . . ' Col. Morrison insisted upon your having a good room.' . . . Upon my soul it was damned ' civil ' in Lamb, because, as I said to you, it was quite gratuitous, and for many, many years we have been very spiteful blades to each other. . . ."

" Dublin, Septr. 11th.

" Well, tonight I am off for Duncannon per Mail to Waterford. . . .

" On Saturday . . . I dined . . . at Lord Francis Leveson's,* and I must say once and for all, that greater civility I defy any one to receive than I have done from him, his rib, and from Lady Charlotte. Our company was the Jerseys, Lady Cloncurry, *Lady Morgan*,† Miss Latouche, and the Men I forget. The Morgan was of course the Lioness. She was dying for a display, but Lord Jersey who was on one side of her was so cursedly affraid of her, that he was nearer crying than trying to bring her out. . . . My fun was in making my playfellow Miss Latouche *burst* at

* Afterwards 1st Earl of Ellesmere. Now Chief Secretary.

† Sydney, Lady Morgan, a very successful novelist of Irish life (1783–1859).

20

Mother Morgan who was just opposite to us. In person she resembles a tetotum. Her face and neck were painted a bright red, her bonnet was of the same colour in silk, and circular in shape, turned up all round at the edge, with four red feathers at equal distance from each other, drooping, or rather flowing from the bonnet like water. Her attachment to the colour was shown in her gown, and descended even to her shoes. We had a very agreeable day altogether. Lord Francis took me aside before dinner to tell me who the Company was for fear of accidents, and it was well he did so, as Miss Latouche fell to my lot, and I might as well have talked to her of Wm. Lamb as of any body else whereas it turned out that dear Miss Latouche was own sister to Lady Brandon that Lamb is in the Crim: Con: with.* . . ."

" Bessborough, Sept. 13th.

" . . . This is a charming place ; I ought to say *as to its position and surrounding scenery*—magnificent. The House itself is a handsome Grey stone House, in shape and size like Howick as *it was*. It was built in 1745, and the Lord Bessborough who built it, showed his taste in his selection of the spot for doing it. Its South Front is on a slope in the Park, with a very handsome and very wide terrace. . . .

" Duncannon is all kindness and intelligence, and My Lady all amiability. . . ."

" Sept. 14th.

" . . . There are from 14 to 20 children of the Duncannons † here, all most amiable and *white*. The eldest son, a young man grown, and a capital

* Lord Brandon was non-suited.

† John William, afterwards 4th Earl of Bessborough, married Lady Maria Fane, daughter of 10th Earl of Westmorland. They had thirteen children.

fellow with the best manners. Miss Ponsonby,* the eldest of the race, seems too a most good, refined, amiable person, tho' in appearance a striking and yet unfavorable likeness to her Grandmother Bessborough, even in her advanced years. A Mr. Fane, brother to the Brussels Fane, is a visitor here at present, and a stupid, pompous, rum, touch he is, and Mr. McDonald, son of the man at the Horse Guards, is another visitor, and then we have Mr. Gurney who has £800 a year as steward and for managing the property, and who turns out to have been in the same college with myself at Cambridge, and a man I knew a little of formerly. . . .

" . . . This climate is such that *myrtles* grow out of doors all the year round without protection of any kind, and are now in the highest beauty, as you would see if the *posy* I am now wearing was placed before your eyes. The little girls tap at my door twice a day with a bunch of this article. We are now all going to Church. . . ."

" Sept. 19th.

" . . . My delight in this place remains unabated. Lady Duncannon is a charming person, her life here is devoted to looking after everybody, and in making them *clean*, and comfortable in their persons, cloaths, cottages, and everything, and her success is great indeed. *He too* in addition to his greater qualities is all after their cleanliness too. I wish you had seen us walking up Pilltown last Saturday. Good old Irish usage in cottages and indeed houses is to place the dirt and filth of the house at the entrance instead of behind it, and this was reformed in every house but one as we walked thro', and Duncannon having called the old woman out of this one told her he *would not*

* Georgiana, married Rev. S. Bourke.

have that filth remain in that place, and she must remove it out of sight ; to which she was pleased to reply, ' Well, my dear, if you do but walk by next Tuesday not a bit of the dirt shall you see remaining, and as for the matter of that, now in your Honor's presence will I lay the first stone of my new back yard,' and away she went with a huge stone in both hands. . . .

" Yesterday Duncannon presided in the same room at his Petty Sessions, and I was as much struck with his good sense as with the effect that his presence and impartial administration of justice must produce upon the great population of these parts.

" The History of this family may be said to be the history of ill fated Ireland. Duncannon's great Grandfather began building this house in 1745, he finished it in 1755, and lived in it till 1757 (two years), when he died. His Son left Ireland when 18 years old, and having never seen it more, died in 1792. Upon that event his Son, the present Lord Bessborough, made his first visit to the place, and he is not certain whether it was *two* or *three* days he staid here, but it was one or the other. In 1808, he and Lady Bessborough came a tour to *the Lake of Killarney*, and having taken their own house in their way either going or coming, they were so pleased with it as to stay here a *week*, and once more in 1812 having come over to see the young Duke of Devonshire at Lismore, when his Father died, they were here a month. So that from 1757 to 1825, 68 years, the family was [here] 5 weeks and two days. . . . My dears, it is absenteeism on the part of Landlords, and the havoc that middle men make with their property that plays the very devil. . . . I think the 2nd. girl * here (a very tall

* Augusta, married, first, William, Earl of Kerry; secondly, Hon. Charles Gore. Bishop Charles Gore was her youngest son.

MARIA, VISCOUNTESS DUNCANNON.
From a painting by Sir Thomas Lawrence, P.R.A., in the possession of
the Earl of Bessborough, at Stansted.

[To face p. 286.

one of 14 or 15) is likely to be as beautiful a woman as
one shall see, and so very amiable too.   They all are,
both girls and boys, and Mother and Father ;   and
all that is quite charming.   I am happy, however, to
say there are but 12 of them.   I'll tell you a curious
pint.   Miss Ponsonby (upon whose judgement I have
perfect reliance) has a school at Roehampton as well as
here, and she says the difference in her scholars is
perfectly astonishing, her Irish ones are not only so
much quicker in learning, but so very much more
desirous of doing so than her English ones.   She says
it is an absolute pleasure to teach the former.   The
Mother is divine. . . .''

" Sept. 20th.

" I don't know that I have anything to say to you
today except it is to laud and magnify Lady Duncannon.   After luncheon yesterday she asked me if I
would go with her to *Mountain Grove*. . . . My Lady's
mode of travelling is on a little poney, she sitting
sideways in a chair saddle ;   one of the little girls was
on another poney ;   My Lord and I sauntered on foot
by her side.   She got off and went into different
cottages as we went.   She gives prizes for the *cleanest*
cottages, and as the time is approaching when the
Curate is to decide this point, she put her Cottagers
in mind of it, but there is a simplicity and interest
and kindness in every communication of hers with the
people here, and on their part a natural unreserved
confidential kind of return to it, that is striking to
the greatest degree ;   add to which that the manners
of both men and women are *perfect*, and much more
French than English.

" Mountain Grove is protected from depredation
by a gentleman of the name of *Fahy*, with a salary of

£10 per annum. He lives alone by its side, and such is his reputation for strength and match in fight, that neither man nor men have ever dared to touch a stick upon his premises. . . . I was charmed with his agility in an enormous great coat at an age of nearly 70. . . . As it was Lady Duncannon's first visit *this* year, he was delighted to see her, so with his hat in his hand he said, ' You are welcome to Mountain Grove, My Lady,' and when he would *lead* her poney thro' any brook, which she wanted him not to do so, all the answer she got was, ' I am not tender, My Lady.' . . . I have thought it right just to give you this literal morning's rural tour of Lady Duncannon's here for the purpose of comparison with a morning's outing of her Sister, Lady Jersey, in London. She is so neat too always, and so pretty, so sweet tempered with her children, and every body else, and so happy. Then whether she understands what she reads, it is not for me to say, but she *does* read, and very good books too, and now I think I have given you a sufficient dose of domestic matter. . . ."

" Sept. 22nd.

" . . . My affection for Dear Bessborough remains to the last. . . .

" . . . We dined an hour earlier yesterday because our two eldest boys had to go 20 miles after dinner to catch the packet below Waterford, and to go by her to Milford Haven. The eldest, Johnny,* aged 19, going to his private tutor, and Freddy,† aged 13, going to a school at Dulwich where there are 12 boys. They are charming creatures, as they are all. Miss Ponsonby aged 21, very dumpy and homely, mais

* 5th Earl.
† 6th Earl. Well known as a cricketer at Harrow and a founder of I.Z.

très aimable, Gussy,* aged 14, very tall with a most beautiful face and countenance. . . . Two girls 9 and 10, one the image of her Aunt, Lady Caroline Lamb, but both pretty enough ; two boys 7 and 8, then two little girls and an infant Hercules of a boy†, all running about, and all the merriest, sweetest tempered children possible ; the second boy is at Sea. . . .

" I think I never had a *greater benefit* than in this house. . . ."

Creevey's tour next took him to Killarney Lakes, and to Lord Donoughmore's at Knocklofty.

" Kilfane, Oct. 4th.

" . . . Mrs. Power . . . is quite charming, and so is her married Daughter, Mrs. Burton. She, poor thing, has but one eye, the other having been put out by play with a Sister and Brother ; barring this, she is beautiful, and in manner sweetness itself, and *quite Irish*. Mr. Power is a man of 50, straight as an arrow and 6 feet high at least, very handsome must have been . . . and a perfectly well-bred man of the world. Bad as the day was, he had been ahunting with his hounds, and when we arrived had gone to bed. He appeared, however, before dinner, and I should think we sat down to it 16 or 18. . . . The dinner was incomparable. Mrs. Power says I *shall* have a receipt for the soup, and she has just given me with her own hand a book very difficult to get, relating to their Kilkenny Theatricals. . . . This House was Head Quarters. These Plays were acted for 3 weeks every autumn at Kilkenny, and for 20 years together the men were amateurs, the Ladies professional ones from Dublin. It was here that Mr. Becher and Miss

* Augusta.
† Spencer, afterwards Sir S. Ponsonby-Fane, of I.Z. fame.

O'Neill acted lovers together till they married.
Tommy Moore and other Wits were actors. The
receipts for the 3 weeks were £1,200, £700 paid everything, and £500 went to Charities. Grattan and his
family used to be here. Was there ever? and all
this in revolutionary Ireland. . . .

" This is an admirable house, excellent Library,
and capital collection of books. A beautiful Park
very well stocked with deer and mirth, hospitality
and good humour. . . ."

" Morrison's Hotel, Oct. 6th.

" . . . To attempt doing justice to the Power
family is really beyond my ability, such quiet, well-
bred hospitality on his part, and so much *hart* (as she
calls it) on hers. . . . We had a haunch of venison
each day, and a succession of visitors. It is a very
populous neighbourhood, I mean of families, and as I
observed before, he is the most popular man in the
County of Kilkenny. . . .

" . . . He has 5 sons and 2 Daughters. The
Eldest is gone to Corfu in despair on account of Miss
Ponsonby having refused him. What a damned fool
she must be ; every one speaks of him as perfection,
both in looks and merit of every description. *She*
was left at Bessborough. . . .

" . . . I have been to pay my respects at the
Castle. Lord Francis was engaged, but I saw
Greville, who asked me to dine at the Secretary's
today, but I told him where I was going. . . . Charles
Greville won £1,300 at Doncaster. . . ."

" Bessborough, Oct. 24th.

" . . . Let me see what gleanings I have from
Kilfane.

" Mrs. Power is charmingly *Irish*, and indeed so is

every one who *lives* in Ireland. *She* is the image of
old Lady Ponsonby in perpetual flying about, and
activity, and the neatness of her in everything is
beyond. . . .

" . . . The Butler, *John Cain*, the best of servants,
of 30 years standing, and with all the privileges of
such long service . . . occasionally gives his opinion
whilst waiting at dinner. A little time since, Lord
Geo. Beresford dining at Kilfane and declining either
to eat or drink something for fear of gout, Mrs.
Power gave it as her opinion that low living was very
bad for the gout, upon which John Cain was pleased
to observe, ' All I can say is, that is not what you say
to my Master.' . . . I (by myself) heard the following
dialogue between Mrs. Power and John Cain as I was
getting up on Wednesday ; she, speaking out of her
window across a court, ' John Cain, is Biddy Cash
there ? ' ' No, she is not, why should she ? ' ' Will
you try.' ' Yes, I'll try.' In abt. 5 mins. encore,
' John Cain, is Biddy Cash there ? ' ' No, and as I
said before, why should she ? ' ' *Try*,' is always
enough for trying to find a thing. . . .

" Talking of Irish people, let me go back to
Glendelough. I walked on by myself past the ruins
about a mile, to enjoy the nearer acquaintance of that
Black Mountain that overhangs the lake, and a ragged
little boy followed me to instruct me in its history. . . .
Having pointed out to me St. Niven's or Kiven's bed
at the bottom of the Mountain . . . he said, ' Have
you ever heard Tommy Moore's verses about it,' and
upon me saying ' No,' he recited the whole of his
melody upon this subject (and which Miss Ponsonby
played and sung for me last night) and I was so astonished at the feeling with which this little Irish beggar
recited these lines, that I made him repeat them to

me three times over.   By the bye, I did not know till
last night that ' The meeting of the waters ' and Vale
of Avoca made another subject for a melody of
Moore's.

"In coming from Kilfane on Wednesday, Lady
Duncannon, her maid and me, we came post about 7
or 8 miles, and then our own horsemen and coachmen
met us to bring us the remaining 15 or 16. . . .

"In crossing our own Mountain for 5 or six miles
there was not a man on the road (and it is very
populous) who had not something to say to Lady
Duncannon. ' Welcome home to you, Lady Duncannon,' ' Safely home to you, Lady Duncannon,'
and very often ' Welcome home (or safely home) to
you, *good* Lady Duncannon. . . .' "

" Dublin, Nov. 15th.

" . . . Yesterday, we had a nice domestic little
snug party at the Errolls' in the Castle, Lord and Lady
Wm. Paget, Berkeley Paget, his Wife and Daughter,
another dragoon Paget, Lyster and myself, and in
the evening Lady Cecilia Latouche, and her Daughter,
and a very jubby day we had, Lady Erroll playing and
singing her Mother's kind of songs in the evening ;
the merits inferior I must admit to her divine original,
and yet certainly like her ; the whole to conclude
with a game at fright. . . .

" Don't you think Lady Duncannon's note to me
a very pretty one ? *Spencer* * is a young giant of a
boy under 5 years old, and in petticoats.   He and the
other two boys would see me half way to Pilltown the
day I left Bessborough, without their hats.   It would
do you good to hear Lady Duncannon express her
terrors of the Seftons ; that Lady Sefton is so ' *awfull.*'

* Sir Spencer Ponsonby Fane.

' But the young Ladies,' said I ? ' Oh,' said she,
' they are all awful, and tho' Lord Sefton is all
politeness in his own house, one always feels certain
he is quizzing one all the time, and I was never so
terrified of anything as going to stay at Stoke.' To
be sure there is some difference between Lady Sef-ton
and Lady Duncannon. I should like to see the
former selling cloaths to poor people without shoes
and stockings for four or five hours every Saturday. . . ."

" Croxteth, Decr. 6th.

" . . . I intended, you know, to come here by last
Tuesday's Chester Mail, but having learnt that it was
the custom of that coach to be upset about twice a
week, and having *by perfect accident* discovered that
there was a daily coach that passed at $\frac{1}{2}$ past nine in
the morning by Kinmel to Liverpool, you won't be
surprised that I availed myself of this discovery, and
came by this coach last Wednesday. We stopt an
hour and a half at Chester, then there was a little
delay in crossing the Mersey in the steam boat, and
the whole to conclude with a Liverpool hackney coach
that was not very *lively*, as dear Pat would say, and
ran me very fine for my dinner. . . .

" I was much struck on this occasion with the
different manner of Earl Sefton, and Taffy Hughes.
The day I got to Kinmel, I said before dinner to Taffy,
' Have I the same bedroom, Hughes, that I had the
last time ? ' ' Indeed I cannot tell you, but we will
soon know if you will ring the bell.' How like our
Pat Duke of Leinster.

" Well, I had written to Sefton saying I should be
here by breakfast last Wednesday, so arriving as I did
at seven, and every servant being then occupied in
putting the dinner on the table, the Pet with his quick

ears heard my crawling coach, and I saw him coming down the stairs, and he was out of the house with, ' It's you, old Fellow ! ' before my man could get down from his coach ; then there was such a hollowing for my own footman Charles that brought him in no time ; then, ' You have your own room that you had last time,' and my portmanteau being up in a jiffy, he (my Lord) would help me to unstrap it, and in short, tho' the dinner was on the table, I dressed and was quite in time for sufficient turtle, and all other good things. The party assembled I found to be My Lord and My Lady, the three young Ladies and Berkeley, Mr. and Mrs. Smythe-Owen, Mr. and Mrs. Strickland, (the latter a parlez-vous, and by far the handsomest, best dressed woman I ever saw, . . .) so it was all mighty well, and Lady Louisa in the course of the evening told me, she really believed Papa would not have come to Croxteth at all if I had not been coming.   Was there ever ? . . .

    " Have you ever heard that Lady Derby is pro-nounced to have an incurable disease, an ossification or some other fatal affection of the heart. . . . I went there to call yesterday, and as I walked up towards the house, perceiving Lord Derby peeping at me thro' a distant window to make out who I was, I purposely loitered, and turned about in all directions, in order that he might recognise me, and so I hoped let me in ; and so it was, for I was admitted in an instant, and he met me in the hall, and having asked, of course, directly after Lady Derby, he said, ' She is a little better today, and *will see you.*'   I sat, however, a long time with him and Mr. Phipps Hornby before I saw her, and when I did so, it was for a very short time before she got into her carriage ; but during the short time she played her part brilliantly. I said, ' I'm glad to hear you are better today.' ' Thank you,' she said, and nodded her head at me in a way that no one could misunderstand for ' I'm going to die,' she then put out her hand a second time and said, ' Will you come and see us ? ', to which of course I said ' with great pleasure,' and when little Derby said, ' When will you come, Creevey ? ' I said ' next week ' ; and I mean to go. . . ."

" Knowsley, Dec. 13th.

" Knowsley without Lady Derby is like a house with all the fires and candles put out.

But *she* still shines tho' out of sight,
For she has carried off the light
And left us dark in blackest night.

2

And never more shall Countess reign
O'er Knowsley and its Stanley train
So bright as this from Drury Lane.

" Sublime, is it not ? but the poor player, I fear, can never show for good again. . . ."

" Whitehall, Dec. 22nd.

" Well, after all, *home* is *home*, be it ever so homely. I left Croxteth about 2 o'clock on Saturday. Bad as the day was, my Lord *would* drive me and my portmanteau in the shooting carriage to the ' Saracen's Head Pot Ale House ' on the Prescot road to catch the *Umpire*, and as we were a quarter of an hour before our time he *would* wait with me in that fashionable hotel till the coach came up, and so see me off. I mention this *pint* to show the terms on which we parted ; then, the *Ladies* informed me they were *all* making up a Xmas-basket for *my* Ladies, and the *young people*, and it was to start today. . . . *This pint* again will shew you, that it's all mighty well with *all* the worthy family. My journey was . . . rather dawdling and time . . . pressing, I laid hold of a *Jarvey* at Islington, and such an artist could not have been selected in the whole town, for he absolutely flew with me, and well it was so, for we dine at ½ past six now-a-days, and they had begun dinner, but Mrs. Taylor left hers and came out upon the steps to meet me, and to bring me in by force, dorty as of course I was, so it was all very well, and ' damned fair ' in Mrs. Taylor after all our snubs ; and Fergy was here, and also Harry Vane, and an Oxonian pedagogue of Michael's.

" After dinner, I of course retired to my toilette, then returned, had two kisses of Lady Glengall, played at cards till one o'clock, won three pounds, and went to bed, and so ended my campaign from Croxteth.

" I am off now to take my place in a coach to the '*Place Ladies,*' * as we are always full this Xmas time."

* His step-daughters at Rivenhall Place.

CHAPTER XIV

1829

THE second act of Creevey's drama drew to a close with 1829 and the curtain falls on the drawing-room scene with the Man-of-fashion playing his part to a sparkling finale. Suddenly, secretly and in the public view inexplicably, the Duke of Wellington surrendered on the question of Catholic Emancipation, forcing both Peel and the King to join in his reluctant conversion. Neither the King nor the Tory party rallied from the blow, and the way was cleared for a new act, in which Mr. Creevey might play a minor but different rôle.

Creevey to Miss Ord

"Whitehall, Feby. 4th.

" . . . Fergy and Lady Glengall and Henry Vane came in the evening. Sefton . . . had told Taylor he should come down to see me in the evening. . . . He and my Lady have been to Witley (Ld. Foley's) . . . on their way up from Croxteth, and his account of Witley is *beyond*. You know, they have not one farthing of income, and the splendour of every thing far surpasses what he found there two years ago. Four servants out of livery, and every thing else in proportion, but dear *Lady* Foley for my money. She never appears in the morning, but just before dinner. A groom of the Chamber dresses up a great chair in the Drawing Room for her with a shawl and great white satin cloak, then a table covered with red velvet and a deep gold fringe round it, and a tray being placed on this table, with every species of watch, smelling bottle &c., &c. . . . In the evening she presides in the same state at a *Hazard* table, a game that she and her second daughter (aged 16) are very fond of. Here again, the same red velvet table is placed by her side, but instead of the bijouterie, a gold tray is placed upon it, deeply laden with gold and silver money, every piece of which has been *washed and cleaned* by the Butler. . . . They call their game *chicken* Hazard, but when I mention that Lord Sefton lost £160 one night at it, I think our old brown hen would not be too strong a name for it. . . . Alvanley who was there, played off one of my . . . jokes. Old Dow. Cork was of the party, and in constant communication by post with old Dow. Elcho at Cheltenham, so having given one of her letters to be franked, and left it for that purpose on the table, Alvanley inserted a slip of paper into the letter, saying that since writing the letter poor Lady Cork had suddenly expired, and then made Gen. Anson frank it, without telling him what he'd done. Sefton left Witley the same day, so has yet to learn how dear old Elcho bore the death of dear old Cork.

" Well, the Catholic question is really settled after all. Sefton knows all the details from Greville. Wellington went to see the King last Monday week, and told him the thing *must* be, and Prinney struck without making any fight to signify. The only points under discussion at present are, whether the [offices of] Lord Lieutenant of Ireland, and the two Chancellors of England and Ireland ought not to be excepted from being filled by *Catholics*, and it is thought that even these offices will be left open for all. Was there ever ? The Beau in his first interview with the Archbishop of Canterbury asked him what his feelings were, and he said they were against further concession,

but that he should not oppose anything that was
proposed by his Grace, and he *ventured* to give the
same as the opinion of the rest of the Bishops.   They
are neat articles, are they not ?   The Catholic
Association is, of course, to be put down, to which
neither O'Connell nor any other possible Pat will, of
course, have any objection. . . ."

" Brooks's, Feby. 13th.

" . . . We dined yesterday, you know, at the
General's * and rum enough it was.   The only spark
of life was in Lord Robert Spencer, aged 84.

" I did not mention that at our dinner at Rogers's
the day before, we had some profane joking with
Scroop about his taking his seat in the Lords. . . .
I suggested the propriety of his being accompanied to
the Lords by a procession, to which Brougham added
—with *crucifixes*, which was rather going it, but it
seemed to give no offence, so there being four enormous
Catholic Candles on the table, I suggested their being
immediately blown out, and kept for the procession,
which was very favorably received, as was a joke of
mine upon a *Green Goose* in the 2nd. course.   It had
the flattest breast and body I ever saw, so much so
that I observed either *Burke or Hare*† must have lain
upon it.

" Here *is* Scroop, and he says, ' I was afraid you
would have shown me up in the " Morning Journal "
after your jokes the other night.' . . ."

" March 7th.

" . . . During dinner . . . Sefton said, ' I should
like of all things for Creevey to go to Harrington

* Sir R. Ferguson's.
    † The celebrated murderers who supplied bodies for the dissecting-
table.   They drugged and crushed the life out of their victims.

21

House. I'm sure he'd be so much amused with the whole thing—the house as well as the acting.' . . . We found old Lord Harrington * sitting in a chair, and alone . . . a large sofa making the front of the audience, and vis a vis the stage curtains. . . . Four rows *I think* of sofas and chairs made the accommodation for the audience, and my counting made the company 50, which I am sure was very near the mark. Nothing could exceed the comfort of it, in light, atmosphere, and everything else. The first piece was ' *The day after the wedding,*' from the French—a shrew of a lady who in her tantrums breaks and tears everything to pieces, and who is eventually tamed by her husband affecting the same dispositions, and being equally successful in his destruction of their property. The Lady was Miss Elphinstone,† daughter of Lady Keith that was Miss Thrale out of Madam Piozzi—an ugly little tit as you'll see ; the Husband was Phipps, a Brother of Normanby, and of much fame at this theatre, more than I think he is entitled to, tho' very fair. A Brother of the Lady's was a younger Wortley who did what he had to do to perfection, and sung capitally. The two remaining personages in the piece were Francis Molyneux and Lady Caroline Stanhope. . . .

" Of Company there were the two young Foleys and their Father ; two Kinnairds ; two Lady Seymours, the Duke of Somerset's ‡ Daughters, (and more inferior articles you won't often see), that extraordinary Miss Jennings (that was a beauty of 35 years ago). . . . Minny Seymour§ next to me, and apologis-

* 3rd Earl. He died in Sept. of that year.
† Georgina, married Hon. Augustus Villiers. Her mother was Dr. Johnson's favourite, " Queenie." Her half-sister, Margaret, married M. de Flahault.
‡ 11th Duke.   § Mrs. Fitzherbert's adopted daughter.

ing for having left Mrs. Fitzherbert, who had but just come up from Brighton. Dawson in the back row flirting with the young Colman in the absence of old Seymour. . . . Old Harrington supported by young Lyndoch * on one side, aged 83, and Burdett on the other ; Wm. Lamb alias Lord Melbourne sitting next to Sefton asleep ; Dow. Salisbury gayer than ever. . . ."

" March 9th.

" . . . I went to Lady Duncannon's, he having told me that *Penny* complained I never came. I found her surrounded with her children, just the same as at Bessborough, except that here they seem all in a prison. I don't wonder at their passionate preference for liberty and Ireland. . . .

" From her, I made my first visit to Lady Grey, who came this day week, and having received messages from her by Sefton, as well as from Lady Georgiana at the Opera on Saturday reproaching me for not coming. For an artificial tip top fine Lady as you know she is, she is much cleverer than the general quality click, and to myself really civil, so we had a very good conversation. . . . *He* came in, and was very natural, and in the same good spirits as he came first to London, so I think it must be she who has taken him out of the hands of the croaking Whigs whom she continues to detest ; nor is her enmity to Sefton at all abated notwithstanding his unabated toadying of them, man, woman and child. . . .

" . . . Michael and I entertained at dinner yesterday, Lord Radnor,† Sir James McDonald, Geo. Ponsonby, and Fer-gy. Folky is off for Paris today (of course

* Gen. Lord Lynedoch.

† Lord Folkestone had succeeded his father as 3rd Earl the previous year.

per coach), having left his Countess there. I went to bed before 12 for a wonder, and walked about my room, thinking of the dinners and *Coffee* that Folky had had out of us in his time, and of the *slight* intercourse in these days between him and me. . . .

"Jersey just tells me (but desiring me not to tell it) that Wellington told her (Ly. Jersey) that he had complained to the King of the Duke of Cumberland about this Catholic measure, and stated particular things he had done. Upon which the King reproached the D. of C. who positively denied the charge to be true; upon which they were put face to face in the Royal presence, and as the Duke of W. said to Lady Jersey, 'I could not tell the fellow he lied, but I went on saying to the King that every syllable of what I told him I knew to be true.' . . ."

"March 14th."

"I had a very good day at Lord Grey's yesterday. The Seftons; Tierney; Ld. Durham and Sydney Smith. Grey uttered various sentiments, which could not have been very agreeable to Lord Sefton or Ld. Durham, such as the destruction of the Whig Party two years ago, &c. &c., and many more *such* things, but all said in a very gay and good humoured manner, and without any *bile*.

"It is really quite pleasant to see him apparently so happy. I was sorry I got no Politics with *Her*, because she always behaves to me as if she thought me a *real*, and not an occasional, friend."

"Sulby, March 22nd.

"Well, so the Beau has had My Lord Winchilsea out,* and very near done him too. His ball went

* The Duke of Wellington had fought a duel with Lord Winchilsea.

through My Lord's coat, *it is said*. Never Puppy more richly deserved it than Ld. Winchilsea. . . .''

" Newmarket, April 22nd.

" . . . We have one of the Russians at dinner again to-day, and a very curious fellow he is, to say nothing of his name—*Matuscewitz*. He never was in England till about 3 months ago, and speaks English so well as to be quite up to all the expressions that belong to Hunting, Racing, or anything else. He is sent from St. Petersburg to settle the question with us of the new Greek Boundary, and is said to possess extraordinary talents, so say the Lievens. This Diplomat seems to make the most of his time. He was living at Melton when I was there, hunting whenever he could find hounds, riding as hard as any one, and giving any prices for horses. . . . He went with Lord Sefton, Lord Jersey, and myself thro' our stable on Monday, and being attended by Edwards our . . . trainer, the Russian observed to him, ' I had a horse out of your stable that win me a great race at Petersburgh, " *Sharper*," ' whom Edwards remembered perfectly well. ' I run (continued the Russ:) two English Horses, " Sharper " and " Mina," against two Cossacks on Tartar Horses.' ' And over what distance ? ' said I ; ' 43 miles,' said he, and they did it, or " Sharper " did it, in 2 hours 53 minutes." . . . Both Jersey and Sefton remembered the Race as a well authenticated event in the ' Sporting world.'

" We are all as amiable here as ever we can be, I mean in our own family, and My Lady and I have a regular set to at Ecarté till twelve, after our men disperse. I thought Sefton looking very ill the day I came, but he is improved since. Last night was the first one that he played Whist at the rooms. He said to me in the morning, ' I really am tired of my ill luck. I lost £10,000 at Whist last year.' ' To whom,' said I. ' Why, to such men as Duncombe, Montrose.' . . ."

" June 5th.

" I came from Banstead as I said I would, tho' various devices were used to keep me, and I had a very agreeable dinner at Kingstown. It is a great country house at old Brompton, buried in trees, and ornamented with cows.

" We had Ld. and Ly. Leitrim ; Ld. and Ly. Rosebery ; Lady — Clements, Ferguson and Stephenson. I am engaged to Ly. Rosebery to spend some time with her in Scotland to meet her Mother, Dow. Anson. Ly. Leitrim is a showy Irish touch, not so handsome as her sister, Ly. Charlemont, but with more to say, and very handy and agreeable. I am happy to say no fellow can make himself a bigger fool than our Northumberland* in Dublin, and Ly. Leitrim appreciated most justly the name they have given him in Dublin. . . .

" We all go to Stoke for Ascot week, either 16 or 18 strangers. I believe no Ladies but the Duchess of Richmond. . . .

" My belief is that neither the King nor the Beau will have anything to do with Grey, and considering the trash Wellington chuses to carry on his Government, Ld. Grey has reason to be proud of his exclusion. Every one tells me that the House of Commons never was in such a state from the gross incapacity of the Ministerial men in it. Then Copley † (they will have it) is in some damnable scrape, and can't remain. . . ."

* At that time Lord-Lieutenant.
† Lord Chancellor Lyndhurst.

"Stoke, June 19th.

"A beautiful race indeed yesterday, and 'Zingalee' proved decidedly to be the first Race Horse of the times in which he lives. . . .

"Lord Chesterfield was here yesterday morning from the Royal Cottage before breakfast to acquaint Charles Greville that he had bought 'Zingalee' during the night for £2,500, an event you know of great importance to us Turf Men. Another event of not less importance took place during yesterday, which was a communication from the Sovereign thro' Lord Mount-Charles to Jersey, that he wished to live as a *Nibber*,* and brother *Leg* with our Pet.† Whether this fraternal embrace takes place today in Prinney's stand is not yet certain, but of course it is at hand, and that *pint* once accomplished I think Nummy's turn must come next, for the day before yesterday for fun's sake I tried to make Prinney see me, and am sure succeeded, for I was quite alone, and distinctly saw him fix his eyes upon me, and as they are not as good as formerly, he got his glass and measured me from top to toe. Then he always makes Jersey, or the Duke of Richmond, or any other of our house repeat to him every one's name that is in this house.

"Pet won the £25 lottery yesterday having drawn 'Zingalee,' which is all very well for entertaining us as he has done all this week with his turtle, and every thing else. Never man did the thing as he does or makes it answer more compleatly in gaiety and every thing else, to say nothing of Berkeley Craven and myself being sent every day to the Races in our Barouche and four posters."

* I.e. Neighbour.
† Lord Sefton. Stoke Farm was close to Windsor Park.

" We had Lord Grey, Tierney, the George Ponsonbys, Lord Robert, Chas. Greville and Luttrell. I had a very pleasant *coze* with Grey in the evening, in which I complimented him upon his present proud and independant position, and he said he was much happier than if he was in Office, mixed up as he must be at present with many persons for whose characters he had great contempt."

" July 1st.

" Decidedly the cleverest fellow I have heard of a long time is one who clearly seeing how the weather would turn out on Saturday for the Horticultural Fete, having speculated largely in *Clogs*, repaired to that scene of pleasure with a large waggon full, and it is said disposed of them all at double their value. Poor *Gunter* says the Ladies drank so freely to keep the cold out, that he shall be a decided loser by his contract."

"Sept. 14th.

" . . . I doat upon Calais,* and always did. It is now much more like itself than when I was there 5 years ago. Boulogne is the great depot of English, and has taken off, I suppose, what settlers there were at Calais. I had my soup, a charming sole, Frecandeau in Sorrell, Mutton Cutlets with sauce piquante, a beautiful roast Fowl, an omlette Suisse (I don't know the sex of an omlet), Cheese, Peaches, G. gages, Cakes and Biscuits—prix 4 francs, a bottle of wine 2½ francs, and this in the best hotel possible."

" Stoke, Sept. 20th.

" . . . Charles Greville came here yesterday. He sees the King, you know, whenever there is a Council

* Creevey had paid a flying visit to Calais.

held. He (the King) is at present quite blind of one eye, and the other is going, and when it is gone he is to be couched, and it is supposed will be cured, but he is very low about himself. He is at the Cottage, and his mind is quite made up *never to live in the Castle*, which considering the hundreds of thousands which have been expended upon it inside and out is not amiss. He says it is *too public*, so I take for granted the new Palace at Pimlico * will share the same fate.

" Old Conyngham kissed hands for the Round Tower in Windsor Castle within an hour after the King received the account of Ld. Harrington's death."

" Sept. 22nd.

" . . . I have finished the first volume of Bourienne, and I hate him. He is a villain, and a mean one. . . .

" Lady Maria has done me such a nice portrait of Croxteth, that I am really quite surprised how brick and mortar only can make so pretty a picture, and if you come to that, having admired very much a ribbon in Lady Sefton's cap before she put on her mourning for Lord Harrington, and which I called a real *Dresden*, she presented me yesterday with two sorts of the same, one broad and one narrow, which she had sent for from her Milliner on purpose, and I flatter myself it will become Mrs. Hamilton very much. I am very fond of it, as you may suppose. . . .

" What a pity I was not here when Charles Greville had in his possession the correspondence between Lord Chancellor Lyndhurst, and the Duke of Cumberland concerning the attempted *Rape* by the latter of Dear Lady Lyndhurst !† . . . Our Greville

* Buckingham Palace was rebuilt by Nash and Blore from Buckingham House between 1825 and 1837. Aiton laid out the garden.

† The facts of this case are well set out in Mr. R. Fulford's *Royal Dukes*. The *locus classicus* is, of course, Greville's *Memoirs*.

always takes a very decided line upon all subjects, and having learnt, as he thought from good authority, that Lyndhurst had much the worst of it in their correspondence, he said so wherever he went, till, one fine day in walking on Wimbledon Common, the female Lyndhurst passed him in a Barouche, and asked him to step in, and having heard from others what his opinion was, proceeded to set him right, and the next Council that was held at Windsor, business being over, my Lord Chancellor took the Clerk aside, and said, as he understood Lady Lyndhurst had been talking to him about his correspondence with the D. of C., he had brought the letters with him, and he was quite at liberty to read them, and return them at his convenience.   Punch brought them here, and the Pet says Lyndhurst cuts a capital figure.   The facts of the case are that the Duke having made a morning call upon My Lady, avails himself of that occasion to make the most furious attack upon the Lord Chancellor's conduct and politics on the Catholic Question, and others, and the storm being over he proceeded to handle my Lady equally roughly in a very different kind of way, so much so that she rung the bell and had him shown the door.   She did not tell her Hubby for four or five days, and did not mean to tell him at all, but it got out by the servants, and being once out, Cumberland like a very sensible man writes in a very high tone to Lyndhurst demanding a denial under his hand of the whole transaction, and which Lyndhurst with equal firmness refuses to do ; but of course considering the *Parties* and the case altogether he does not go to publick battle with him upon the subject, and he concludes by laying the whole correspondence before the King who highly approves his *discreet* conduct on this occasion. . . . Our Punch being now juste-au-fait with the real state of the case was equally loud in publick and private versus the Duke of Cumberland, till another fine day comes to him . . . a message from the Duke of Cumberland, '*very civil*,' hearing of his unfavourable opinion respecting the late correspondence, and begging the favor of Mr. Greville to call upon him . . ., but our Punch was not to be so caught, and so from this house he wrote as Sefton says a most capital letter . . . declining altogether any communication with the Duke of Cumberland personally or otherwise, and so it ended. It is supposed the Duke begun his correspondence with Lyndhurst under the conviction that my Lady had never blabbed . . ."

" Newmarket, Oct. 1st.

" . . . Here we are, all writing according to custom after dinner. Duke and Duchess of Richmond*; Jersey; Lord Geo. Bentinck†; Greville; and John Mills. Apropos to the latter, *Mills*, he is a member of the *Yacht* Club, and has a *Yacht*, and I am engaged to him for next June at Cowes bound for any place in Europe I choose to name. It is a thing I have long wished for, and if I live and am well, will certainly keep him to his mark.

" Certainly this young Duchess of Richmond from the little I have seen of her and the other young female grandees, is decidedly the most natural, best mannered and best looking for a mother of such a family. . . ."

" Newmarket, Oct. 13th.

" . . . Lady Worcester‡ told a capital story of some expedition from Walmer to see some Castle 12 or 14

* 5th Duke, married Caroline, daughter of Marquis of Anglesey.
† Son of 4th Duke of Portland ; the well-known politician.
‡ Emily, second wife of 7th Duke of Beaufort. Niece of the Duke of Wellington.

miles off, and in doing which having to go thro' some
nearly impossible road, they all stuck fast, two carriages of men and women, and had all to turn out and
walk up to their knees in mud a mile or two to a
neighbouring town, Sandwich, when the Beau's delight was to buy the ladies shoes and stockings of a
tolerably homely salesman as you may suppose, and
in which they came home, but his great delight of all
was to see my Lord Chancellor* attempting to help my
Lord Privy Seal (Roslyn) in this dirty lane, and by
' *backing* ' or clumsiness of some kind, knocking him
over, and tumbling upon him. It certainly was a
pity I did not get amongst these Lads. His Niece
knows the Beau to a nicety, and describes him
capitally. I wonder what kind of a tit this other
niece of his is that's coming to breakfast—Lady
Euston ? Nous verrons, so ta, ta.

" No more the Beau's Niece than you are, I mean
this Lady Euston,† but a Daughter of Admiral
Berkeley, and a cousin of Lady Sef-ton's, and considering her fame for beauty, I think a mighty poor
business. Large enough, it's true, but r-a-a-lly for a
beauty it's *too*. Her Sister Lady Hardy beats her
easy. . . ."

" London, Oct. 19th.

" Lord Essex has just asked me to dine with him
tomorrow, but I have taken my place for Liverpool,
and hope to be at my Sister's at Edge Hill in time to
drink Andrew's ‡ health in her excellent Port on
Wednesday.

" We dine early today in Arlington Street. I am

---

* Lyndhurst.

† Lady Euston and Lady Hardy (wife of Admiral Sir Thomas) were
daughters of Sir Geo. C. Berkeley and his wife Emily Lennox.

‡ Anne Hamilton's son.

curious to see or rather *hear* Fanny Kemble, for her forte they say is her beautiful voice."

" October 20th.

" Well, according to the Earl and myself, Fanny Kemble is *no go*. A very nice girl, and her coming out as she does to prop her Family, gives a great interest to her, and makes one wish most sincerely for her success, but she has no force, and I can't help thinking with her pretty manner and *pleasing* voice (for it is nothing more than pleasing) that she would do better in Comedy than Tragedy."

" Knowsley, Novr. 1st.

" It is really very agreeable being here, I mean principally on account of Lord Derby. I never saw the agreeableness as well as perspecuity of his understanding to such advantage. Lady Derby with all her jokes, agreeableness and real fun drove all natural subjects out of the field for Dramatic Piety and twaddle, and *he* followed her in everything, so that now he is his own natural self again, reads the papers from beginning to end . . . and comments . . . with the skill of a Master. Then he shews in his innocent, natural way much more knowledge upon all subjects than I thought he possessed. I may be a partial witness from his extreme politeness and attention to myself. . . ."

" Knowsley, Nov. 3rd.

" No indeed, I think it would be base in me if I was not to begin to relent, and to proclaim my relentance with respect to Edward Stanley. He has just given me a sharp canter of five and twenty miles to see the *Via* duct. . . .

" I was to ride a horse of Lord Derby's of great worth in all ways, and the little fellow came out to see me mount, and said, ' You'll find that horse carry you very well, Creevey, he is the only one of my Hunters I have kept, and I shall never get upon his back,' and a charming horse he was, and Edward was as coddling and carefull of me all the way as if he had been Holyoak, my *Nevvy*. In short, never fellow got more petted by all the worthy family than I am, the little Earl always at the head of them. . . ."

" Croxteth, Nov. 7th.

" As the worthy family of this House kept changing their day for leaving London, I made up my mind for leaving Knowsley on Thursday for Edge Hill, lest my staying longer at Lord Derby's might look like making a convenience of him, so I was not sorry at receiving the enclosed note from *Mull* on Thursday morning before I was out of my bed, and of course I came here, and joined my *Brothers* * and Cousin Craven. The latter is Lady Craven's second son, and is in Henry's regiment. I walked in yesterday to see my Sister,† and on my return and about a quarter of a mile from this house, I saw various white handkerchiefs flying from out of windows here, and which of course were instantly answered by my own from the end of my stick, and very hearty were the congratulations from each branch of the family, who had arrived about an hour before, but let me not omit to mention that my leave taking of Lord Derby was everything I could wish ; he again thanking me for coming to him, saying again ' *how good* ' it was in me. . . ."

" November 14th.

" Montrond told me he knew *Josephine* well, and that a more vulgar, common kind of person could not

* The Molyneux.   † Miss Creevey in Liverpool.

be found.   He's a comical chap, he'll scarcely allow
any Frenchman any merit ;   England is his passion,
or his *professed* one.   He swears that all Englishmen
down to the lowest are fifty times better behaved and
more civil than French ones.   Whilst I think of it, let
me mention a fact respecting our Prinney told to De
Ros by the Beau himself.   He won't open any letter
that is not folded up in some damned extraordinary
conundrum manner possible, so according to the Beau,
he and his two Secretaries, Algy Greville and Drummond, were two hours trying to do it right, at the end
of which time, he (W) observed, was there ever any
thing equal to this, wasting two hours upon such
damned nonsense, and then after all by God ! I can't
do it.   Just at this moment a clerk or servant came
in to tell *Algy* that *Mrs.* Algy was waiting in the
carriage for him, so Wellington said, ' Drummond, let
us have her in, and see what she can make of this note
folding,' and she was had in accordingly, and what is
more, solved the riddle.   He, *Prinney*, must be mad.
He tells almost daily how he won the Cup at Goodwood by *his own* riding.   ' I kept the old Mare back
till I was within fifty yards from home, and then, by
God ! I made such a rush with her, &c. &c.'   He tells
likewise, in the presence of Wellington, how *he* gained
the battle of Salamanca by bringing up a Regiment of
heavy German Cavalry when *things were looking very
ill indeed.*   De Ros asked the Beau if it was really
true that he had said this in his presence, and the
other said ' *quite so.*' . . ."

Creevey's handwriting.   The specimen given overleaf shows Creevey
at his best.   Sir Herbert Maxwell justly described his general pen-
manship as " simply execrable," and acknowledged a public debt to
Miss Ord, who copied out a large part of the collection and so rescued
from inevitable oblivion many names and allusions.

FACSIMILE OF CREEVEY'S HANDWRITING.

PART III

PLACE-MAN

CHAPTER XV

1830

GEORGE THE IV died at last in the night of June 25, 1830, and the Duke of Clarence packed off his homely belongings from Bushey to Windsor with unrestrained pleasure in his new consequence. The demise of the Crown necessitated a general election, and Wellington's Tory Government made a brief appearance in the new Act. But the day of the Whigs was dawning at last and Reform was in the air. The Tories faded out in the fierce smoke of the fires lit by the mob, and in autumn, with doubt in his heart, the King sent for Lord Grey, and the pale Whigs " crept out again to feel the sun," after a quarter of a century in opposition. Lord Grey assumed office in November, and that trusty lance, Mr. Creevey, was not forgotten in the great divide.

After a tantalising delay, he received at last in the Treasurership of the Ordnance a Christmas plum pudding very much to his taste, for all that he was turned sixty-two. And now old scores were written off and party rifts were closed. Who now so trustworthy, so loyal in friendship, as Wickedshifts, *alias* Lord Chancellor Brougham, *alias* Guy Vaux?

Creevey to Miss Ord

"March 26th, 1830.

" No ! to say that a thing is as good as a play, would be a feeble illustration indeed of the *benefit* Mrs. Will'm. and ' the Lights ' * had last night at Old Sally's.† I dined you know with the Seftons, the only stranger was George Anson, who came when

* Mrs. William Brandling and two daughters, Creevey's nieces by marriage.
† Lady Salisbury.

dinner was nearly over, and whose apology for being so late was, that he had been riding with Creevey's pretty relations in the Park.

" We were at the Play before the curtain drew up. Portia has nothing that can shew off any powers Fanny Kemble may have, but I still think little of her compared with her fame, and that she would do very well in Comedy.*

" The hour of my appointment with Mrs. William and ' the Lights ' being 11, I walked from Covent Garden, and at that hour took up my position by a fireplace in the Inner Hall, and was presently joined by Sefton, who whether from curiosity or kindness (I believe the latter) waited with me ten minutes till the Squadron came in sight, and then by his desire was introduced.   I took Mary the younger under my arm, and My Lord walking by the side of the others, up we mounted the Stairs, and into the rooms we entered. The crowd was very great, but round the first corner of the first room were seated (I believe by design) Lady Sefton and her Daughters, for they immediately left their seats, and having at Lady Sefton's request been made acquainted, there was no civility or rather kindness they did not show our Squadron whenever they came near them the remainder of the Drum. This alone you know would have put us in Port, and it was followed by the most universal and *intense* admiration in every room we passed thro', but Sally's card table, My Dear, was the scene.   No, I never shall forget it.   It was her only card table, and in a corner ; Sally in a seat accessible to her company with *Slice* † for her partner ; Lord John Fitzroy with his back to us with Mrs. Stanhope for *his* partner.   So

* Crevey held strong but confused opinions on the Drama.
† Duke of Gloucester.

having surveyed my ground, and observing people taken up and presented to Sally, up I went too, and said that with her permission I had brought Mrs. and the Miss Brandlings, and I assure you she rose from her seat most graciously, and three better *curtesies* in line were never made than by Mrs. William and Lights, and then came *the* scene.   Down went Slice's cards upon the table, and I declare I think he did not touch them again for five minutes ; fixing his eyes with all his might and main upon the Lights, and then devouring Lord John with his whispering enquiries, as to who they were. . . . I assure you I never saw girls so looked at and admired in my life.   The Duchess of Gloucester seemed *almost* as much struck as Slice, and she got Lady Cowley to enquire which was the eldest, what their ages were, and which was *thought* the prettiest.   Not at all *Royal*, was it ? . . . In the midst of all this, I had a very satisfactory conversation with Dear Lord Hill about Sandhurst. He always asks you know about Anne and her children,* and I told him that it might turn out that her boy would go to Sandhurst, and I asked him what he thought of it, and he said most favourably. . . ."

" June 3rd.

" I dined at Lord Durham's, and tho' we had only Sir Hedworth Williamson, a Calcutta Attorney General, he (Lambton), Lady Louisa and Miss Lambton, it was the jolliest day I ever had in that house. ' King Jog ' is so very amiable at present, and she was improved in vivacity.   *He* is all for running in

* Anne's husband, Lt.-Col. Andrew Hamilton, had died in 1821. Her son, Andrew, died in 1835 at the age of 18.   Her daughter, Anne, married in 1842 John A. Blackett and, succeeding her uncle William Ord, brought Whitfield and the Creevey MSS. to their present owner, Mr. John Blackett-Ord.

upon the Beau out of hand, and I am quite certain considers the Government as his own. I asked him what place he meant to give that *feeble* devil, Lansdowne, and he went into fits of laughing."

" June 4th.

" . . . I had been down at Whitehall, and in passing my Hotel in my way home the Waiter pursued me without his hat, saying, ' Here are two letters for you, Sir, *that may be of consequence.* The Earl of Radnor seemed to wish much to see you.' So he gave me your letter, and Folky's note. At all events, the Countess can't have blown me up for the ' *laxity* ' of my conversation with her last Monday. . . ."

" Brooks's. June 5th.

" . . . I was with Folky of course by 12, and it was as I supposed. He told me he had an inclination to bring in Cobbett, and asked my sincere opinion, which I gave against him, and with my reasons, and he decided against it. He then said he had thought of bringing in *Shaw Le Fevre.** . . . I could only say, you know, that he was a very good man ; he then said, ' Perhaps it would be agreeable to yourself to be in ? ', to which comical suggestion I muttered something as to *that* being at his pleasure—that it was certainly no sacrifice to me to be out. . . .

" I went direct to Sefton as I had promised to do, and he was *convulsed* at this conduct of Radnor altogether, abused me like a pick-pocket for not having done myself justice, and said I should write a note to him directly to set myself right, so I came here and wrote one, took it back for his approval, which he gave, and by this time I apprehend it has reached the Earl of Radnor. . . ."

* Afterwards Speaker.

"June 8th.

" . . . Respecting Folky. . . . It is quite impossible to conceive any conduct more *idiotic* or meaner than his on this occasion to me. I have had no answer from him to my note, and I can't say I expected it. . . Supposing him to do as he ought, I doubt, as you do, whether it would add to my happiness. I think I could say altogether that it *would not*, but it would be some *little* triumph over other mean devils ; it would afford the privilege of franking, and then it would amuse the children to have the ' *decayed Member* ' restored. This, I think, is all my case, and one that in all probability will never be realized.* . . .

" June 17th.

" Mrs. Taylor sees Ly. Conyngham's daily letters from Windsor to her Brother. On Sunday Halford † told her his opinion was that the King would die either that day or night ; on Tuesday she says to her infinite astonishment she found him to be so much better as to be really very much as formerly, and he told her what he wished to have done at the *Cottage* as he meant to remove there as soon as he could, being sure it would do him good. What a man he is for strength ! "

" June 22nd.

" . . . I . . . looked in at Crockford's, and took a *cheerful Crayfish* with *Erroll* who was quite as crazy and comfortable as when we met in Ireland. He and My Lady are living with her Father, *Billy*.‡ Erroll's account is that the latter, Billy, has a real affection [for Prinney], and that he never returns home after

* He got a seat in 1831.
† Sir Henry, physician to George IV. He was present at the opening of Charles I.'s coffin and abstracted the famous cervical vertebra.
‡ Duke of Clarence.

seeing him without being greatly affected and crying like a child. Then he describes the domestic habits of Bushey as of great *simplicity*. The favourite amusement of our future Sovereign being ' *Pope Joan* ' at which he plays every night, but will never trust himself beyond the stake of one shilling. The Duchess is a great *worker*, and carries on that occupation by the land table, whilst Billy and the young ones go on with their Pope. When I said, ' the time must be near at hand when the Duke must be King, and that I trusted that I should see him Ld. Chamberlain or Lord Steward,' he replied very naturally, ' I hope so.' "

"Stoke, August 22nd.

" . . . Yesterday was as gay a day in point of weather, scenery and events as one could possibly see or wish to see. Francis and I started on horseback about one to see the humours of the dinner in the long walk of Windsor Park, which was to take place at two. Upon passing the approach to the Castle in Windsor Town, we saw the Royal carriages coming in procession down from it. . . . So having taken a position with our horses' tails looking down a bye street, and our faces commanding each carriage as it passed, we prepared for action. The first carriage, *open*, contained the Queen, and Betty Humbug* on one side and Billy and Sister Gusty† opposite with their backs to the horses. I had met my Sovereign the day before in his little phaeton with *Wyatt* and had a good stare from him. . . .

" The next carriage was *not* open and contained Mrs. Gloucester and Lady Jersey one side, little Sussex opposite. I made my reverence to the

* Elizabeth, Landgravine of Hesse-Homburg, 1770–1840. Daughter of George III.
† William IV and Princess Augusta (1768–1840).

latter with such humility and solemnity that like the
King he involuntarily was taking his hat off to return
my salute, when all at once recognising my face, he
put his head out of the window, and at the full
stretch of that gentle pipe of his hollowed out, ' Oh
you old Vagabond ! What the devil are you doing
here ? ' I need not add how much I rose in the
estimation of the surrounding crowd, from this unexpected burst of Royal familiarity, nor was my fame
diminished by about the fifth or sixth carriage—open
and containing Lord and Lady Erroll. They had
seen me some time before they came up, and I
deported myself with such becoming gravity, treating
them quite as Royalties, that they were actually in
fits. Her Mother, our *Nell*, never laughed more
heartily or seemed more happy. *He* hollowed out
' Lady Erroll says you don't know her,' but I thank
you I never relaxed a muscle or presumed to cover
myself in their presence, and off they went roaring.
Our Francis is pleased to say, it was one of the best
scenes he ever saw. I was excessively pleased with
the two Royal boys* in their phaeton together, but not
so with that villain Cumberland who drove the
Duchess in a phaeton. Altogether it was a charming
turn out.

" At the entrance of the Park Billy got out and
walked thro' the crowd, and as you may suppose was
not a little applauded. . . . Terrace and Flower
Garden were open to all the world. . . . We could
hear the people saying perpetually, ' This is something
like. What a change ! Who could ever have thought
of this ? ' The suite of Drawing Rooms in which the
Company assembled before dinner all look into this
garden, so we could see and distinguish every one. . . .

* Prince George of Cumberland and Prince George of Cambridge.

" After dinner Billy rose, but desired every one to remain seated and the men to fill their glasses. He then proposed our Beau's health, observing that it was the anniversary of the Battle of Vimeira, the first of these splendid victories &c. &c., and Sefton says he did it as well as possible. It was seen by all around the reception this toast met with from the Duke of Cumberland who was turning his glass upside down, and that damned *Slice* Gloucester passed the bottle without helping himself. Sussex said in the evening to Lord Sefton, ' Did you see that insolent scoundrel, the Duke of Cumberland, turn his glass down, he ought to be turned out of the Castle.' . . ."

" Liverpool, Septr. 23rd.

" We slept at Conway on Monday, at Chester on Tuesday, and got here about 3 o'clock. We drove through Kinmel Park and I made Mrs. Taylor get out for half an hour, tho' she had no previous acquaintance with Charlotte.*

" Our visit answered extremely. We found little Sussex and ' *Ciss* ' in high force.

" Here is Lady Glengall having come from Manchester to breakfast by railroad and steam. She has been off and on the road for the last three weeks. What think you of her having picked up in this very Hotel the Duchess de Berri, and as she knew her of course in Paris, they had a regular *go* or *lark* of it, railroad, hackney coaches, &c. &c. . . .

" Little Sussex whilst sitting next to Mrs. Taylor at Luncheon at Kinmel said, ' You'll be glad to hear, *Ma'am*, that the King has continued to Mrs. Fitzherbert the same pension she had before.' ' I'm very

* Wife of Col. Hughes (afterwards Lord Dinorben) of Kinmel. She constantly entertained the Duke of Sussex.

glad of it, Sir, it does his Majesty great honor.'   ' Oh, Ma'am ! the whole family made a " *pint of it*." ' . . ."

Earl of Sefton to Creevey

" November 17th.

" Everything is going on smoothly. Nothing could be more agreeable to Grey than the King's reception. He put himself entirely in his hands, without any restriction.

" You will be pleased at some of the arrangements. Of course Palmerston, Melbourne and Co. join.

" Burn this as I have no *right* to tell anything. Anglesey, Ld. Lt. of Ireland ; this charms me. Richmond, Master Genl. of the Ordnance.

" I can tell you nothing more at present. Grey is now with the King, and I shall see him tonight, and will write to you every day, but upon my soul you are *too* not to come.

" My whole occupation is, between ourselves, to keep Bm. [Brougham] quiet. He is very difficult, but I hope it will do."

" Nov. 19th.

" . . . Brougham is Chancellor ! . . . At the meeting last night, changes took place, Lansdowne and Holland declined the Foreign Office. The enclosed is now fixed, and goes on to the King this even: . . ."

" Treasury	Ld. Grey.
President	Lansdowne.
Chancellor	B.
Foreign	Palmerston.
Home	Melbourne.
Colonies	Goderich.
Admiralty	Graham.

P. Seal	Durham.
Exchequer	Althorp.
India	C. Grant.
Duchy	Holland.
Atty. Genl.	Denman.

Albemarle Buck Hounds.   Ha ! ha ! "

"Nov. 21st.

" Start the moment you receive this, in a post chaise, and arrive at this house with your portmanteau. I hope you will be here by 3 o'clock.   You may rely upon me for not sending for you on a wild goose chase. . . ."

Creevey to Miss Ord
"Whitehall, Nov. 22nd.

" Well, I was in Arlington Street before *two* (what pens I have got here) and found the Ladies all as merry as Grigs. . . . My Lord was instantly sent for to Brooks's, and when he arrived we withdrew to his room.   It seems Lord Grey and *Lord* Brougham dined there yesterday, and much was said about *me*, I mean at dinner, both the Lords being extremely desirous I should have a *berth*, and at last Grey said, ' Do take the book and look at the *Ordnance*, the places there have not been disposed of yet.'   So it turns out there are four, each worth about £1,200 a year. . . . A capital start this.   Don't count your chickens as yet, My dear.   If it is made a point that I am to be in the House of Commons, I *can't*, and *won't* go there if I am to vote against *Reform*. . . ."

"Nov. 25th.

" . . . I am an ungrateful wretch, to Sefton in particular, to have my interest so consulted almost against my will, whilst those around me, and who are already in Parliament, are perfectly furious at being neglected. Oh dear, oh dear ! what a spoony ! . . .

" I walked down today, for fun, to see Lord Chancellor Brougham in the bowels in his Court of Chancery, but the crowd was much too great for me to get thro', so I was obliged to put up with *Vice* Chancellor *Wizard*,* to whom he has given one of the great places in the Court. . . .

" Upon going to the Lords, I found Sefton had also seen *Vaux*† and had learnt from him that he had been today to Earl Grey expressly about my business, and that all was right ; then Sefton and I went to him in his private room, and he confirmed the same thing to me, and nothing could exceed his kindness, so all I want is the official notice from Grey.   The other 3 offices in the Ordnance are filled, but I like mine *much* the best, and indeed better than any other, and as far as I can see, no going into Parliament."

" Nov. 26th.

" . . . I have not done anything like justice to the friendly manner yesterday of Lord Chancellor Brougham, and Vauxhall. . . .

" Supposing myself to be in *port* about my *berth*, as Vaux assured me I was, what do you suppose are the two points I think most about ?   The first very much on Annie's account, I mean the *Colour* of the *official boxes*.   The next is, that I understand the Treasurer has an apartment of his own in the *Tower*, which I am sure I would *doat* upon.   The office you know is in Pall Mall, the fine house next to Leopold's.   I can't suppose that the Treasurer *franks* by virtue of his

* Vizard, Brougham's and Creevey's lawyer.
† Brougham took the title of Lord Brougham and Vaux, giving Creevey an opportunity to coin another nickname, " Guy Vaux."

office, but *that* is always managed some way or other in every publick office. . . .

" Now I am *dry*, I think except that Montrond brought old Talleyrand into Crockford's the other night, and such a fellow I never in my life beheld. He has *two skins*, one hanging over the other like a loose shirt, and for hair and *poudre* and *pig tail*, *I* never approached within a hundred miles of him. He can scarcely drag one leg after the other, but when seated, you see a *fire* in his eyes that does much for him in *bowing* and *backing*. As he hobbled along he was every thing *I* could wish. . . ."

" Dec. 8th.

" Well, would you believe it that after all that has passed, I am *floor'd*.

" After dining at Dudley's yesterday I went to Crocky's* in hopes and expectation of Sefton coming in, which he did, and the moment I saw his face, I knew my fate. He took me to a sequestered spot and told me that things looked very ill for me ; that Brougham had dined at Lord Essex's as well as Lord Grey, and that he, B, had taken him, G, into another room to pin him about me, that the Earl said he was so beset by people who insisted upon the necessity of the person who held the office being in Parliament, that he could not give it me. Sefton heard Brougham resist this with all his might and insist upon it that I was most shamefully used. This is all Sefton knew, and as I have no note from Brougham this morning, *it is quite enough*. If you wish to know the true and real state of my *fillings* upon this occasion, I can solemnly declare that they are without a single *ripple*. Reflection makes me regret it on your accounts, all

* Crockford's.

because I *did* wish to be of some use to the Firm in
return for so many past favors.   I am sorry too on
Lord Sefton's account.   He was really quite an
object. . . .

" Do you know that even now, on this very day of
disappointment, I am a happier, much happier man
than Dudley with all his wealth, and in his splendid
house.   I was really quite sorry for him.   I had him
at last, and quite alone and to myself, and could see
distinctly how depressed and changed he was from
former times. . . .

" I just came up here to show my excellent family
that I was not depressed, and Sefton being out, I am
with Mama, Lady Maria, and Lady Louisa.   They
knew my fate, and are very pretty about it of course."

" Dec. 18th.

" Well, Barry My Dear, so William the fourth's
pleasure was taken yesterday by Earl Grey, whether
' *Rowland* ' might mount his Ordnance Mare or not, and
our Sovereign was pleased to assent most graciously,
but our reforming, retrenching Government have
docked my Mare's mane and tail most cruelly.   All
the Ordnance places are reduced to £1,000 each, and
what of that ?   To a man like me, that sum is as good
as £1,500, and then I like to come in as a real reformer,
and above all I like my company ;   that is, Grey and
Althorp—as the heads of Treasury and of Finance.

" I dined yesterday and went to the Play as you
know with my young people, and just before it was all
over our Earl came in from Talleyrand's dinner where
Earl Grey was, and the latter came up to him, and
told him what pleasure it had been to him to give my
name in to the King, and told him at the same time of
the reduction in the salary.   The more I think of this

business, the more I am struck with the humour and good luck of it altogether. . . .

" . . . I shall call in the course of the day upon both Lord Grey and Ellice. The former told Sefton that it must be a very gratifying thing to Creevey, that throughout this business he had not only had no enemy, but that every one had been for him, and no one more so than Althorp and Duncannon. Now is it not r-a-a-lly too ? . . .

" I have been to the Treasury. Ellice was out, but I found Earl Grey, and had a charming tête à tête with him. Nothing could exceed the prettyness of his manner, and if you come to that, it is £1,200 and not £1,000 a year my salary is reduced to. . . .

" I have just come from Arlington Street. Reeves can't take me in, so I shall try *Durham's** I think. . . . "

" Dec. 20th.

" . . . I asked at the Ordnance for Mr. Holmes,† and was told he had not been there for a fortnight, and most probably was at his office in the *Tower*. What a charming sound ! I have the greatest passion for the Tower ; what a nice walk, and what a shop for *an historian* to *explore* all its contents and antiquities ; I only hope there is a bedroom too. Then I am told, I have an office at *Woolwich*. Altogether I think there is nothing so nice as this Ordnance, and its different subjects. When I told the friendly Duncannon yesterday that I now could afford to hire a Cabriolet, and come down and see Lady Duncannon, ' Oh ! ' said he, ' she is delighted at your appointment,

---

* Mrs. Durham, of Bury Street, became Creevey's landlady for several years.

† William Holmes ; died 1851. Creevey's predecessor, famous as a Tory Whip.

because you must *now* come to Ireland.' ' How ? '
' Oh, you have an office in Dublin, and must come
once a year. Holmes always did, and I have the
pleasure to tell you that your travelling expenses are
paid.' Now Barry, my dear, all I say is this, was
there ever ? . . ."

Earl of Sefton to Creevey

" December 26th.

" . . . You overrate my services. I was of no further
use than in keeping attention alive. No man ever had
a more zealous set of friends. We shall do very well,
I have no doubt, if we can weather the reform question. . . .

" Mind you get a *handy* lodging, not above 3
minutes walk from your family at 7 o'clock. . . ."

23

CHAPTER XVI

1831

GREY secured an increased majority at the General Election following the dissolution in the spring of 1831. On July 8th the Reform Bill passed its second reading in the Commons by a majority of 136. Grey introduced it into the House of Lords at a moment when the temper of the nation was at fever heat. The coronation brought a brief respite in the storm and enabled the King to realise how much the immediate interests of the monarchy depended on the passage into law of the Bill. But Grey refused to whittle it down to a mouthful which the Tory peers would swallow, and in October it was rejected on second reading in the Upper House by forty-one votes.

Parliament was prorogued and Creevey paid a visit to his Dublin office. At the close of the year the mob relieved its pent-up fury in the Bristol riots.

Creevey to Miss Ord

" *Tower*, Jany. 17th, 1831.

" Well, *here* I am you see. Billy came for me according to appointment, and we went to the Bank together, where the Cashier of the Government Department was in waiting for me, a large book lying open for me to write my name in as successor to Billy, and a new banking book lying by its side with ' Thos. Creevey, H.M. Treasurer of the Ordnance ' written upon its outside as well as within. My Patent being entered there at the Bank, brought by Crofts (who is a charming man), and then a sum of £30,000 and upwards was transferred into my name as my account with the Bank. . . . I can't say much for the vivacity of my room, but what of that ?   It is like a steward's room on the ground floor of Thorndon, Holkham, or Wentworth ; the building being an *enormous* one.   A Beefeater in his velvet hat and *sweet peas* in it, to let me in and out, and portraits of the Lions* in the way to my office as large as life.   It is now 3 o'clock at which hour we pay no more bills upon us, so I shall set out and see how long it takes me to walk to Charing Cross. . . .

" Well, here I am at *Durham,* and a neater, cleaner, nicer, more respectable apartment than the one I am writing in I defy London to produce.   It took me 55 minutes to walk from the Tower to Charing Cross. The Lions gave me three cheers as I passed their office. . . ."

" Jan. 18th.

". . . I had a very good day at Ellice's yesterday, Earl Grey and Lady Georgiana, Wood and Lady Mary, Melbourne, Althorp, Sir J. Graham, Kempt, our Michael, Denison and Aby. Roberts.   Grey looked uncommonly well, and was in the highest glee.   He called out to me from the top of the table, and asked if I had got my official coat made to be presented in to the King, and I said no, and that I had no intention of going to Court. ' Oh ! but you must,' said he, ' and I shall present you ' ; so again I said I would not, and that I was sure after having abused the King as I had done in the House of Commons, he would much rather have nothing to do with me. ' Quite the contrary,' said Grey, ' for he told me he approved of your appointment very much, and that you were

---

* Henry III built the Lion Tower. The Tower menagerie was increased again in 1822, but the last of the animals were removed to the Zoo in 1834.

a very old Friend of his.' Now raally was there ever ?
For Billy to turn out a *friend* too after all.   Is it not
too ?   I had a good deal of private talk with the Earl
in the evening about Mrs. Taylor, and about Michael.
I told him every thing, and I have little doubt the
little idiot will be a Privy Counsellor. . . . Grey told
me that Vaux is in constant correspondence with the
King, and that the delight of the latter with his new
crony is quite unbounded. . . .

" Do you know that my name is wrong spelt in the
patent, Creevy* not Creevey. . . ."

"Jany. 23rd.

" . . . When I got to my lodgings yesterday evening,
I found the accompanying letter from Lady Louisa
Molyneux, the principal merit of which is the kindness
of herself and race.   I look forward with serious
pleasure to that constant intercourse, which my new
position must necessarily afford me, with my *real*,
worthy and sincerely friendly family. . . .

". . . I found a fine assembly at Ly. Grey's . . .
As I was leaning over the banisters of the staircase in
deep conversation with Lord Charlemont, having
received a considerable shot in the back, and so turning about quick to ascertain the assailant, ' *It is only
me, Creevey,*' said the young Frog† . . . putting out
his hand. ' God bless you, and goodnight to you,'
and off he went ; so surely if the rain will let me I
must go and write my name at his Hotel.   His last
familiarity was the prettier because, in our preceding
conversation, I found myself pulling his coat about,
as I did Lord Hill's the first time I saw him at
Cambray.

* A common contemporary mistake, *vide* Lord Colchester's *Memoirs*.
† The Prince of Orange.   Belgium revolted Aug. 1830.

MARY ELIZABETH, COUNTESS GREY
From a miniature in the possession of Mrs. Lascelles,
at Woolbeding.

[*To face p.* 334.

" . . . I had a most friendly meeting with *Alava*,* and was quite as much pleased with him as I ever have been. *Too* be sure, to have seen Alava, the representative of Spain to the Frog at Brussels, and to see these exiles as private strangers here last night was rather striking, to say nothing of meeting them at Lord *Grey's* instead of the *Beau's* to whom they both belong. . . . I never saw Lady Grey look better, and her behaviour to me was what it uniformly is, downright patronising friendliness, and last not least, let me mention *Vaux* who entered in the eleventh hour with Miss Spalding under his arm, and whom he introduced to me under the name of ' his daughter.' . . .

" . . . I can't omit mentioning that the friend of my youth *Palmerston* could not think of letting me pass last night, tho' at two yards distance, without the most tender squeeze of the hand, and to say nothing of Auckland and Sister Emily." †

Lady Louisa Molyneux to Creevey

" It is so many hours since your family have seen you, that they have some hopes you will come to breakfast."

Creevey to Miss Ord

" Jany. 25th.

" . . . We had a very pleasant dinner yesterday, Sir Thos. and Lady Hardy‡ (he is at the Admiralty you know) ; Geo. Dundas, (another Admiralty Lord) ; Lady Morley, Lord Jn. Russell ; . . . Spring Rice ;

* Creevey thus describes Alava : " The representative of Spain at the Court of the Bourbons and at Wellington's Headquarters also— a most upright and incomparable man." " The Frog " is William Ist.

† Emily Eden, author of *The Semi-Attached Couple*, etc., kept house for her brother during his Vice-royalty in India.

‡ " Nelson's Hardy " married Emily, daughter of his chief on the N. American Station, Sir Geo. Cranfield Berkeley.

Michael ; Howick ; F. Molyneux and others. You may not think this very promising material, but Grey's great spirits, and the incessant jaw of Lady Morley * kept all alive, and in the evening *she* desired to be introduced to me properly, and to strike up a cronyship. . . . she must have both talents and fun, and the Greys all swear by her, but for myself I think the first impression of her is odious . . . an eternal clack accompanied with the most boisterous shouts of laughter. . . . We were interrupted by the arrival of the *Duchess De Dino,*† so it was all mighty well, and another time will do quite as well. As for *Dino*, villain as she is, I never saw anyone more striking or imposing. Her *eyes* brilliant beyond all example, her face extremely handsome, her figure that of perfect youth, tho' she has a Son married, her manners the most natural for a French woman I ever saw, and quite perfect, and her dress the same. And yet to think of this devil living as Mistress with old Talleyrand, the Uncle of her husband, and having three or four children by him. Was there ever ? . . .

" I had some excellent conversation with *Flaugh*‡ (how the devil is his name spelt ?). He is very confident all will go well in France, and his opinion is, of course, old Talleyrand's.§ . . .

". . . *John Bull* of last Sunday . . . says, ' And so our old friend in his *grey knit pantaloons and black gaiters* is come to life again in the character of Treasurer of the Ordnance, Mr. Creevey,' and then *John* proceeds to belabour Jimmy McKintosh‖ with-

* Frances Talbot, second wife of 1st Earl.
† Talleyrand's niece.
‡ Flahault.
§ He was Talleyrand's natural son.
‖ Sir James Mackintosh, lawyer and philosopher. He died four months later.

out mercy for taking a place at the India Board which
I, Mr. Creevey, moved to abolish as useless, and for
which motion, he, Jimmy, himself voted.   It was Lord
Grey who told me this before everybody, in fits of
laughing at the attack upon my wardrobe, and still
more at the leathering of Jimmy. . . .

" The day after the Seftons dined at old Talleyrand's, the latter in an interview with his Cook the
next morning praised him greatly for his dinner, and
said how much Lord Sefton had been pleased, and he
was the best judge in England.*   ' Ah ! ' said the
Cook, ' c'est une famille tres aimable, . . . and tous
les *petits Seftons* sont tous si gourmands.'   I don't
give the French right.† . . .

" The face of that wicked Dido or Dino was one
of the *most agreeable* I ever saw."

" Feby. 2nd.

" Well, we have got a little *privy* of our own at
Whitehall, i.e., a Privy Counsellor.   When I got to
dinner there yesterday Michael showed me a letter
he had received per post from Lord Grey at Brighton,
and a very pretty one it was indeed.   The substance
was that he had named Taylor to the King as a very
proper person to be one of his Privy Council, a suggestion that His Majesty received most graciously.
. . . Why, the house would scarcely hold him, and
he never ceased saying that yesterday was *decidedly*
the happiest day of his life. . . ."

" Tower, Feby. 26th.

" . . . As I dined at Ld. Sefton's yesterday, and
we were alone after dinner, we fell upon the subject
that is uppermost with every one, the unqualified

* He was the patron of the famous Ude.
† Creevey's French is often worse.

failure of Althorp, the utter impossibility of putting him on his legs again, and in short, the absolute necessity of *replacing* him, and then Sefton said from all he saw of what was going on, he thought *Stanley* would be the man.   I won't stop here to discuss the merits of such a change, but go on with the Earl, who added, ' But there is a much more serious subject than that, and one that may prove much more fatal to the administration.'   Alarming enough, you will say, so says I, ' What is that ? ' ' Have you seen " The Times " Newspaper for the last 3 or 4 days ? ' ' No.' ' Because there is a systematic attack upon Grey, and panegyrics upon Brougham with a comparison between them to the prejudice of the *former*.   Brougham's late advancement of . . . Masters in Chancery is selected as a case in point.   The Lord Chancellor, it is said, had two brothers Lawyers, but he thinks it his duty to give this patronage to the old practitioners in his Court.   How unlike the *Nepotism* of Lord Grey.' Now you must know, Barry, that this word *Nepotism* as meaning relationship is known to be Brougham's *own word*, and it is equally known that William Brougham, the youngest brother and a clever chap, is a regular writer in ' The Times.'   Under such circumstances Lord Grey is deeply impressed with the idea that those attacks come from Brougham himself. . . .

" Well, another £23 earned this week. . . . If the Government will but linger on for some weeks, the sum gained *for me* is considerable. . . ."

" March 2nd.

" For once I abandon all sordid motives ; what is £3. 15. 0 a day to me ?   *For the present at least* I can live upon the pleasure.   I feel that Lord Grey has done himself such immortal honor, I am too proud of belonging to him, and to a Government that has for ever knocked out the eyes of all the Nomination Borough Men. Poor Niffy Naffy Cleveland, poor dawdling Fol-ky, you might both of you as well have given me a last turn, but I'm glad you did not ; it suits my feelings better to laugh at, and despise you. My obligations to poor Bob and Lord Thanet were great, and the recollection of them is a sincere pleasure. To think of that low lived Twitch Bernard,* he is floor'd too, thank God ! If there is one thing more humourous than another in this projected Reform, it is the delicacy with which the right of voting is treated in such Boroughs as are still to send Members. . . .

" . . . At Crocky's last night, it was a decided Anti-reform concern and numerous. . . . But thank God in the face of every one of these worthies, and in his manner of talking too, there was an evident misgiving and despair that so sweeping a measure should *ever have been proposed* by any Minister. Indeed ! ah there's the rub, my boys, because as sure as my name is Diddy Creevey, this sweeping plan of Reform never will be for a moment lost sight of, from the time of its birth, and that it *must* and *will* be carried, but as you say, Barry, When ? . . . "

" March 3rd.

" Well, and what think you of our Reform plan ? . . . I quite long to see Lord Grey. What a charming thing for the old ' grey knit pantaloons and black gaiters ' to have come out again for such a triumph as this. . . .

" . . . Meetings are called in all the Parishes in

* 12th Duke of Norfolk.

London and Westminster to testify their gratitude to the Government.

" Dear Lord Cleveland loses every close seat he has, and yet to my infinite surprise Ly. Augusta told me last night at Ly. Salisbury's that her Father would support the Bill. . . . If you would really like to see the effect of this Reform Bill upon the r-a-a-lly grave and reflecting mind, you should have seen your Squire Western with me yesterday. After having looked me through with *awe* for some minutes he said, ' Did you ever hear of such a plan of Reform as this in the World ? ' ' Never.' ' It is quite impossible it ever can be carried, Creevey.' ' It is as sure to be carried as we are now in this room,' and I added that if it should fail by a few votes, a dissolution would very soon put that to rights. He then said he did not know what to do, that Maldon was to lose a Member, and that he *dare* not vote for that. In short, I never saw a man in a greater *quandary* in my life. . . ."

" March 11th.

" . . . I said nothing, I think, of Lord Grey except that he was as pretty behaved to me as ever he could be, altho' at dinner on Thursday he begun with a very different and much graver manner than he had ever shown before. ' Upon my life ! Creevey, you *must* go to Court, you are very wrong in not doing so.' ' And am I,' said I, ' to pay £120 for my cloaths to go in ? ' ' No,' said he, ' it is only the dress of Privy Councillors &c. that costs so much,' and Lady Mary Wood added that Mr. Wood's dress (which is the same as mine is to be) cost £40, and so Grey is to take me in my new livery to the King on Wednesday week, and to the Queen the first Drawingroom afterwards.

To the first I go in *Blue pantaloons*, an immense broad
gold lace stripe down the sides, and BOOTS.   To the
Queen I go in *white* serrididles, white silk stockings,
shoes and *gilt* buckles, and a hat with *feathers* all
round the edges.   Thank God !   Mrs. Durham lends
me the hat, sword, shoes and knee buckles—they
belong to a lodger of hers now out of Town. . . .

" What think you of old Talleyrand, Montrond,
Sefton and myself playing seven or eight rubbers
together for 3 nights together, old Talley and I frequently partners ?   Sefton complimented me much
upon the *steadiness* of my play, and as in *my little* way
I picked up four pounds, it not only paid my *chay* out,
but I treated myself with another back, and gave
Luttrell a seat back in it, and set him down at Holland
House gate.   Apropos to Holland House, Luttrell
showed me before breakfast yesterday a letter from
My Lady. . . . She says in it, ' Pray give my kind
love to Mr. Creevey, and do persuade him if you can
to dine here and stay all night tomorrow or Tuesday,
or any other day he likes.   He knows how very much
we like him, and how desirous we are of living more
with him than we do, and *then I owe him much for
the different acts of kindness he has shown on various
former occasions to me and mine.*'   Now since the
world began, was there ever ? . . . Sefton instructed
the Dino as to all my brutal conduct to Lady Holland,
but both Dino and Montrond were much pleased with
this history of my rebellion, having both witnessed
the airs she gave herself at different times at Paris. . . .

" . . . From Stoke . . . we all went to see
Windsor Castle, the King having so settled it with
Sefton.   He told the latter he had no partiality for a
Frenchman, and still less (as he seemed to insinuate)
for Talley ; but tho' he would not see him, himself,

Sir F. Watson should have his orders to show Mnsr. Talleyrand and the rest of Lady Sefton's party the whole of the Castle. The Queen, too, I should think, would have had no turn for any *private* meeting with the Dino. . . . When we drove into the Court in the interior what should we see but the whole court in the act of mounting their horses and carriages, so of course our carriages took up a position as far removed from the Royalties as we could, and there we saw the whole concern. I was perfectly surprised at the Queen's pretty figure on horseback. . . .

" . . . Old Talleyrand was exceedingly pleased, and said it was much handsomer than Fountain-bleau. . . ."

Earl of Radnor to Creevey

" April 20th.

" Pray call on me in the course of the morning tomorrow, (Thursday), or Friday ; as soon after 10 as suits you will suit me."

Creevey to Miss Ord

" April 21st.

" . . . Well, I was at my post at Fol-ky's this morning, and it was as I supposed. . . . He said he had every reason to suppose in the event of a dissolution, that both his Downton seats would be vacant, as Shaw Lefevre was to stand for Hampshire, and his brother Philip for Cricklade, but that whichever was vacant was at my service. . . .

" Notwithstanding my face, I went both to old Sally's and Almack's last night. The first was rubbishy to the greatest degree, and the latter, after some time, a great deal too crowded. . . . I found Mrs. Durham just returned from the Play in a silk gown, and one bracelet studded with precious stones ; we

had a cheerful glass of gin and water together, which
was her present.

" . . . Only think that before I close this it will
be decided whether Mr. Diddy is to be a man or a
mouse. . . ."

" April 25th.

" . . . Here . . . is your Saturday's letter—full of
your natural rejoicing at our Billy's courage and
fidelity.* ' Where is my Crown ? ' said he as he was
preparing to enter the House of Lords, and as Lord
Hastings who carried it was preparing to put it on his
head, the King took it from him, put it himself on his
head, observing at the time that no one should crown
him but himself, and having done this, he said to
Lord Grey, ' Now, My Lord, the coronation is over,'
and again he said out loud, ' Lord Grey, carry the
sword of state,' as he did, standing by his side on
the throne whilst he read his admirable speech.   You
must know that in former times our Billy has often
been heard to say that if ever he was King he would
never submit to be crowned by those fellows the
Bishops, and it is supposed that his putting the Crown
on himself the other day, and adding that the Coronation was then over, had to do with the same sentiment,
and that very likely he don't mean to have a
Coronation.

" The whole Town thro' which I passed in my way
here is getting ready for an illumination tonight—
the Mansion House raally beyond. . . ."

" April 27th.

" It was really a curious sight in my way here to
see the almost universal attempt from Charing Cross

* The King was very popular now as a result of his action in
dissolving Parliament.   The reference is to the opening ceremony.

to this Tower to get up something more than mere
lights for the illumination this evening. Portraits of
William and Adelaide, sea pieces, flags without end
from windows and tops of houses. ' Reform ' in all
shapes, and devices, &c. In short, it is quite impossible to see the thing, and not be perfectly convinced
that the great mass of London, great shop-keepers and
small, take an intense interest in our Bill, so the Lord
send it may answer. . . .''

" April 28th.

" . . . James Brougham and myself are to be
returned for Downton next Wednesday. . . .''

"April 29th.

" . . . I learnt from my Patron that going to
Downton was quite out of the question, a practice
never heard of. What a nice place ! To have two
such, Appleby and Downton ; really for old School
Lane it is too. He asked me if I would be returned
as T.C. of Rivenhall Place but I preferred *Bury Street*,
thinking the other would have been foolish. . . .''

" May 7th.

" Was there ever anything like our success in
County Elections ? In Essex, Bedfordshire, in
Huntingdonshire, (a new man and Reformer beating
the Duke of Manchester) ; Lord Ed. Somerset has
struck for Gloucestershire, Lord Robt. Manners for
Leicestershire. To sum all, Lord Lonsdale consents to
let a Reformer come into his hitherto pocket county of
Westmoreland.

" I foresee that the loss of the Durham seat will be
a lasting sore place to the Taylors—to her particularly.

" In ' The Star ' of last night there is a truly
affecting article. In congratulating the country on

the defeat of various anti-Reformers it likewise con-
gratulates them ' upon the return to Parliament of
that honest Member, Mr. Creevey, for Downton.' . . ."

" May 26th.

" Andrew * is really capital in his letter, and it is
a very great pleasure to see him enter so heartily into
this change.   I have no doubt he feels he is at a kind
of stand still where he is as to the *World*, and is
anxious to see it on a larger scale.   I remember
distinctly that it was the same feeling that made me
bother my Mother into sending me from Liverpool,
South, and I was then older by a good part of a year
than Andrew is now.   If Sandhurst suits his disposition and he is happy there, which I have no doubt he
will be, I am quite sure it is much the most *rational*
education that the country can supply. . . ."

" Brooks's, June 15th.

" As I mean to be at the Honorable House at 2
today to take my seat, I am cutting the Tower, you
see.

" I dined with the Ladies in Arlington Street
yesterday, Baron Sefton † of Croxteth dining at
Holland House, and we Ladies all went to the Opera ;
not however so early that I had not time enough to
pick up from our Francis after dinner much of his
news from the Foreign Office.   *He* thinks Palmerston
will resign that office, . . . he has received a very
great affront . . . from Brougham. . . . When a
Head of a Department receives a dispatch . . . it
goes its round in an official box to all the other Cabinet
Ministers.   Upon a late occasion when some document

* His nephew, Andrew Hamilton.
† Lord Sefton had received a U.K. peerage.

of this kind from Palmerston's office was making its round, and had reached Brougham, the latter in forwarding it, was pleased to accompany it with some observations of his own in writing, and the most adverse possible to Palmerston ; when this came to the ears of the latter, you can't be surprised at his flying out, and the notion in the office is that he will resign, and *Lambton* alias Durham is talked of as his successor. . . . Sooner or later Brougham and Lord Durham must capsize the Government and ruin Lord Grey. . . .

" The Ladies yesterday gave me a capital account of Papa at the Bazaar. . . . When the Queen arrived she was received by the Stewards, it is true, but the collection of people in the room for the purpose of seeing her was so immense that the Stewards found it utterly impossible to conduct her in. . . . When I mention the names of Lord Lansdowne and Lord Cawdor as two of the most active of the Stewards, you will conclude that poor Queen Adelaide was not in a very hopefull way in this dead lock. However, the Stewards had the good sense to turn their eyes towards Sefton, and by common consent implored his succour. Sefton only consented upon being armed with one of the official *H*osier sticks, and this being done, he placed himself in front of her Majesty, and began his march ; the success of which is represented as having been miraculous—his constant and *loud* observation was ' Ladies, it is as much as my place is worth not to make room for the Queen, and do it I must,' and do it he did, by forcibly taking them in handfulls and stowing them away as he could, and yet he was so full of his jokes all the time that the victims themselves were even in good humour, and so must our Adelaide have been, for being once landed in the place prepared for her where Lady Sef-ton went to pay her respects to her, she kissed her. . . ."

" House of Commons, June 21st.

" So here I am again you see in the old shop, or rather in the new one to me. Its Library has been built since my last reign and is the best and most agreeable room in London.

" Well, I dined with my fellow servants [at Althorp's] yesterday, about 33 in number . . . I went in full fig, and I assure you altogether I had a very pleasant day. All whom I knew, and who were much the greater part of the Company, seemed as if they were really pleased at having got a merry old fellow and friend amongst them again. I assure you there was no end to the *petting* I received. It seemed as if I was recognised as the only dealer in Fun amongst the whole concern, and even my pushing a snuff box across the table after dinner with my *sword* was very graciously received. So much for Puff. . . ."

" June 29th.

" It is quite in vain for me to attempt describing the disgust with which the Honorable House continues to fill me—such a set of low devils. However, in some respects it may be useful to one, I drink much less wine, and keep much better hours, and I can take my own time of dining, which is about 6. . . .

" Poor Duncannon has enough upon his hands. He and the Duke of Sussex are *two*, the former as Surveyor of the Crown Lands, and the latter as Ranger of the Parks. The latter busy blockhead has taken to cutting down trees in Hyde Park, and has a turn for *planting*, neither of which he has the least right to, it belonging to the Woods and Forests, and he is extremely indignant at Duncannon having stopt him.

24

So to have his revenge, his Keepers are shooting dogs all day in Hyde Park upon the ground of their running after the King's deer. People have had their dogs shot at a few yards distance from them, and it is said there is going to be a breeze in the House of Lords about it. What a charming thing *Power* is. This is the first time little Sussex ever had it, and a charming use he seems inclined to make of it. . . ."

"July 11th.

" . . . *Rothschild* had dined at Sally's, and during dinner had received an express from Brussels with the news of Leopold being elected King. This he immediately sent down to Talleyrand and Grey, the former dining in Downing Street, and it was their first intelligence of the event. Sally had sent in to tell Sefton, and it was confirmed by the Ladies when they came home. This is really a great event, and another one of not less importance is that the French Elections turn out most favourably in the return of *Moderate* men and supporters of Casimir's Government. In the present state of the World this is of the first consequence, and allow me to add, to no persons more than to you female French Fundholders. . . ."

"July 13th.

" *No*, Barry, don't talk to me of an ' *Egg*,' an Egg that I may or may not ever want ; an Egg that I may or may not ever use. What I *do want* is the present pleasure of contributing my mite for the first time to the amusement of my benefactresses—the Place Ladies. . . ."

"July 22nd.

" Well, you see by the paper that we were close pressed last night about Our Downton. . . . Downton *was* in Schedule B.—that is to return one Member, but my wrong-headed . . . Patron said that it would still be impossible for him and his family not to return this one Member, and therefore to remove this scandal or temptation for ever, he kindly requested that the people of Downton should have no representative at all, by being placed in Schedule A. . . .

" In my way down to the Honorable I met Earl Grey walking up from the Lords in his white hat, and with one of his boys on each arm. It really was a pretty sight, they looked all three so happy. He made me turn about with them, and we talked of the destruction of our game, the 6 brace of prime Boroughs, the preceding night with great delight on his part. In crossing a street we were all nearly run down by Lord Lansdowne in his chaise and a pair of post horses, so I said, ' Bless me ! upon what rural excursion is the President of the Council starting at this time ? ' ' Oh ! ' said Grey, ' he is going to eat his Cheese-cake [?] at Richmond.' Very disrespectful to the Roscius, was it not ?

" We are to begin Reform tonight. . . ."

" House of Lords, Sept. 1st.

" Well, I hope I have done nothing wrong, but I have promised Lord Plunket that Andrew should be his Page at the Coronation. . . . I came in here for the chance of seeing Brougham, and as Lord Plunket came up to coze with me, I asked if any business was going on, and he said, ' No, I am only waiting for the Duke of Richmond to tell me if he has been able to get me a Page for the [Coronation] of whom I am urgently in want.' Then came in the Duke and said he had not succeeded, and then came up Sefton who said Spalding was to be Brougham's, and advised me at once to close with Plunket, telling Plunket at the same time that he would have much the finest and handsomest boy for a Page at the Coronation, and P. professed to be under the greatest obligations to me. Since then Sefton and I have been in Brougham's Private Room, and he most good-naturedly sent for the man who arranges the dress in every respect for the Pages. A scarlet tunic with standing collar and black stock, no waistcoat, white breeches and silk stockings, gilt buckles both knees and shoes, and a blue sash—expence under £20, a perfect fleebite, and if Mama consents, it will be the happiest moment of my life. . . ."

" Septr. 22nd.

" . . . So you see our Reform Bill is at last launched, and with a miraculous majority all things considered, viz., that Schedule A. and B. were all voters, that several voted for the 2nd. reading to see if it could be mended in Committee, and then voted against it last night ; to say nothing of our loss of newly created Peers, and by new elections. In short, the victory in our House is perfect, and the country will never consent that *their* Bill shall be defeated by the Lords, but nous verrons. . . .

" I am come to be ready to attend our Bill to the Lords, and by all appearances we shall have a rare bluster of Reformers to accompany our ' Pea and Thimble ' Lord John. . . ."

" Oct. 10th.

" All is bustle and excitement, the streets in the neighbourhood lined with constables without end to protect the Lords, and more especially the *Bishops*. 30 thousand of the Parish of Marybone met today in Regent's Park, and by far the greatest and most respectable Westminster meeting ever known took place today likewise.   The object the same in all— to support the Government, and to *renew* the Bill.

" A riot at Derby, and the goal broke open, *this* is bad.   The country in a state of desperation in all directions, i.e., in all the Towns.   Lord Dudley's house in Warwickshire said to be destroyed, and believed.   Devilish long faces in our Tories, I can tell you, and well may they be so.* . . .

" . . . I hear Grey is in very good spirits.   He is with his Sovereign at Windsor today."

" Ordnance Office, Dublin, Novr. 21st.

" . . . We are to have a good party in the park today, Duke of Leinster, the Lords Charlemont, Leitrim, Plunket, and Cloncurry, Stanley of course, and the tiers état.   Blake takes me out, and brings me back. . . .

" . . . Our Irish Survey Establishment about four miles out from Dublin . . . is by far the most perfect establishment you can imagine. . . . It is the head quarters for the general Survey now going on in Ireland, which is ten times more minute than that of England.   Fifty maps perhaps for a single county when it is a large one—containing every parish or home-land, I might almost say every house.   Then in *books* is contained the history (that is the *statistical* history) of every parish, its soil, productions &c. &c., and in various cabinets is contained a portion of its mountainous substances. . . . As the County of Derry is the only one finished, they produced a sheet of it, and most beautiful it was, and *raally* it was funny enough that the most conspicuous home land of this sheet was ' *Creeve*donel,' so I could not help, you

* The Bill was rejected by 41 votes in the Lords.

know, claiming my property, coming from the North of Ireland as my Father did, and it led to some fun. . . ."

" Croxteth, November 26th.

" What happiness it is to live with either of one's own two families.

" I never saw our Earl in greater, *real happy* spirits than he is.   He on horseback, and the Ladies and I in a poney carriage and on foot have been following the shooters, i.e., the 3 sons, Mr. Hopwood, Aug's. Craven, and a brother officer of Berkeley's, till it was dark; and Sefton was delighted at the brilliant day's sport.   I said to Ly. Sefton how much better it was for him than to import those plundering swindlers who used to come and shoot his game, and get all they could out of him, and she said she quite agreed with me."

CHAPTER XVII

1832-3

REFORM BILL year was in truth less exciting than its predecessor. Grey persuaded the hesitant King to agree to a defined creation of peers, if needed to ensure the passage of the Bill through the Lords. But on April 14th, by a majority of nine votes, the unaugmented House passed the second reading. Suffering defeat, however, in the Committee Stage, the Government resigned, after Grey had failed to secure from the King powers for the creation of new peers wider than those to which he was already pledged. No other alternative being found practicable, King William recalled the Whig Ministry, and gave way to its demands. Thereupon the bulk of the Tory Peers, acknowledging defeat, let the Bill pass, and it received the Royal Assent on June 7th.

Creevey to Miss Ord

"Tower, Feby. 27th, 1832.

" . . . We had a comical party enough at Goodrich's [Lord Goderich] on Friday ; *our* Chief (Kempt)* had been caught up by some earlier invitation, and so had Lord Hill, so we Inferiors of the Ordnance— Kennedy, Duncan, Maberley and School Lane were there, and of Soldiers—Lord Fitzroy Somerset, Sir Willoughby Gordon,† Harry Grey, *Sir Hudson Lowe,*‡ General McDonald, . . . and 7 or 8 officials . . . My chief crony was *Gordon* whom I have always hated

---

* General Sir James Kempt commanded 8th Brigade at Waterloo. Master-General of Ordnance 1834-38.

† General Sir James Willoughby Gordon, Bart (1773-1851). Q.M.G. at Horse Guards.

‡ Bonaparte's gaoler at St. Helena was hated by the Whigs.

with considerable ardour, but as on this occasion he devoted himself exclusively to me, and as he was full of entertaining and sarcastic anecdotes relating to the Duke of Kent and the *late King*, he amused me very much.   Indeed, he was by no means amiss in his jokes upon his cousin, the Duke of Northumberland.   I was a little put to it when I entered the room, upon seeing Sir Hudson Lowe there, but I soon made up my mind to persevere in cutting him, for which Harry Grey said I was quite right, and if you come to that, I never saw any officer speak to him the whole day. Goodrich asked him to drink a glass of wine, and that was all the notice I saw taken of him by any one.

" It promised to be so foggy when I went there that I arranged with Durham that he should be there by ten with a coach, but the fog had then set in so intensely that he could not find his way till 20 minutes after, and when I got in, tho' assailed by a linkboy, I was above half an hour in finding my way to Bury Street. . . .

" . . . If the Bill is lost by Grey not using his power to make new Peers . . . even his *life* will not be safe ; to such a pitch is the reforming part of the press now goading the publick on this subject. Lord Ponsonby and Ellice were both of my opinion. . . ."

" Stoke, April 29th.

" . . . I found on my arrival here that Brougham had been most dreadfully out of spirits when here, tho' somewhat better the last two days, but according to Sefton—a perfectly altered man. He contrived however to *sleep* at night, which he had not been able to accomplish for some time before. He was here six days, and on one of them went over to see the King . . . *There* does not seem to have been

anything of their *first* good fellowship and *fun*, and
what there was of *politicks*, was more than suspicious.
He [the King] was prodigiously up at the 2nd. reading of the Reform Bill having been carried in the
Lords without any new Peers, and took great credit
to himself for having always predicted that it would
be so. . . . He did not ask Brougham to dine, nor
has he taken the least notice of the Seftons. . . .
What people are at the Castle are all *conservatives* of
the most ultra cast, and the Queen is said to be working heaven and earth on their behalf. Sefton wrote
to Lord Grey telling him he thought he ought not
to leave the Royal Camp entirely in possession of the
enemy at such a period, . . . to which Grey replied
very naturally that he knew all the mischief that
might arise from the present state of things at
Windsor, but that he could not intrude himself *without
an invitation. . . .*"

Defeated in the Lords on Lyndhurst's motion in
Committee, the Ministry resigned in view of the King's
refusal to enlarge the powers for creating the necessary peerages. But no alternative could be found.

" May 16th.

" From all I have learnt of yesterday's transac-
tions, when Wellington had announced to the King
that all his efforts to make an administration had
failed, the King *wrote* to Lord Grey, which in itself was
not civil, as he ought to have sent for him ; the
substance of the letter related to him, Lord Grey,
carrying the Reform Bill, but suggesting alterations
of some kind or other, and the *tone* of the letter not
over civil. To this letter, after it had been submitted to the Cabinet, an answer was returned by
Grey worthy of himself and his position, i.e., as firm

as a rock to his *Bill*. All that was further known last night was, that a great meeting of the Tories was held at Apsley House to whom it was stated by Wellington that the King was resolved to make no new batch of Peers on any account. After the conduct of these villains in consenting to advocate this Bill themselves, there ought to be no occasion for Lord Grey to ask the King for any such creation, but in order to meet a repetition of their villainy, it is absolutely necessary Lord Grey should have this power, and be assured that he will not start again without it. It is said Lord Grey has been with the King this morning, and, if so, of course must have been sent for. . . .

" Only think of little Derby (aged 80) being just now at the Levee presenting with Lord Sefton the Liverpool Reform Address to King Billy.

" You will see by today's papers that every Ambassador dined with the King yesterday ; they were expressly invited to meet his *New Ministers*. Upon your soul ! ' Where hast thou been all the day, My Boy Billy ? ' Did you never hear me sing that air amongst others of my Liverpool Juvenile favorites ? "

" Bury Street.

" Well, having seen Sefton passing by Brooks's window on his way from the Levee, I lost no time in following him, and found him in the midst of his Ladies ; so when I entered he called out with a loud voice, ' Good.' Again, ' Good.' So in descending to particulars, he had seen all the Ministers standing by the King as Ministers, and Grey looking more happy, he said, than ever he saw him in his life, and when Sefton came in contact with Holland, he said, ' Come, just tell me in a word. Is it bad or good ? ' and Holland said, ' *Good*.' Then again in passing Althorp,

Sefton said, ' Well, I pity *you*,' to which Althorp said,
' Yes, and after ordering my new gun too, and thinking I was going to have a real good shooting season.'

" The only other thing I know is that Grey had an
audience of the King for two hours before the Levee,
so there can be no doubt they are in again, and when
Ld. Grey could look so happy, one knows he is in
upon his own honest terms."

" Bury Street.

" Of all modern inventions recommend me to
Cabs. I picked up one in Cheapside, and absolutely
flew here. . . .

" *Mull** opened the Ball at the Palace on Friday
with Ly. Georgiana Grey, and the King told Princess
Lieven he was the best dancer in the room ; a compliment, which the young Ladies say is owing to
Mull *going it* or dancing rather like a *Sailor* when in
roaring spirits. When the Royalties came out of the
Supper room about half past one, a period when they
generally retire to rest, Billy laid hold of his first love,
Lady Sef-ton, and I was asked to guess how long he
sat by Mama in close conversation—only *one hour and
three quarters*. The Queen sent her Chamberlain to
him repeatedly to ask if he would not go to bed, to
which he always replied, ' Not *yet*,' and turning to
Lady Sefton said, ' You know I should lose you,
Madam, in that case.' "

The peers capitulated and the Reform Bill received the Royal Assent on June 7th. It became
necessary for Creevey to look round for a new seat.

" June 21st.

" Wonders . . . will never cease . . . *Old School
Lane* is in the new Parliament to be Member for

* Lord Molyneux.

Finsbury. Duncannon and Ellice have just been to announce this to me. It is Lord Grey and Lord Brougham's doing, their recommendation to this new District of that old, staunch and tried Reformer— Thos. Creevey, Esq. It is to be settled tonight, and the whole announced in print. Now all I ask is *this*, was there ever ? . . ."

" August 6th.

" *Dispatch*, My Dear, is the life and soul of business. I wish Andrew had seen me start from Kelvedon. After walking about for half or three quarters of an hour, a vehicle came rattling thro' the place, in which I was lucky enough to get a place. It is a new Ipswich coach called the '*Quicksilver*'! It is very near the ground to prevent it from upsetting, I presume, for altho' it has only two horses it goes at the rate of 12 miles an hour. . . . A gentleman behind dressed in scarlet . . . plays every possible tune on his bugle all the way. . . . The whole population from Kelvedon to Whitechapel turned out of their houses or windows to see. Dogs, cats, and horses were put to flight at our approach, and even waggon horses trotted off with their loads, so enchanted were they, or so frightened, by our speed or our musick. They change their horses every five miles, but it is quite impossible it can last ; they will either be stopt by some accident or indicted as a nuisance. . . ."

One by one the " faithful " secured their long-deferred rewards and Creevey's cronies assumed their blushing honours.

Sefton had received an English peerage, Brougham was Lord Chancellor, Michael Angelo Taylor, for three years Creevey's host and for decades the host of the Advanced Whig Party, had been fobbed off with a Privy Councillorship in lieu of the longed-for peerage,

and now Western, the champion of the agricultural
interests, the Squire, the Turkey, Stiff-rump Western,
transferred his stock of elaborate platitudes to the
Upper House.

Creevey was entrenched in his Tower, and more
concerned with its dicky and antiquated defences
against retrenchment than with the political situation.   He found no seat in the reformed Parliament,
and his interest in its doings now began steadily to
decline.   In the autumn he found occasion for another
dash to Ireland and " dear Bessborough."

Lady L. Molyneux to Creevey

" Jan. 7th. 1833.

" *Mr. Western, a peer.*   Am I the first to inform
you of that fact ?   Lord Cleveland and Lord Stafford,
Dukes.   This comes by to-day's post from Mr. Wood
to Papa. . . ."

Creevey to Miss Ord

" Tower, DEAR Tower, Jany. 12th.

" . . . I might as well say a word of the new
furniture in Downing Street at Earl Grey's, everything therein being all spick span new.   The two
principal Drawing Rooms opening into each other
are papered with a pattern of your Drawing Room
ground, and a large *gold* rose or flower of some kind.
. . . The curtains are yellow silk, . . . as gay and
handsome as possible. . . .

" . . . Grey . . . was low, both about his health
and the *perpetual applications to* him for promotion
in some shape or other.   He said I could have no
conception of it ; then he added he was equally
beset by people's *advice*, and that every man thought
himself the best fitted to be Minister of the country.
He talked of Western, and said, of course *I* must be
pleased with his peerage, and indeed if you come to

that, I am for ever congratulated upon my *old and intimate friend's* promotion, so I take it all mighty well. Grey asked me who he meant to leave his property to, and I said he had sent for me whenever he was ill for the last thirty years to ask my advice upon that subject, but that I did not think he had made up his mind even yet.

" . . . I, of course, was on the alert to find out if any other peerages were on the stocks for defeated County Candidates, and my mind was much relieved when Grey said, he should have liked very much to have recommended Sir Thos. Baring for a peerage as the head of that family, and as an additional mortification to Alic, but his having sons to succeed him *put that quite out of the question.* Western being a single man, and at his time of life, added to his service of two and forty years in the field, made it quite another thing. . . . "

" Feby. 27th.

" I have been an atrocious correspondent of late, but *raally* cold after cold quite disables one from writing, and then I think in the midst of your furnishing* you can't miss me much. . . .

" As I have been rather remiss once, or indeed twice, of late in not staying to the end of the ballet at the opera to be of use to my Ladies, I was determined to do my duty last night, and as my patron, the Earl of Essex,† found I was going there, he would take no denial of landing me there. In our way there he said, ' Creevey, Grey dines with me on Friday, will you meet him ? ' and when I said, ' With great

---

* The ladies had left Rivenhall and bought a freehold house at Cheltenham on Creevey's advice.

† George, 5th Earl, became Creevey's chief crony in the last years.

pleasure,' he added, ' And if you see Sefton tonight, secure him too.' When I reached my box the four Ladies in front were Lady Sefton, Lady Cowley, one of the Hardy girls, and Lady Caroline, (her three sisters being all disabled). When Sefton came in, which he always does from the Dandy Box below a short time before all is over, I could see in an instant the satisfaction it gave the Pet to see me there, and on what account, so he began with his endearments of, ' Where do you dine, Old Fellow, on Thursday ? You never come to Crockford's, do come tonight,' so when the thing ended, which by great curtailments it was made to do at ¼ *past one*, I had to perform my part. My Lord handed down Lady Cowley, and I Lady Sef-ton, and the two young ones had Francis and C. Grenfell, and having performed my task I walked to Crockford's, and the flood of mud of the morning was much abated, not so my hoarseness which had gained upon me considerably, but I was very temperate indeed, and having looked over Sefton and seen him win £1,200, I left him and his resort of virtue about ¼ after three, and on waking this morning I found my *voice* again as fresh as a four year old, and every other symptom in a corresponding state of improvement. . . .

" Enter Major Hamilton * armed *cap-a-pie* (or epie, how do you spell it ?) just come from the presence of his Sovereign, . . . he looks so *very*, VERY well and handsome. As for Mrs. Durham she can scarcely keep her lips off him. King Billy must have been struck with him, for he said, ' You are a young man,' and then he bid one of his attendants observe the Waterloo Medal. . . .

* Anne's brother-in-law, Alexander, 73rd Regt. ; Ensign at Waterloo.

" Enter the Treasurer's Messenger from the Tower with Miss Ord's letter from 1, *Lansdowne Terrace.*

" Nothing gives me more sincere pleasure than the satisfaction you express with your new house, and which of course ought to increase every day that it is nearer being all furnished. . . .

" . . . I have the pleasure of informing you that your first letter from No. 1 came free with its circular red mark, and only little black canal on it with

Penny post Cheltenham

" March 11th.

" . . . Our Friday's dinner with the Chancellor, tho' a very natural agreeable thing, was not as frisky as I expected. . . .

" We went up to dear Lady Vaux's* before dinner, and drunk tea with her after, and she was quite as frightful and languishing as ever. Miss Spalding dined with us, and the little girl was in the Drawing-room. Her colour has been greatly exaggerated. She looked a very sensible, interesting little thing with her eyes and ears all about her. . . .

" Yesterday at Kensington we had the Dinorbins and Bulkeley Williams, Annis Williams and her Sister Pierce and her Husband, Lord Uxbridge, Lord Baltimore (young Mary Brandling's friend), Count Daneskield (The Dane), John Grey and myself, not excepting the Lord in waiting—Lord John Churchill, who Lady Bulkeley told me is making violent love to Fanny Hughes, with the entire approbation of herself and parents. Of course *Ciss*† was there, and every

* Brougham took the title of Lord Brougham and Vaux, the latter an ancient barony to which he claimed to be heir-general.

† The Duke of Sussex's first wife, Lady Augusta Murray, died in 1830. Their marriage had been declared void in 1794. In 1832 the Duke married Lady Cecilia.

inch a Princess. Suss : handed her out, and she sat
next him, and it was very amusing to see how distinctly she showed herself to be his wife, and the
mistress of the house. . . .

" I have never mentioned poor Dudley's death.
He has left Mrs. Wm. Spenser £800 a year, and £30,000
amongst her children. . . . He has left £2,000 a year
to *Lady Lyndhurst*, so it is said, but more of this will
be known in a day or two. It seems that upon one
occasion when Dudley's mother thought he was going
to be married, she sent him her Diamonds for his
Bride, and they are known to have been very magnificent ones, so as they were never afterwards returned,
there has been a great search made after the box that
contained them, which at last is found, but alas !
pretty much in the state of Lucy Locket's pocket,
when Kitty Fisher found it—the devil a diamond in
it.

" It is said that our Stanley has a rare flogging in
store for Joe Hume tonight. I hope he may lay it on
the puppy well. . . ."

Viscount Althorp * *to Creevey*

"Downing Street, April 5th.

" My Dear Creevey,

" This is a very disagreeable note for me to write
to you, but it must be done. I see clearly that we
cannot defend the existence of the office of the
Treasurer of the Ordnance. We have fought off the
evil day . . . but with the present House of Commons this will not do . . . I felt myself obliged to
speak to Lord Grey about it. . . . He felt it very

* " More of a grazier than a statesman," yet loved and respected as
" the very model of the English country gentleman, ardently desiring
the good of his country," Lord Althorp, afterwards 3rd Earl Spencer,
was a fine product (and typical) of his day and class.

25

much, and you and I have so long worked together,
. . . that I can assure you I never was more sorry for
any thing of the kind in my life. . . ."

Creevey to Viscount Althorp

"Bury Street, April 5th.

" No note from you can be ' disagreeable ' to me,
because you never do anything that is not perfectly
right. You are very kind in your expression of
regret at being obliged to sacrifice my office. I can
assure you I value such feelings on your part more
than I do my office. . . .

" I beg to repeat my obligation to you for the kind
manner in which you have communicated to me this
absolutely necessary act of justice and economy. . . ."

Creevey to Miss Ord

" *Tower*—no longer ' *Dear* Tower ' but
Tower, *Oh dear.*
" April 6th.

" Well, what of that, ' 'tis but in vain for soldiers
to complain,' and my short lived Military Career has
afforded me many, very many *agreements* (as our
Michael often says), and then again, it has in fact
lasted longer than I expected. . . .

" As I have always heard that Ladies should wear
something *new* on Easter Sunday, I had got four little,
very little pets of handkerchiefs for the Place Ladies
and Annie, which please me by their *gaiety*, tho' in
fact such trifles. Then whilst buying them at
Lewis's I rather fell in love with the pretty *colour* of a
gown, indeed I believe it was a *Robe* and made at
Paris as such, and I thought it was peculiarly suited
to Mrs. Hamilton, and so I bought it for her, and very
very cheap I thought it, and *paid for*, honour
bright. . ."

"April 20th.

" Many thanks to you, my pretty, for your daily accounts of your invalids. . . .

" What think you of 24 being ill in Duncannon's family. . . .

" The humble individual, who has now the honour of addressing you, has never been entirely free from it,* nor ever *much* affected by it. I had rather a threat one morning this week having waked about seven with considerable pain in every limb of me, but I was not to be done in that way, so having buried myself in the middle of the bed for three or four hours till I was as wet as a drowned rat, I rose as fresh as a four year old. . . ."

"May 20th.

" . . . There was no Lady Grey's on Friday on account of the Queen's Ball. Adelaide is an ex-cellent waltzer, it seems, and she waltzed or *V*altzed (which is it ?) with both young Orléans and the Duke of Brunswick.

" . . . Young Brunswick is much offended at playing second fiddle to young Orléans, and says that as *reigning* Duke he ought to rank first. On this account *he* would not attend the Review the other day, and he is to have another for his own self this week after the Frenchman is off.

" Upon the last occasion, when the Duke of Wellington saluted the Duke of Orléans at the Head of his own Regiment as its Colonel, Orléans broke ground, and said to the Beau he had received nothing but honors since his arrival in England, but that the greatest of all was reserved for that day, and which he had just received. Well done, *parlez vous !* A

* Influenza.

capital contrast with the Beau pointing at his broken windows, was it not ?

" Then the Dino* is everything one could wish in her anxiety for all going right. The Queen of France wrote to her begging she would be a *Mentor* to the youthful Orléans whilst here ; on which account she told the Seftons *she did not dance in his presence, thinking it unbecoming the character of a Mentor ;* but at the Queen's Ball when Adelaide was asked to dance, she replied that she could not if she was the only married woman, so the Dino was asked to stand up to remove this difficulty, and the Mentor for that once complied. . . ."

" May 23rd.

" . . . Last night I went in again to Lady Grey's, and I am quite sure never was there any thing so well timed as this visit of mine. . . . There sat Elizabeth Bulteel, and Lady Mary Wood on a sofa, and at a table before them were seated Countess Grey, and the Duchess of Sutherland,† ci devant Stafford, and not a soul else, except Wood in the corner of another room with a diplomat. Never was anything more visible or more funny than the *relief* my arrival was to Lady Grey ; ' Oh, dear Mr. Creevey, how nice and good in you to come to me. Do pray come and sit in this chair next to me.' As I was quite in the humour for answering the whip forthwith, it was as good as a play to see old Sutherland moving her huge derrière by slow and dignified degrees about in her chair, so as to come into action if necessary, I having utterly defeated the tête-à-tête between her and Lady

---

* Talleyrand's niece, Duchesse de Dino, acted as hostess at the French Embassy.

† Elizabeth, the Countess-Duchess ; married George, Marquis of Stafford, created 1st Duke of Sutherland in January of this year.

Grey, to the evident and unspeakable delight of the latter, who, if I ever appeared to be stirring, always said, ' *Pray*, Mr. Creevey, don't think of stirring.' . . ."

" June 8th.

" . . . I had two charming days at Windsor. Col. Ferguson you know is there with his Regiment of Guards, and whilst they are quartered there, he has hired the house in the College of one of the Canons, Dr. Stopford, and in this house I was. There never was such a position for actual beauty, and the most striking and charming associations. The house stands on the pent of the hill near the top, commanding old Father Thames, and young Eton Boys in their boats on it. Eton College and its chapel, and all the beautiful country about it, to say nothing of Stoke Church steeple, in the churchyard of which lies Gray whose descriptions of this scene will never die. Then I could hear the organ of St. George's Chapel whilst I was dressing, and had not fifty yards to go to be present and hear the Anthem in it before I went to the Races. Then again the North Terrace was open to me about 50 yards further, with the Castle by my side. In short, such a spot to feast one's eyes, and employ one's mind in reminiscences, the country cannot furnish. . . . Our dining men were all Guardsmen, and my two playfellows in particular Lord Charles Wellesley (the Beau's second son) and young Lord Louvaine. The first is the image of his Father in manner and voice, and two better behaved or *heartier* young ones I have never seen. You ought to have seen the care they took of me on the race course, and above all that I should have my due share of the eatables and drinkables. . . . I never spent two more agreeable days in my life, and when we returned to Windsor yesterday about half past six, my little cart from Slough was at the door, and I was at Stoke before My Lord and My Lady arrived from Town. So it was all mighty well. . . ."

" July 4th.

" . . . Yesterday, you know, was Lady Holland's benefit at ' Essex's.' As the Cabinet always dine together on Wednesday, she invites herself out on those days, as she can't bear being left alone. Altho' it was her own doing my being asked to meet her, . . . according to Sefton, I was to be very roughly handled by her in return for my late perfidy in neither going to her as I promised, or sending any excuse, and this too, as she told Sefton, after her maid, Mrs. Brown, had taken such pains *in making my bed* AS SHE KNEW I LIKED IT. . . . When dinner was announced, ' Essex ' took out Lady Mary, and Lady Holland putting her arm thro' mine said, ' Come, take me,' and as we dined most punctually Duncannon, Charles Fox, LeMarchant, and some one else did not come till we were set down. . . . Old Madagascar was much more civil to myself than to Essex. She began by complaining he had no fire for her, then she was very badly helped to turtle, and said so, and condemned it with great reason as being both bad, and ill dressed, and when he helped her to some venison, she said it was much too hard for her digestion, and sent it away. When she . . . left us after dinner, she said, ' Lord Essex, have you ordered the fire to be lighted in the next room ? ' and upon his saying, ' No,' she said, ' Then I shall light it myself,' and accordingly it was all alive O when we went to Coffee. . . . Lady H. had lighted it with Essex's notes from the card rack on or over the chimney. . . ."

" Septr. 11th.

" . . . I must just give you a little more of our
Diplomatic Party at Stoke last week. . . . The . . .
great subject that was handled by our Princess Lieven
and the Dino was, being *bored* and the protection
against it, and I assure you the discussion was most
animated. The Lieven's creed was that she *would
not* be bored, and the Dino's that she *could not*. The
Russian avowed that the instant a person began to
bore her, she got up and left him, and that nothing
could or should extort any civility from her at the
expence of being bored ; so the Dino said, ' What do
you do when you stay at Windsor with the Queen ? '
' Oh ! ' said the other, ' Elle m'amuse,' which I think
was very *low* ; she ought to have said *that* was her
trade—civility to crowned heads, particularly to those
she was Ambassadress to. Then the modest Lieven
said, ' She knew in return she must bore people herself, for she had observed that at dinners she was the
only person who had ever an empty chair next to her,
and that she was always sure of one if there was a
place to spare ' ; ' but,' said the Dino, ' that is from
the fear of people lest they should bore *you*. The
Dino said that from her infancy she had always had
civility to every one impressed upon her most strongly
as her first lesson, and that from having always
practised it, she did not know what boring meant.
She mentioned a curious fact of old (or, as she said,
Mons'r) Talleyrand, viz., that he hated to be left
quite alone, that he preferred the company of the
most stupid companion to such solitude, and she
added that when there was more than one such
person, it was understood between them that she was
to take the most stupid to herself, and that she often
did so for hours without any *gène* to herself. (Is that

right ?) As the Lieven could not be shaken in her
own hostility to civility, the Dino tried for a compromise with her in favor, at least, of *parent* or *un mari*,
to which the Lieven made her last reply, ' J'ai un
grand respect pour mon mari, mais il m'incommode,'
so that ended it, but it was really very curious, and
very entertaining. . . ."

" Bessborough, Oct. 30th.

" . . . It is not the outside of this house alone
that is so interesting to me ; perhaps there is no
such treasure in the United Kingdom for a *Memoir
Man* to fall in with as Duncannon. He is in constant
correspondence with Sir Herbert Taylor,* which in
truth is with the King, about the state of Ireland, the
question of tithes &c. &c.   He had an excellent letter
from Taylor yesterday with various messages and
opinions in it from the King on publick matters. Then
as the Board of Works in England is now united with
the Woods and Forests, Duncannon† manages all the
palaces, so yesterday brought him a collection of
patterns *for him to* choose out (such manufacture !) for
the furniture of the Queen's apartments in Buckingham House. Lady Duncannon and I were quite
agreed about which she should have, but Duncannon
would not hear of it as being much too dear ; he
would not go beyond six shillings a yard. Then he
had the devil's own trouble with the Duchess of Kent,
who bothers his and Lord Grey's and the King's life
out with the perpetual demands she makes for
alterations, additions, furniture, &c. &c. on her
Royal Residence. In short, there is no end of her
bother. Then Duncannon is now in the most con-

* Lt.-Gen. : Surveyor-General of Ordnance : became Private Secretary
to William IV.
† He was then Commissioner of Woods and Forests.

fidential correspondence with Ld. Grey about the
latter's wishing to *resign* his office, ditto with Althorp
on the same *pint*.   Duncannon has shown me all the
correspondence without reserve.   The letters are all
copied by his Daughter into a book, but I have seen
the originals.   Then he is in the same confidential
correspondence with Wellesley upon the projected
measure of the latter for Ireland and I am quite
astonished at the liberal views of Wellesley, and the
great talents he displays in stating them. . . .

" Our only company is the young Lord Kerry,*
Lansdowne's son, and Miss Augusta's intended
husband.   He is, *I think*, a nice young man, not very
lively as far as I see, and *she* less so, but very pretty.
Would you believe it, that altho' the Lansdownes
were here the other day, *He* never mentioned the subject, nor had he ever before to Duncannon, and as
the latter told me, *he* never should begin it.   It is
all settled between the two Mothers, but he, Lansdowne, having, as he says, made up his mind *eight
years* ago that his son should not marry till he was 23
years old, and as he is not to attain that age till next
March, the Marquis won't hear of the marriage taking
place before that period.   Was there ever such a
damned fool, as Duncannon and I both agree ? . . . "

" Nov. 2nd.

" . . . I told you of the correspondence going on
between Lord Grey and Duncannon when I arrived
here, the subject of it being no less than Lord Grey's
intense desire to give up the Government, that is, his
position in it. . . .

" This brings me to Duncannon's correspondence

* William Thomas.   The marriage took place in March 1834.   He
died in 1836.   Lady Kerry married Hon. Charles Gore in 1845.

with Sir Herbert Taylor, or in truth with the King. The latter has been under an impression for some months past that Lord Grey's Government, at least *his position in it*, hangs by a thread, and he shows great anxiety as to his probable successor. His own man is *Lansdowne.* . . .

" This brings me back again to Durham. *He* too knows that Lord Grey's Government hangs by a thread, and he is deliberately doing all he can to drive him to resign, *and to succeed him.* The villain is perfectly restored to health by Quin, the Quack Doctor, and he modestly avows that political occupation is his object, and that he will have it. . . . As he has quarrelled openly with most of the present Government, he can expect no support from them, nor can one have a conception how a man so generally odious as he is, can find support from any quarter, *except one*, and that one is demonstrably his game. I mean the Duchess of Kent, and her Daughter. His attentions to them in the Isle of Wight this summer convinced me he had his views upon them, but here again our invaluable Duncannon has the connection in proof. Sir John Conroy, the Duchess's present man, is in constant correspondence with Duncannon on her behalf. She is the most restless, persevering, troublesome devil possible, neither the King nor Lord Grey will answer her applications any more, and every thing is referred to Duncannon. In return, thro' Conroy to Duncannon, she expresses the most violent indignation both against the King and Grey, considers and states that as Mother of the Princess Victoria she is entitled as *matter of right* to every thing she asks, that she will receive nothing as matter of favor &c., and Conroy upon more than one occasion has had the folly to add that her Royal Highness having consulted the Earl of Durham had the entire sanction of his opinion in her favor. Was there ever ? . . .

" I could write volumes in favor of *every one* in this house, the Father and Mother, six Daughters, and four Sons, with two of the latter articles besides now in England. I am very much disposed too in favor of our young Earl of Kerry. A more natural, unaffected young man I have never seen, and I have just been expressing my delight to Ly. Duncannon that I can't discover in him in any one respect the slightest resemblance to his Father. She laughed (and could not do more). . . ."

Lady Louisa Molyneux to Creevey

" Stoke.

" . . . We have had one more dinner at the Castle for the opening of the Waterloo Gallery, in which they dined, using St. George's Hall as a Drawing Room, which when comfortably furnished has all the appearance of a snug boudoir. We concluded the anniversary of some victory had been selected for the occasion, and upon consulting *history* could find no such event on the 14th of October since the Battle of Hastings, which of course we took as a personal compliment, but neither William the Conqueror nor any of his followers were mentioned.

" . . . Our party was a little agitated (but not the less gay) by the arrival from Antigua of the consent of Sir Evan Macgregor to his son's marriage with Mary Hardy,* which was immediately followed by the young gentleman himself. We were much pleased with him, and they are to spend their honeymoon here. . . ."

* Daughter of Sir Thomas.

Creevey to Miss Ord

" . . . It was my intention to be off tomorrow morning, but in the middle of yesterday comes to me a card of invitation from My Lord and Lady Lieutenant to dinner yesterday, and of course I went. . . . After we had been there some time, enter their excellencies arm in arm as King and Queen, bowing condescendingly to their little circle till the little Marquis with his piercing eyes said, ' That is Mr. Creevey, I'm sure,' and then coming forward he took hold of my hand with both of his and said, ' I am glad we have caught you at last, Mr. Creevey '; then her excellency* put her hand out to shake with me, but she was, or meant to be, every inch a Queen the whole day. As dinner was announced the moment the Viceroys were ready, Wellesley on handing out the Queen called out, ' Mr. Creevey, let me have you on my left side at dinner as I have a great deal to say to you,' he having his deaf ear to her Majesty, and I assure you from the time we sat down for a couple of hours, I should say, the Marquis and I had such an incessant run of jokes and stories that we quite convulsed all our household. There is a charming son of Lord Grey's in the household, and I shall never forget his delight. In spirits and accuracy in recollection, quotation &c. &c. Wellesley might be *twenty* instead of 75. We went on long after Mrs. Viceroy had left the room, and he having gone out before, he had told Lady Wellesley, as she told me, that I had made him laugh more than he had done for ages. She looked handsomer than I ever saw her, and would willingly have conquered

* Lady Wellesley was formerly Mrs. Paterson, an American. Her sister was the 1st wife of Jerome Bonaparte, King of Westphalia.

herself and been comfortable with me, but dare not.
. . . I suppose she has promised Queen Adelaide
that as her representative she would keep herself up.
Ld. Geo. Hill and all the others quite smoke it, and
in truth it is both great folly and vulgarity in her.
Nevertheless, I dine there again tomorrow at his
request. . . ."

CHAPTER XVIII

1834

In 1834 the Whig Ministry was split, in part by the intrigues of Brougham, over Irish policy, and the Coercion Bill gave Grey the opportunity he had come to welcome of retiring from public life. Before he handed over patronage for ever, he was happy to offer his old friend Creevey a secure anchorage for the rest of his life. Creevey, who sincerely admired Grey as a man and not as a bestower of patronage, gives a charming picture of the Prime Minister of Reform in the first days of his retirement.

Governments came and went. Melbourne succeeded Grey, but went out in November, when, on Wellington's advice, Sir Robert Peel was summoned from Rome. Wellington acted as Pooh-bah until Peel reached England at the end of the year, and the piquant situation gave the Whigs a rich banquet of gossip and speculation. But Commissioner Creevey merely toyed with this fare. It is noticeable that in reckoning the date of Peel's arrival, he was estimating the chances in a race between the new Premier and the last instalment of his salary from the Ordnance Department.

A very rare autograph is included in the letters of this year, the only example of Miss Creevey's hand-writing in the huge collection of papers. Short as her letter is, it gives a clear picture of a stiff, prim, and sometimes disapproving spinster of the middle class, whom naughty boys of whatever age are apt to hold in awe, especially when material expectations depend on good conduct.

Earl of Sefton to Creevey

" Jany. 9th, 1834.

" With so many real friends as you have *in high quarters* I cannot consider you as thrown upon the wide world. I have not a doubt that something permanent will be found for you, but even your present situation does not appear hopeless. . . ."

Creevey to Miss Ord

"Jany. 21st.

"When I wrote last to you I was not aware that *Auckland* was to be promoted to a new place in the Exchequer, in consequence of Lord Grenville's death, and the termination of his place as Auditor of the Exchequer. This produces a vacancy in Auckland's present office of Auditor of Greenwich Hospital. I have, of course, been turning in my mind who was likely to get it, and yesterday I thought I might as well just look into the Town for the chance of seeing Ellice or Duncannon, so I went down to the War Office where I found the former. After some general conversation about our Ministers &c. &c. he said, ' You know, Creevey, that Auckland's place at Greenwich is vacant, and either you or Geo. Ponsonby is to have it, and I think it will be you. Do go now to Lord Grey and he will talk to you about it,' so I said, ' I shall do no such thing. I am not going to set myself up against a Brother of Lady Grey's.' ' Oh ! ' he said, ' Lord Grey would much rather you had it, because he is sure George is too idle to attend to it, and then I tell him the Press will never let him alone if he makes another appointment in his own family.' Of course I told him if it was given to me I should like it most extremely. . . . It will be curious enough if George Ponsonby gets it, for he is compelled to give up his present office of Lord of the Treasury worth £1,200 a year, upon the express ground of his incompetency. . . . However, one *must* suppose that he *will*, and I must kick my heels without it, for

Ellice says there is not a doubt of my present pet place being put an end to on the 5th of April next. This is rather tantalising, is it not ? However, ' 'tis but in vain for placemen to complain,' so ta, ta, My Dears all. . . ."

Earl of Sefton to Creevey

" Jany. 24th.

" . . . It is impossible not to admire the delicacy with which you declined calling upon Grey when Ellice urged you to do so ; who must have known what was best for you to do, but, to be sure, £800 a year for life with a house, rent and tax free at Greenwich, was not worth thinking of. After all, what is money, and independence for life ? You have, thank God ! a soul above such considerations. I cannot help, however, fancying this trumpery thing will be forced down your delicate throat, whether you will or not. I am very sorry I am not in Town to assure you there will be no disgrace in your taking it, even at the expense of Lady Grey's Brother. . . ."

Creevey to Miss Ord

" Jany. 31st.

" . . . I received a note from Kempt saying he dined at ½ past 6, and I was sure there was only one person in London or the world that could fix their own time for dining, and that at the eleventh hour too—Lady Holland—and so it was, and Lady Georgiana Grey came with her Father as the companion for her. We had a stupidish day enough, but I closed it, I think, rather cleverly. I asked Lady Georgiana if she should like to look in at the Seftons on her way home, and she said very much, if Papa did not object. . . . Soon after that they rose to take leave, and I said, ' What do you say to just looking in at the Seftons? ' and he having looked at Lady G., and she said she should like it much, in we all got, and when arrived in Arlington Street, Grey said, ' Come, Creevey, you must go in first ; we are your company.' So having admonished the servants to announce me only, all my family with one accord arose to accost me, and after many hearty shakes I said, ' I am not come alone, I have brought with me a Lady and Gentleman from the country, and in entered Lady G. and our own Prime Minister in his Star and Ribbon, and Garter and all, and the result was most successful, and if you come to that I think the whole performance was not amiss for old School Lane. . . ."

" Feby. 24th.

" Well, I suppose my Dears I must begin with my *cupping* first, and it is an operation that I doat upon ; the only drawback is that one does not *see* what is going on except by the flare of those little burnfires they put into little glass beehives, and then turn them down upon one's back under lock and key. Mr. Watkin of Savile Row who has the honour to cup all the nobility and gentry of the West End, arrived at 11 on Saturday night, precisely at the same moment with Freeman, and a genteeler man, with a more beautiful set of teeth, I know nowhere. Mrs. Durham was, of course, quite ready with her hot water basins, and *rags*, and we were in action in no time. ' Upon my word, Sir,' said the insinuating Watkin, ' there is not a young man in all London can produce more beautiful blood than yours.' Freeman too was very handsome on the same subject. *My* notion had been that cupping was a *dibbling* operation, and was therefore not a little

26

astonished to hear Watkin and Freeman observe,
' *that* makes twenty-two ounces,' and Freeman said,
' We will stop if you please.' . . . Would you advise
me to be proud ' of the blood in my veins ? ' . . . My
cough is dying away. . . . He is pleased to puff my
constitution very much as well as my blood, and re-
commends me much to be *good to it* in future.   One
of his prescriptions I approve of much, namely, that
when I dine (as I do always) at ½ past 7, I am to take
a single mutton chop, and a single glass of sherry in
the middle of the day.   He is a great enemy of
champaigne, and above all of mixtures, and as you
may suppose much in favour of *moderate quantities* of
whatever you drink, so it's all mighty well, and I
intend to be a very good *boy* from henceforth. . . .

" . . . I rather regret also having been obliged to
miss Earl Durham's last Thursday.   Ly. Durham
gave a very agreeable and indeed funny account of it
in Downing Street.   The heroine of the piece was
Miss Martineau.   You are, I dare say, aware of her
great fame as a writer of little popular essays upon
political economy, and from the success of which she
has relieved a long tribe of younger sisters and
brothers from poverty, suddenly brought upon them
by the imprudence of a Father.   Ly. Durham described her as very agreeable tho' compelled to use
two trumpets, the one for her immediate neighbours,
the other so long that she could shoot it out, not only
across the dinner table but the room, and then collect
anything you have to say to her, and reply to it.
Her writings have made such an impression in
America that she has received a regular invitation
from ' *the Union* ' to come and see and settle with
them, and she is going.

" Whether the two Yankees who dined at Lord

Durham's likewise were delegates sent in pursuit of her, I know not, but they return in the same ship with her, and her trumpets. . . ."

" March 7th.

" When a man has *two* swelled faces, I trust it will be considered as some little apology for idleness in letter writing, and yet I have no pain in either, merely *stiffness* and *distortion*. I dined nevertheless at the Duke of Norfolk's yesterday with Lords Grey, Carlisle, Durham, Lansdowne, Cawdor, Stafford, Surrey, Duncannon, &c. &c., and I was temperance itself, and yet the left cheek has shot ahead considerably this morning, so that positively I will not touch meat to-day, and with the least allowance possible of wine. . . .

" This nomination by Lord John Russell of *Gleig** to be Chaplain at Chelsea Hospital has made people absolutely furious. That it should have made all Kentish men so is most natural, as he took the most active part in every way at the last General Election against the Whig Candidates for Kent. It is said to be Lady William Russell's influence over Lord John that procured this appointment, and she is a bitter Tory. Was there ever ?

" As for this promotion of Murray McGregor who married the youngest Miss Hardy, there is more made of it than it deserves. Lord John is the *hitherto* unsuccessful lover of Emily Hardy. The youngest sister is lately married to this young McGregor, son of Sir something McGregor, Governor of Antigua. It was supposed they would have a competence to start with, whereas they have not a sou, and John Russell has given him a common clerkship in the Pay Office.

---

* Rev. Geo. Gleig, author of " A Life of the Duke of Wellington " and " The Subaltern," served as a soldier in the Peninsula and at Waterloo. A strong opponent of the Reform Bill.

This is all, and if it had not been coupled with the Gleig case would have gone for nothing, tho' the family of McGregor in the Co. of Perth election were quite as violent against the Whig candidate as Gleig in Kent. . . .

" I reckon with confidence upon keeping my *good ear*. Freeman syringed it again yesterday, and it is going on as well as possible. I am not certain that Freeman does not give me too much physic. . . . I am a perfectly different man in every thing requiring any exertion, such as going up and down stairs, getting in and out of coaches. I have been fancying for months past from the bother and clumsiness with which I accomplished these different operations that it was the effect of age, and on that account thought little of it, whereas now, upon all such occasions, I am at least as active as I was ten years ago. . . .

" . . . You know the artificial terms that the whifling Lansdowne and I are upon, so I was rather curious to see yesterday if Lord Kerry's *apparent* admiration of my jokes at Bessborough had reached the Roscius. As you may imagine I did not put myself in his way, but having caught me with his glass, he came up to me, and putting out (not his hand) but one finger, said, ' How are you, Creevey ? You have been in Ireland lately at Bessborough.' ' Yes,' said I, ' where I had the pleasure of making Lord Kerry's acquaintance.' ' Oh,' said the Marquis, ' I believe it was from [him] I heard of you.' . . . Which was very handsome, you know, after having dined with us twice a week regularly in times gone by. . . .''

" March 25th.

" . . . Sunday at Lady Holland's was *beyond* ; I mean as to her capricious *muggery* from the moment I

went in. ' Creevey, you remember Brown, my maid ;
do go and see her.   I am sure she will be delighted to
see you ! ' So away we went into My Lady's bedroom,
and found Brown, and a female apprentice. ' Brown,
you remember Mr. Creevey ?   How kind he always
was to me at Brighton,' upon which Brown, by no
means inferior to her Mistress in muggery, said, ' Yes,
My Lady, I well remember Mr. Creevey's kindness to
you at Brighton, but dear me ! Sir, you don't look a
day older than when I saw you there.'   ' Ah ! Brown,'
said Lady Holland, ' is it not so ?   Indeed, Creevey, it
is quite a pleasure to see you look so well,' and by way
of beating Brown she said, ' I see no difference in you
from the day I first saw you ' ; so much for *cupping*,
for everybody says the same thing. . . ."

Earl Grey to Creevey

" 8th July.

" Lord Grey presents his compliments to Mr.
Creevey, and will be much obliged to him if he could
make it convenient to call upon him in Downing
Street before 5 o'clock today."

Creevey to Miss Ord

" July 11th.

" . . . My faithful *Cab-man** was in constant communication yesterday with both Grey and Brougham
respecting myself and Greenwich.   He learnt from
Lord Grey that on the day he sent for me . . . he
had taken the King's pleasure upon my appointment as Auditor of Greenwich, and which His Majesty
was pleased to approve of most graciously, so according to established rule, *that* is done, even if a New
Government—a Tory one—was to come in tomorrow ;

* Lord Sefton.

but the hitch is that Auckland and his *Sisters* are mighty fond of the house and the garden, and the flowers, and he is kind enough to offer to do the business of the office for nothing if he may keep the house, thus modestly depriving Government of their patronage, and myself of the salary. . . .

" Sefton was present last night in the Lords when Brougham called Auckland to him on the Woolsack and abused him like a pickpocket for treating the Government in this manner, and the man they were all so anxious to see in that place. ' Who is that ? ' said Auckland. ' Why, Creevey to be sure, who is Lord Grey's first object, and so he is with all of us.' . . . The villain Auckland . . . whispered or muttered something like, ' then he supposed he must give it up.' . . . ."

" . . . Taylor is dead. I called in my way down to Downing Street between 1 and 2 today, and he had been dead about a quarter of an hour. In my return I saw the cook (Cardwell) in the street, who told me he (Taylor) had not suffered the least pain. I asked after Mrs. Taylor, and he said she was pretty well. . . .

" . . . Do you know, I think I shall live permanently at Greenwich when once I get my house. I get fonder of the notion every day. I must have a *single room* somewhere in London to dress or sleep in occasionally, but as for a permanent lodging *by the year*, I mean to have no such thing. The notion of having a house of one's own over one's head in such a position, and with such advantages ! *Is it not too ?* How I long to see it. . . ."

" July 17th.

" . . . Sefton . . . learnt from Auckland . . . the salary was a *good* six hundred a year, and that altogether to *live there* the place is worth a good *thousand a year*, i.e., with no taxes, coal, candles, &c. &c. It is only *bread* and not *meat* that you have at the contract price. You have a Greenwich Pensioner for a servant whom you pay six pence a day ; that is the fixed price by Law, and you may have as many as you like at the same rate. Some of them, Auckland says, are very clever in the *kitchen*. But what gratifies as well as amuses Sefton the most is that *I shall be entitled to medical advice gratis*. As to the House, I don't stand in need of Auckland's or Essex's testimony in its favour, for Sir Thomas and Lady Hardy and their two Daughters go into it today, the Governor's House being at present unroofed and undergoing repair. So I think if the Governor of Greenwich himself, and Lady Sef-ton's own cousin— Lady Hardy—can be content to live in Old School Lane's house, its proprietor, Mr. Nummy, may live there too. . . ."

"July 18th.

" Barry, My Dear, don't tear or destroy the frank containing this note because it is

' *My House* '

at Greenwich just sketched off by Auckland as we were talking over matters, and he says he can't draw.

" You go up steps or stairs to the first, or living floor, and the kitchen and servants rooms are above. . . . Auckland says it is a very pretty house, and that his Father and Mother and five children lived in it for years before they succeeded to the other one. There *is* a garden, but it is a small one. . . . The River is a good deal further off than it appears in the drawing, but you see its relative position with the house. . . .

" I was shown in to the Miss Edens, and, as I told them, I looked about the room before I sat down to see if there was an Assassin concealed to murder me for taking their place from them, and we were all very jolly, and who should come in but Tierney, and we became more and more jolly still ; so it was all mighty well, you know. Miss Eden says there is very good society indeed at Greenwich composed of the different families on the establishment.

" I am delighted to find that the *small beer* is incomparable, and that we brew once a month. Nothing so nice to my palate as *New* Beer, all at contract prices. Thank God ! we are all out of the reach of Parliament. We live upon our own, without a stiver of publick money to be voted for us by that infernal House of Commons headed by Joe Hume.* . . ."

" July 22nd.

" . . . Suppose I was to run *stuffy* and not tell you where I have just been—at no other place than *Greenwich. Dear, Dear, Dearest* Lord and Lady Sefton, the Ladies Louisa, Katherine, and myself. . . . I am part of the Hospital, my rooms in the midst of Corinthian Pillars, the last corner of the right side of the quadrangle from the river. Looking from the river, four windows on that side of the quadrangle before you turn the corner, all commanding the river, and not one hundred yards from it. All the rooms so lofty, so clean. Oh dear, oh dear ! you must contrive to make it hold you. Such a distinguished passage that is, quite a walk for me. You don't mind the wash house and garden being a little out of the hospital, and the 3-stall stable and coach

* Joseph Hume (1777–1855) ; preached retrenchment *and* reform.

GREENWICH HOSPITAL AND PARK, SHOWING LONDON IN THE DISTANCE.

From a drawing by W. Westall, R.A.

[*To face p.* 386.

house 100 yards off likewise? Two rooms above the
coach house, one with a fire place and an excellent
loft besides. Such a charming kitchen range, water
laid in all over the house, two perfect waterclosets. . . ."

" August 2nd.

" . . . I send you the first official summons to Mr.
Commissioner Creevey for a Board Day at Greenwich.
Mr. *Secretary Lethbridge* had called here to take my
Patent with him to Greenwich, and had told Mrs.
Durham he believed there would be a Board on
Wednesday, but nothing of sufficient importance to
bring Mr. Creevey, if he was otherwise engaged. . . .
Is not this first act of mine a curious one—laying out
a nursery garden at *Alston*, or on *Alston Moor* of all
places in the world. Oh dear, oh dear! who would
have thought it, when old Sheridan and Charles
Warren and Tom Sheridan and I were larking and
fighting the battle of the Pyramids there 3 and thirty
years ago. . . .

" We had a great dinner of 30 people at little
Sussex's yesterday, all for Lord Grey and Lady Grey
too. I went with Lord and Lady Sefton. I think
we had five Dukes at least, and the Duke of Devonshire and another one missing.

" Lord James Fitzroy *was* Ly. Radnor's man, and
she has often told me that it was I alone who prevented her going off with him, which I take for
granted was a *lie*. . . ."

" Septr. 12th.

" . . . I was at dinner at Crocky's by half past
seven, and I praised it so much that *Monsr. Ude**
having heard from the waiters of my commendations,
came up to make me a speech of thanks, and then

* Lord Sefton's former chef became the genius of Crockford's.

winked and spoke low about people finding fault, and
I dare say longed to say particularly *those who don't
pay*, and then he asked after and talked about our
common friend, Lord Sefton. . . .

"Today . . . at Greenwich again, and I am
charmed with my temporary apartments—any thing
so beautifully clean, airy and in such order in every
way I defy any one to find.

"Lethbridge said that Sir Thos. Hardy having
heard I was to be at Greenwich today had expressed
a desire to see me, and of course I meant to call on
him, and Dee (the Clerk of the Works) in going over
the apartments with me said, ' Sir Thomas Hardy
had been already over them this morning, and said
he liked them better than those below.'   Just at this
time Lethbridge conducted the Dear Sailor up all the
stairs to me, and he shook hands with me in the
prettiest manner, and said he was quite ashamed of
keeping me out of my own apartments.   In short,
the face as well as manners of Nelson's Captain of the
Fleet were worth his weight in Gold. . . .

"I told Sir Thos. Hardy that under Ld. Sefton's
advice I had talked to, and meant to adopt the
counsel of Poodle Byng as to furnishing my apartments, and he laughed and said he thought the
Poodle over estimated his talent in that line, and that
he would bet Lady Hardy against him as a much
better manager in that respect. . . ."

Lady Hardy to Creevey

"Sept. 14th.

"Sir Thomas says you wished to know from me
the address of an upholsterer that would be less expensive, and equally good as the fashionable ones . . .
There is a good repository for furniture nearly

opposite Conduit Street in *Regent Street*.   I think the
name is Willan & Hart, but it is an open warehouse
with a great deal of furniture in the door and window,
and I bought some, and found them reasonable and
good.

" For objects of *taste* and good bedding &c. I
employ *Tratt & Atfield* in Lower Brook Street, and
found them very civil and more reasonable than I
expected, but not what could be called *bargains*.

" For Carpets and Curtains, I should certainly
say Graham of Holborn. . . ."

Creevey to Miss Ord

" Stoke, Septr. 29th.

" . . . I part company with Mrs. Durham the end
of this week, and heartily glad I am to do so.   I am
sick of her dirt.   We are, however, very good friends,
and she sees, I am sure now, her folly most clearly in
not having taken me as a Lodger *by the year*, as Mrs.
Hurrell used to do, and of course for much less
money. . . .

" I wrote to my Sister on Saturday to say I should
be at Croxton on Saturday next.   I think I shall go
on the following Saturday to Longford (Radnor's)
and then give Mrs. Taylor some days in the three
succeeding weeks, being always at Greenwich and the
Tower the three last days in each week. . . ."

" Oct. 8th.

" . . . My journey to Croxton* altogether was
ultra-successful. . . . We sat down 20 to dinner yesterday in Squires, Squiresses, and Parsons and their Ribs.
My Sister wore on two of the days two different gowns
of my donation, a satin and a silk, which were pronounced beautiful.   I never saw the said Sister better

* Croxton Park, where Miss Creevey was on a visit.

in my life, and for *chat* with all the world she is unrivalled. . . ."

Miss Creevey to Creevey

"Croxton Park, October 15th.

" MY DEAR BROTHER,

" Your magnificence is quite astounding ; you might be of Royal blood to bestow thirteen shillings upon your man in waiting for four night's lodging. However, if you had told him to have given half-a-crown to each of the housemaids for the trouble they had in making your bed, fire, &c., to say nothing of your sickness, there would have been plenty left for the trouble of bringing up water, and your shoes to your room to that tall gawky lad. However, you have made a great impression, both in the Drawing-room and elsewhere. Dear Charlotte talks of you in raptures, and the youths and old Newton are equally enthusiastic. . . .

" I leave here on the 22nd or 23rd for Miss Heinglemarn's, where I perhaps may stop a week with her, and after that time I hope to be favored with a letter from you directed to me at Edge Hill.

" I told you a great story about game from Lord Sefton's, for upon questioning Mary I found I had had both hares and pheasants in great abundance, and that it was the last winter but one I did not get any, owing to the new game laws.

" . . . I intended going on the Monday, but Charlotte will not hear of it, so as I expect to be tired, I shall rest on Wednesday and start on Thursday. Mr. Newton has offered me his carriage as far as Kimbolton, which I shall most gladly avail myself of. . . .

" Believe me, ever most
" truly yours,
" J. CREEVEY."

Creevey to Miss Ord

"*York*, Nov. 2nd.

" . . . When you travel next all night, and in a mail, don't forget to provide yourself with some *patent woollen* stockings that won't shrink. My *Woosteads* were very warm to the feet, but they *tickled the legs* so that I did not like the prospect of that in a coach for so long a time, so yesterday I invested a slight capital in Patent *Wools*, and they are *divine*—soft as milk and warm as a toast. My feet were never the least cold all the way, which they have always been before, and tho' the weather is not severe, still night is night, and November is November. These dear stockings have '*patent*' engraved upon them at the top in large letters with a portrait, and other ornamental paintings. . . .

" Poor Lord Grey ! I shall long to hear what he says. His letter to Lambton that was used by him at Glasgow was a regular broadside into Brougham, but Lambton by this new Reform manifesto of his has destroyed all the advantage he had over Beelzebub. . . ."

"Howick, Nov. 4th.

" Welcome to Howick, My Dear. . . .

" I left York at five last night, and was at Alnwick by five this morning, went to bed till 10, then got up, breakfasted and walked over here, all the chaises at Alnwick being gone to a wedding at Belford. I was most of the day yesterday in the *Minster* at York, and was delighted with every part of it, and such *songsters* I never heard, but the building itself is beyond all praise of mine, I mean the interior. . . ."

" Nov. 9th.

" . . . When Lady Grey expresses her belief that
B. did not mean that Lord Grey should go out,* she
adds, ' Observe, I don't think the better of him for
it ; on the contrary, I have a worse opinion of him
than ever.' She told me that when they paid their
leave taking visit at Windsor, after Lord Grey's
retirement, and just before they left London, the
King, having Lady Grey next to him at dinner, was
expressing to her his deep regret at losing such a
faithful and able Counsellor as Lord Grey, whose
place could not be supplied, and took occasion to
observe upon the difference between him and his
Lord Chancellor in terms not very flattering to the
latter.

" By the way, . . . when the Recorder's Report
from the Old Bailey &c. was laid before the King and
his Privy Council of Ministers, Brougham took
occasion to observe to His Majesty that he thought
this report ought to be laid before him more frequently . . . The King replied, ' He quite agreed
with the Lord Chancellor, and desired that his own
personal convenience might never be thought of, for
that in fact *he never made long and distant tours in
the country*, but was always on the spot in London, or
Windsor, or Brighton.' Was that not well done by
our Billy, versus the *Tourist?* †

" Lady Grey still overflows with Lord Grey's reception in *Scotland*, and well she may, but I tell her
she has greater homage still to come to him, by that
feeling which *must* show itself more and more, and
from day to day, viz., that the only man to keep the

* Grey's resignation was unquestionably due to Brougham's intrigues
over the Coercion Bill.
    † The reference is to Brougham's "progresses," notably that through
Scotland. He took the Great Seal with him.

Country straight, within and without, is gone, and
that it is utterly impossible to supply his place. *He*
talks to me very naturally, and with great regret that
there is no rising young man who by talent, position
and character is made to have any command in either
House of Parliament or the Country. With any thing
like manner and management he thinks Stanley
might have done it, but that his recent conduct has
made it nearly hopeless. . . .

" It is curious to hear Lord Grey speculating
upon what the conduct of the Government will be on
this occasion—whether they will have the *firmness* to
resist these radical propositions of Lambton's, or not,
and he seems to think they won't. To be sure, when
one thinks of the quarter from which the *firmness* is
to come, it makes one either laugh or sick. Old
Auckland and Old Aber, and Hobhouse, and Spring
Rice or even Duncannon ! Oh dear, oh dear !

" Poor Melbourne, I pity him, but what can he do,
raw as he is in the concern, and with such a crew ? It
is quite clear to me that if the Government shows itself
at all *loose* in its treatment of this new and extended
Reform by Ld. Durham, it will find Lord Grey highly
conservative. . . .

" I forgot to mention how pleased both Lord and
Lady Grey were with Lords Erroll and Elphinstone's
coming on purpose from *Windsor* to Ld. Grey's
dinner at Edinbro', the one a Lord of the Bed Chamber
to the King, the other Master of the Horse to the
Queen and son-in-law to the King. They came and
returned immediately after dinner, and if you come to
that, I'll dress now for my dinner with Ld. Grey too. . .

" It is impossible for me to describe to you, what
appears to me to be the real happiness of Lord Grey,
and I feel sure I am a great God-send to both him and

her. To be sure, when I see Geo. Ponsonby here, of
whom his Sister tells me *she is very fond*, when I see
Lord Grey kiss *Di* as he did when she came, and tell
her he was waiting for her to *cut his hair*, which she
has since done ; the Daughter too of Mrs. Bouverie,
and the *adopted* one, at least, of Lord Robert ; when
I hear George talk of being here *forty* years ago upon
his Sister's marriage ; when, I say, I put all these
things together, and know that Lord Grey at the close
of his political life had the power of making a provision
for these near connections of his, the most wanted and
the most suited to them, and yet that he should have
conferred this last favour of his upon myself ; upon
my soul ! I am lost in astonishment to think of it. . . ."

" Nov. 10th.

" Well, I have said so much of Lord Grey that I
think it is time to say a little more of Lady Grey, and
yet I can never say too much of *him*, of his happy
tranquility of mind. To hear him say at breakfast,
' Well, Creevey, what will you have for dinner today ? ' Then his enjoyment of his dinner, and *of my
approbation of it ;* the whole to conclude with our
shilling *cribbage* at night, in which he displays as
much energy as he ever could have done as Prime
Minister. The only complaint I hear from him, is
his being *tired* after walking, and he certainly does
not walk as far and as fast as he did when I was here
seven years ago. . . .

" We breakfast to a minute at *ten*, and dinner
ditto at half past six. Such hours suit me much
better than the Seftons' and so do the dinners too,
much, in that it is perfect living, and I am delighted
with everything. . . .

" Well then, now for a little about Lady Grey.

She seems always most happy to have a little private
chat with me, which is both flattering and very agreeable to me. She says she is occupied in writing or
copying into a book, all the letters she ever received
from Lord Grey, and that she has never destroyed
one. This correspondence began just *before they were
married*. I need not say that she copies only the
publick parts of such letters, and in the first ones
there is much of the state trials at the Old Bailey of
Tooke, *Thelwall*, &c. &c., at all of which Lord Grey
attended. Then she says for several years he went
from here to London for some months in the Spring
to attend Parliament, and leaving her here. During
these absences he used to write to her almost daily
an account of all that was passing. She says that this
correspondence, or rather these letters of his, fill many
boxes. Her object is to have every thing in readiness
to put into Lord Howick's hand for *ulterior* use.

" In talking of letters she said there were none
that were better written or that had given her greater
pleasure than your Mother's, and that she had had
the greatest regret in destroying them, but that your
Mother had desired her to burn them, from observations made in them about the Whitbreads, Sheri-
dans, &c. &c. and from a wish that they should never
reach any other person. . . ."

" Novr. 18th.

" Rather a bore to have no letters or newspapers
from London today in such times as these. Lord
Grey, however, had a few lines from Melbourne, which
he put into my hands to read. The contents were
that Wellington is Prime Minister, that *Hudson*,
Private Secretary to Sir Herbert Taylor, left London
for Italy on Sunday in pursuit of Peel, and that
Melbourne received the King's commands on Sunday

27

to summon a Cabinet Council for yesterday, and for the three Secretaries of State to deliver up their seals of office. Who are to be their successors was unknown to Melbourne. Lord Grey thinks that from this rapidity in going to work, they must have known that Lord Spencer's death would break up the Government,* and were preparing for it, as his state of health for some time past made his early death quite certain. . . .

" No Sefton yet, but it is only half past five. They are very much wanted indeed, for I never saw any one more bored or more fairly done than Lady Grey is with these two young women—the Russell and the Fitzclarence, to say nothing of the Duke of Bedford himself. . . .

" Well, here is all my own family, and a charming meeting with them.

" A note from Brougham to Sefton waiting for him to say that he *and the City* are going with such an address to the King as will shake him on the throne. Was there ever ? . . ."

" Nov. 19th.

" Well, Lord Grey's letters today go no further than making Wellington Prime Minister, *till Peel decides whether he will take that office*, and Wellington is likewise Secretary of State for the Home Department *at present;* his real destination being the Foreign Secretaryship, but he is already up to the chin in the Home Department in reading Irish correspondence. . . ."

" Novr. 30th.

" . . . It was well I was stopt yesterday from going into any comparison of the way of living in my

* Taking Lord Althorp to the Lords.

two benefactors—Earls Sefton and Grey. I mean
no disparagement to the former who has uniformly
been to me the most constant, active and *powerful*
friend that man could have, all I mean to say is *this* :
Lord Sefton carves out his day by rule, for his own
fixed purposes. He makes *every body* breakfast at
eleven or half past, the object being *double*—to have
an *attendance* and a *meal* to make a break in the day
of *an hour*, and to make an exact rest for the stomach
against half past seven.

" By the arrival of newspapers before breakfast,
and of the morning ones again between breakfast and
dinner, the arrival of the *fish*, visiting the kitchen, a
good deal of ennui is cleared away *for a very clever
man*, and (if it can be accomplished) an importation
of tip top swindlers for the evening, and till 3 or 4 in
the morning, to carry away some hundred pounds
from him to London the next day, has created the
necessary supply of excitement *for a very clever man*.
Now this is all literally true ; then comes our other
Earl, after all his *ultra* excitement as first Minister
of State, success without end, ill usage without end,
come to an anchor at 70 years of age, and his political
life closed ; without a particle of ennui, or apparently
a grievance of any kind, breakfasting *naturally* at ten
for sustenance, and leaving to every one to follow the
same course, or not, according to their pleasure ;
always cheerful and communicative, and absconding
when he likes ; the same at luncheon, and I can add
no more than that he seems the happiest of men
without any, the least calculated, division of his time,
arrangement of his victuals, or *purveying* of his
company. . . .

" . . . If you had seen him walk with all us *young*
things today, and the pleasure he had in making

Creevey jump over a ditch ; indeed it is high time I was gone, for I feel that I compromise *the dignity of my character* on making him laugh so much, and yet it is such a delight to see him so pleased and happy. . . .

" Whilst we were at luncheon today, I thought I would recollect the contents of it.   I can swear to two hot roast fowls, two hot roast partridges, a dish of hot beef steaks, a cold pheasant, partridge pie, &c. . . . We had only at dinner, two soups, and two fishes, a round of beef at one end, a leg of mutton at the other, a roast turkey at one side and I forget what at the other, with three entrées on each side ; woodcocks, snipes, plovers in the *second* course ; red herring devil, cream cheese, &c. de plus. . . .

" *Peel* went from Florence for Rome and Naples on the 14*th,* so he can't be here I think for a fortnight yet—tant mieux.   I make sure of weathering the present month, and *raally* think I shall *crib* something out of the *next one.* . . ."

                                    " Brooks's, Decr. 29th.

" . . . Well, Barry, what comes next ?   Are our Whigs to turn out any thing like *correct* in their estimate of the New Parliament ?   I believe they will *not,* but still I cannot but believe that the New Government will be in a minority in the new parliament.   I know, too, for a positive fact, that Peel and Wellington are at this very moment at daggers drawn.   The former claims and will have the whole and absolute patronage of the Government, and will submit to no interferences from the Beau. . . .

" I lived at Greenwich on Saturday, and spent my evening (tea &c.) with the Hardys, i.e., Sir Thomas, My Lady, and Miss Hardy.   Miss Emily was missing. I discovered a new property in Sir Thomas—a turn for ' de joke.'   I never saw the dear little old Seaman laugh in greater earnest than I made him three or four times.

" Yesterday, I was in my fine pew again all alone, and I feel myself a truly great man when I am there. We have two Divines who always do duty, and such has been the effect of my attendance that yesterday I had not been ten minutes returned from Church, when Dr. Cole (one of these Clergymen) came, as he said, to *pay his respects to me,* so I made him sit down and be very cozy, and he told me all about Dear Mrs. Cole. . . . The way to know every one there (I mean belonging to the Hospital) is to be at Church on Sunday. People walk about after Church, and Lady Hardy is as handy as a cat in introducing one to any body one wants.

" I dined at Holland's yesterday with the Tanker-villes, Melbourne, Auckland, Thompson. Holland and I are *raal* cronys. I had seen Melbourne before, and had thanked him for his kindness to Walsham, altho' he had dropped thro' at last. ' Ah ! ' Melbourne said, ' I thought it would have done.' . . ."

Countess Grey to Creevey

" Decr. 28th.

" . . . You *know* I am not by nature a Radical, yet I am rapidly becoming one, or any thing else that may be most opposed to the horrid Tories. I am delighted at their appointments—one more outrageous than another—because I hope they may hasten the overthrow of the Ministry.

" I have received a *blow* this morning in hearing that Ld. Roden* (the most effective of all) has retired. It is a pity, but they will no doubt find somebody to act in the same spirit. And what do you

* 3rd Earl. He lived till 1870.

think of our most gracious Sovereign, and of his toasts ? I give him up, and were he to come back to the Whigs tomorrow, all confidence in him must be over for ever. Perhaps this is for the best, and that a King should always, in fact, be dealt with as a secret enemy.

" I used sometimes to think Ld. G's. affection for ours a little too romantic, and he has proved how little he deserved it.

" You say, you very much admire Mr. Stanley's speech ; and Ld. G. praises it as much as you do. I was much gratified by his compliment to him, and approved much of all the good advice which he gave to the young men at the University. But as to any expression of political opinions, it seemed to me as cautious and innocent as Sir R. Peel's manifesto,* and equally capable of being construed one way as the other. . . .

" . . . Poor Ld. John ! *he* first upsets the coach, and I believe with all his good intentions it would be better if he could neither speak nor write. This observation comes with an ill grace at this moment from me, whose principle it is that a woman ought not to hazard a word upon politics, yet here have I been prosing these two sheets of paper. . . .

" We have missed you and the Seftons most dreadfully, and no day passes without our lamenting you. Do you think you will ever all meet here again ? Ld. G. has been a little complaining, but I hope it does not signify.

" God bless you ! My dear Mr. Creevey. . . ."

* " The Tamworth Manifesto."

CHAPTER XIX

1835–36

CREEVEY was in his 67th year and his iron constitution was breaking up. He had no doubt taxed its resources, and the fashionable doctors were now carrying on the work with their fashionable remedies. His old friends were dropping out one by one. He had already survived a majority of his intimates, Currie, Whitbread, Romilly, and Michael Angelo Taylor, under whose roof he lived for nearly three years. This year died Mrs. Taylor and Lady Dinorben and his sister, Miss Creevey.

But the greatest among Creevey's natural gifts was his power of absorption, to the exclusion of all other thoughts, in his newest possession. Whether it was his latest pamphlet on Reform, or a newly-published Memoir, his room in the Tower or his garden at Greenwich, it was thrilling and all-sufficient.

Ill-health, increasing deafness, the loss of friends, were misfortunes grievous enough, but not so grievous as to damp his ardour for his latest toy or his hopes for the future. He was hard at work preparing his house at Greenwich, now vacated by the Hardys, for the reception of his stepdaughters. It was his design to live principally at Greenwich for the rest of his life, and in that haven, which for half the year at least one or other of his beloved Ords was to share with him, to write the History of his life and times for which he had long prepared material. For the rest, he would keep a bedroom in London for use when some specially attractive invitation tempted him back to St. James's.

By the terms of his sister's will he received a welcome increase in income, and for the remainder of his days was assured of £1000 a year, a rent-free house, and a number of useful perquisites. He accordingly watched the development of the political drama with more amusement than anxiety.

Peel had arrived from Rome and issued his Tamworth Manifesto, which revealed a willingness to continue the policy of social reform. In the general election, albeit the Tories gained much ground, he returned to office with a minority which implied early defeat. Before the year was out, the Whigs were back again under Melbourne with most of the leaders in their old places. Only for Brougham was no place found.

Sir R. C. Ferguson to Creevey

"Jany. 14th, 1835.

" Vane, who is in great distress, has expressed a wish that you should be informed of the death of poor Mrs. Taylor,* which took place about ½ an hour ago. . . ."

Creevey to Miss Ord

"Jany. 16th.

" What dear things Omnibusses are ! I was at Greenwich at 2 o'clock ; then came in one to Charing Cross, . . . then got into an omnibus at the top of St. James's Street in Piccadilly, and went to Lad Lane in the City, . . . then got into another Omnibus and was landed in the same place in Piccadilly—whole cost of the day *two shillings*. . . .

" Did not I mention that I went to Mrs. Taylor's about 10 days ago ? Dined and slept there, but she could not see me, tho' she ordered for my dinner what she knew I liked. . . ."

"Jany. 17th.

" . . . It is *raally* marvellous the way in which our Dear Tower *sticks* to me. It seems to me that it must be *Monday* or *Tuesday week* before I am summoned to surrender.

* Mrs. Taylor was the daughter of Sir Harry Vane, 1st Bart., by Frances Tempest.

" I wonder when poor Mrs. Taylor is to be buried. I have written to Jack to know, and to say how de-sirous I am of attending *if I can*. . . .

" The wretch Palmerston is done in Hampshire, and so is Sir George Murray* in Perthshire. If you come to that, no one more richly deserved the punish-ment than the latter. . . ."

" Jany. 30th.

" You would have heard from me before, Barry, but I have been out of sorts for some days past. I went to Greenwich on Sunday to meet Lady Hardy *without my great coat ;* I did the same on Monday after physick, and I was violently assailed by a cold for my folly. . . .

" Well, at the expiration of these elections, the Tories are in my opinion dead beat, and every part of the press that is devoted to them clearly shows it. Our Doctors make out that flinging every least wavering, timid Whig into the ranks of the Tories, there will be a dead majority of 70 against them, whereas no Government can conduct the House of Commons thro' any session without at least the same majority of 70 in their favour, and that in such times as these, little enough too. It is settled that an attempt to storm Sutton as Speaker is to be made, with Abercromby for his substitute. *My own opinion* is, and it is as yet quite my own, that Sutton will not stand this, but be off, probably to the Lords, if he is not actually beaten.† He will be so bespatter'd and

---

* A successful soldier and politician. Sat for Perth, but was defeated in the by-election necessitated by his appointment as Master-General of Ordnance. Was Colonial Secretary under the Duke of Wellington, 1828-30.

† James Abercromby (Lord Dunfermline) was chosen amid intense party excitement by a ten-votes majority, and proved an excellent Speaker. Manners-Sutton was created Viscount Canterbury.

will leave such a *huge* number of votes against him that he never could consent, (gentleman as he is), to preside over such a body if by accident he ever wins. . . ."

" Jany. 31st.

" . . . We had Lord and Lady Kerry at dinner yesterday, and she is really quite beautiful with all the good nature apparently as when I knew her as a child in Ireland. . . .

" Well, you see Aber: is our Whig Nag for the Speaker's chair, and there are some very good observations upon his pretentions in ' The Morning Post ' of to-day, not omitting his accepting from the Duke of Wellington £4,000 a year as Chief Baron of Scotland, and then again a pension of £2,000 a year for his life in compensation for giving up an office in which there was nothing to do. I dare say you have often heard me declare my opinion, that after this extraordinary favor conferred by the Beau upon Aber :, the latter, as a man of honor, ought never to have taken his seat in the House of Commons again as a politician. . . .

" Here is Lord Charles Churchill* by my side, arrived from Kinmel last night with the Duke,† his Master. Poor Hughes ‡ was left as composed as could be expected. . . ."

" Feby. 6th.

" . . . *Tuesday* . . . I dined with Lady Holland, the only other company being Auckland and P. Thompson. When dinner was announced she said, ' Give me your arm, Creevey.' ' Impossible,' said I, ' in the presence of a Peer and Privy Counsellor.'

---

* Son of 5th Duke of Marlborough.
† Of Sussex.
‡ Lord Dinorben. The reference is to Lady Dinorben's funeral.

' Come along,' said she, and I was placed accordingly
at the head of the table with the dear *Creeter* by my
side.   I had my suspicion that I was to pay for my
elevation in some way or other, so in the middle of
dinner she said, ' Go with me tonight, Creevey, to
Drury Lane at 10 o'clock to see the *Horses* in ' Arthur's
Round Table.'   I struck at once like a man and said,
' With great pleasure,' tho' waiting till 10 when you
dine at 6 is no joke, nor did the HORSES seem to
promise any very high intellectual treat for one's
reward.   Our time between dinner and 10 was pretty
well employed by Lady Holland in abusing old Allen,
and *his horrid temper ;* how he forbore *shying* the
first thing he could lay hold of at her head I can't
imagine.   He did occasionally stop and look at her
with eyes of thunder, but nothing came of it, and the
carriage was announced, a large coach, and I was made
to sit by My Lady's side, Allen opposite.   We had
scarcely left the door when we passed her Doctor's
coach (Hammic,* the Greys' Doctor, and Baronet). . . .
His carriage . . . was ordered to follow ours, and she
took him into her box at Drury Lane to have his
advice about herself. . . ."

"Feby. 11th.

" I am very much set up with a letter I had from
Lady Grey on Monday in which she tells me that
Lord Grey desires her to tell me that he quite agrees
with me upon *all* subjects ; so that you see I am
rather a Jeroboam with myself at present. . . . On
Saturday I dined with Essex and on Sunday with
little Sussex ; he and his Rib being both in mourning
for poor Charlotte†—a very small party and very

* Sir Stephen Hammick, Surgeon to George IV and William IV and
to the Whig nobility.   He lived till 1867.
† Lady Dinorben.

agreeable. For Saturday I had a note from my never failing friend Ly. Holland, asking me to dine with her on Monday to meet a party she knew would suit me, and that I should like, and so I went, and the party *was to have been* the D. and Duchess of Bedford, Duke of Norfolk, Medim (the Russian Ambassador) and Ld. Granville. The Duchess had a cold and could not come, all the rest did, and I had a great benefit ; *Brother Bedford* and I are actually one. At night, before I came away, Madagascar asked me before every one, to dine there both to-day and on Saturday next. The latter I shall do, and at *Scroop's* * on Sunday. . . .

" Wickedshifts is not yet arrived but expected daily. Young Mr. Ord is here, and as busy as ' *Bloks Wife* ' (as my Mother used to say) in assisting in making out the lists between Aber. and Sutton. . . ."

" May 19th.

" . . . I am rather hurried for time, having just returned from going over Buckingham Palace with Lords Duncannon, Grey, and Sefton, and being to dine in Arlington Street at half past six for the Opera. . . .

" . . . I *do* flatter myself that things do begin to look favorable as to your intentions of coming to me soon. As to my *sheeting*, can you do with two pair of sheets a piece for your four best beds, ditto pillow cases &c. &c., and two pair of sheets a piece for the three maids' beds upstairs, and for Eddy's bed in his pantry ? Will this do ? because if it will, I am your man. . . . Your *Plate* I shall accept the loan of most gratefully as I should be at a dead-lock without it. Will 4 dozen *Towells* be enough ? 12 breakfast table-

* 12th Duke of Norfolk.

cloths, and 4 dinner ones ? Suggest anything you think me likely to forget. . . ."

" May 26th.

" . . . When you impeach me for my lavishness in furniture, are you prepared to know, that the bed and window furniture of yours and Eleanor's bed rooms actually costs *sixpence* a yard ? Can you say a word after that ? Tell Eleanor with my love, that she . . . will find our Park very beautiful just now, and I trust it would do her great good, as indeed I hope our old Father Thames would do, who rolls by us every day as fresh as when he first started from your seven springs, and still quite capable of carrying any weight. . . . From the bottom of my stair case it is not ten yards to Sir Christopher Wren's colonade under which you go to the gate, cross the High Road ten yards more, and then . . . thro' our beautiful school ground, and by a private door into the Park. . . . I hope our warm baths may be of use to her. Lady Hardy, I believe, uses them constantly. . . .

" I dined again at Mull's on Sunday with Ladies Louisa and Kate, the rest of the family being at Stoke, and we went to the Greys' in the evening, and the footman called out, ' Mr. Creevey and the Ladies Molyneux,' which was all very well. . . . There had been a dinner party as usual, and I was rather sorry that one of the guests had left the Drawing Room just before we arrived—*Lucien Bonaparte*. Alava, I believe, was the only other Foreigner, the rest being Richmonds, Stanleys, Sutherlands, &c. whom I found there. A flock of admirers surrounded the three neat'ns—the sisters Norton, Blackwood and Seymour.* I am afraid it is too good fun to be true

* The three beautiful daughters of Thomas Sheridan, Mrs. Norton, Lady Dufferin, and the Duchess of Somerset.

that old Colhoun* Grant is to prosecute these sisters
for a conspiracy in robbing him of his Daughter for
the benefit of their Brother, but they say it *is* true.
I am glad the young gentleman's name is really
Brinsley ; it keeps alive the talent of the family
name. . . .

"I dined yesterday at Essex's to meet Brougham
who was as silent as he could possibly be, but old
Rogers† who was there agreed with me, that all was
false and hollow. Duncannon too was there. He
told me two months ago in the same room that there
would be no difficulty in forming a Government and
carrying it on, if the then existing one was but fairly
out. The last event has since taken place, and the
New Government is already at a deadlock, what about
in particular I can't make out, but Duncannon admits the fact in the most unqualified manner. . . ."

"June 9th.

"If you *do* start tomorrow, I think the post will
find you before that event takes place, and I wish you
to bring with you, ' *Creevey's Pamphlets.*' In addition to that valuable work you would oblige me very
much by bringing me such *dokiments* upon publick
subjects as I have at different times communicated
to you. I have always a floating kind of idea of
' *putting pen to paper* ' (as Skin Flint always says)
once more, and by way of a winding up. When I
look at my materials I can see what they are worth.
At all events I could find amusement in retracing my
life, and I am sure I shall never have so good a retreat
for that purpose as my own room at Greenwich. . . .

"Oh! that you could have seen the beauty of

* Lt.-General Sir Colquhoun Grant, of Frampton, Dorset. His
daughter married R. B. Sheridan in 1834.
† Samuel Rogers (1763-1855). Banker, poet and conversationalist.

Greenwich Park and every thing about it yesterday. . . .

"I dined at home on Mutton Chops and a very
good dinner I had, and I liked the appearance of my
new maid very much. She is named *Emma*, and
came yesterday. . . ."

"Edge Hill, August 3rd.

"I started by the London *Tantivy* yesterday a
little before 8, and was at Birmingham a little before
8 at night, a distance of 120 miles, and got into the
Birmingham Mail for Liverpool about ten minutes
after that, and was here by seven this morning,
another 100 miles. . . . My Sister died within the
hour that letter was written, which I received on
Saturday at Greenwich. My two female Cousins are
here, and the eldest one, aged forty-five about, is a
most useful ally. She has long kept an Uncle's
house ; the other is feeble enough. My Co-executor
too has been here (Tom Newton) and we have been
over my Sister's will together. . . . Everything is
given to myself for my life ; so the account will stand
thus—our Corporation annuity of £175 per annum of
course survives to me, but as I have received £100
hitherto per annum from it, I only get £75 *now*. She
has two houses her own absolute property from which
I shall get £50 a year and £30 ; then she and I have
between us four houses which produce £130 a year,
and as I have never received a farthing from that
source, this is all new. Then again as the stables to
this house produce £30 a year, the house must surely
produce £50, which will be likewise new to me. Lastly,
an annuity of £20 a year which my Sister had, survives to me, so it stands . . . £355 or £455 with my
old Corporation £100. . . ."

" Well, the Notary and Tom Newton and *Phoebe Barrington* and myself have just settled our concerns. I don't know whether I mentioned yesterday that the said Phoebe is an executrix of my Sister's Will, and very glad I am she is so ; for she is as handy and correct as ever she can be. . . . Indeed, the said Phoebe produced me this morning two receipts, one for £25 lent by my Sister within the last year to her Uncle with whom she lives, and another for £50 lent by my Sister to my other Cousin (the Dawdler). . . . The Notary . . . thinks he can let me go on Saturday or Sunday. At all events I reckon upon being at Greenwich the beginning of next week.

" So how are you all, and how is the *Garden* ? . . . "

The **next day**, August 5th, Creevey signed his own Will, of which something will be said hereafter.

" August 6th.

" My Sister was buried yesterday. I was accompanied to her Funeral by Tom Newton and Mr. Hodgson, the latter is a Clergyman who lives at Crosby about 7 or 8 miles off ; he married for his second Wife an own Cousin of ours by whom he had *Dawdle*. . . .

" . . . I have done the greatest injustice to . . . Dawdle ; . . . with a little *Pewit* of a face and manner, she is as manly and correct a little chap as I have seen this many a day. . . . *Her* Mother (my own Cousin likewise) tho' of excellent parents, was of a terribly low and degraded nature, and she married a *Butcher* very near to Market Harbro :

" Upon *riding* from Cambridge to Liverpool in 1792, forty three years ago, I enquired and found out the Butcher's residence ; my Cousin was dead, the

Butcher was out, and the *Executrix*, a child of two years old, was playing at the shop door, so I gave her a guinea, and departed, but the Butcher pursued me on horseback, and caught me the next day at Derby. The *Executrix* has a most lively recollection of this Guinea transaction. . . ."

Countess Grey to Creevey

"Howick, Nov. 1st.

" . . . I should very much like to know how you do, and what you are about ? I hope you are well yourself, and that Mrs. Hamilton and her Sisters are so too, that you are not tired of Greenwich, and yet do not forget Howick and its little Burn, and all the nonsense we used to talk ? . . .

" . . . The principal cause of my writing to you, and my venturing to do so, will I hope prove to you how entirely I rely upon your friendship. . . . I am very much distressed about my boy, William, who is with Mr. Soames, the Clergyman at Greenwich. . . . Mr. Soames has written to Ld. G. to complain that William has of late spent much of his time in playing at Billiards with a young acquaintance who is just come from Eton, full of the expensive ideas which boys contract at that school. He very justly objects to the waste of time in such an occupation, and still more to the bad company he is likely to meet in a public billiard room, of which he cannot have half such a horror as I have. . . . The dread I have of his making disreputable acquaintances and being drawn by them into profligacy and extravagance makes me quite miserable.

" . . . Dear Mr. Creevey, I think if you are good enough to interest yourself about my poor boy, you may be of essential service to him. He will, I am

28

sure, respect your advice, and you may guard him from many dangers in such a place as Greenwich, where I imagine he may too easily get into bad company. At the same time I should be very sorry to have his Father's displeasure known, or to have his character hurt by talking of my uneasiness to any body but yourself. I beg you will in particular avoid mentioning it to the Hardys, who are great gossips, and might unintentionally do him mischief. . . .

" God bless you. . . ."

Creevey to Miss Ord

"Brooks's, Dec. 14th.

" I think I must begin with the last part of your letter first, as you say there that your *fillings* are hurt at no mention having been made by me of . . . *your own house* at Greenwich. I can only say that Mary's report to me was that she *cried* for three whole days after you went, and Emma for the whole week. With respect to myself, it has really become *your own house*, and no longer mine, for I am quite sure nothing on earth could make me eat or sleep in it again till you return to it. If therefore, you wish to keep up my character as a Greenwich *Resident* Commissioner, you cannot fail to live there for at least six months out of the twelve. . . .

" Nothing is found yet of poor old Dow: Salisbury.* The Insurance Offices are in possession of the ruins and are fortifying the walls before any excavation takes place. What a singular thing that she should have been the only person in this wing, her maid being at tea with the other Ladies' maids at the time. She had lighted her Mistress's Candles for

---

* Emily Mary, Marchioness of Salisbury, was burned to death at Hatfield when the west wing was destroyed by fire on Nov. 27th, 1835.

dressing time, with which, or with the fire, no doubt
the old woman had set fire to herself. She was for
ever falling from feebleness, and the wonder is she
was never destroyed before. . . .

" Today I dine again at the Seftons with the
Tankervilles, the Hollands, and the old customary
Rogers, Luttrell, Creevey and Charles Greville.

" As you may suppose, I am always at my post on
Board days at Greenwich. On the Thursday before
last I returned with a posy of two of the sweetest
roses I ever smelt ; the production of one of your new
planted trees. I have got too another _Pear_ Tree
given me by Lady Sefton, originally from Howick, and
Lady Sefton gave Lady Hardy and myself each of us
one, so they travelled from Stoke together, and Lady
Hardy's gardener was graciously pleased to come and
plant mine himself in my own garden. . . ."

" Decr. 18th.

" . . . Yesterday I had the lively Duke of Devonshire at Essex's, he and Clifford* and myself in a row
was not amiss for _Deafy's_, but I beat them both easy
as to hearing. . . .

" What a singular fellow Melbourne is to be the
chief of a Government in such a storm. He dined
at Sefton's on Tuesday, and as we sat about the fire
after dinner I said there was a passage in O'Connell's
letter to the Reformers of Ireland that looked like a
squeak, and as if he did not feel quite as sure of his
birds as formerly ; to which Melbourne replied in
his way, ' God, it is a curious thing, two or three
people have made the same remark to me,' and then
after pausing he said, in his own way again, ' _God !_

* Adm. Sir Augustus. He had no connection with the barony of
Clifford brought in by the 4th Duke's marriage in 1748. He was a
natural son of the 5th Duke by Lady E. Foster.

perhaps it is so.'   Not amiss for a Prime Minister to
be so playful on his own downfall, is it ?   I have just
talked over the subject with Lord Clifden since I
begun this letter, a very clever man, and I am much
struck with his reply to my supposition of O'Connell's
deserting the Whigs whenever it suits his temper to do
so.   Lord Clifden says, ' He never can desert them,
because he knows that Peel and Hardinge * would
succeed them, and that they would twist the rope
about O'Connell's neck without further ceremony.'

" Lady Holland was in the sulks all the day at
Sefton's because Melbourne was not there in time
to hand her out to dinner, and when he did come was
on the other side of the table. . . ."

"Decr. 28th.

" . . . I go on as usual living upon *Elymosinary*
(is that spelt right ?) food without being ever compelled to put into Crocky's, but Sefton has of late
been made by his Doctor to dine at *four* o'clock some
days, and on such occasions I have dined with the
Ladies, and when he dines with us, it is always at a
quarter before seven, and he and I have a pint of
Claret a piece set before each of us as our exclusive property as well as *allowance*. . . . He took me, one of the
evenings I dined there last week, to see our new Play
House in King Street next to Almack's or Willis's ;
where we had no difficulty (even at half price) in
having a stage box entirely to ourselves, so little
resorted to is this new synagogue of Braham's, but his
crew is so horribly defective in every kind of talent,
that was he a Christian instead of a Jew he could not
have a better fate.   The house itself is by far the
most beautiful Playhouse in London.   What Ladies
were in the boxes were all of the *Israelitish* faith,

* F.M. Sir Henry.   Irish Secretary in Peel's 1835 Administration.

running very large, and very dressy, their heads profusely ornamented with Mountain Ash red berries. . . .

" You may have seen or heard that most of the
jewels, diamonds, &c. which old Lady Salisbury took
with her to Hatfield have been found, but I dare say
you have *not* heard that all the most valuable of them
turn out to be the property of *Pawnbrokers* till they
are redeemed by payment of the sums for which they
were pawned.   She has been some time at this trade,
and so when she wanted her finery to show off, they
were *lent* to her upon giving a due receipt for them.
You may suppose I get this from the fountain head,
Lady Cowley to Sefton, and him to me.   She sold two
thousand a year of her jointures a few months ago
only to a notorious money lender, so *he* can't have
made a good thing of her. . . ."

" 17, Jermyn Street, Feby. 6th.

" A second* fit of the gout in so short a time for
so young a customer may be considered as rather
trop, but . . . it . . . still preserves its unassuming
position *below*. . . . Freeman says I must have
wrenched the ankle of my damaged leg . . . for it
took fire instantly with great inflammation, and
brought down gout in both feet.   However . . . I
never was happier in my life than I am now.   I am
now in my elbow chair in my Drawing Room for the
first time, having had a whiting, a boiled chicken, and
an apple tart for my dinner, tho' I can't say I eat
vivaciously.   I have the best victuals London can
afford of all kinds within ten yards of me, and the
best cook within the house to dress them, and many
thanks for your kind offer, but I find these extra
drains quite within my Greenwich means. . .

* He had his first experience of gout this year.

" I take in ' The Chronicle ' by day, and ' The Courier ' by night, and am enchanted with the opening of the Session.   The King's speech was unrivalled. There never was such a one before, tho' that sneaking Roscius Lansdowne made Melbourne adopt Wellington's amendment.   Thank God ! however, our boys in the Commons were not to be done in that way, notwithstanding Master Stanley and his dirty tricks. However, I see as clear as possible Ireland will have a Municipal Reform Bill, and then if I am alive, as sure as my name is Thomas, I will go and see her for the first time in her life *a Nation, a nation.* . . ."

"Feby. 26th.

" I am truly sorry to hear of your sufferings from the toothache.   As for your coming to Greenwich, you know as well as I do that my apartments there are *yours*, and to be used at all times as your own. I was there yesterday, and the weather being fine, I gave directions to our little Clerk of the Works to see to have the staircase painted forthwith, . . . but there is quite time enough to stop that . . . if you should come. . . . You will find Mary Vinicome but a wretched cook compared with your own, and I am affraid you will find Greenwich at this season a very inconvenient distance from your dentist.   I have never ate or slept there since the day you left it. . . .

" I dined yesterday with the Hardys &c. &c. at Sefton's.   The former returned from Paris a week ago in ecstasies with their visit there.

" On Wednesday I dined at Minto's in full fig, with the Navy, and it was decidedly the handsomest and best managed entertainment I have ever seen in any official house.   I suppose his having been our

Ambassador at Berlin got him into the habit of such entertainments.

" I continue to dine with my benefactor, Essex, twice or thrice a week, and with Sefton about as often. . . ."

"Stoke, April 8th.

" You must abuse me very much, I fear, for not having written from here before, but *raally* I have had nothing to write about. Such an Easter for *weather*, I presume, was never known before. Luttrell and I came down in our chay on Sunday, and well it was we did so, for we came thro' torrents of rain, and an open concern from Slough would have finished us. I found only Mr. and Lady Georgiana Mitford, Berkeley and Charles Grenfell ; a young Stopford, and a young Seymour, with old Rogers were the next importation, then Cumming, the M.P. for Riga (as Sefton calls him) and lastly De Ros and Alvanley who came yesterday. . . . Mitford's extraordinary talents for singing make his sole attraction, as in other respects he is an effeminate imbecile. *Her* hold on this family is having been a flirt of Francis,* but as she seems quite as ready to flirt with old Sefton himself, Lady Sef-ton whispers to me that she is a little coquette, and that by her good will she never should come into the house again. Poor Lady Sef-ton ! I never knew her *jealous* before. She is a Daughter of Lord Ashburnham, and they are as poor as Job ; they came last from Cheltenham where they lived some time. . . ."

"May 9th.

" . . . We were all in great alarm on Saturday and yesterday in the belief that Norton was proceeding

* Her marriage to Mr. H. R. Mitford was dissolved and she married Francis Molyneux in 1842.

in an action against *Melbourne*, a crim: con: case, but I believe it is not so.* . . ."

"Sept. 16th.

" . . . Cashiobury† rather differs from Stoke as to hours, breakfast punctually at *nine*, dinner half past six, and after coffee and tea a floating écarté at a shilling ahead for every one to come in that likes, and our Earl retires punctually at half past ten.   All this was mightily to my mind.

" Essex is a man of very few words for *compliments;* but I took it as a real civility when he said, ' I ordered for you, Creevey, the room that poor George Tierney was so fond of, and always had ' ; and certainly a more perfect apartment no man ever had. Essex and Lady Holland were growling at one another all the time, but she was always the aggressor. Melbourne and Holland were all good nature and gaiety. The only drawback to my amusement was owing to my great folly in walking on Monday to see the Birmingham Rail Road now making, being about four miles there and back, which has made me dead lame, with a good deal of pain. . . ."

Lady Louisa Molyneux to Creevey
"Frankfort, October 1st.

" . . . I was delighted to see your field of Waterloo, and looked with great interest at every step of the way to it.   It is easy now to take a good view of the whole ground from the top of an enormous mound, on which they have had the presumption to place a gigantic Belgian Lion in commemoration of the battle. . . .

---

* It was unfortunately true. The action was tried on June 23rd, and both parties were acquitted.   Mrs. Norton was a Sheridan.
† Lord Essex's.

" We slept at Namur, Liège, 2 nights at Aix-la-Chapelle, Cologne, Coblentz, and Wiesbaden, mostly at excellent Inns. . . .

" We were surprised as we were driving through Rudesheim. . . . to be called to from a window to stop by Ly. Cowper, who was on a junket from Wiesbaden.   Poor Ld. Cowper crawled out, and is a miserable sight, but he spoke cheerfully. . . .

" Lady Jersey has been making herself ridiculous all over the Continent in her pursuit of Royalty. She is the subject of everybody's conversation—English and Foreign, particularly as she has gone about relating her complaints against Ly. Pembroke who followed her with her story. . . ."

Creevey to Miss Ord

"October 14th.

" . . . I, of course, was at Greenwich yesterday, and you know how to appreciate my *fillings* when I learnt from our Receiver . . . that a *vein of lead ore* supposed for years and years past to be somewhere incog under Langley . . . has turned up at last in all its beauty a richer ore in appearance than any one known in its neighbourhood, and this you know with lead at £27 a *fodder* . . . is not amiss. . . . I *knew* little Essex would not leave me out, and here he is, and *today's* dinner at least is safe.   What a nice man he is !

" Really people talk of nobody being in town ; why what would you have ?   Here are the Duke of Argyle, Earl of Essex, Lord Fitzalan, Sir Leith Hay, and a Commissioner of Greenwich Hospital all at the same table. . . ."

" . . . I dined at Stephenson's yesterday with our Argyle, Codringtons* male and female (My eye ! what a bore Navarino himself is), Charley Gore,† &c.

" . . . We shall have the *Pet* and his litter back de suite. . . .

" Miss Hardy who is in constant correspondence with Lady Caroline‡ says that the marriage is to take place immediately upon their return here ; at which of course the relations who are in London—the Hardys and the CREEVEYS—must all attend. . . ."

" Oct. 22nd.

" I told you how I broke my engagement with Madagascar for Thursday. I was to have called for Charley Gore (John Russell's Secretary, you know) and so I cheated him as well as the Hollands ; notwithstanding which I had a letter with the lark from Gore yesterday saying that, faithless as I was, I would be forgiven if I dined there yesterday. . . . I *went* escorted by . . Gore and Anson (Melbourne's private Secretary) and found the company just set down to dinner. . . . As soon as I could look about me I recognised besides the family faces those of Lord Minto, Luttrell and my two aides de camp, but the rest were quite new to me. On the other side of Lord Holland sat a very good looking, good natured, rollicking, *fleshy* lady, rather like Lady Erroll, and I directly found from Lord Holland's manner that I was to be agreeable to her, and so I tried, and when the strong Spanish wine came, which Holland men-

* Admiral Sir Edward. He was handsomely rewarded for his victory at Navarino.
† Hon. Charles Gore.
‡ Lady C. Molyneux married Charles Towneley this year. Creevey could not endure him.

tions in his note to me, the lady said she wished Mr.
Creevey would ask her to drink a glass of it with her—
a penance which you know Mr. Nummy would not
object to.   Well, but who do you suppose the lady
was ?   No other than Lady Holland's Daughter,*
and not only that but *the* Daughter of whom the
funeral was got up by her Mother to torment and
punish her Father, Sir Godfrey Webster.   On the
opposite side of the table was a very free and easy,
vulgar-looking, talking gentleman, who drove Lady
Holland into perpetual distortions and gesticulations,
at the space this gentleman occupied in our dinner,
and who do you suppose he was ?   Why My Lady's
Son-in-law, Husband to my jolly friend, and by
name Sir —— Pellew, a sailor, and the second son of
the Lord Exmouth. . . .''

" Nov. 29th.

" . . . Aye, aye ! 'a friend in need is a friend
indeed,' so here is our original *Barney* to frank this
letter for you.   I dined with him and Earl Surrey at
Mr. Powell's yesterday, and I thought the Earl rather
less odious than usual, but the Earl of all others for
my money is Earl Sefton.   He *raally* cannot live
without me. . . .

" Of course I dine there today, as I did on Sunday
with the Mites—Lord and Lady John Russell ;
Melbourne was to have been there, but his Son died
that morning.

" I accommodate Essex as often as I can, but not
as often as I could wish. . . .

" Does your paper give you any hint upon the
subject which now occupies a leading place in our

* Harriet Webster, married the Hon. Sir Fleetwood Pellew.

West End town's talk? De Ros's cheating as detected and *exposed* by George Payne, and two others—Brooke Greville and Cummings. It was so fully established to every one's belief here, that it was supposed De Ros, who went abroad imme- diately after, would never return, but here he is, and, as he says, to face it at once and prove the falsehood of the charge.* . . . In the meantime De Ros goes lower and lower in publick estimation as well he may. . . ."

* During this cause célèbre, Lord Campbell, then Attorney- General, unfairly aspersed Payne's character and afterwards apologised.

CHAPTER XX

1837-38

STRANGE but true, the letters to Miss Ord of the last full year of his life make up as huge a bundle as any. Creevey was much tied to his rooms in Jermyn Street with severe colds and frequent attacks of gout and influenza, but if the matter of his discourse was less exciting, his spritely style continued to the very end, his interest and optimism suffering no decline. When he was well enough, he dined out as of old, chiefly with Sefton and Essex, and he continued, though more rarely, his country house visits. He survived William IV and lived into our own times, to leave us his picture—a very appreciative study—of the laughing, friendly, dignified young Victoria; and in recording the intense interest with which every detail concerning her was received in Society, he clearly shows the significance then attached to the new era. For the rest, Creevey derived a great deal of amusement from the publication of various memoirs and records of events of his day. But his own *magnum opus* made no progress.

He was well enough to spend his last Christmas at Holkham, where his energy in a country dance was only equalled by that of his eighty-five years old host.

Then he returned to 17, Jermyn Street, as cheerful, as hopeful, as full of interest as ever, to keep his last engagement.

"Feby. 15th, 1837.

" . . . . Barry, I am still to a certain degree *influenza'd*. I am *feeble* in body and mind. . . .

" I dined at our Ellice's * on Saturday, and a very

* Edward ("Bear") Ellice, of Invergarry, was an influential Whig politician and had large interests in Canada. He married, first, a sister of Lord Grey's; secondly, Lord Leicester's widow.

nice merry party we had. He has taken Goderich's house in Arlington Street for the season. . . . Ellice has not moved from Carlton Terrace to Arlington Street yet. The dispute between the two Nibbers, Sefton and Salisbury, about *building on their own*, has played the devil with the value of Goderich's house, as his next nibber, Lord Dundas, runs into two thirds of his garden (slip as it is) and may build upon it accordingly.

" A very nice dinner at our *Barney's* on Sunday to eight only, but excellent company, tho' not perhaps so *moral* as our *eighteen* who dined together at Sefton's on Monday, such as D'Orsay,* Alvanley, Ld. Allen, Tom Duncombe, &c. Was there ever ? However, yesterday we were purity itself at the same house, being all alone and the only gamblers myself and Lady Sefton to whom, I am sorry to say, I lost three shillings.

" What an exhibition de Ros's trial was for all the parties concerned. Poor George Payne, I must always feel sorry for him. . . . It was shameful in the Attorney-General showing him up as he did. . . .''

" Jermyn Street, Feby. 25th.

" . . . At the last Egham Races, our Gracious Sovereign being present, he called out, ' Ld. Albemarle, come here, quick, quick, quick ! ' ; so having come to his side, the King said, ' Do tell me who that man is,' pointing to someone in an open carriage. ' That, Sir,' replied Albemarle, ' is Count D'Orsay.' ' I had a notion it was,' said the King, ' but I am very blind ; ' and then mustering all his energy he said, ' *Damn him.*' I trust that this was a compliment to the whole French Nation as well as D'Orsay and

* D'Orsay and Lady Blessington now lived together in London.

dictated by the natural feelings of an honest English sailor. I have reported it duly to Sefton, Standish, Allen and other friends of D'Orsay, and it is very much approved of. . . ."

"March 18th.

" . . . On Sunday I dined with my Essex, being taken there and brought back by *Old Wickedshifts*. . . . We had Denman, Secretary Stanley, and others at Essex's that day, and altogether it answered so well that Duncannon, Ellice and Stanley suggested to me privately that in their opinion another friendly meeting might be very useful. . . . Our Bruffam asked me to dine with him alone, as yesterday, and to go on with our *book*,* which as you may suppose I was too happy to comply with. . . . Lady Brougham has not only been visible but as active with her legs as with her tongue. Brougham's hatred of her, *absolute hatred*, is too visible. . . .

" Well, having dined at 6¼, and dear Lady Brougham having only remained the accustomed time after dinner, we took to our book, and what time do you think it was when I first looked at my watch ? Just a quarter of an hour past *twelve*, and then there was much left for another *treat*. . . . A great portion of these letters contain the Royal personal criticism upon politicians and candidates for office. When Fox first took office under Lord North in 1771 or thereabouts, altho' he was about 23 years only, the King wrote of him as a gambler without principle. . . . About the same time he writes, ' I must object to *Captain Fitzpatrick* being in my household. I don't like admitting *Gamblers* into my family.' He

* Brougham's collection of papers beginning with the very interesting correspondence between George III and Lord North. Creevey tells Miss Ord that Brougham had them from Lady Charlotte Lindsay.

is almost savage in his hatred of Lord Chatham. He says, ' Was Mr. Pitt reduced to a state of absolute decrepitude, or was he entirely disabled from ever appearing on the public stage again, I should not object to some provision being made for his second son, but Mr. Pitt has used me so shamefully that I never can forgive him as long as he remains in publick life.' He is quite at home in every part of his dominion, and with every body in it. He is quite against Hastings and Barwell in India, and is most favorable to the three Commissioners who were sent there in 1773 or four,—Mounsey,* Clavering and Francis, and he is particular in his approbation of Francis, and of his *abilities*. So it is clear that *he* did not think our Phil was the author of *Junius*, tho' from his letters being discontinued at that time Francis has been supposed to be their author. Altho' Melville was then a young politician, being Lord Advocate of Scotland, the King writes that, ' altho' he has had more done for him than any other man, there was still no end to his rapacity.' He has a hit too at *Scotland* as the favorite soil for plunder. . . . About 1778 he began to be restless as to the result of the American War, and you clearly collect that Lord North is always warning him and preparing him for submission. . . . He has a Spy at the French Court who writes under the name of *Wentworth*, who prepares him regularly for the rupture with that country, and being completely bothered with the growing storm altogether, he seems to take fresh courage when he writes to Lord North to this effect that ' the conduct of France and Spain, &c., will be a sufficient excuse for his withdrawing his troops from America, and then, that they may *pounce* (I think that is his

* ? Monson.

own word) upon the French Islands in the West Indies as a proper punishment for the perfidy of the French Monarch.'   And here I think I must close George the 3rd and Lord North for *today*. . . .''

                                         " Stoke, August 5th.

" Lady Sefton has a letter from Lady Cowley today with an account of her dinner at *Viccy's* one day this week. The company was principally Ambassadors and diplomats with their wives. *Madame Mère* (as Lady Cowley calls the Duchess of Kent) was according to her quite in the back ground (and a very sensible woman, says I, for her pains).   The Queen, she said, was excessively civil to every one, had excellent manners, but was *Royal* (and quite right, little Vic, too, I say again) ; then Lady Cowley adds that in the evening the Queen relaxed, and that nothing could be more amiable and agreeable than she was. Can you wish for a better account of a little tit of 18 made all at once into a Queen ? She wore the Ribbon and Star, and a massy gold garter on her arm.   I got a very good sight of her the other night.   I was in my walk in St. James's Park, playing with my *ducks*, when I saw a movement to the Palace, and I saw likewise the barouche and two outriders entering the gates, so I joined my fellows at the outside of the rails to see my little Sovereign.   I stood at the centre openwork gates, and with my long eyes could see her distinctly walk to the carriage, and was surprised to see her look so much taller than I had fancied from her look- ing so little in the carriage.   She passed my gate at a foot's pace, and then coming out of *our* gate, she passed me quite close again, and she looked even pretty with a most agreeable smile and the prettiest manner possible to us all without any *acting*.   After

29

she had got into the carriage the Duchess of Kent
followed, and then a lady who sat opposite. So, as
we of the British publick are always full of our obligations, various voices called out, ' That's the little
Queen, God bless her ! ' Then again, ' That's her
Mother, the Duchess of Kent ! ', but when the third
Lady came, they were all at fault, and many cried
out, ' What Lady is that ? ' and a man in the crowd
said, ' *That's the nurse,*' at which we all laughed very
much.

" Poor dear Lady Sefton !   What would she give
to go to a dinner, or even to a *tea*, at *Viccy's !* . . ."

"Sept. 6th.

" . . . Let me see what tidings I have for you of
little *Vic.* . . . On Saturday Berkeley Molyneux drove
Lady Kate, Miss Grenfell and myself over to Windsor
and having got out of the carriage we ranged on one
side of the road close to the gate thro' which she was
to pass ; so on they came, a smart pace, and as I
should say nearly 20 in number—the King of Belgium,
Vic and Duchess of Kent in the first row, but the Boss
King very gallantly held his horse in a little to let his
Queen Niece be first, and they passed so close that we
could hear Vic say to her Mother, ' That is not one of
the Ladies Molyneux (meaning Miss Grenfell) ; who
is it ? ' and as I stood, of course, with my hat off,
the Duchess of Kent was pleased to make me a very
gracious bow, which I returned.   I was quite delighted with *Vicky* in every way.   She looks infinitely
better on horseback than in any other way ; she was
dressed so nicely too, and her manner *quite perfect.*

" I saw Melbourne and Lansdowne in the group,
but not to speak to. . . .

" *Vick* is employed a great part of the day with

Melbourne upon State affairs, and in the evening for
general relaxation and amusement the Duchess of
Kent introduces a box of *letters, initials,* from which
to make words, or by way of a change *maps* to dissect
and put together again. What an innocent Court
at all events ! I don't wonder Miss Cocks asking
Lady Tavistock if she might walk out. ' Where, my
dear ? ' said Lady T. ' *Into the town.*' . . .

    " She told me a very pretty thing of Vic. George
the Fourth had the bust of the Duke of Bedford removed out of the long gallery, and the first day
Tavistock went to Windsor, he found it restored ; all
her own doing without a word to anyone. . . ."

"Stoke, Sept. 15th.

    " . . . Melbourne was here for an hour at least on
Wednesday whilst I was away. . . . The Young
Ladies thought him grave. All they could get out
of him about the Queen was that she did not like
the country, that she likes town better. . . . Yesterday I had the pleasure of coming down with her and
her party from Kensington as far as Colnbrook. . . .
It seems the Royalties had been shopping, or making
morning visits in London, and they changed horses in
the street at Kensington, and they overtook me in
two carriages before I got thro' Kensington, and as I
had no one in my coach I had a capital view of little
Vic, and was stuck close to them till they changed
horses at Cranford Bridge when we passed them, and
then they passed us, and we parted at Colnbrook,
having enjoyed the Royal presence for sixteen miles.
She had no escort, and in the second carriage poor
Lady Tavistock & Co. had only post horses. Vic was
at one time talking, and I was particularly struck with
the firmness of her mouth and manner. I contrived

to catch her eye in taking off my hat, and she made quite a suitable reply for a stage coach.

" Lady Maria and Kate are gone over to call at the Castle on Lady Tavistock, so I won't conclude this till I see if they bring any news.

" . . . I have taken to riding hugely, and like it prodigiously, only I sprained myself one day in getting on . . . but now, having acquired the art of mounting perfectly, Sefton said, ' How is it you manage it ? ' ' Oh ! ' says I, ' I no longer attempt to mount my horse by climbing up his side, but I get upon a place which is higher than his back, and then let myself down upon the *roof*,' and he was pleased to approve very much. . . .

" Here is Lady Maria, and the trip to London yesterday was merely a lark of Vic's to shew the Belgian Queen her Palace, and to drive about the town. . . ."

" Sept. 22nd.

" . . . Lady Tavistock came over once again with a couple of young ones, a Lady —— Stopford, and Miss Lister, the former belonging to the Duchess of Kent, the latter to the Queen. The Lister was full of regrets that she did not see more of the Queen. She was so good-natured to her whenever she *did* see her, which was only occasionally, as she (Vic) was walking or *running* thro' the Gallery. She (Lister) was in hopes to have been of the party when the Queens took their lark to London that day, but our Queen laughed and said, ' I shan't take the *children*.' *Too* be sure, neither the children nor the adult females see much of her, for she neither breakfasts with them nor attends at luncheon ; then she is employed most of the morning with Melbourne, rides at four with her female staff pretty much in the rear, dines at half

past seven, and leaves the drawing room at half past
ten—all clock work, so the young ones have not much
time for a *romp* with their mistress.   Miss Murray is
much blown up by her fellow maidservants for having
said the other day at luncheon, that it was the only
house she was ever in where there was neither news
nor *gossip*. . . .

" . . . One should think that the universal impression of . . . the firmness of the Queen, would
create for her a great degree of personal power, the
advantages of which must be shared by her Ministers,
but the Tory feeling of the country runs so high, and
the Church and Magistracy are so powerfully entrenched in their strongholds, that one can scarcely
reason upon even this Queen, let her remain ever so
good and steady, making any decided head against
them, at least at present. . . ."

"Sept. 25th.

" . . . I dined yesterday at my Essex's, and with
a new artist, at least so to me—Hayter the younger,
and a very modest and agreeable man he is.   He was
the most interesting to me from having just left
Windsor where the Queen has been sitting to him for
her picture on the Throne. . . . He is, like everyone
else, quite in love with her, and he spoke most scien-
tifically of the extraordinary character of her eye.   He
considers her as a truly great personage as to understanding, and with the most amiable and attractive
manner possible.   He heard a conversation between
Coburg [King of the Belgians] and her in German,
and tho' a very indifferent hand at that language, he
understood it enough to find there was a difference of
opinion between the Uncle and niece, and that the
latter kept her own.   He saw a great deal of both the
King and Queen of the Belgians, and was greatly

pleased with both, and he said that they had both expressed to him again and again their high opinion of Lord Melbourne. . . ."

"Oct. 1st.

" . . . Berkeley drove us over to Windsor one day, up to the Castle door, his object being to write the names of Her Majesty's two Colonels in her book, but the porter said in my hearing, ' The Queen, Sir, has no book ; there is one for the Duchess of Kent,' so Berkeley was obliged to be content with that. As to her *marrying*—Hayter said the day I met him, that it seemed to be quite a settled opinion with the Coburgs at least, that the Queen did not mean to marry for some years.

" I have seen several officers who were present at her review of the troops at Windsor the other day, and they are all enchanted with her. She wore the old Windsor uniform with the Star and Ribbon of her order, and a foraging cap with a broad gold laced band, and looked, they say, inimitable. I must say I should have liked to see *her* ride down the line, and between the ranks with old Fatty Lord Hill, and examining the men and their accoutrements to see that all was right. . . ."

"Brighton, October 11th.

" . . . Well, as you may suppose, we were all openmouthed and openeared when Francis* returned from the Pavilion on Monday. It was a very small party and Francis the only strange visitor except Melbourne, if he can be called so. As Francis had never kissed hands that ceremony was gone thro' first. He was told several times by different func-

* Molyneux. The Seftons were staying in Brighton ; the Queen at the Pavilion.

tionaries that he was to sit next to the Duchess of Kent. This done, the Queen put out her hand to Lord Melbourne to be conducted by him to dinner, and out they all went and seated themselves. For five minutes or so the atmosphere was rather lowering, then out came the sun and all was perfect sunshine till they parted. You know what a *rollicking* laugher Melbourne is ; he went his usual pace the whole time, and upon all subjects ; that is, common ones, and *Vic* it seems is nearly as much for ' *de laugh* ' as her Minister, and in quite as hearty a way. I want Francis to recollect (but he can't) upon what occasion it was that Vic said, ' My Mama has spoilt me,' and to which Mama replied, ' No, my dear, I have not spoilt you.' I am excessively fond of this, altho' I am ignorant of its application. At dinner the Duchess of Kent and our Frankfort discussed German Princes and Princesses, and a difference of opinion having arisen between the said Duchess and Francis as to the sex of some very young German baby, the Duchess maintaining it was a girl, and Francis that it was a boy, the Duchess said, ' We had better refer it to the Queen who knows all about such things much better than I do,' so being referred to, she said at once, ' It was a boy,' but, she added, she did not think it of the least consequence, and this said with a laugh too, which you know was rather profane for so serious a subject. . . .

" . . . Upon opening a card table drawer . . . a Phillidor upon Chess was found. ' Oh ! give me that,' said Melbourne, ' I never saw one in my life,' upon which the Queen said to him, ' That is very good indeed in you who have quoted the book to me fifty times at least.' These are but sorry scraps, you'll say, of our little Vic, but in a day or two I hope to get you some more, for between ourselves I am going to dine at our own Pavilion, and with dear little Vic herself *tomorrow*. . . . Henry Cavendish was the bearer of the message to Lady Sefton, and one or more of the Ladies, and as the Queen always saw Mr. Creevey with them, she requested his company too, and all this without the formality of a card. . . ."

Lady Louisa Molyneux to Creevey

" . . . We have not profited much by our friends at Court. . . . but we have one great feature in Lady Foley. She called here yesterday, and finding Maria at home alone, she took her out driving. She was dressed in the finest white muslin gown, with a blue satin spencer, a man's shirt, full-collar and neck-cloth, over which a white domino, a man's hat, and a double thick green veil which she never raised even in the room. She desired her coachman to drive wherever the fashion was, and in this attire Maria accompanied her up and down the Parade. She was in the highest spirits, and with all her finery she drove to a stableman's to look for ponies to drive, declaring she was the best whip in England ; . . . when Maria suggested the possibility of her being asked to dine at the Pavilion, she flourished her smelling bottle and said, ' I suppose one need not go if one is dangerously ill.' She was great on the subject of the way she would dress herself for riding if she was Queen, with her horse's head covered with jewels, and herself in scarlet. . . .

" Lord Melbourne has just called. . . . He complains very much of having a sad ' washy ' set of ladies, and says they are always ill. . . .

" We had a splendid arrival of Germans at Byam House last night. The Princess Augusta of Saxony, who required so many beds no hotel could take her in. She refused to marry the Emperor of Austria twice, and Napoleon once ; has a hundred thousand a year, and finer pearls and diamonds than anybody in the world.

" The John Russells are at the Bedford, and dine every day at the Pavilion. He has such a bad cold that there is not even his voice left of him. . . ."

" London, Nov. 10th.

" . . . Everything within and without the Guild-hall, and throughout the whole day went off to everybody's unqualified satisfaction ! always ex-cepting one occurrence, and which is really most provoking—that old Goose Sussex would have his *Gosling* Ciss invited to the banquet* : he wanted blank admissions for two Ladies (her and Lady Gore) but the city authorities said, ' No ! the Queen shall have no one to meet her at dinner who will not give their names,' and to that they stuck after much fighting. . . .

" . . . I have no patience with those idiots *Suss and Ciss* for getting into such a mess and upon such an occasion as dear little Vic's day of trial and of triumph. The thing altogether can't fail of being very advantageous for the Government ; so young a creature as Vic to have the courage to face her whole London population, to act her part so perfectly to the life, and never in the least to overact it, can't fail of leaving an impression that must require some very adverse acts indeed to weaken. Her Ministers *must* profit by this more or less, and the Tories show *they* think so by their dejected looks or snarling ob-servations. . . .

" I dined . . . yesterday with Sir David Wilkie,

* The State Banquet to the Queen at Guildhall.

who, you know, is the Queen's painter, and had dined in the Guildhall the day before. His broad Scotch description of the finery of the Queen's *boudoir*, in the room or out of the room, got up for her at the Guildhall was really beyond, and he said she has a *face*, a voice and manner that would have done honor to any of old who swore by the *solemn league and covenant.*

" . . . I am so interrupted by the kind enquiries of my *great* friends that I don't know whether I shall be able to finish this letter. First my Lord Lieutenant of Ireland must have a coze with me, and then our Ambassador to all the Russias must compliment me upon my *youthful* appearance, and then to discuss little *Vic* with me. You know he is quite at home in that family, and of course an authority, as to all that passes in it, and he told me that on Thursday night after the Guildhall Fête, Viccy was in bed before eleven, and that when Madame Lutzen went into her room the next morning at nine, she had never wakened. She has contrived so, or will do it, that Lady Caroline Barrington shall have a *permanent* residence about her, and Durham says that he knows that all these repeated proofs of her kind consideration for others are all her own exclusive acts. . . ."

" Holkham, Jany. 3rd, 1838.

" . . . I am much better than I was, tho' I was never bad, and at present I am not *quite* well. I live mostly in my charming bedroom on the ground floor with a door at hand to go out of the house if I like it, and another equally near for nameless purposes. A maid lights my fire at seven punctually, and my water is in my room at eight. The attention of my maid in refreshing my fire thro' the day, almost

H.R.H. DUKE OF SUSSEX.
From a lithograph by E. Desmaisons, 1841.

[*To face p.* 436.

hourly, is raally beyond, and I can never forget Lady Anson's* liberality in the way she has permitted me to partake of her *blue pill, black doze,* &c. . . .

" With all Melbourne's gaiety, Ellice describes his situation as really pitiable ; that according to his own account to Ellice, *he has no one to lean upon,* and for which reason he is for ever sending for him, Ellice. He feels quite certain that after all the secessions which have taken place since the formation of Lord Grey's Government, any further going out would destroy the Government, and yet the trumpery which composes it is always threatening him with this step. That false, palavering, and evil Jack the Painter † did them mischief without end in every part of his late management of the Civil List Bill, and Pension Concern, and yet he was always for resigning because he knew there was no one to supply his place. . . .

" In mentioning the name of little Vic it would be unpardonable not to state what I hear as a certain fact, viz., that Dr. Headlam has been made Mayor of Newcastle for the express purpose of doing honor to the town, and affording pleasure to the Queen when he receives her as Mayor on her way to Scotland next summer.

" I retract any skit I may have been guilty of at the expence of Lady Eliz. Stanhope.‡ She is full of good sense, and a most accurate observer of persons, and she has been and is a most valuable ally to me here. . . .

" I wish Miss Dutton was here—a Daughter of

* Lord Leicester's daughter, Anne, by his first marriage. She married 1st Viscount Anson.

† Rt. Hon. T. Spring-Rice.

‡ Another of Lord Leicester's daughters by the first marriage ; married John Spencer Stanhope.

Lord Sherborne, and a lady quite up to the mark in the humorous line.   She was here a short time lately with the Stevensons, the American Ambassador and his wife, who seem to have been admirably calculated for sport, particularly the lady, who always got someone to loosen girths when she left the diningroom, attributing her swollen condition to grapes, (not *gripes*, but *grapes*). . . ."

"Holkham, Jany. 7th.

" . . . I am sure Ellice communicates his correspondence to no one in this house but me.   He had another dispatch yesterday from Aber., whose back is very much up by a letter he has received from Melbourne, which more than insinuates that Aber. behaved ill to the Government in giving up the Speakership, but which nevertheless he means to do in the course of the session.   Ellice supposes that *Jack the Painter* will succeed him, and then at all events there will be a Speaker so affable as to be sure to please.

" Lyndhurst (who you know is a wag) says of Rice that when he goes down to the House, he first shakes hands with both the door-keepers at the outside of the House, then with every member of each side within the House, promises something to everyone, and gives it to none. . . .

" We have had another great household Ball here the night before last, and Lord Leicester danced again with a Lady staying here—Lady Beauchamp.   I declined taking the field again, as did my inseparable dear Dow. Anson.

" Lord Leicester took me a drive yesterday in his post chaise to show me improvements, and then to follow the shooters. . . .

" I forget whether I told you in my last letter any
of Lady Elizabeth's stories of the Stevensons, the
American Ambassador and his Rib, when they were
here. I am affraid of repeating them twice, but
talking with her on the same subject I said, ' The
other Yankee who used to be here a great deal, Mr.
Paterson, Lady Wellesley's Husband, was a good,
vulgar fellow too, was he not ? ' and upon her saying,
' Yes,' I said, ' Recollect a specimen for me,' so she
replied, ' Why, he was going on talking one day in a
manner that she, Mrs. Paterson, did not approve of,
and she tried by some indication under the table to
stop him, upon which he said, " Mrs. *P.*, I wish you
would keep your legs to yourself. I know very well
what I am about, so mind your own business." Only
think of the contrast in *manners* at least between the
American savage, and his polished successor—our
dandy little Marquis. . . ."

" Jermyn Street, Jany. 17th.

" . . . I concluded my campaign . . . at Holkham
with the greatest success. . . .

" . . . You will see from Lady Louisa's notes, that
her Father continues in the same [periods] of painful
depressions. . . . He sent for me, when, putting out
his hand to me and bursting out crying, he said,
' Excuse me, Creevey, troubling you in this manner,
but promise me to be kind to the Ladies in the next
room—to Lady Sefton and her Daughters. *My
living*, I assure you, is quite out of the question. As
far as money goes, the Ladies will, I may say, be
magnificently provided for. Lady Sefton will have
between £7,000 and £8,000 a year, and the girls in
proportion, but do promise to be kind to them.' What
a cruel state of mind to be in, if, what all his Doctors

pronounce to be literally true is in fact so, he has not a shadow of complaint about him. . . .

" Lady Louisa's remarks upon the wretch Lady Charlotte Bury and her book * are perfectly just. I know no name that is bad enough for her.

" I trust you saw Henry Webster's letter in ' The Times ' newspaper of one day last week vindicating his Mother, Madagascar, *by name* against the anonymous description of her in the book, and she burying her child, or rather a kid in lieu of her child, to deceive her husband, Sir Godfrey, and so to drive him to cut his throat. All these facts are admitted to be true by a son defending his mother, the authoress of them. . . ."

" Jermyn Street, Jany. 27th.

" . . . I dined at the Woods at the Admiralty on Wednesday, dinner at half past five o'clock, and saw young *Keane*† in ' Hamlet ' at Drury Lane afterwards. Ladies—Lady Mary and Lady Caroline Barrington ; gentlemen—Morpeth, Sir Parker, Lord of the Admiralty ; Fred Grey, Wood and me. (Dear Lady Mary !) *marrow-bones* on purpose for Mr. Creevey ! From Keane's first appearance and first speech I resolved to look at him no more, but I did, and he certainly improved *perhaps* to *mediocrity*, certainly never beyond it, but it is a most difficult part, and the poor man is a scarecrow, but the applause of a most crowded audience was almost beyond belief. . . .

" I dined with my Essex yesterday, his dear

* " Diary illustrative of the times of George IV " had just appeared anonymously.

† Charles, son of the famous Edmund Kean. He began on Jan. 8th, 1838, under Bunn at Drury Lane, a three weeks' engagement at £50 a night, playing *Hamlet* and *Richard II*.

Countess * having been *buried* the day before.   Today
I am going to dine tête-à-tête with our *Barney*. . . .

"Sefton continues very much the same ; days of
wretchedness with mighty poor intervals of sunshine,
if such can ever be called so. . . ."

"17, Jermyn Street, Feby. 3rd.

"'Helloa my dear Mr. Nummy!' I hear all you
Ladies exclaim, 'where is your frank, when there are
so many M.P.'s of both Houses in town?' The truth
is, My Dear, I can't catch them.   I returned from
Greenwich on Thursday with a chill, even more than
the one I had at Mrs. Aubrey's at Brussels, so I had
my bed made as [soon as] possible, and this is the
first time I have been out of it.   Freeman says I am
going (*sic*) and shall be quite well again in a few
days. . . ."

Thus, unconsciously prophetic, consciously hopeful as ever, the ready writer laid his pen away.   It is
the last letter in the collection in Creevey's handwriting.   A few hours later, on the fifth of February,
1838, on the eve of the new Session, he died very
suddenly, wanting exactly one month of seventy
years.†
Louisa Molyneux, in the final letter in the collection, charmingly writes his fit epitaph ; and so
his two "families" are left to their memories of
"dear Mr. Creevey" and "dearest Nummy."

* Formerly Mrs. Stephenson.   Old Lord Essex re-married within
3 months Catherine Stephens, the actress, who survived till 1882.
† It may be of interest to record the dates of death of his surviving
intimates.
Lord Sefton died in November of the same year, 1838.   Lord Essex
in 1839.   Lord Grey in 1845.   Miss Ord in 1853.   Lady Grey in 1861.
Lord Brougham lived until 1868.
Probably the last survivor of those mentioned by Creevey in his
letters was Sir Spencer Ponsonby Fane (the "young giant Spencer" of
Bessborough days) who survived vigorously until 1915.

Lady Louisa Molyneux to Miss Ord

" Feb. 8th.

" . . . No time can ever efface from my mind the feelings of respect and attachment to his memory, nor of gratitude for his constant kindness, which has added to all the pleasures, and diminished all the sorrows, of my life. . . ."

There are no details of his death among his papers, but Greville in his *Memoirs* (under date Feb. 20th, 1838) supplies a long and rather curious account, which is quoted in full by Sir Herbert Maxwell in his introduction. According to Greville, Creevey died suddenly, and, none of his relations being at hand, Lord Sefton got in touch with the family solicitor, Vizard, and had all his papers sealed up. Creevey had left as his executrix and residuary legatee " a woman who had lived with him for four years as his mistress " ; the cash value of the estate was not more than £400, but the papers potentially " exceedingly valuable, for he kept a copious diary for thirty-six years." According to Greville again, the papers held in their lamentable orthography the reputations of Brougham and one or two more of the old gang. Greville hints that Brougham himself came close on the heels of Sefton and that these two and the lawyer between them negotiated with the unknown executrix to buy the diaries of her, Vizard taking possession of them *pro tem.* Sir Herbert Maxwell's conclusion is that, if the diary existed as a continuous whole, Brougham succeeded in getting away, or making away, with such part of it as was " damaging." *
Hear Greville, echoing the sentiments of the age of privilege, on this point :

* If he did so, which I doubt, it was labour lost. He left that reputation for consistently single-minded statesmanship which he so carefully protected in his Autobiography (*Life and Times of Henry Brougham*), still in the hands of Miss Ord. In his vast and largely un-published correspondence with Creevey, a cynical opportunism which justifies his nicknames, is revealed. He barely mentioned Creevey's name in the Autobiography.

" The most extraordinary part of the affair is that the woman has behaved with the utmost delicacy and propriety, has shown no mercenary disposition, but expressed her desire to be guided by the wishes . . . of Creevey's friends. . . . Here is a strange situation in which to find a rectitude of conduct, a moral sentiment, a grateful and disinterested liberality which would do honour to the highest birth. . . ."

What reliance was to be placed on this record of Greville's ? I have been at some pains to test it and have in part succeeded. Two or three statements always aroused in me a suspicion which I could wish were justified. Who was this woman ? And what grounds were there for insisting that she was Creevey's mistress ? There is not much to suggest in all the length and breadth of the papers that Creevey was given to tread that irregular way. Was it in the probabilities that at the age of sixty-six, when his health was failing, he suddenly took a mistress ?—or a new mistress ? To the end of September, 1834, we know that he was happy under the care of " Mother " Durham, and he first dates letters from 17, Jermyn St. only in January, 1836. Certainly, therefore, Creevey was not keeping house (as opposed to " living with ") the woman for *four* years before his death. And, though it was conceivable, it seemed improbable that he left his effects and the few hundreds at his disposal to the woman under whose roof he occasionally lived during the last two years of his life. Whether she was his mistress or his landlady, and what her name was, were not to be learned from his papers. I have, however, traced his will, and think the relevant parts of the document of sufficient interest to set out :

" I Thomas Creevey of Greenwich Hospital in the County of Kent being one of the Commissioners thereof do hereby declare this to be my last will & testament I . . . bequeath unto my friend William Vizard Esq

30

Solicitor of Lincoln's Inn Fields . . . all that my undivided moiety of a freehold messuage . . . situated at Edgehill . . . in the County of Lancaster and all my undivided moiety in certain leasehold houses stables and other hereditaments situated in Bury Street & Lydia Ann Street in the Town of Liverpool all of which . . . were devised & bequeathed to me . . . by John Eaton Esquire formerly of the said Edgehill before mentioned . . . upon trust to . . . sell all the said premises . . . and as to all sums of money to arise from such sale . . . the said William Vizard . . . shall . . . pay out of the same the sum of two hundred pounds to William Wallace Currie Esquire now due to him upon my bond & in the next place pay out of the same funds the further sums of four hundred pounds and four hundred pounds to the Earl of Sefton & to General Sir Ronald Crawford Ferguson respectively being now due & owing by me upon my bond etc and if there should be any surplus remaining after the payment of these my just debts then I . . . bequeath the same together with all & every part of the furniture in my present appartments in Greenwich Hospital aforesaid & all and every other personal PROPERTY of which I may die possessed unto Mrs Emma Murray now residing at number seventeen Jermyn Street St. James' London her heirs etc for ever.   In witness etc this 5th day of August 1835. . . ."

In the light of Creevey's will, Greville's testimony must be accepted as in part at any rate accurate and fair.

There is no doubt that Mrs. Emma Murray was living at No. 17 when Creevey lodged there during the last two years of his life, and she it was undoubtedly who ministered to his wants and smoothed

his pillow.   He must, moreover, have known her for
some years previously, since he signed a will in her
favour in August, 1835, on the day before his sister's
funeral.   It is not possible to state with certainty
who she was or what was their relationship.   Something perhaps near the truth is contained in a letter
written by Sefton to Creevey on Jan. 12th, 1828.   He
says :

"Think of my good fortune in seeing one of
Michael's [Taylor's] letters in his beautiful handwriting
open on the table at Brooks'.   My eye was attracted
by the words 'Sausages' and 'Murray, 20 something
Pall Mall' . . . We had it all out at night, and
Mrs. Taylor was in fits, Taylor swaggering and
swearing he thanked God he had a fund which he
did and could devote to women."

Taylor and Creevey were close friends.   Creevey
long lived in Taylor's house, and it is not impossible
that he took over one of Taylor's liabilities.

On the whole, the will confirms in other respects
one's good opinion of Creevey.   That he should have
died in debt to the tune of a trifling £1000, if one consider the loose finance of his age and the great wealth
and devotion of many of his friends, is a sign of
strength (restraint and independence) rather than of
weakness.   The will makes no specific mention of
papers, though any documents in the Treasurer's
rooms at Greenwich or in Jermyn Street would fall
into residue, since there was no specific bequest to
Bessy Ord.   The question remains : what papers,
considered by Creevey to be valuable, lay in his rooms
to fall into the residuary bequest ?   That he should
have left to Emma Murray any papers which he himself
thought valuable, is hard to believe, since we know
that he retained his faculties, and the affection of
Bessy Ord, to the very end.   Years before he had
made Miss Ord aware that he regarded *her* as his
literary executrix and, as is well known, she had

frequent recourse to his papers, having re-copied a mass of them ; a large part of that great bulk of manuscripts which Sir Herbert went through before me were presumably already in her keeping. It is, therefore, strange if Creevey (who had one eye on posterity) left any valuable papers outside the control of the one educated person whom he had trained up to deal with them. On the other hand, his death was bound to give rise to gossip concerning scandalous papers, for all his life he had been credited with the power for evil of a Recording Angel. Myself I suspect Miss Ord had the papers which mattered.

So died Thomas Creevey, something of a mystery for all his frankness and verbosity, something of a solitary for all his wide acquaintance. He lies buried in the old Cemetery in the grounds of the Royal Hospital School* at Greenwich, and his name is recorded on the monument in the grounds.

*   *   *   *   *

What is a fair estimate of the man ? It would be generally agreed that the most prominent features in his character were an insatiable interest in the human drama and inexhaustible spirits to keep that interest alive. As an observer and critic of social and political life his energy knew no bounds ; he spilled gallons of ink and poured out millions of words year after year in his hobby. No trouble could possibly be too great, for never, never could his tongue or fingers keep pace with his enthusiasm.

Lytton Strachey, drawing on the only data available when he wrote, rather summarily dismisses him as a mischievous imp, an opportunist and a toady.

An imp, an ape or a toady he certainly was not. His ability and intellect were not of the first rank, but they were above the average in the political life of his day. He became an experienced and telling speaker, and was ready and apt in debate, with any amount of courage or truculence to back his opinions. A shrewd-

* On the south, or Park, side of the street which divides the Hospital property.

ness, resourcefulness and common sense, which even his enemies admitted, enhanced those qualities and won him the life-long respect of a number of first-rate contemporaries of both parties.   It is inconceivable that Wellington would have given such proof of respect to a mere toady or that Grey would have been at pains to conserve with a tame-cat a life-long friendship, which their correspondence proves to have been dignified with mutual regard and confidence, or that Brougham, whom Creevey lashed repeatedly, would have returned again and again to canvass the opinions of a man of no ability.   These were in their very different ways front-rank men.   To lesser men, such as Sefton, Bennet and Folkestone, Creevey's friendship was indispensable and they relied on him as guide and philosopher as well as boon-companion in their broad fun and boisterous revels.

There is no sort of justification for connecting him with " littleness," physically or mentally.   In stature he was of normal height, thick-set and latterly stout ; in face humorous, cheerful, kindly and handsome. Had he been small in mind, he would surely not have fastened diminutive nicknames on himself, called himself and suffered himself to be called by his wife's family, " Diddy " and " Nummy " and " Little Creevey," and so on.   And it would be impossible to find a man in his position who was less of a toady and a snob, or, indeed, more reckless of making enemies in the ranks of those to whom he looked for advance- ment and hospitality.   All his life, it is true, he took a boyish pride in retailing to his family his social triumphs ; but then his heart was incorrigibly young. The man who revelled in the splendours of Raby and the gilding and cuisine of Goodwood, would cheer- fully deny himself the aristocratic luxury of Croxteth to attend his sister's supper party in a little house in Liverpool, and return to delight the company at the Seftons' with an account of how he made the turkey " do duty " for all the hungry guests.

Living, as he did, constantly among the richest and most fortunate of the privileged class, he was devoid of

envy and never dreamed of bemoaning his own poverty
or of concealing his humble origin and connections.
The ducal patron whose interest gained Creevey his
seat in Parliament received a lecture such as Addison
might have given his stepson, when he preferred to him
a nominee who had financial claims. Indeed, Creevey
was a man of remarkably independent mind.

Quick-tempered and not thin-skinned, swift to
anger and not so swift to forgiveness, he was little
given to sentiment, but was by no means a hard-
hearted man. There is no doubt that his tongue
ran away with him. His head was hot while his
heart was cool, and Melbourne's judgment of the man,
that he was " very shrewd, but exceedingly bitter
and malignant," must be accepted as just, though it
must not be forgotten that in the politics of his day
bitterness and malignancy were common among large-
minded and otherwise charitable men. There is good
evidence that (politics apart) he was balanced and
philosophical. In the years of his poverty, in his
periods of privacy, in his inexpensive lodgings, he
was as serene and cheerful and well occupied as in his
days of plenty and power. He loved good literature,
showed a deep appreciation of natural beauty and
works of art, and, for a man of very rudimentary
education in the humanities, was remarkably interested in political and social history. He was content, when nothing else offered, to sit in the sun and
contemplate, and though he was seldom thrown of
necessity on his own resources for company, his was
the happy nature that could make solitude interesting.

In a word, the secret of his constant cheerfulness
was an absorbing interest which never failed him, in
life and men and in his own career and hobbies ; his
latest friendship, his latest triumph, his latest pursuit,
was perfection until another, succeeding it, took from
it all point and sparkle ; and that cheerfulness, march-
ing gaily along with a natural courage, optimism and
good health, made him a welcome guest wherever he
went. As husband, stepfather, brother, grandfather,
he was an unqualified success, receiving as much

affection as he bestowed, conceiving no trouble too great to benefit those he loved. Indeed, his family life was an idyll and the world's coarse thumb never tarnished his ideals. He could recognise and worship a saint among women and distinguish between a great lady and an important. All his life he won and held young and old, men, women and children, by the charm of his social gifts.

The best contemporary portrait of him is to be found in Lord Broughton's " Recollection of a Long Life." * Creevey naturally was not to everybody's taste as a country-house guest and did not appeal to the fastidious and scholarly mind of John Cam Hobhouse, who set a high standard on the obligations of friendship and believed in reticence. But, making all allowances, Lord Broughton's criticism must be regarded as just and illuminating and may fitly stand as a summing-up by an able, if unsympathetic, contemporary. Writing from Lambton in 1824, he says of Creevey : " I cannot say I formed an agreeable opinion of this gentleman from his visit to Lambton. He seemed to me a very wag, and one who would let no principle of any kind stand in the way of his joke. When he had no jest to excite laughter, he tried grimaces. He spared no one, and he fell foul of Lambton's pedigree, which our host had indiscreetly left on the library table. One of his constant topics was the absurdities of Michael Angelo Taylor, with whom he live more than with any other man. All this is true ; but of Creevey's superior abilities there can be no doubt. He had a strong and a quick memory and that lively perception of the ridiculous which goes to make an entertaining man. Raillery of the present and detraction of the absent were his weapons for general talk ; but when serious he showed sound and honest views, both of public and private duties, and discovered qualities which might adorn a higher character than he had endeavoured to acquire. . . ."

In assessing his merits as a historian, it is fair

* Vol. iii. pp. 80–81.

to say that Creevey's records of political events are, on the whole, fairly accurate even when compared with parallel records compiled by authoritative contemporaries of the opposite party (such as Abbot), and his judgments are very little exploded by our now accepted historical views. Gronow somewhere describes him as accuracy itself. On the other hand, in matters of no moment, in purely social gossip, he would pass on what he heard without troubling to sift the truth, though he was careful to correct misstatements when they came to his notice.

Assuredly he was an opportunist. What proportion of men with their way to make in life can be entirely acquitted of the charge, whatever profession they adopt ? The profession of politics is sometimes vaguely assumed to rest on a higher plane, although common experience and a reading of history do little to justify the assumption. Creevey at any rate scorned to cloak his opportunism with hypocrisy.

Nevertheless, the Galahad of politics will shake his head over him, as Councillor Barlow shook his head over Denry, the Card (of Arnold Bennett's creation). He will question whether Creevey or his intimates ever set cause before self, even the cause of Reform, and will ask : " What's he done ? What great cause is he identified with ? "

Some readers may perhaps speak up for Thomas Creevey and complete the quotation : " He's identified with the great cause of cheering us all up."

It is a task never yet accomplished but by men of independent character, of humanity and of courage.

THE END

INDEX

INDEX

A

Abbot, Rt. Hon. Charles (Lord Colchester), v, 241, 449
Abercromby, Rt. Hon. James, 63, 67, 83, 253 ; defeats Manners-Sutton for Speakership, 403–404
Addington, Rt. Hon. Henry (Lord Sidmouth), 16–20, 26, 55
Adelaide, Queen, 322, 346, 357 ; valsing, 365
Alava, Gen. Ricardo de, Spanish Ambassador and soldier ; on Wellington, 239–40 ; 335, 407
" All the Talents " Ministry, 26 et seq.
Allen, Dr. John, 25, 126 ; Lady Holland abuses, 405
Almack's, 151, 189, 199
Alten, Gen. Count, 80
Althorp, Viscount, 27 ; Chancellor of Exchequer, 329–30 ; 347, 357 ; and C.'s post, 363 and note ; succeeds his father, 396
Alvanley, Lord, 186, 280 ; his joke on Lady Elcho, 298 ; 424
Anson, Dow. Viscountess (née Coke) ; kindness to C., 437–438
Antrim, Countess of, 199
Aremberg, Prince Pierre d', 280
Arundel Castle, 270–71 ; owls in keep, 270
Arundel, Earl of (13th Duke of Norfolk), 194
Ascot, 196, 212–213, 264–265, 305
Athol case, note on, 24
Aubrey, Sir John, 65
Auckland, 2nd Lord, 153, 195, 335 ; retires from Greenwich, 377 ; 384–385 ; 404
Augusta, Princess, 197, 215, 262, 322
Austen, Jane, Emma published, 97
Austria, Emperor of, 95

B

Baillie, Dr., 98
Baker, George, 161, 166

Barclay's Brewery, effect of gin drinking on, 261
Barden Tower, 168
Baring, Alexander (1st Lord Ashburton), 99
Baring, Sir Thomas, question of peerage for, 360
Barnes, General Sir Edward, Adjt.-Gen., 73, 75, 78–81, 87, 88
Barningham, 243
Bathurst, 3rd Earl, 211 ; at Howick, 250 ; on C., 258
Bathurst, Countess, 212, 250
Beaumont, Mr., M.P. for Northumberland, 190
Bedford, John, 6th Duke of, 82, 106, 112, 126 ; at Howick, 396 ; 406
Bennet, Lady Emma, 215–216
Bennet, Hon. H. G., 56, 64, 70, 74, 81, 82, 98, 103, 106, 116, 117, 129, 130, 138, 139, 162
Bentinck, Lord George, 161, 309
Berri, Duchesse de, at Liverpool, 324
Bessborough, Fredk., 3rd Earl of, 171
Bessborough, the Duncannons at, 284–289, 290–292, 370–373
Binning, Lord, 139, 140
Bland, Dow. Lady, on Devonshire House, 220 ; card-playing methods, 220–221
Bloomfield, Sir Benjamin, 149
Bloomfield, Lady, 149
Blücher, Prince, 92, 93
Bolton Abbey, 166, 168
Bonaparte, Napoleon, 23, 36 ; abdicates, 72 ; lands in France, 73, 74, 75, 83, 85, 86, 90 ; surrenders to Maitland, 93 ; St. Helena, 96 ; 153, 154
Bouverie, Hon. Mrs. E. (Lady R. Spencer), 18, 272
Bouverie, Miss Frances, 272, 273
Bowyer, Robert, painter, 173
Brand, Gen. Hon. Henry (21st Lord Dacre), 104, 202
Brandling, Charles, 181 ; death, 224–225

Brandling, Mrs. William and daughters, 247; their success at Lady Salisbury's, 317–319
Brandon, Lady, and Melbourne, 284
Brandreth, Dr., 20
Brighton, 23–25; its rapid growth, 115–116; 383; and Queen Victoria, 432–434
Brooks's Club, 237, 253, 262; and *passim*.
Brougham, Henry (1st Lord Brougham and Vaux), v, 40, 52; some account of, 53, 54; Liverpool Election, 57–66 *passim*; Creevey's trial, 69, 70; 83, 97, 99, 104, 107, 108, 123–125; Queen's trial, 127–131; 136–138, 141–143, 147; Durham clergy, 154–156; 161, 163, 177, 178, 186, 188, 194, 214, 219, 222, 242, 250, 251; offer of Chief Baron, 252; 260, 299; Chancellor, 325–328; "Vaux," 335; and *The Times*, 338; and Palmerston, 345, 354; Coercion Bill intrigues, 376; and Grey, 391; and William IV, 392; shelved, 402; 406, 408; his papers of George III, 425; actions at C.'s death, 442
Brougham, Mrs., 142, 147, 152, 178, 214; "Lady B. and Vaux," 362; B.'s hatred of, 425
Brougham, James, 214, 249; returned with C. for Downton, 344
Brunswick, Duke of, 218; jealousy of Orléans, 365
Brussels, 72–90 *passim*; 418
Buckingham Palace, 307, 406
Buckinghamshire, Earl of, 98
Burdett, Sir Francis, 14, 20, 42, 45, 47, 48, 51, 125; imprisoned, 137; 178
Burgoyne, Sir John Fox, 42
Burrell, Sir Walter, 271
Bury, Lady Charlotte. Her published disclosures, 440
Byng, Mrs. George, 65, 185
Byng, G., M.P. ("Poodle"), 217, 388

C

Calais, C.'s visit and dinner, 306
Calcraft, Rt. Hon. John, 58, 63

Caledon, Countess of, 150
Callings, Mrs., C.'s jest on, 246
Cambridge University, Queen's and Trinity, 5, 6; Petty contests, 27; 238
Campbell, Sir John (Lord Campbell), conduct in de Ros case, 422
Canning, Rt. Hon. George, 19, 41, 44, 45, 53–56; Liverpool election, 59–62; 103, 105, 106, 111; his dilemma in 1822, 158–163; 166, 177, 178; succeeds Liverpool as premier, 232; 237–239; death, 243
Canning, Miss, 158
Canning, Sir Stratford, at Newcome's school, 5
Cantley, near Doncaster, 7, 200–202, 210, 215–222
Caroline, Queen, 53; 65–68; goes abroad, 72; 82, 104; return and trial, relations with Brougham, 122–131; 135–138; at Abbey, 141–142; death, 143–144
Cashiobury (Lord Essex's), 418
Castlereagh, Viscount, 41, 45, 67, 74; the green bag, 129; 137; suicide, 148, 155
Castlereagh, Viscountess, Paris 1815, 95
Cavendish, Lord George, 221
Chandos, Marquis of, 198
Charlotte, Queen, 82
Charlotte, Princess, 98
Chatham, 2nd Earl of, Walcheren Expedition, 46
Chichester, Earl of, 49
Chiffney, Bill, Lord Darlington's trainer, 242–243
Chronicle, The, 416
Churchill, Lord Charles, and Duke of Sussex, 404
Churchill, Lord John, and Fanny Hughes, 362
Churchill, Lord William, 215
Cintra, Convention of, 39–40
Clancarty, Earl of, 94
Clarence, H.R.H. Duke of. *See* William IV.
Clarence, H.R.H. Duchess of. *See* Adelaide, Queen.
Clarke, Mrs., 44; *The Rival Princes*, 47–50
Clifford, Lady Ann (Countess of Pembroke), 169, 170, 172

Clifford, Admiral Sir Augustus, 413 and note
Clive, Dr., 30
Cobbett, William, 32, 39, 45, 48 ; Newgate Prison ; on India, 50 ; on law of libel, 71 ; 320
Codrington, Admiral Sir Edward, " Navarino," 420
Colborne, Sir John, 179
Coleshill House, 48, 49
Conyngham, 1st Marquis, 189, 242, 307
Conyngham, Marchioness, 126, 212, 228, 321
Conyngham, Lord Francis, 189
Copley, Sir John and Lady. *See* Lyndhurst
Copley, Sir Joseph, 149, 158, 166, 219, 221
Copley, Miss Maria, 158–161, 171, 188, 219
Coronation of George IV., 141–142 ; of William IV., 343
Coutts, Mrs. *See* St. Albans, Duchess of.
Coutts' Bank, 216
Covent Garden Theatre, 182
Cowdray Park, 272–273 ; the Woolbeding fountain, the Montagus and Poyntz, 279
Cowley, Countess, gossip about Hatfield fire, 415 ; dinner with the Queen, 427
Cowper, Earl, 247 ; at Wiesbaden, 419
Cowper, Countess, 212, 247 ; at Wiesbaden, 419
Craven, Hon. Berkeley, 305
Craven, Hon. George Augustus, 312
Craven, Hon. Keppel, 138
Craven, 6th Lord, 151
Creevey, Eleanor (Mrs. Thomas Creevey), 7 ; marries Creevey, 10 ; 11, 19 ; Brighton, 23–24 ; 29, 34, 39, 45, 46, 50, 52, 54, 55, 59 ; letters on Creevey's libel case, 66–70 ; 90 ; illness and death, 97–111 ; letters at Howick, 395
Creevey, Miss Jane, 4, 207, 254 ; her drum, 255 ; 310, 312, 376 ; at Croxton, 389 ; letter to C., 390 ; her death and will, 409–411 ; her cousins *ibid.*
Creevey, Thomas. Principal events and dates : born 1768.

B.A. Cambridge 1789. Called to Bar by Gray's Inn 1794. Married Mrs. Ord 1802. M.P. Thetford 1802. Secretary, Board of Control, in " Talents " Ministry 1806–7. Contested Liverpool 1812. Convicted of Libel 1813. Settled in Brussels 1814. Death of Mrs. Creevey in Brussels 1818. Lost seat at Thetford 1818. Returned to England 1819. Returned for Appleby 1820. Lost seat at Lord Thanet's death 1825. Whigs return to power. Appointed Treasurer, Ordnance, 1830. Returned for Downton with James Brougham 1831. Retired from politics 1832. Appointed Treasurer, Greenwich Hospital, on abolition of Ordnance office 1834. His sister died 1835. Death 1838.
His finances. From his marriage to his death, except for the twelve-year period 1818–1830, his income from all sources was never less than £1,000 a year. For short periods it was much more. For his private income, *see* pages 409 and 444.
His profession. He continued to practise on the Chancery side until he obtained office in 1806.
Politics. The Whigs remained continuously in opposition from 1807 to 1830. References to C.'s speeches on Ceylon and on India are on pages 17 and 51 ; to his political pamphlets, on pages 124 *et. seq.* and 225
Creevey, William, 3, 4, 5
Creevey, Mrs. William, 3, 4, 5, 12, 406
Crockford's, 321, 328, 339 ; Sefton's winnings, 361 ; Ude and C., 387–388
Croxteth, 63, 173, 229–230, 251, 293–295, 352
Cumberland, H.R.H. Duke of, his marriage, 82 ; 234, 266 ; and Wellington, 302 ; assault on Lady Lyndhurst, 307–309 ; 323
Cumberland, H.R.H. Prince George of, 264, 323
Cumberland Lodge, household ball at, 189

Currie, Dr. James, 5, 7, 8, 9, 11, 13, 18, 19 ; his death, 24 ; 36

D

Dallas, Sir Robert, 22
Darlington, Countess of, 188, 208–210, 213, 219, 231, 248, 249, 259
Darlington, Earl of (1st Duke of Cleveland), 165, 188, 208–210, 213, 219, 224 ; his arms, 249 ; 259 ; loss of patronage, 339–340
Dawson, Massey, M.P., 145
Denison, J. H. (brother of Lady Conyngham), 149, 185
Derby, the, 195
Derby, 7th Earl of. Note on Athol case, 24
Derby, 12th Earl of, 22, 39, 41, 57, 62, 195, 204, 205, 294–295, 311, 356
Derby, Countess of (Eliza Farren), 205, 294–295, 311
Devonshire, 6th Duke of, 112, 188, 216, 218, 221, 413
Dino, Duchesse de, Talleyrand's niece, 336, 342 ; and Queen Adelaide, 366 ; on boredom, 369
Dolphin Inn, Chichester, 268 ; its excellent fare, 271
Dorset, Duke of, 189, 243
Downing St., No. 10. Its furnishing, 359
Drury Lane, 175
Dublin, the Castle, 283, 292, 351 ; Wellesleys at, 374–375
Dudley, 1st Earl of (9th Lord Ward), buys Witley, 231 ; 240 ; and Lady Lyndhurst, 252, 255 ; foreign secretary, 262, 329 ; his death and will, 363
Dumaresq, Capt., A-D.C. to Gen. Byng, 89, 262
Duncannon, Maria, Viscountess, 236, 257 ; at Bessborough, 284–289, 292, 330, 370–373
Duncannon, Viscount (4th Earl of Bessborough), 151, 152, 171, 185, 189, 196, 214 ; at Bessboro', 284–289, 330 ; quarrel with Sussex, 347 ; influenza in family, 365 ; and Sir H. Taylor, 370–373 ; 408
Duncombe, Thomas, M.P., 165, 201, 252, 265, 304, 424

Dunstanville, Lord de, 194
Durham Cathedral libel, 154–156
Durham, Earl of. *See* Lambton, J. G.
Durham, Mrs., C.'s landlady, 330, 361 ; as nurse, 379 ; C. leaves her, 389 ; 443

E

Earle, Thomas, of Liverpool, 61, 62
Eaton, John, and Mrs. (Creevey's uncle and aunt), 5, 22, 104, 111, 125, 207 ; C.'s will, 444
Ebrington, Viscount (2nd Earl Fortescue), 204
Eden, Hon. Emily, 335, 386
Edinburgh, George IV's visit to, 157–158
Egremont, 3rd Earl of, 258, 269, 273–279
Eldon, Earl of, refuses to serve under Canning, 232
Ellenborough, 1st Lord, 68, 70
Ellice, Edward, of Invergarry, 271, 330, 333 ; mentions Greenwich to C., 377 ; 423 and note
Ellice, Lady Hannah (*née* Grey), 271
Ellis, Charles (Lord Seaford), 61
Elphinstone, Hon. Georgina, 300
Elphinstone, Hon. W. F., Chairman East India Company, 34
Erroll, 18th Earl of, 236, 292, 321, 323, 394
Erroll, Countess of, daughter of William IV, 236, 292, 321, 323
Erskine, 1st Lord, 10, 20, 51, 56
Erskine, Hon. E. S., 79, 81
Essex, 5th Earl of, 127, 310, 360 ; and Lady Holland, 368 ; 408 ; at Cashiobury, 418, 419 ; wife's death and his remarriage, 440–441
Essex, Countess of (Mrs. Stephenson), her death, 440–441
Este, Sir Augustus D.', son of H.R.H. Duke of Sussex, 194, 214
Esterhazy, Prince, Austrian Ambassador, 176, 180, 255
Eton College, 8, 182, 265 ; C.'s love of, 367
Euston, Countess of, 310
Evatt, Major, 80

Exeter, 2nd Marquis of, 180
Exeter, Marchioness of (*née* Poyntz), 180, 271, 279

F

Fabvier, Col., 187
Fawkener, Mr., Secretary Privy Council, 18
Fawkener, Sir E., footnote 18
Fawkes, Miss Maria, 166, 170
Felix Hall, Kelvedon, 8, 133
Ferguson, Major-Gen. Sir R., of Raith, 139, 157, 171, 195–196, 296, 299, 301, 304 ; loan to C., mentioned in will, 444
Fitzherbert, Mrs., 24, 69, 114, 115, 301 ; pension continued by William IV, 324
Fitzpatrick, Gen., 30, 32
Fitzroy, Lord Charles, 221
Fitzwilliam, 4th Earl, 30, 98, 247
Flahault, Comte de, 149
Flahault, Comtesse de (Lady Keith), 149
Foley, 3rd Lord, 164 ; extravagance, 231
Foley, Lady, her extravagance, 230–231 ; again, 297–298
Folkestone, Viscount (3rd Earl of Radnor), Mrs. Clarke's revelations, 47–49, 64, 124, 126, 134, 259, 301, 320–321 ; offers Downton to C., 342
Fonblanque, Jasper, 65
Fortescue, Hon. George, 204
Fox, Rt. Hon. Charles James, 15, 16, 17, 19–21 ; " All-the-talents," 26 ; his death, 29–33, 116–117
Fox, Hon. Mrs., 29, 30

G

Gascoigne, Gen. Bamber, M.P. for Liverpool, 15, 53, 60, 108, 112
George III., 18, 26 ; on Fox's death, 30; 40; insane, 51; death, 122 ; and his Ministers, the Brougham papers on, 425–427
George IV., 21, 24, 31 ; Fox's death, 33 ; Regency, 51–54 ; 65, 72, 82 ; Bonaparte's appeal to, 93, 96 ; 102, 104, 115 ; strange behaviour, 126 ; coronation, 135 ; Queen Caroline's death, 142–143 ; visit to Curragh,

144–146 ; 148, 157, 163, 166, 179 ; illness, 182 ; household dinner, 189 ; health, 211 ; fishing, 227, 229 ; and Lady Salisbury, 228 ; 234 ; and Canning, 237, 241 ; Chiffney and, 242 ; last Government, 257; health, 262 ; Ascot, 264 ; and Greville, 267 ; dinner to " brother jockeys," 268 ; admits Catholics, 297–299 ; Ascot, 305 ; dislike of Windsor Castle, 307 ; how he won Salamanca! 313 ; death, 317, 321
Gleig, Rev. George, author, Lord John's appointment of, 381
Glengall, Countess of, 114 ; account of George IV at Curragh, 144–146 ; 150, 151, 152, 175, 186, 296, 324
Gloucester, H.R.H. Duke of, 197, 318–319, 324
Gloucester, H.R.H. Duchess of, 197, 228, 262, 319, 322
Gloucester, Princess Sophia of, 102, 197
Goderich, Lord, succeeds Canning, 232–233 ; resigns, 256 ; 353, 424
Goodwood House, 269–270
Goodwood Races, 267–269
Gordon, Gen. Sir Willoughby, 353, 354
Gore, Hon. Charles, brother of 4th Earl of Arran, 286 note ; 371 note ; Lord John's secretary, 420
Gore, Bishop Charles, 286 note
Grafton, 4th Duke of, 93, 196
Grant, Sir Colquhoun, his daughter's marriage to young Sheridan, 408
Granville, 1st Earl (Lord Granville Leveson-Gower), 61, 175, 239, 406
Graves, 2nd Lord, 158
Gray's Inn, 5, 6, 11
Greenwich Hospital, Treasurership, C. hears of vacancy, 377 ; 378 ; appointed, 383 ; his house at, 384–387, 388, 406–407, 411–413, 443 ; C.'s grave at, 446 and note
Grenfell, Charles Pascoe, 173, 224
Grenfell, Lady Georgiana, daughter of 2nd Earl of Sefton, death, 224, 226

Grenville, William Wyndham, 1st Lord, 26, 41, 51 ; refusal to serve with Perceval, 53–56

Gresley, Sir Roger, 202

Gresley, Lady Sophia, 202

Greville, Charles, diarist, v, 161, 236, 246, 255, 262 ; sulks, 265 ; Secretary for Jamaica, 267 ; 278, 290, 307 ; Cumberland and Lady Lyndhurst, 307–309 ; account of C.'s death and will, 442–443

Greville, Lady Charlotte, 76, 161, 172, 283

Grey, Charles, 2nd Earl, 6, 7, 8, 17 ; " All-the-talents," 26–27 ; Viscount Howick, 32 ; 34, 37, 40, 41, 45, 51 ; refusal to join Perceval, 53–56 ; 67–68, 123, 138, 159–160, 184, 190, 203, 214, 240 ; on Canning's death, 243–244 ; 250, 251, 256, 259, 260, 263, 301, 302, 317 ; summoned at last, 325 ; his government, 325–327 ; C.'s post, 329 ; Reform Bill struggle 1831, 332–352 passim ; the Bill passed, 353–357 ; wish to retire, 371–372 ; Coercion Bill, Grey resigns, 376 ; and C.'s post at Greenwich, 377 ; 378–379 ; 383, 386 ; and Brougham, 391 ; in retirement, 391–398 ; 405

Grey, Countess (wife of 2nd Earl), 240, 260, 301–302 ; party at, 334–335 ; C.'s intervention, 366–367 ; at Howick, 391–398 ; to C. on politics, 399 ; asks a favour of C., 411–412

Grey, Lady Georgiana, 254 ; at Palace Ball, 357 ; 378–379

Grey, Henry (3rd Earl). See Howick, Viscount

Grey, John, Capt., 82, 90

Gronow, Rees Howell, memoir writer, v ; on C., 449

Guardian and Evening Reporter, 106

Guiche, Comtesse de, 200

Guildhall, banquet to Queen Victoria, 435–436

H

Halford, Sir Henry, 321

Hamilton, Alexander, Major, brother of following, 101, 361

Hamilton, Andrew, Lt.-Col., at Waterloo, 73, 74, 75, 77, 79, 80, 86, 88 ; in Paris, 91–96 ; marries Miss Ord, 98, 101 ; 131

Hamilton, Mrs. Andrew (Anne Ord), marriage 98, 100–101 ; 109, 110, 115, 259, 307, 319, 364

Hamilton, Andrew (Anne's son), 310, 345 ; page at Coronation, 349

Hamilton, Lady Anne, in attendance on Queen Caroline, 128, 141

Hammick, Sir Stephen, and Lady Holland, 405

Hardinge, F.-M. Sir Henry, 414 and note

Hardwicke, 3rd Earl of, reported dead, 150–151

Hardy, Admiral Sir Thomas, 335 and note ; 373, 385, 388, 398 ; " gossips," 412 ; 416

Hardy, Lady (neé Berkeley), 310, 335, 385, 388–389, 398, 403, 406 ; " gossips," 412 ; 416

Hardy, Miss Emily, Lord John Russell and, 381, 389

Hardy, Miss Mary, marriage to Mr. Macgregor, 373, 381, 398

Harewood House, 167

Harley, Lady Anne, 187

Harrington, 3rd Earl of, 199, 299–301 ; death, 307

Harrington House, theatricals, 299–301

Harvey, Mr., on field of Waterloo, 81, 94

Hatfield House, fire at, 412–413, 415

Hatfield, attempt to assassinate George III, 198

Hawkesbury, Lord. See Liverpool, 2nd Earl of.

Hayter, Sir George, painter, impressions of Queen Victoria 431–432

Heath, Dr., 8

Hertford, Marchioness of, 126

Hervey, Lord, son of Marquis of Bristol, 211

Hesse, Capt., Waterloo, 81, 89 ; attending Queen Caroline, 141

Hill, Lord Arthur, at Waterloo, 81 ; 186, 196, 197, 235 ; with Lady Salisbury, 265

Hill, General, 1st Viscount, 319, 334, 353 ; at Queen Victoria's review, 432

Hobhouse, John Cam (Lord Broughton), v ; his picture of C., 449
Holkham, 423, 436–439
Holland, 3rd Lord, 29, 33, 44, 49, 51, 325, 356, 398, 420–421
Holland, Lady (Elizabeth Vassall), 25, 30, 76, 97, 101, 177, 215, 233, 237 ; gratitude to C., 341 ; bad manners at Lord Essex, 368 ; 378, 383, 404–405 ; and her doctor, 405 ; 406, 418, 420–421 ; Lady C. Bury's disclosures on, 440
Holland House, 177–178, 237 ; Lady H.'s maid, Brown, 383 ; 420–421
Holland, Sir Henry, 143
Holly Lodge (Duke of St. Albans'), party at, 265–266
Holmes, William, Treasurer of Ordnance, 330
Hood, 2nd Viscount, 141, 144
Hood, Viscountess, 141
Horner, Francis, M.P., 98, 105
Howick, Viscount. See Grey, Charles, 2nd Earl
Howick (House), 159, 250 ; Lord Grey at home, 391–398
Howick, Henry, Viscount (son of 2nd Earl Grey), 24, 223 ; stands for Winchelsea, 224 ; 353
Hughes, W. J. (Lord Dinorben), 132, 293, 404
Hughes, Mrs. (Lady Dinorben), 324 ; her death, 404
Hughes-Ball, Mrs., 213
Hume, Joseph, M.P., 363, 386
Huntley, Marchioness of, 199
Huskisson, Rt. Hon. W., 44, 105, 232, 235, 239, 244
Hutchinson, Lord, 128

I

Ibbetson, Sir Henry, 167
Income Tax, 27, 97, 100
Influenza, its ravages, 365
Inverness, Duchess of. See Underwood, Lady Cecilia

J

Jersey, 5th Earl of, 152, 195, 236 ; and George IV, 268 ; 283
Jersey, Sarah, Countess of, 123, 136, 152, 180, 183, 185, 236,

283 ; compared with Lady Duncannon, 288 ; 322 ; her behaviour abroad, 419
Johnstone, George, M.P., 67
Juarenais, Marquis de, at Brussels, 79, 80
Juarenais, Marquise de, 79, 80

K

Kean, Charles, actor, C.'s poor opinion of, 440
Kemble, Fanny, 311 ; C.'s poor opinion of, 318
Kensington, 2nd Lord, 151, 235
Kensington Palace, 194
Kent, H.R.H. Duchess of, 234 ; her demands on Bd. of Works, 370 ; and Conroy, 372 ; "Madame Mère," 427 ; at the Pavilion, 432-434
Keppel, Sir W., 189
Kerry, William Thomas, Earl of, 371, 373, 382, 404
Kilfane, Co. Kilkenny, the Powers at, 289–292
King, Lord, 20, 186
King, Mr. and Mrs. (née Wyndham), 275
Kinmel, St. Asaph's, 205, 324
Kinnaird, 8th Lord, 128, 187
Kirkpatrick, Mr., of Liverpool, C.'s libel on, 66
Knighton, Sir W., 189
Knowsley, 39, 62, 204, 295, 311

L

Lade, Sir John, 227
Lake, Richard, C. counsel in his law suit, 22
Lamb, Hon. Mrs. George, 183
Lamb, Rt. Hon. William (Lord Melbourne), 280, 283–284, 301, 325 ; succeeds Grey in 1834, 376 ; his difficulties, 393 ; 395–396, 398 ; cynicism, 413–414 ; Mrs. Norton, 417–418 ; and Queen Victoria, 429, 430, 433–434 ; 437
Lamb, Lady Caroline (née Ponsonby), wife of above, "Glenarvon," 102 ; 289
Lambton, J. G. (1st Earl of Durham), "King Jog," 106, 128, 139 ; at Doncaster, 160–166, 179, 183, 200, 201–203, 214, 215, 217, 222–223, 256 ;

Lord Durham, 258, 263, 319; plots against Government, 346; again, 372; Miss Martineau, 380–381; 391

Lambton, Lady Louisa (Countess of Durham), 159, 161, 214, 223, 319, 380–381

Lambton, William, 190

Lambton, Mrs. William, 203, 223

Lambton Castle, 202–204; a large house-party, 222–223; the gas fails, 223

Lansdowne, 3rd Marquis of (Lord Henry Petty), " The Roscius," 19, 20, 23, 26; Chancellor of Exchequer, 27, 33; marriage, 39; 55, 63, 112; on Castlereagh's suicide, 150; and Canning, 232; 240–242, 256, 319, 325, 349; on Lord Kerry's engagement, 371; 382, 416

Lascelles, Hon. William S., M.P., 165

Latouche, Miss, 283–284, 292

Lauderdale, 8th Earl of, 40, 102, 126, 186

La Valette, Marquis de, 98

Lawrence, Sir Thomas, 247

Le Blanc, Mr. Justice, 70

Leeds, Duchess of, 200

Legh, Thomas, of Lyme, 79

Leicester, 1st Earl of, at Holkham, 423, 436–439

Leinster, 3rd Duke of, 144–146

Lemon, Miss, 194

Lennox, Lady Sarah, 75

Leopold, King of the Belgians, 266; elected King, 348; and Queen Victoria, 428, 431, 432

Leveson, Lord Francis (1st Earl of Ellesmere), 172, 283, 290

Lieven, Princess, note 180, 181, 247–248; on boredom, 369

Lieven, Prince, Russian Ambassador, 184, 248

Lindsay, Lady Charlotte, gift of papers to Brougham, 425 and note;

Liverpool, 4, 7, 9, 11, 15, 17, 22, 23; election, 53–63; Sefton's land dispute, 230; 324; Reform address, 356; 444

Liverpool, 2nd Earl of (formerly Lord Hawkesbury), 16; succeeds Perceval as premier, 54; 103; Bill of deprivation, 131–132; 143; and Canning, 163;

last year as premier, 224; resigns, 232

London University, Brougham's work for, 238

Londonderry, 2nd Marquis of. See Castlereagh, Viscount.

Londonderry, 3rd Marquis of, 219

Londonderry, Marchioness of, 199, 200, 203, 218, 251

Louis XVIII, 72, 74, 83, 94–95

Lowe, Sir Hudson, 96, 154; unpopularity with Whigs, 353–354

Lowther Castle, 162, 235, 246

Lumley, Mrs., 222

Lushington, Stephen, 143, 214

Luttrell, Henry, his wit, 280; 413, 417, 420

Lyndhurst, Lord, 253, 304; and Cumberland, 307–309, 310

Lyndhurst, Lady, 252; Cumberland's assault, 307–309; Lord Dudley's will, 363

Lynedoch, Gen. Lord, 301

M

Mackintosh, Sir James, 10, 13, 113, 336

MacMahon, Sir John, 31, 33

Maitland, Sir Peregrine, note 75, 83

Mandeville, Viscount, 171

Manners-Sutton, Archbishop of Canterbury, 241

Manners-Sutton, Charles, 1st Viscount Canterbury, 241; and Abercromby, 403

Mansfield, Countess of, 199, 219

Mansion House (1824), 191–193

Martin, Admiral, 151

Martineau, Miss Harriet, at Lord Durham's, 380–381

Matuscewitz, M., his race-horse Sharper, 303

Maxwell, Rt. Hon. Sir Herbert, v to ix, 3, 232; views on C.'s diary, 442

Mayo, 4th Earl of, 145

Meath, 10th Earl of, 145

Melbourne, Viscount. See Lamb, Rt. Hon. W.

Melville, Lord, impeachment, 23

Middleton Park, Bicester, 123, 126

Milbank, Lady Augusta, 164, 200, 202, 209, 214, 246

Milbank, Mark, of Thorp Perrow,

165, 203, 214; and the candle, 223; 246
Mills, John, M.P., 201, 309
Milton, Viscount, 247
Minto, Earl of, 416–417, 420
Mitford, Mr. and Lady Georgiana, 417 and note
Moira, Earl of (Marquis of Hastings), 51, 54–56
Molyneux, Viscount, 252, 264–265; opens Palace Ball, 357; 407
Molyneux, Hon. Berkeley, at Windsor, 428, 432
Molyneux, Hon. Francis, 213, 237, 300, 322, 337, 361; marriage, 427 note; dines with Queen Victoria, 432–434
Molyneux, Lady Maria, 213, 237; picture of Croxteth, 307; 329, 337, 430
Molyneux, Lady Louisa, 215, 237, 252, 253, 329, 334–335, 337, 407; Frankfort, 418–419; writes Creevey's "epitaph," 441–442
Molyneux, Lady Caroline, 237, 279, 361; marries C. Towneley, 420
Molyneux, Lady Katherine, 407, 428
Moniteur newspaper, on Canning's death, 243
Montgomery, Sir William, 65
Montrond, Count, 252; on books, 264; 281; on Josephine, 312–313; 328, 341
Montrose, Duke of, 234
Moore, Capt. Graham, 7, 19, 35, 37, 43; view on Walcheren, 45–46; 47, 65
Moore, James, his defence of his brother, Sir John, 43–44
Moore, Sir John, 7; his death, 41–44
Moore, Thomas, 290–292
Morgan, Sydney, Lady, 283–284
Morley, Countess of, 199
Morning Journal, 299
Morning Post, 85, 135; on Abercromby, 404
Morpeth, Viscount, 32
Motteux, M., 272
"Mountain, The," Advanced Whig Party, 73, 232
Murray, Mrs. Emma, C.'s mistress? 442; C.'s bequest to, 443–444; her identity, 445
Murray, Sir George, and Perthshire, 403

N

Nagle, Sir Edmund, 189
Navarino, battle of, 253, 255, 257, 420
Nelson, Horatio, Viscount, death, 24
Newcastle, Dow. Duchess of, 199, 215, 278–290
Newcastle-on-Tyne, and Dr. Headlam, 437
Newcome's School, Hackney, "Old School Lane," 5, 8, 205, 345
Newmarket, 303, 309
Nicholson, Margaret, would-be assassin, in Bedlam, 198
Norfolk, 11th Duke of, "the Jockey," 10, 34, 54
Norfolk, 12th Duke of, "Scroop," etc., 107; Creevey's strong letter about Thetford, 112–114; 194, 260; at Rogers' dinner, 299; loss of Boroughs, 339; 406; and Lord Surrey, 421, 424
Normanby, Marchioness of, 223
North, Dudley, 59
Northumberland, Duke of, Lord-Lieutenant of Ireland, 304, 354
Norton, Hon. Mrs. (*née* Sheridan), 407–408; and Melbourne, 417–418 note
Nugent, Lord, 194

O

O'Brien, Dennis, 32
O'Connell, Daniel, 299; and Melbourne, 413–414
Ockham Park, Ripley, 186
O'Meara's "Voice from St. Helena," 152–154
O'Neill, Miss, actress (Lady Becher), Kilkenny Players, 289–290
Orange, Prince of, 91, 334
Ord, Anne. *See* Hamilton, Mrs. Andrew
Ord, Charles, Mrs. Creevey's younger son, 69, 77, 81
Ord, Mrs. (Eleanor). *See* Creevey, Mrs.
Ord, Eleanor, 23, 36, 68; at Brussels, 72–96; at Rivenhall, 251, 296; move to Cheltenham, 362, 406; Greenwich, 412
Ord, Elizabeth (Bessy or

" Barry "), Creevey's chief correspondent, 23, 29, 31–34, 36 ; at Brussels during Waterloo, 72–96 ; her mother's death, 100–13 ; thereafter *passim*.
Ord, Mrs. James, 246
Ord, William, 12, 46, 55, 85, 90, 100, 102, 108, 110
Ordnance, Treasurership of, C.'s appointment to, 326–331 ; first impressions of, 332–333 ; Althorp's letter on retrenchment of, 364–365
Orléans, Duke of, dances with Queen Adelaide, 365 ; tribute to Wellington, *ibid.*
Orsay, Comte Alfred d', William IV's dislike of, 424 and note.
Ossulston, Lord (6th Earl of Tankerville), 84–85, 180, 185, 216
Oxford, Countess of, 187

P

Palmerston, Viscount, 232–233, 244, 325, 335 ; anger with Brougham, 345; 403
Paris, after Waterloo, 91–96 ; 416
Parnell, Henry (1st Lord Congleton), 67
Parr, Dr., 10
Payne, George, 201 ; at Ascot, 264 ; de Ros case, 422, 424
Peel, Sir Robert, 156, 159–160 ; and Canning, 232 ; 235, 245 ; summoned from Rome, 376, 395–396 ; Tamworth manifesto, 400 ; 402 ; and O'Connell, 414
Peninsular War, 36–37, 45
Perceval, Rt. Hon. Spencer, Premier, 41 ; remains in power at Regency, 53–54
Percy, Earl, 32
Petre, 10th Lord, 10, 13, 113–114
Petre, Julia, Lady, widow of 9th Lord, 59, 65, 250
Petre, Mary, Lady, wife of 10th Lord, 14, 34, 59, 92
Petre, Hon. R. E., " Dear Eddard," 164, 201
Petty, Lord Henry. See Lansdowne, 3rd Marquis of
Petworth House, 273 ; its early hours, its servants, 275 ; account of pictures, 274, 276–278
Phillimore, J., 105

Phillips, Sir Richard, 48
Phillips, Mr., succeeds C. at Thetford, 113
Phillpots, Rev. Henry, Durham clergy libel, 154 and note.
Pitt, Rt. Hon. William, 15, 16 ; his return, 17–22 ; death blow, 23 ; death, 26
Plunket, William, 1st Lord, 178
Ponsonby, Hon. Augusta (Countess of Kerry), 257, 286, 289 ; and Lord Kerry, 371, 404
Ponsonby, Hon. Frederick, 247, 288
Ponsonby, Hon. George, note 54 ; 261, 271, 301 ; C.'s rival for Greenwich, 377 ; at Howick, 394
Ponsonby, Hon. Mrs. George, 271, 273, 394
Ponsonby, Rt. Hon. George, Leader of Whig Party, 54, 82, 106
Ponsonby, Hon. Georgiana, 285, 287, 288, 290, 291 ; her father's secretary, 371
Ponsonby, John (1st Visc. P.), 34
Ponsonby, Hon. John (5th Earl of Bessborough), 288
Ponsonby, Hon. Spencer, 289, 292, 441 note.
Ponsonby, Hon. William (Lord de Mauley), 261
Portarlington, 2nd Earl of, 144–146
Portland, 3rd Duke of, Premier, 27 ; 36, 43–44
Portugal, 35–38
Power, Mr. and Mrs., of Kilfane, 289–292
Powlett, Lady Caroline, 170–171, 200
Poyntz, William Stephen, of Cowdray, 271–273, 279
Prussia, King of, 72
Prussians, in Paris, 94
Public vehicles, 282, 354, 357–358 ; comfort of woollen stockings in, 390

R

Raby Castle, 208–210, 248
Race-horses, *Belzone*, 264 ; *Bobadilla*, 269 ; *Canteen*, 218 ; *Cedric*, 217 ; *Fleur de Lys*, 265 ; *Maria*, 267; *Sharper*, 303; *Zingalee*, 305

Radnor, 3rd Earl of. *See* Folkestone, Viscount.
Reform Bill, 332–357 *passim*.
Reichstadt, Duc de, 176
Richmond, Duchess of (*née* Gordon), Brussels ball, 86, 186; and Mr. Tighe, 211
Richmond, 5th Duke of, son of above, 211, 268–270, 309
Richmond, Duchess of (wife of 5th Duke), 268–270, 309
Rio de Janeiro, British Fleet at, 37–38
Rivenhall, Essex, 8, 121
Roden, 3rd Earl of, 399
Rogers, Samuel, 272, 280, 299, 408
Romille, Cecilia de, Bolton Abbey history, 168
Romilly, Sir Samuel, 7, 22, 24, 63, 65, 68, 106, 113
Ros, Lord de, 255; and George IV, 313; the cards scandal, 422, 424
Ros, Lady de, 151
Roscoe, W., 57, 60, 62, 64, 108
Roslyn, 2nd Earl of, 140, 157 and note; 179, 195, 214, 310
Russell, Lord John, 30, 31, 97, 225, 239; the Bill, 350; and Gleig, 381; Lady Grey on, 400; 421; at the Bedford, Brighton, 435
Russell, Lady William, influence over Lord John, 381
Russia, Emperor of, 72
Rutland, 5th Duke of, 196

S

St. Albans, 9th Duke of, 216, 266–267
St. Albans, Duchess of (Harriet Mellon, formerly Mrs. Coutts), 216, 217; party at Holly Lodge, 265–267
St. Vincent, Earl, his papers left to Brougham, 181
Salisbury, Mary Amelia, Marchioness of, 197, 215; arrives at Stoke, 227–228; her dinner party, 235; at Ascot and Eton, 265; 278–290, 301, 317–319; burned to death, 412–413, 415
Salisbury, 2nd Marquis of, 228; Arlington St. dispute, 424
Sandwich, Countess of, 183

Scarlett, Sir James (1st Lord Abinger), 7, 13, 18, 22, 36, 108, 136, 137, 155
Scott, Sir Walter, 148
Sefton, Countess of, wife of 2nd Earl, 136, 151, 184, 187, 213; C.'s comfort, 230; 233, 268–274, 292, 307, 318, 329; and William IV, 357; 361, 396–397, 417; and Queen Victoria, 428; 430, 437
Sefton, 1st Earl of, Creevey's parentage, 3–4
Sefton, 2nd Earl of, 22, 57, 59, 62, 83, 99, 104, 106–110; defeated at Liverpool, 111–112; 125, 128, 132, 138, 140, 149, 150, 177, 185; at the Derby, 195; 198; and Mde de Guiche, 200; 204, 213; daughter's death, 224; his grief, 225–230; 233, 251–253 255, 268–274, 293–295, 301; losses at whist, 304; 318, 324–331, 337; U.K. peerage, 345; 352; winnings, 361; on C.'s chances for Greenwich, 378; at Howick, 396–397; 414; abroad, 418–419; 421; a rake's dinner, 424; his expectation of death, 439–440; 441 note; actions on C.'s death; mention in C.'s will, 442–444
Seymour, Lady (*née* Sheridan), and her sisters, 407–408
Seymour, Miss Minnie, Mrs. Fitzherbert's adopted daughter, 300
Seymour, Lord Robert, governor of Bedlam, 198
Shelley, Sir John, wins Derby with *Cedric*, 196, 217
Sheridan, Charles, 50
Sheridan, Rt. Hon. R. B., 20, 23; at Fox's death, 31–32; 35, 46, 50, 52; Moore's Life of, 222
Sheridan, Mrs. R. B. (*née* Ogle), note 50
Sheridan, R. B. (grandson of R. B. above), marries Miss Grant, 407–408
Sheridan, Mrs. Thomas, 199
Shipley, William, Dean of St. Asaph's, famous libel action, 205; 206
Sicard, Mr., sent to Queen Caroline, 128

Smith, John, 138

Smith, Sir Sidney, senior officer at the Tagus and Rio, 35–39

Smith, Rev. Sydney, "a boisterous mountebank," 258; 302

Smythe-Owen, Mr., of Condover, 282, 294

Somerset, Lord Charles, 271, 275

Somerset, 11th Duke of, 300

Southill Park, 64-65

Spalding, Miss, Lady Brougham's daughter, 362

Sparrow, Miss, 171

Spencer, Lord Robert, 30, 213, 258, 267, 272–279, 299

Spencer, Lady Robert. See Bouverie, Mrs.

Spring Rice, Rt. Hon. T., 239, 437 and note.

Stael, M. de, 179

Stanhope, Lady Elizabeth (née Coke), 437 and note

Stanley, Lord (13th Earl of Derby, 1834), 59, 195, 204

Stanley, Hon. Edward (14th Earl of Derby, 1851), 311; and Hume, 363; Grey on, 393

Star, The, newspaper, 344-345

Stephenson, Henry, 161, 214; note on parentage, 234; 262, 304, 420

Stevenson, Mr. and Mrs., American Ambassador, anecdote of, 438–439

Stewart, Lord, 199

Stoke Farm, Windsor, 182, 187; for Ascot, 212; 215, 226–229, 263, 273, 305–307, 322; Dino and Lieven at, 369; 417; 427–432

Strachey, Lytton, vi; on C. note 10; his estimate of C., 446

Strangford, Lord, quarrel with Sir S. Smith, 35–39

Stuart, Sir Charles, 233

Stuart, Lady Elizabeth, 151

Sumner, Holme, M.P., 137

Sussex, H.R.H. Duke of, 153; at Lambton, 158–161; at Cantley, 162–165; 179, 189; at Mansion House, 192–194; 197, 209, 213, 218; Duke of York's funeral, 233–234; 259, 266, 322, 324; quarrel with Duncannon, 347–348; dinner at Kensington after marriage to Lady Cecilia, 262–263; a

dinner for Grey, 386; 405; at Guildhall Banquet, 435

Sutherland, Elizabeth, Duchess of, and Lady Grey, 366 and note.

T

Talleyrand, Prince de, 328, 336, 337; at Windsor, 341–342; hatred of solitude, 369

Tankerville, 6th Earl of. See Ossulston, Lord

Tankerville, Countess of (Corise de Grammont), 180, 215, 223

Tarleton, Mr., M.P., Liverpool Dock Bill, 22

Tavistock, Marchioness of, in attendance on Queen Victoria, 429–430; the Queen's thought for, 429

Taylor, Sir Herbert, 189, 370–373

Taylor, Michael Angelo, 7, 149, 162, 178, 186, 195, 196, 209, 210, 214; C. lodges with him, 224, 301; appointed P.C., 334, 337; death, 384; and "Mrs. Murray," 445

Taylor, Mrs. M. A. (née Vane), 148, 175, 183, 187, 201, 210, 213, 216, 218, 223, 224, 231, 248, 265–266, 296, 324, 384; death, 402–403

Thanet, 9th Earl of, 122, 125, 151, 185; dies, 208

Thanet, 10th Earl of, 213

Thetford, C.'s first constituency, 10, 59; C. loses seat, 107, 112–115

Thornton, Col., 189

Thurlow, Lord, 24

Tierney, Rt. Hon. George, 34, 40, 44, 82, 98, 105, 113; as leader of party, 116–117; 137–138

Tighe, W. F., of Woodstock, and Lady Louisa, Duchess of Richmond on, 211

Times, The, 105, 136; circulation, 175–176; "best written paper," 225; Barnes of, 234; puff of Brougham, 246; 256; attack on Grey, 338; Brougham influence, ibid.

Tindal, Sir Nicholas, and C.'s trial, 69

Tooke, Rev. J. Horne, 20, and note

U

Ude, M., famous chef, on Duke of York, 231 ; at Crockford's, 387
Underwood, Lady Cecilia 2nd wife of H.R.H. Duke of Sussex, 250, 324 ; marriage to Duke of Sussex and dinner party, 362–363 and note; 405 ; refused invitation to Guildhall, 435

V

Vane, Sir Harry, 296, 297
Vane, Jack, 214, 402
Vansittart, Rt. Hon. Nicholas (1st Lord Bexley), Chancellor of Exchequer, 16
Vauxhall, 151
Victoria, Queen, 372, 423 ; first impressions of, at State dinner, 427–428 ; riding at Windsor, 428 ; Melbourne on, 429 ; expedition to Kensington, 429–430 ; and her maids, 430 ; Hayter's impressions, 431 ; and Leopold, 431–432 ; at review, 432 ; Melbourne and, at Brighton, 433–434 ; Melbourne on the Court, 434 ; at Guildhall Banquet, 435 ; Wilkie on, 435–436 ; and Dr. Headlam, 437
Vigoureux, Col., 90
Vizard, C.'s and Brougham's lawyer, 207 ; Vice-Chancellor, 327 ; seals up C.'s papers, 442 ; C.'s executor, 443–444
Voltaire, 10

W

Waithman, Robert, Lord Mayor of London, 51–52, 192
Walcheren Expedition, 45–46
Wardle, Col., M.P., his enquiry, 42–43 and note, 44 ; Mrs. Clarke, 48–49 and note.
Warrender, Sir George, 139, 140, 258–259
Waterloo campaign, 72–96
Webster, J. Wedderburn, panic before Waterloo, 73, 76
Webster, Miss H. (Lady Holland's daughter), marries Sir F. Pellew, 420–421 and note
Wellesley, Sir Arthur (1st Duke of Wellington), C.'s relations

with, 36–37 ; Convention of Cintra, 39–40 ; 41, 45 ; Waterloo campaign, 73–96 *passim* ; Verona, 148 ; C.'s memo. on, 153 ; Hudson Lowe, 154 ; ill at Beauvais, 166 ; Vienna, 170 ; 176–177 ; and Lady Jersey, 183 ; at Ascot, 197 ; 212 ; resigns with Liverpool, 232 ; succeeds Goderich, 233 ; 239 ; Alava on, 240 ; 244 ; "reformer," 259 ; overworked, 262 ; admits Catholics, 297–298 ; and Cumberland, 302 ; duel with Winchilsea, 303 ; at Walmer, 310 ; 319, 324, 355 ; tribute from Orléans, 365–366 ; Premier again, 395 ; 404
Wellesley, Lord Charles, 2nd son of Duke of Wellington, 367
Wellesley, Marquis, 37, 40 ; offer to Grey and Grenville, 53–56 ; Duncannon's praise of, 371 ; at the Castle, Dublin, 374–375
Wellesley, Marchioness (formerly Mrs. Paterson), at the Castle, Dublin, 374–375 note ; and Mr. Paterson, his uncouth manners, 439
Wellington, 1st Duke of. See Wellesley, Sir Arthur
Wentworth Woodhouse, 247
Western, Charles C., 8, 10, 11, 34, 100, 121, 133, 134, 137, 151 ; on Reform, 340 ; receives peerage, 359
Westmorland, 10th Earl of, 55
Wetherell, Sir Charles, 136
Wharfedale, 167–168
Whishaw, J., M.P., 64, 126
Whitbread, Lady Elizabeth, 75, 84, 85, 97
Whitbread, Samuel, M.P. (of Southill), 15, 24, 27, 37 ; leader of advanced Whigs, 41 ; on Melville and Duke of York enquiries, 42–43 ; 44, 52, 54 ; at Southill, 64–65 ; 66–68 ; 74 ; suicide, 83–85
Whitbread, S. C., marries Julia Brand, note 202
Wilbraham, George, 204
Wilde, Thomas (1st Lord Truro), 143
Wilkie, Sir David, impression of Queen Victoria, 435–436
William IV. (Duke of Clarence),

at York's funeral, 234; 262; succeeds to Throne, 317, 321; at Bushey and Windsor, 322–324; sends for Grey, 325; and Reform Bill, 332–357 *passim*; opens Parliament, 343; and Hamilton, 361; and Brougham, 392

William I, of Holland, "The Frog," 335

Wilson, Sir Robert, " Jaffà," 151; and Murat, 221

Winchilsea, Earl of, duel with Wellington, 302–303

Windham, Rt. Hon. W., 30

Windsor Castle, 182, 188–189; Wyatt's improvements, 226; 322–324, 341, 367; Waterloo Gallery, 373; 392; Queen Victoria at, 428–432

" Windsor Express," 188–189

Wingfield, William, 258

Witley Court, Worcestershire, 230–231, 297–298

Wivell, Abraham, artist, 173, 177

Wood, Alderman, and Queen Caroline, 128, 129

Wood, Lady Mary, 128

Woolbeding, Midhurst, 30, 261, 267, 269–273; fountain, 278–279

Worcester, Marchioness of, at Walmer, 309–310

Wortley, James Stuart- (1st Lord Wharncliffe), 67, 246

Wyatt or Wyatville, Sir Jeffry, architect, work at Windsor, 226, 322

Wyndham, George, 1st Lord Leconfield, note 269, 275

Wyndham, the Misses, 275

Wynn, Charles Watkin Williams, 105

Y

Yarmouth, Earl of, 67

York, H.R.H. Duke of, 163, 189, 196; his new house, 212; funeral and debts, 233–234

York Minster, 391

Printed in Great Britain by
Hazell, Watson & Viney, Ltd., London and Aylesbury.